A

CRITICAL INQUIRY

INTO

ANTIENT ARMOUR.

Sir Samuel Rush Meyrick

A

CRITICAL INQUIRY

INTO

ANTIENT ARMOUR,

AS IT EXISTED IN EUROPE, BUT PARTICULARLY IN

ENGLAND,

FROM THE NORMAN CONQUEST TO THE REIGN OF

KING CHARLES II.

WITH

A GLOSSARY OF MILITARY TERMS OF THE MIDDLE AGES.

IN THREE VOLUMES.

BY

SIR SAMUEL RUSH MEYRICK, LL.D. AND F.S.A.

VOL. II.

This Edition Originally Published :
    London : Robert Jennings. No 2, Poultry: 1824

This Edition :
    Barrie : RNU Press : 2018

Re-Typset in: Garamond Premier Pro®

Book Design & Layout: © David Edwards (RNU Press)
Cover Art: © David Edwards

Republished by RNU Press
111 Widgeon St.
Barrie, ON, L4N 8W2
www.rnupress.com

RNU PRESS

ISBN: 978-1-989434-01-7

This book is printed on acid-free paper.

Vol. 1. ISBN 978-1-989434-00-0
Vol. 2. ISBN 978-1-989434-01-7
Vol. 3. ISBN 978-1-989434-02-4

CONTENTS

LIST OF PLATES

A CRITICAL INQUIRY

INTO

ANTIENT ARMOUR.

Edward the Third.

1327.

DWARD immediately on his accession, though of comparatively a tender age, was so impressed with whatever was connected with the martial character of his country, which he knew would be cherished by nothing better than liberty, that in the very first year of his reign a statute was passed respecting the posse comitatiis, which might be termed a declaration of individual freedom. The section of the act[1] to which I allude runs thus: Item le roy vœt desormes nul soit charge de soi armer, autrement qu'il ne soleit en temps de ces auncestres roys d'Engleterre. Et que nul soient distreintz d'aler hors de leur countez, si non par cause de nécessité de sodeyne venue des estraunges enemys en roialme, et adonques soit fait corne ad este fait avant ces heures par defens du roialme. "Also the king wills, from henceforth, that no one be at the charge of arming himself otherwise than has been the custom in the time of our ancestors kings of England. And that no one shall be compelled to go out of his county, ex-

---

[1] Stat. 1 Edward III, c. 5.

cept on account of necessity, arising from the sudden invasion of strange enemies in the kingdom, and then the same shall be done as formerly in defence of the kingdom."

This king too introduced a practice, which was constantly followed by his successors, of engaging with his subjects and other persons by indenture to furnish soldiers at certain wages. Most of our armies from this time, therefore, consisted of stipendiary troops. The terms soldier and stipendiary are etymologically the same: the first being derived from solde, *pay*; and the latter from stipendium, *wages* or *hire*. Nevertheless custom has established a difference; the soldier signifying one of the constitutional military, while the stipendiary implies one of the indented troops.

The utility of the hobilers became so evident, that during this reign they were in the greatest request. In a table, describing the garrison at Calais in the year 1350, there were sub comite Kildariæ bannerets 1, knights 1, esquires 38, hobilers 27. Sub. dom. Reginaldo Cobliam bannerets 1, knights 6, hobilers 19, archers on horse 24, archers on foote 32. Sub. dom. Fulcone de la Freigus Hibernico bannerets 1, knights 1, esquires 18, hobilers 14. By their tenure they were bound to maintain a little nag, for the convenience of giving notice on the sea coast of any invasion or peril; hence they were stationed at Portsmouth and other maritime garrisons. In the year 1345 their pay was established and put on the same footing as that of the archers.[2] Hitherto we have seen that the hobilers and archers were distinct; during this reign, however, there were hobiler-archers. Thus we have a writ:[3] Pro warda maris tempore guerræ, pro hoberariis sagittariis inveniendis. "For the protection of the sea in time of war, for finding hoberary (hobilary) archers." Again: Pro expensis factis circa constabularies laborantes ad eligendum et ducendum prædictos hobilarios sagittarios.[4] "For expenses incurred for constables' labour in choosing and conducting the aforesaid hobilary-archers."

The arms and appointments of a hobiler, as directed by Edward III, were a horse, a hauketon or armour of plate, a basinet, iron gauntlets, a sword knife, and lance.[5]

Camden[6] says, " In old times there were set horsemen at parts, in many

---

[2] Stat. 2nd the 18th of Edward III, c. 7. Et que gentes d'armes hobilers et archiers estus pour aller en la service le Roi d'Angleterre soient as gages le roy, &c.

[3] Rot. Parl. 21st Edward III.

[4] Wm. Thorn in 1364.

[5] Yelverton MS. formerly in the library of Thomas Astle.

[6] Brit. fol. 273.

places, whom our ancestors called hobelers, who in the day should give notice of the enemies approach;" and, according to Spelman,[7] this species of troops lasted till the time of Henry VIII, when they were succeeded by the demi-launcers.

Thus an army at this time consisted of the commander-in-chief, on whom attended a chaplain, a physician, and a crier; the different leaders of the respective bands, who had each their bannerers or standard bearers, from the king to the banneret; the knights with their esquires, and the men at arms with their sergeants. The cavalry was thus composed of men at arms, hobilers, and mounted archers. Under these were the infantry, who consisted of spearmen, bowmen, cross-bowmen, and pavissers, to which were also attached gunners and artillers, pavylers,[8] mynours, armerers, &c.[9]

The bannerets and knights made a considerable figure in the armies: and the title of the former was particularly honourable, because it was conferred only on the field of battle as the reward of valour.

The men at arms, a title which had been in former reigns sometimes conferred on the heavy-armed infantry, under this became of a mixed character, expressing the knights fighting both on horseback and on foot. They often performed their chief service while dismounted, and then got on their horses to pursue the enemy. Froissart calls them not only gens d'armes but lances,[10] from their being armed with this weapon; and this latter name became afterwards peculiarly appropriated to them, as was that of demi-lances to the hobilers. He also describes these last as hommes armez montez sur petites naguenees,[11] "armed men mounted upon little nags."[12] Hollinslied,[13] speaking of the battle of Aulroy, the 38th of Edward III, A.D. 1365, informs us, that "the Frenchmen after the manner of that age, every man hadde cutte his speare (as then they used, at what time they should join battaile) to the length of five foote, and a short axe hanging at his side. At the firste encounter, there was a sore battaile, and truelie the archers shotte right fiercelie, howbeit their shotte did but little hurte to the Frenchemenne, they were

---

[7] Vocab. in voce.

[8] Or paviloners, those who pitched the tents; a duty now performed by the pioneers.

[9] MS. Chrono in Harl. lib. marked 53.

[10] Thus among the Rotuli Scotiœ, 15th Edward III, is a command from the king to John de Cherleton and others, to raise homines ad lances et sagittarios in North Wales; andd a similar one to Rhys ab Grufydd in South Wales, dated Tower of London, 14th October, 1341.

[11] Qu. Is not hackney a corruption of naguenée?

[12] Vol. III.

[13] Chron. p. 970.

so well armed and paveshed. The archers perceiving that, (being bigge men and light[14]) cast away their bowes and entred in amongst the Frenchemenne that bare axes, and plucked them out of their handes, and therewith fought right hardly."

Edward III found it necessary to enjoin the practice of the bow, by two mandates during his reign.[15] At this time a painted bow sold for one shilling and sixpence, and a white or unpainted one for a shilling. Arrows were sold at one shilling . and twopence per sheaf, each sheaf consisting of twenty-four, if they had sharpened points, or piles, as they were technically termed; but if blunt-headed, they were only one shilling per sheaf. The iron from which the best points were made is said to have been that of anchor flukes. At the battle of Poictiers the English archers resupplied their quivers by drawing the arrows from the dead bodies of their enemies.

When Lionel Earl of Clarence[16] went with an army into Ireland, he took with him many mounted archers, whose pay was sixpence a day each man, esquires in the same army were rated one shilling each per diem, knights two shillings, and bannerets four. There were also some archers at fourpence a day, these, therefore, probably served on foot. There is a schedule of pay in French attached to a man-datur,[17] dated Redyng, 20th March, 1347, among the Rotuli Scotiæ, in which the sums are nearly the same.

In the Supplement to Du Cange's Glossary various kinds of cross-bows are thus enumerated, from an account in the year 1338, of Barth[w], du Drach. They consist of the arbaleste de cor et d'if, of horn and yew; arbaleste a tour, the winding crossbow; à hausse-pié, with a running knot (or, perhaps, to raise with the foot); a tailler, for cutting weapons or barbed arrows;[18] and a baudrier or baudreer, with leathern thongs. The use of these thongs we learn from a letter remissory, dated 1358: Symon Patroullardi dixit Johanni ipsius famulo, quòd dictam balistam ten-deret cum manibus, qui nequivit hoc facere, sed bauderium accepit et earn tetendit.

"Simon Patroullardi told his servant John to bend the said cross-bow with his hands, but he declined this, and taking a bauderium (or appara-

---

[14] Active.

[15] Tbe words are: Arcubus et sagittis vel pilettis aut boItis, "with bows and arrows, or pilettes (short small javelins, or more probably pellets) or bolts."

[16] Son of Edward III.

[17] It is entitled Mandatur quod stipendia solvantur magnatibus et aliis ad invadendum Scotiam profecturis; et notantur stipendia singulis solvenda. See R. S. [120] p. 691.

[18] See one of these with the cutting barbes PI. XLIV1 taken from a specimen in the collection of Llewelyn Meyriek, Esq.

tus with leathern thongs) at once bent it." In an inquisition, dated 1363, we'meet with balista de reverso, but in what manner it acted we are not informed.

The Genœse were at all times most celebrated for the skilful management of the cross-bow. The success which attended the Christians at the siege of Jerusalem, in 1100, is attributed principally to the mechanical talents of this people. In the beginning of the thirteenth and until the middle of the fifteenth century crossbowmen are uniformly mentioned as part of the Genœse troops. From Justiniano we learn that, in the year 1225, twenty arbalesters mounted, and one hundred on foot, with cross-bows of horn, were then employed in the army of the state.[19] Five hundred were sent against the Milanese, in 1245, and these unfortunate men being placed in front of the lines were taken prisoners by the enemy, who, to revenge the havoc done by their bows, cruelly punished each with the loss of an eye, and the amputation of an arm.[20]

The greatest number however of these troops, which appears to have been ever introduced into the field, was at the battle of Cressy, in 1346, in which engagement the foremost rank of the French army was composed of 15,000 Genœse crossbowmen.

Notwithstanding their ill success in this battle they do not seem to have at all lost their reputation, for in the very next year we find that Charles Earl of Blois had, at the siege of Le Roche de Rien, no less than two thousand in his army. So in the Chronicle of Bertrand du Guesclin we read:

> Dix sept mille furent armez sur les concois[21]
> Sans les arbalestriers, qui furent Genevois.

> "Seventeen thousand were armed on the
> Without reckoning the cross-bowmen, who were Genœse."

Indeed the cross-bowmen of Paris were held in such esteem, that their presence was deemed necessary to give proper eclat to the friendly combats that took place in 1349, at Lille, in Flanders.

Edward III, though he wished principally to encourage the long-bow, in which the English seem naturally to have excelled, could not help seeing the advantages which might be derived from the arbalest. The shortness

---

[19] "Venti ballestrieri a cavello et cento ballestrieri a piede con le ballestre di como." Annali di Genoa, p. 75.

[20] Thesau. Hist. Ital. Grrevii et Burmanni,

[21] I am totally at a loss to make out the meaning of this word.

of its range and the length of time required between each discharge rendered it much inferior to the long-bow, but the great exactness of its shot, and its convenience on horseback were evident. In the year 1363 the king, therefore, wrote to the sheriffs of London, and ordered that "they should cause public proclamation to be made, that every citizen, at leisure times and holidays, should use in their recreations bows and arrows and pellets or bolts (both of which last imply the use of the cross-bow), and learn the art of shooting."

Indeed, for the encouragement of its practice, we read of matches being made in different parts of Europe, called Ludi ad Ballistam, and prizes given to the most skilful cross-bowmen. Thus in letters remissory, dated 1382, Gautier de Moncliel escuier, chastellain, et garde du chastel d'Estaples, pour bien de paix et nourrir amour entre les compagnons du dit cliastel jouans d'arbaleste, et pour plus entretenir et accoustumer icellui jeu, donne un espervier d'argent au mieux jouant de l'arbaleste, avec certains autres pris et joiaux, et eust icellui chastellain fait ce savoir, et signifier paravant le dit jeu en plusieurs lieux, pourquoy plusieurs com-paignons et arbalestriers du pays feussent venus en la dite ville d'Estaples au dit jour, et eussent joué d'arbalestes. "Walter de Monchel, esquire, castellan, and keeper of the castle of Estaples, for the encouragement of tranquillity and regard for each other among the companions of the said castle, who delight in the arbalest, and for their better instruction and experience in that game, gives a silver hawk to the best shot with the arbalest, with certain other prizes and entertainments; and this castellan had this made known and proclaimed, before the game took place, in several places, on which account many companions and arbalesters went from the country into the said town of Estaples on the said day, and there shot with their arbalestes."

The costume of the cross-bowmen at this period may be seen in an illuminated MS. in the British Museum.[22] They wear on their heads scullcaps, and plate armour on their legs and arms, while their bodies are protected by jacks with large pendent sleeves.

During this reign the cross-bowmen seem first to have been protected by pavisers, or men who held before them a very large shield, which was called a pavise. Thus we read in Thomas Walsingliam:[23] Venientem contra eum cum 7 militibus electis armatorum, aliisque armatis, pavisariis ac balistariis in numéro excessivo. "Coming against him with seven chosen knights

---

[22] In the Sloane library, marked 2433.
[23] In Edwardi tertii.

from the army, and other armed men, with pavisers and cross-bowmen, in immense numbers." So in an account of Du Drac, the French treasurer of war, dated 1350, occurs: M. Savari de Vivone Sire de Tors chev. banner-et, pour luy 5 chev. bacheliers, 36 escuyers au prix, 10 arehiers à cheval et un pavessier à pié. "M. Savari de Vivone, sire of Tors, knight banneret, for him five knights batchelors, thirty-six esquires at a certain price, ten archers mounted, and one paviser on foot." Pavises are thus mentioned in a deed, dated 1345: Quod in dictis galeis sunt in qualibet CC homines CLXXX pavesii cc lanceæ, &c. "Because in each of the aforesaid galleys are two hundred men, one hundred and eighty pavisers, two hundred lances," &c. In a deed, dated 1359, it is said: Et dimittere debeat unam pavesem de pavesibus ipsius, &c. "And he ought to spare one pavise from liis collection." Lastly, in a charter, dated 1377, occurs: Videlicet balistas, viratones, pavesia et alia quaecumque arnesia. "Namely, cross-bows, viratons,[24] pavises, and other harness whatsœver."

From these quotations we may learn how very prevalent they had become; and, from the Chronicle of Bertrand du Guesclin, that they were protected by large bands of iron, as he says:

Arbalestes, pavas et fors escus bandez.

"Cross-bows, pavises, and strong shields banded."

These bands or edgings of iron appear in the illuminated copies of Froissart; but from other authorities we find that they were otherwise embellished,[25] and in Henry the Fourth's time charged with armorial bearings, as in a deed, dated 1405,[26] we read of viginti et novem pavisses cum armis Sancti Georgii depictos et quin-decim pavises cum armis Oxoniae et Deverosse depictos. "Twenty-nine pavises, with the arms of St. George painted on them; and fifteen pavises, with the arms of Oxford and Devereux."

The seal of Edward III represents him with a cylindrical helmet, and a knight's cap on its top, on which is standing a lion, his crest. He wears a short surcoat with sleeves to his elbow, which also opening in front has much the resemblance of a jacket. The surcoat of Philip de Valois, as repre-

---

[24] The viretons were arrows having the feathers put on them diagonally, so as to occasion their turning in the air when shot. Some of these, from Genoa, are in the armoury of Llewelyn Meyrick, Esq. and represented in Pl. XLIV.

[25] Thus Octavo de S. Gelais, in Viridario honoris, or le Vergier d'honneur, speaks of pavois dorez, "gilt pavises."

[26] In Rymer's Fœdera.

sented by Montfaucon,[27] has also short wide sleeves; and that of Bertrand du Guesclin, on his monument at the cathedral of St. Denis, is exactly like Edward the Third's, except that, instead of being opened at the bottom, it has buttons down the front.[28] The seal of Robert de Bruce, king of Scotland, represents him in gamboised armour, which, as has been observed, had obtained a high degree of estimation in that country, but he wears the usual helmet of this period, which was pointed.

In this age of heroism we meet with instances of females appearing in armour. Thus Froissart tells us, that "the Earl of Montfort being a prisoner at Paris, the Countess, who possessed the courage of a man and the heart of a lion, defended the castle of Hennibon, belonging to the Earl; clothed herself in armour, and mounted on a charger, galloped up and down the streets encouraging the inhabitants; ordered the ladies and women to unpave the streets, and cany the stones to the ramparts, and throw them on their enemies; and she had pots of quicklime brought her for that purpose." He further relates, that "the Countess of Montfort's fleet being attacked by the Genœse and Spaniards, she proved herself equal to a man, for she had the heart of a lion, and with a rusty sharp sword in her hand combated bravely." Knighton, under the year 1348, tells us, that it was the practice for ladies to attend tournaments on horseback, when they appeared with their girdles handsomely ornamented with gold and silver, in imitation of the military belts, habentes cultellos, quos daggerios vulgariter dicunt, in powchiis desuper impositis, &c. "having knives, commonly called daggers, placed in powches before them."

We may judge of the effect of the stones which the Countess of Montfort ordered the women to collect from other instances mentioned by Froissart. Thus, "At the siege of Aubouton, Baldwin de Beaufort, an esquire of Hainault, received so violent a blow from a large stone, that his shield was split by it, and his arm broken, which forced him to retire." Again, speaking of an attack made by the Earl of Hainault and his uncle, he says: "They fought most valiantly, and spared none, each of them at his place received two such blows from stones thrown down upon them, that then- helmets were split through, and themselves quite stunned." The monumental effigy of John of Eltham, who died in 1329, has afforded the subject of Pl. xxxi. He is habited according to the fashion at the commencement of this reign, for a considerable change took place before its close. He has on his

[27] Mon. Fr. Pl. CIV. Fig. 1.
28 See Montf. Mon. Fr. Pl. CXXIV. Fig. 2.

head a conical cervelliere, to which is attached the gorget that appears covered with silk. On this cap is his coronet, and below it a vandyked drapery, which not only is an elegant ornament, but serves to attach the gorget of mail. His hauberk is cut into a point before, which just reaches to his knees. It is without sleeves, as he has plate-armour on his arms as well as his legs. At his elbows are round plates, and his gauntlets are composed of several pieces sewn on his gloves.[29] Underneath this hauberk is seen the hauketon, above it the pourpoint, and over this the cyclas, which reached behind to the calves of the legs, while in front it came but just below the abdomen, being open on each side to the hips. It is kept confined by a small ornamented girdle, while the chief splendour was bestowed on the great sword-belt. The sword-sheath is studded over, the pommel and cross-bar adorned with lions' heads. His spurs are of the pryck-kind, the leathers of which, as well as his genou-illieres, are much ornamented. On his arm is his shield, which shews that the length had been much diminished. The edge of the pourpoint terminates in foliage with much taste, and, as observed, is here represented as worn over the armour. The hauketon or lioqueton, which is underneath, finished in a puckered skirt. It was not unusual for this garment to be worn sometimes under the hauberk as well as at others as armour by itself. Thus in the Roman de Gaydon, an old warrior is described as having—

Sor l'auqueton vest l'auberk-jazerant.

"Upon his hoketon put a jazerant-hauberk."

And in another passage of the same work it is said:

Sor L'auqueton, qui d'or fu pointurez,
Vesti l'auberc, qui fut fort et serrez.

"On his hoketon, which was stitched with gold,
He put on his hauberk, which was strong and compact."

The utility of this under garment is thus stated in the Chronicle of Bertrand du Guesclin:

L'escu li derompi, et le bon jazerant;
Mais le haucton fut fort, qui fut de bouquerant.

---

[29] These are more distinctly represented at the foot of Plate XXXI.

"His shield was pierced, and his good jazerant;
But his hoketon was strong, being of buckram."

Whence we also learn the material which formed its exterior surface. The value of this garment, indeed, in point of protection, was so fully proved, that, like the gambeson, it came to be used as armour by itself. Thus Thomas Walsingham, the historian of this reign, informs us that indutus autem fuit episcopus quadam armatura quam aketon vulgariter appellamus, "a bishop had put on a certain kind of armour, which we commonly call an aketon." So in an ordinance of Oudouard Lord of Hamen, dated 1328, it is said: Se aucuns hustions est fais as armes en la dite ville teles come auqueton, espee, coutel et boucler, &c. "If any dispute with arms should take place in that town, such as hoketon, sword, knife and buckler," &c. Such disturbances were not unusual, as they are thus noticed in Rymer's Fœdera:[30] Aketonis, borcinettis, et aliis hujusmodi armaturis, nocte dieque in villis feriis mercatis ssepissime armati incedunt. "With hoketons, basinets, and such like armour, persons very often come armed into towns, both day and night, to sell their beasts." The following extracts from inventories, taken at Holy Island, point out the usual armour at this period. Anno 1362: Item sunt pro defensione domus: vi bom-baces (i.e. wambaises), iii lancae, i galea cum i pectorale, i par cerotecarum deferro. Anno 1367: In camera: i hawbergeon, ii paria de plates, i par de paunce, i par be[a], de maile de stel . . . . quissens de stele, ij paria cirotecarum de stele, v lancee, i scutum, iii bacinetts, i kett . . vii actons. "In the year 1362: For the defence of the house, six bombaces, three lances, one helmet with a pectoral, and one pair of iron gauntlets. In the year 1367, in the chamber, one liaubergeon, two pairs of plates, one pair of paunces, one pair of sleeves of mail of steel, . . cuisses of steel, two pairs of gauntlets of steel, five lances, one shield, three basinets, one . . . . , seven hoketons."

The following inventory of armour, at Grafton, in the county of Worcester,[31] purports to have been taken after the decease of the first Sir Gilbert Talbot, who is said, by Collins,[32] on the authority of a roll of that period, to have died in the year 1353; but I am strongly disposed to conceive that it must have been long after that date, and that the indorsement which contains the above description is altogether incorrect.

---

[30] Vol. IV, p. 203, col. 1.
[31] The original is in the possession of the Earl of Shrewsbury.
[32] In his Baronage, Vol. III, p. 5.

PLATE XXXI

JOHN DE ELTHAM EARL OF CORNWALL,

A.D. 1329.

In the Armery Howse.

	£i.	s.	d.
Item. A payer of briganders (brigandines) cov'ed (covered) w^t blak velvet, with the slevys and coler (sleeves and collar), price	—	xxvi	vii
Itm vj payer of yomen briganders (these were more particularly termed brigandines, the former being most probably jaze-rant-jackets) cov'ed w^t ledder	—	xxiii	iiij
Itm A curas complete of Flaundris makyng, of the new turne, price	xx	—	—
Itm ij almerys (armuries, armoires, or cases) for harneys, price	—	v	vj
Itm A salet harneyssyd (garnished, or furnished) w^t sylv^r and gylte, price	—	x	—
Itm A coote of fens (coat of fence, or defence) w^t a paier of brokyn bringanders	—	vi	—
Itm In the almery ij payer of legge harnes, vj yoman salettes, a paier of bombardes and camnys (padded breeches and gamnys, jambs or leg-coverings), iiij paier of splentes, the base pte of the legge harneys, ij paier of slevys and xiij gorgettes of mayle, price of all	iij	vj	viij
Itm A standard (a frame or horse) of mayle harnessyd w^t sylv^r and gylte	—	iiij	viij
Itm iij blake byllys (bills) price	—	—	xviii
Sm^d	£i xxvii	iiii	iiii

The armour enumerated in the foregoing I shall not describe in this place for the reason before given.

Very similar to the monument of John of Eltham is that of a knight in Ifield church, Sussex, the only essential difference being gloves of chain-mail instead of plate, and gussets of mail to protect the arm-pits. The effigy in brass of Sir John D'Aubemoun exhibits a fashion of the same kind, as may be seen in his figure represented in Pl. XXXII. The tunic under his hauberk has not, however, a puckered skirt, but appears to be simply of buckram, and this because his armour seems as if gamboised: probably, therefore, it may be the paunce mentioned in the inventory quoted antecedent to the last. Above it, however, is the pourpoint studded with rosettes of metal, and over this the cyclas. Instead of jambs he wears merely greaves or shin-plates to guard his legs; and although he has demi-brassarts to protect the upper part of his arms, he has no vambraces. Below the elbow, indeed, the sleeves of the hauberk reach only half way to the wrist, and are slit up underneath, so that the sleeve of the tunic is left quite visible. This is, perhaps, intend-

PLATE XXXII

SIR JOHN D'AUBERNOUN,

A.D. 1550.

ed to fasten over the military glove when worn. Besides the elbow-pieces are round plates, held on by laces or points as they were called, and similar plates are seen on the shoulders.[33] The basinet on his head, different from the cervelliere, comes lower behind than in front, a fashion that was increased in size towards the close of this reign.

A painting in glass of Ralph Lord Basset, in the east window of Drayton-Basset church, represents him[34] in mixed armour, having a cervelliere on his head, elbow-pieces, and genouillieres, with greaves for his legs, and plates on the upper part of his feet, like Sir John D'Aubernoun. Much in the same style are the two military figures on the front of Exeter cathedral, where we may observe the change which the surcoat underwent to become the cyclas. It is in every respect like it except not being longer behind than in front. These statues have exterior plates over their armour, which is of stitched and padded work, or ouvrage de pourpointerie. Their gauntlets are of plate, and one wears the birrus or large wrapping cloak. He has a moveable visor attached to his basinet, which is uplifted. This appears to be appropriate to the building for which the figure is designed, as Froissart speaks of the Black Prince, in 1367, when praying, having his visor up and joining his hands.[35]

The Chronicle of France, speaking of its king, Charles V, informs us that, Eli ce temps la las coustume des homines estoit, qu'ils s'armoient a bacinez a camail à une pointe ague, à un gros orfray sur les épaulés, et chascun avoit sa hache attachée a son ceinture. "In that time it was the custom with persons to arm themselves with a basinet formed into a sharp point with camail attached, with large embroidery of gold and silver upon the shoulders, and each had his battle-axe attached to his girdle." Sometimes, however, these basinets had an ornament on their peak resembling foliage, as in the specimens of John de Elthain and Sir John D'Aubemoun; but this was liable to the same objection as the nasal in Stephen's time, for from the Chronicle of Bertrand du Guesclin we learn, that it served the enemy as a holdfast. Thus:

> Et Charles est tresbuchiés et navrez laidement,
> Et tirez par le bacin, et prins moult fièrement.

---

[33] These were sometimes termed rouelles.

[34] He is represented with his page holding his war-horse, which is covered with a caparison of his arms.

[35] C. 237.

"And Charles is overthrown, and sadly wounded,
And dragged along by the basinet, and most fiercely taken."

In an account rendered by Stephen de la Fontaine, in the year 1352, is the following item: Pour faire et forger la garnison d'un bacinet, c'est assavoir 35 vervelles 12 bocetes pour le fronteau tout d'or de touche, et une couronne d'or pour mettre sur icelui bacinet dont les fleurons sont de feuilles d'espine, et le cercle diapré de fleur de lys: et pour faire forger la couroye à fermer le dit bacinet, dont les clous sont de bousseaux et de croisettes esmaillées de France. "For causing to be forged the furniture of a basinet, that is to say, thirty-five little loops,[36] twelve little bosses for the forehead part, all of standard gold, and a crown of gold to put upon the same basinet, the foliage of which is composed of thorn-leaves, and a circle diapred with fleur-de-lys: and for causing to be forged the leather strap for making fast the said basinet, the nails of which are headed with bosses and little crosses enamelled with the arms of France." Another item is for a bacinet à visière, and this very ample description is fully borne out by the monumental effigies of this period. The manuscript Roman de Kanor tells us, that bacin ne puet le cop tenir, qn'il ne soit entrées en la coiffe, et le bacins faussés. "The basinet cannot resist a blow so that it shall not enter the coiffe and false basinet."[37]

The coiffe, however, at this time, when worn, was of a smaller or lighter kind, and therefore termed coiffette, and appears to have been of plate. Thus Froissart speaks of cottes de fer, gantelets, coiffettes d'acier, "coats of mail, gauntlets, and coiffettes of steel and in the ordinance of Oudouard Lord of Hamen, in the year 1328, are enumerated haubregon, bacinet, coiffete, ou plate, ou autre armeure semblable. "Haubergeon, basinet, coifette, either of plate or other similar armour."

The splendid manner in which some of the knights at this time chose to have their armour made proved sometimes fatal to them. Thus Froissart tells us, that "Raymond, nephew to Pope Clement, was taken prisoner, but was afterwards put to death for his beautiful armour." This elegant taste has always been prevalent with the Italians.

Gambesons and gamboised armour continued to be worn at this period. Thus, in a roll of the Chamber of Accounts at Paris, in 1332, there is: Item Adse armentario 40 sol, 4 den: pro factione gambesononun. "To Ada, the armourer, 40s 4d for making gambesons from which we learn that they were fabricated by the same persons as made other kinds of armour. In a

---

[36] These are for passing the cord through which attached the camail to it.
[37] Probably the cap underneath the coiffe, which kept it from rubbing the head.

letter of John King of France, in the year 1353,[38] he directs que chascun ait le plus qu'il pourra de chevaux couvers de maailles et de gambaiseure. "That every one hath as many horses as he can covered with mail and with gamboised housings."[39] The seal of Sir Peter de Malo Lacu or Mauley exhibits the mail on his horse under the caparison; and Froissart, speaking of Edward the Third's first campaign in France, describes the barbed horses, and the knights and esquires richly armed.[40]

The gambeson descended to the middle of the thigh, and, as we have seen, had sleeves. The same kind of garment was worn by the women to regulate their shape; but, as Fauchet observes, not so stout or strong either in materials or quilting. In a MS. in the Cotton library,[41] entitled The Pilgrim, is the figure of a woman represented in the gambeson without any other clothing; and it is said that she,

> "Save a gambesoun, was naked."

And speaking of herself she says:

> "And the world I have forsake
> Richesse and alle pocessyonn,
> Save only this gambesoun."

This delineation is copied at the foot of Plate xxxii, and from it we learn that the female gambeson was without sleeves, and stitched horizontally, instead of longitudinally as those of the military.

Armour much in the style of that worn by Sir John D'Aubernoun and Lord Basset is represented on St. George, as depicted in glass, in the eastern window of Wimbledon church, Surrey. His surcoat, instead of being precisely like those in front of Exeter cathedral, is cut into wavy Vandykes at the bottom.

Plate xxxiii represents Sir Oliver de Ingham, copied from his sepulchral effigy in Ingham church, Norfolk. He also wears mixed armour, which is chain-mail covered exteriorly with black plates, the brassarts reaching but half way up from the elbows, and probably, therefore, are what were called

---

[38] Ex Memor. C. Cam. Camput. Paris, fol. 143, r°.

[39] This letter is directed to the burgesses and inhabitants of Nevers, of Chaumont in Bassigny, and other towns, and they are assigned to appear at Compiegne, on the 15th of Lent, to go against the king of England.

[40] P.159.

[41] In the Brit. Museum, marked Tib. A. vii.

braçonniéres. There are round plates placed to cover the outside of the shoulders, and at the bend of the arms, which are gilt, as are also the elbow joints, plates of the gauntlets, the genouillieres, and sollerets, or coverings for the feet. His chauçons or breeches are pourpointed with studs, and he wears the pourpoint over his hauberk. His basinet is made much longer behind than that of Sir John D'Aubernoun, and he wears over the pourpoint the cyclas. He died in the year 1343, and his monumental effigy is carved recumbent, but nearly in the position here represented.

The cyclas was also called ciclaton, siglaton, singlaton, and chigaton. It seems to have been borrowed from the Greeks, by whom it was called κυκλάς, from its fitting close round the body, in which, besides its form, it wholly differed from the surcoat. That of Sir John D'Aubernoun is laced together on both sides. Guillaume le Breton is willing to derive its name from the Cyclades, to the inhabitants of which isles he attributes the invention. He describes it as of

Stamina Phœnicum, serum, Cycladumque labores.

"Phœnician production, silk, and manufactured in the Cyclades."

Matthew Paris tells us, that on the marriage of King Henry III with Eleanor, daughter of Raymond Count of Provence, in 1236, the citizens of London were sericis vestimentis ornati, cycladibus auro textis circumdati, "adorned with silk garments, and enveloped in cyclases woven with gold." Probably, however, at this time the cyclas had not become a military garment; but the Chronicle of Bertrand du Guesclin speaks of a warrior, who rode out before the army by way of challenge, thus accoutred:

Voit son frcre venir, Hanry ot a nom,
Qui devant sa bataille venoit sur un Gascon,
Armez de haubregon, couvert d'un singlaton,
C'estoit Hanris armés à loy de champion.

"He saw his brother come, Henry was his name,
Who advanced before his line on a Gascon horse,
Armed in a haubergeon, covered with a singlaton;
Thus was Henry armed, according to the law respecting champions."

The siglaton was, as we have seen, of silk, and at first, when not emblazoned, of a vermilion colour. Thus the MS. Roman de Garin has:

> Ex par deseure un vermeil ciglaton.

> "And upon it a vermilion ciglaton."

And the Roman de Roncevaux:

> Chascons couvert d'un vermeil syglaton

> "Each covered with a vermilion syglaton."

They were afterwards plaided, whence, in the former of these romances, we read:

> Emprunte pailles et ciglatons plaiés.

> "Borrowed cloaks and plaided cyglatons."

After this they were emblazoned in a similar manner to surcoats.

The form of the cyclas is particularly pointed out in the following words:[42] Cycladem auro textam instar dalmaticæ, et preciosissimi operis quam sub mantello ferebat, etiam auro texto induto. "The cyclas, of woven gold and of most valuable manufacture, was like a dalmatic, and this he placed under his mantle, which was also of woven gold."

The monument of Sir Oliver de Ingham also affords us one of the earliest specimens of the jousting-hehnets of this time, surmounted by its crest, and as this is introduced into Pl. xxxiii, the form will be better understood than from description. Below is the visored basinet, the usual head-covering for battle, of Mercœur, as painted on the wall of St. Stephen's chapel, Westminster.

Edward Prince of Wales, son of Edward III, received the honour of knighthood in the year 1346, being then sixteen years and a month old,[43] and in about six weeks after led the van[44] of the English army at the celebrated battle of Cressy. This line, or battail, as it was antiently called, was thus

---

[42] See the Monachus Pegavensis sub an. 1096.
[43] Barnes, p. 341; Stow. p. 241; Speed, 689.
[44] Froissart, c. 130.

PLATE XXXIII

SIR OLIVER  DE INGHAM.

A.D. 1343.

composed: The archers were drawn up in the form of a herse,[45] about two hundred in front, and forty deep. The usual mode was a column of much greater depth, as the bowmen could shoot their arrows over each other's heads; but on this occasion, as the enemy were far more numerous it was necessary to prevent being out-flanked. The Prince of Wales stood at the bottom of this herse on foot, among his men at arms, in a solid square, having on his left the Earls of Arundel and Northampton, with a force of 7,000 troops, consisting of men at arms, billmen, and archers.

As the object is merely to shew the nature of the troops employed, and their mode of forming, it will not be necessary to pursue any regular account of the battle. I shall, however, notice some incidents that refer more particularly to our subject. Being on their ground, the archers having taken a short repast laid themselves on the grass, with their bows and helmets by their sides, and in this posture expected the approach of the enemy from about nine o'clock in the morning. This enabled them, by being refreshed, to sustain the combat with vigour. The French, on the other hand, were quite fatigued by a long march in their armour, the weight of which was particularly complained of by the Genœse cross-bowmen.[46] John of Luxemburgh King of Bohemia led the van, and was therefore the more immediate competitor of Edward. His division consisted at first of 20,000 men, there being 6,000 Genœse and Italian cross-bowmen, under the command of Carolo Grimaldi and Antonio Doria; but afterwards, at the request of the king of Bohemia, it was increased to 29,000 by the accession of all the Genœse cross-bows, led by Ame Count of Genoa, who were considered collectively as a match for the English archers, and appointed to commence the battle.

It was three o'clock in the afternoon before all the divisions had taken post; and then, as the Genœse were preparing to shoot, there fell a smart shower of rain which for a time delayed their operations. The air soon cleared, the sun was again visible, but it shone strongly and directly in their

---

[45] The herse was an instrument used in fortification, composed of transverse pieces of wood, with spikes projecting from their points of intersection; it was similar to the portcluse or portcullis, and let down over the inner gates by a molinet, to serve as a second protection after the enemy had forced the portcullis and first gate. The word is derived from the French herise, and was probably the adjective, and signified a bristled portcluse or gate-cover. Hurdles were often used instead of herses, to impede the march of cavalry. When troops were drawn up in form of a herse it was generally with their spears projecting from every possible direction .

[46] It has been already shewn, p. 6, from other authorities, that the cross-bowmen wore complete armour.

faces. They discharged their cross-bows, but their correct aim being thence prevented, and their bows losing strength from their strings being relaxed by moisture, it was without execution. The English archers had during the shower put their bows into their cases, so that when withdrawn they were uninjured. One flight of their arrows put the Genœse in disorder, who immediately retreated. The French king, enraged at their cowardice, intemperately cried out, "Slay the rascals!" an order most hastily obeyed, so that the English archers detroyed their enemies thus fighting against each other. Some of the followers of the English army at the same time penetrated this confusion, and with long knives dispatched all they met with without distinction.

After this the Prince of Wales was so warmly attacked, that fears were entertained for his life, but his father, who remained on the reserve, exclaimed: "While my boy is alive let him try to win his own spurs."[47] When victory appeared in favour of the English the King of England joined his gallant son, and the archers were ordered to throw behind them their bows, fall on the flanks, and combat with then-swords. This, however, encouraged the French, who thought, while they did not run the hazard of their lives by distant weapons, they could easily vanquish the English hand to hand.

The Marquis of Moravia, son to the King of Bohemia, was the first to renew the battle; but being wounded in three places, his standard beaten to the ground, and his men falling around him, with much difficulty turned round his horse, stripped off his emblazoned surcoat that he might not be known, and rode out of the field. The royal standard-bearer of France was beaten to the ground, and killed in sight of the king; but while both nations warmly contended for this prize, a French gentleman dismounted from his horse, and at the hazard of his life ript with his sword the banner from the shaft, and, wrapping it round his body, rode off with the object of his valour.[48]

It is said, but it is almost incredible, that the King of Bohemia at the commencement of the battle, though almost blind with age, induced two of his officers to lead him against the English, that "he might deal among them one good stroke with his sword." They fastened the bridles of their horses to

[47] The mark of knighthood. The king himself, previous to the battle, rode along the ranks mounted on a small palfrey, with a white truncheon in his hand, and attended by two marshals.

48 Mezeray, under this year; Froissart and Sleidan's Epist. p. 193; Knighton's History of Edward III, p. 2630; Æn. Syl. Hist. Bohem. c. 32; Gio. Villani Hist. c. 66, p. 879.

his, and being foremost in the charge were killed with their royal master.[49] The standard of the King of Bohemia being taken by the Prince of Wales he ever after bore the same device, being three ostrich feathers on a black ground, each labelled with the words Ich dien, "I serve."[50]

From this time the French began to call the young Prince of Wales Le Neior, or the Black;[51] and in a record, 2d of Richard II, n. 12, he is called the Black Prince. Yet this title does not appear to have originated, as generally supposed, from his wearing black armour, nor is there indeed any thing to shew he ever wore such at all.[52] When, however, he attended at tournaments in France or England,[53] he appeared in a surcoat with a shield, and his horse in a caparison, all black, with the white feathers on them, so that it must have been from the covering of his armour that he was so called.[54] Yet in the field of battle, and on all other occasions, his surcoat or guipon[55] was emblazoned with the arms of England labelled. The terrible effect of his prowess seems to have given another meaning to his epithet, for Froissart,[56] having described the battle of Poictiers, in 1356, adds: "Thus did Edward the Black Prince, now doubly dyed black by the terror of his arms." In that battle the king of France fought with a battle-axe.[57]

The monuments of Sir Guy de Brian at Tewkesbury, and the equestrian statue of Bernabo Visconti at Milan, afford interesting specimens of what may be called mixed armour. For this reason they have been selected to form

---

[49] There does not appear to be any good authority for this.

[50] Sandford's General History, p. 182. Some historians say, that the French had brought into the field their holy banner, called oriflamme, which was a signal of extermination, having been used in the crusades; and that Edward, as a retaliation of sentiment, displayed a burning dragon.

[51] Froissart, c. 131.

[52] In the painting of him, discovered on the wall of St. Stephen's chapel, his armour is gilt; and yet Eustace and Merceur are there represented in black armour. In the illuminated MSS. he also appears in plain steel armour. Thus in the initial letter to this reign, which is taken from the original one of the grant of the dutchy of Acquitaine, by Edward III to the Black Prince, the king appears on a throne of marble ornamented with a frame of gold, but both his armour and that of his son are steel with gilt knee and elbow caps. The grant is in the British Museum, in the Cotton library, marked Nero, D. VII.

[53] Ashmole says, he particularly distinguished himself in the exercise of those knightly sports. See his Order of the Garter, p. 669.

[54] Thus in the Memoires du Guesclin, among the English knights, mention is made of one called the Green Knight, c. 16.

[55] This is still to be seen hanging over his monument at Canterbury Cathedral.

[56] C. 169.

[57] Ibid. c. 162.

Plate xxxiv. Both these warriors are habited in a hauberk, much shortened, one of which terminates in what is called in heraldry vairee, resembling escutcheons of a later period; sometimes this termination was in Vandykes, and sometimes the hauberk was without any, as in Sir Guy de Brian's figure. The hauberk had thus been much shortened, so that it did not extend very much below the fork. One of this kind, though as they were worn to a later period, of what date cannot be so positively asserted, is in the armoury of my son. It had been purchased by a Jew, of an antient family, at Senegalia, near Bologna,[58] in whose possession it had been beyond any of their records. From it we learn that these Vandykes, which are also at the elbows where the sleeves end, are of brass. It also accounts for that furrowed appearance observable in those sculptured on the monumental effigies of this period, for we hence find that it was occasioned by every alternate row of rings only being rivetted, and these not so stout as the solid rings.

On the elbows of Sir Guy de Brian are elbow-caps, and below them several pieces of steel extend longitudinally to the wrists, and seem fastened on some padded work, as that is painted red. On his hands are fingered gauntlets. He is habited also in chausses, having a plate of steel on the front, and another on the side of each thigh, and the same on the legs, the knees being guarded with kneecaps. On his head is the basinet with its camail attached, and at his heels his spurs. The camail is not formed of rings, like the hauberk and chausses, but of wires, which, bent to take the form of rings, extend all round. This cannot be shewn in so small a space as allotted to it in the plate, but is very evident in the monument itself, and accounts for what we often see represented in illuminations of this period,[59] viz: such a stiff appearance in the camail, that when the basinet is put on the ground in the same way as on the head it does not bend under it, but takes the form of a solid. The rings of the hauberk are larger than those of the chausses.

Bernabo Visconti, below the sleeves of his hauberk, has elbow-pieces, on which are oval plates surcharged with his device; and below these vambraces or plate-annour for the lower arms. In the front of his thighs are cuisses, and at the back parallel pieces of steel, which are placed close by the side of each other. Over his knees are genouillieres, and under the bend of the leg

---

[58] The Jew bought it by the ounce, and paid for it forty guineas. It had been Mr. Douce's opinion before be bad beard mine, that this was not of Asiatic manufacture; and though there are in the same collection ten or twelve varieties of Asiatic chain-armour, not one resembles it. Probably, therefore, it is tbe only existing specimen of European chain-mail in this country.

[59] See the initial letter of this reign.

chain-mail. His legs are cased in jambs, or steel boots as they were some-times called, and his feet are guarded by sollerets. The jambs continued, till the time of Edward IV, to follow the line of the ankle at their termination, and the sollerets had pieces attached to them by a hinge to cover the heel.[60] He also wears spurs with large rowels, and on his hands are fingered gaunt-lets. All his plate-armour has on it a handsome border. As he is without his basinet and camail we are enabled to see that the hauberk terminated at the throat with a collar, different from the fashion at the close of the reign of Edward I. Both these figures have under their hauberks convex breastplates with their greatest convexity at the lower part; and over them jupons, or guipons, instead of surcoats, charged with their armorial bearings. These succeeded the cyclas, and were not so long as the hauberk, reaching only to the fork; they were sometimes terminated with elegant fancy work serving as a border, or were cut straight round. They were formed of silk or velvet, as may be observed in that of the Black Prince over his monument at Canter-bury, stuffed with cotton, and like that stitched down in parallel longitudi-nal lines, or quilted as in that of Sir Guy de Brian. These were kept down to their proper place by the military girdle, from which was suspended on the left side the sword, and on the right the dagger.

The guipon, gyppon, or jupas, which is the upper garment worn by the figures in this plate, was called by the French jupon and juppel, by the Ital-ians giupone, and by the Spaniards aljuba. It was of Arabic origin, as indeed this last word implies, and was derived from guibba, which signified the Moorish thorax. It was introduced into England about the middle of this reign,[61] and previous to the grand French and English struggle in Spain. A traveller has lately discovered some Moorish drawings in this last-men-tioned country, which, by exhibiting the Moors in this garment, corrobo-rate the above account of its origin.

Almost all the authorities seem to shew that this was an exterior gar-ment, yet we read in a French letter remissory, dated 1380, of a juppon de bougran, "a buckram juppon and Chaucer, in his Canterbury Tales, speaks of a knight not having time to change his clothes since his journey, who wore a gyppon of fustian, which had become dirty from the use of the hau-bergeon:

---

[60] Such a pair, marked Urban I. H. S. was in the collection exhibited in Pall Mall, of Italian workmanship.

[61] The figure of Robert de Brotherton in the initial to the last reign proves that it had been earlier known, but I believe it is a solitary instance.

PLATE XXXIV

SIR GUY DE BRYAN, & BERNARBO VISCONTI.

A.D. 1365.

"Of fustian he wered a gyppon
All besmotied with his haubergion."

From which we further learn, that the short hauberk was at this time called haubergeon.

It was, however, as before observed, generally of silk or velvet, and succeeded the cyclas, in being worn over the armour. Hence, in the Constitutions of Frederick King of Sicily: Comités, magnates, barones, milites ex uxores eorum possint habere in æstate guarniamentum unum de serico sub eo farsetum vel dublectum, ac juppain de serico. "Counts, peers, barons, knights, and their wives, may have in summer one garment of silk, under that a stuffed garment or doublet, and a juppa of silk." Thus also the monks, by the Reformatio Mellicensis "were not to use shirts of linen but only of wool," nec bambasio vel joppa,[62] "nor of silk or what was used for juppons." Pope Alexander IV having assigned to the Knights Hospitaliters black surcoats, that they might be distinguished from the other brethren of the same order, adds: In bellis autem sive in preeliis utantur jupellis et aliis superinsigniis militaribus, quæ sint coloribus rubei, in quibus etiam crux albi coloris sit in eorum-dem vexilli modum assuta, &c. "But in war or battle they are to use jupells and other military upper insignia, which may be of a red colour, in which also there must be a white cross, sewed in the same manner as on their standards:" so that here it is expressly called an upper garment. Again, in the Annales Genuenses,[63] it is said: Et statim Consul Pisanus cum Bucio ascendit galeam, et posuit in capite elmum et juppirai in dorso. "And immediately the Pisan Consul with Bucius ascended the gallery, and put on his head his helmet, and a juppon on his back." In a manuscript, entitled Miracula Urbani V" P.P. a warrior is spoken of who erat armatus de jupone, de tunica ferrea, et jaque de veluto cum bacineto ligato et stachato ut moris est, braceriis et gantelletis, ense et cultello cinctus, in pondere praedictorum arnesiorum 150 libras; "was armed with a jupon, an iron tunic, and a velvet jacque, with a bacinet fastened with cords to tie, and knotted according to the fashion, with bracers[64] and gauntlets, and a sword and knife appended to the girdle. The weight of the aforesaid armour was 150 pounds." Here the

---

[62] Joppa is the modern name for Jaffa, and therefore it might be supposed that this garment originated there; though I have not met with any authority to countenance such an opinion.

[63] Apud Muratori.

[64] For the lower arm, as on the figures of the last plate. These were the same as those called vambraces.

jupon seems to have been used as an under garment, and its place supplied by the jacque, but in several illuminations[65] it is drawn as worn over the armour, and a mantle or cointisse then thrown over it.

The saddle on which Bernabo Visconti sits is worthy of notice, giving the rider a very high and consequently commanding seat on his horse; the back part is also curiously formed, and the saddle-cloth is very splendid.[66] The stirrups are in the form of gothic elipses, and have just below the leathers two small projecting plates, the use of which is not so very evident. Stirrups were at this time called sautouers, whence Du Cange supposes was derived the sautoir or saltier in heraldry. The Latins of the middle ages termed it strepa and stapha, and the modern Greeks ςκάλα.[67] The manuscript Ceremonial says, that an esquire at a tournament ought not have a sautoir to his saddle. In the account delivered by Estienne de la Fontaine, for the year 1352, under the article "Harness," is the following item: "Pour six livres de soye de plusieures couleurs pour faire las tissus, et aiguillettes ausdits liarnois faire sautouers, et couyeres et tresses a garnir la selle. "For six pounds of silk of several colours to make tissues, and little needles (or tags) for the same harness, to make sautoirs, and joining pieces and twists to garnish the saddle."

At the foot of Plate XXXIV are the locket and chape of the sword of Edward the Black Prince.

Of Sir Guy de Bryan's services there are many proofs; but Rymer has preserved the king's writ, dated 24th of Edward III, A.D. 1350, issued to the treasurer of the Exchequer, directing the payment of 200 marks for life to Guy de Bryan, for his gallant behaviour in the last battle against the French near Calais, and for his prudent bearing of the standard there against the said enemies, and there strenuously, powerfully, and erectly sustaining it.

In the monument of Lord Hastings[68] are brasses representing him and Sir Hugh Hastings. Instead of the camail they are represented as wearing gorgets of chain-mail, and about their necks collars of two plates. They have moveable visors to their basinets, and tilting helmets near them. They have round plates to protect their armpits and elbows, and the chain sleeves of their hauberks further strengthened by plates put on the outside. The sleeves

---

[65] See particularly one in the royal library, in the British Museum, marked 16, G. VI, entitled "Gestes des Roys de France."

[66] It is engraved alone in Plate LXXX.,

[67] The learned have remarked, that stirrups were first used about the time of Constantine the Great.

[68] At Elsyng, in Norfolk.

of the liauketon are also visible in these specimens. The former has merely greaves, while the latter has chausses on his legs. The knee-caps are formed of circular pieces laid over each other smaller and smaller, and terminating in spikes. The basinets have flaps projecting behind.

Perhaps the monumental effigy of Sir Humphrey Littlebury[69] may be considered as one of the earliest specimens of plate-armour. He is habited in an haubergeon without sleeves. On his shoulders are four sliding plates, called espaulieres, below which, under the arms, is seen the gusset of mail, and the same in the bends of the elbows and knees. His arms and legs are completely covered with plate, the cuisses or thigh-pieces having silk coverings studded in the manner of pourpoints. Instead of solid solerets, his feet are protected by little contiguous plates rivetted on cloth, in the same manner as the knight in Plate xxx. The upper parts of his gauntlets are made in the same manner: they have fingers, but are made only to guard the outside of the hand, and therefore buckle at the wrists with straps. His jupon terminates in elegant foliage, and is kept down by a most splendid military girdle. Transversely from above the right hip is placed his sword-belt, also much ornamented, from which is suspended his long sword, the sheath of which has its top and chape embellished with architectural ornaments. From this belt is also suspended the dagger. On his head is the basinet and camail, and underneath his jousting helmet. His shield is of small dimensions, and resembles the architectural arch of this period, inverted: it is charged with two lions passant guardant.

The funereal effigy of John Cockayne, Esq. in Asliburne church, Derbyshire, exhibits him with a short sword at his side, the blade of equal size till near the point. He has cuisses on his thighs, but only greaves to protect his legs. His jupon is somewhat remarkable, having short sleeves which extend just over the shoulders, and ornamented with fringe.

In the quotation from the Federal Constitutions of the king of Sicily, we have found mention made of the doublet. So in one of the wardrobe rolls of Edward III, orders are given to prepare for the king on occasion of a tournament, among other things, a doublet of linen, having round skirts, and about the sleeves a border of long green cloth worked with representations of clouds, with vine branches of gold, and the following motto, dictated by the king himself. "It is as it is." Probably, therefore, the upper garment of John Cockayne is a kind of doublet instead of the jupon. Another specimen of it is to be found on the monumental figure of the renowned Connétable

---

[69] In Holbeach church, Lincolnshire.

du Guesclin, where it appears much like a short surcoat, with loose sleeves not extending so far as the elbows, and made to button down the front.[70] It was called doublet, from its being made of two folds of cloth, and therefore double.

A specimen of the short broad-bladed sword, not very different from that worn by Cockayne, but exactly like those depicted on the walls of the painted chamber, is engraved in the Archæologia.[71] It is taken from an original of the time of Edward III, still preserved at Durham, and which is presented in homage to the bishop of that see when he first takes possession. The wooden hilt remains, and seems to have been formerly covered with wire and velvet: the guard is straight and of metal, as is also the circular pommel, on which are on one side the arms of England, and on the other an eagle displayed.

With respect to cuisses of plate being worn with sleeves of mail, we find the practice noticed in the Roman du Chevalier délibéré:

> Cuissotz, braçonniere de maille
> Avoir te fault, et n'y fais faille.

> "Cuisses and braçonnieres of mail
> Thou shouldest have, and then you cannot fail."

The cuisses are here termed cuissotz; were also called cuissaux, cuissarts, and cuissets.

It was a custom on grand occasions of triumph to expose armour by way of military trophies; hence Knighton, describingJ the entry into London, of Edward the Black Prince with his prisoner the king of France, says, that "in the streets through which they passed the citizens placed in public view their plate, tapestry, and the like; but especially they boasted of their warlike furniture, and exposed that day[72] in their shops, windows, and balconies, such an incredible quantity of bows and arrows, shields, helmets, corselets, breast and back pieces, coats of mail, gauntlets, vambraces, swords, spears, battle-axes, harness for horses, and other armour, both offensive and defensive, that the like had never been seen in memory of man."

The reason of leaving off the long hauberks, and substituting plate-armour, was the weight of the chain-mail with its accompanying garments: indeed it was so great, that sometimes the knights were suffocated in it when

---

[70] See Montfaucon's Mon. Fr. Pl. CXXIV.

[71] Vol. XV, Pl. XXVI.

[72] The 24th May, 1357.

the heat was excessive, for although the plate-annour was very heavy, it was less so than the coat of mail with the wambais, the plastron, and the surcoat, because there was no need of either of the two former under a cuirass of steel; besides, if it was of well-tempered metal it was neither pierced nor bent by the thrust of the lance, nor pushed into the body of the knight as the mailles used to be, if the wambais or hoketon were ever wanting underneath.

But these plates were not always sufficient protection, as Froissart[73] speaks of an esquire who struck his antagonist in such a manner with his sharp and strong glaive, as not only to break his target, but pierce the plates and the hoketon underneath them, and entering his body it reached his heart. Still they were highly esteemed, and are thus spoken of in the Chronicle of Bertrand du Guesclin:

> Ils ont dedans leurs chefs les bacinets fermez
> Les escus a leur cols, dont il i ot assez
> Bonnes plates d'acier et de glaives assez.

> "They had among their chiefs some with closed basinets;
> Their shields at their necks, of which they had plenty;
> Good plates of steel, and plenty of glaives."

The arms and legs having become cased in plate, and pieces of mail, called gussets, at the joints of the limbs found sufficient, the haubergeon was often discarded, and an apron, or petticoat as it was called, of chain-mail only attached to the breast and back plates.

When, therefore, the cuirass was thus worn without any other covering of armour, another invention was applied for the greater convenience of managing the lance. This was a projecting piece, a little curved, fixed on the right breast, and called a lance-rest. Hence Froissart, describing an ambush of the French in the year 1356, says, that after suffering a part of the English force to pass by, "the French came briskly with their spears couched in their rests" to attack them.[74] The old chronicler Stowe, probably copying some writer of the time, says:[75] "At the commencement of the battle of Poictiers, 19th September, 1356, Lord Eustace d'Ambreticourt, being on horseback in

---

[73] Vol. 1, c. 49.
[74] C. 157.
[75] Chrono p. 261.

the English front, laid his spear in his rest,[76] and riding in among the German cuirassiers was so roughly met by the Lord Louis Van Coucibras, that both of them were unhorsed; but the German being wounded in the shoulder could not get up so soon as Sir Eustace, who, rising quickly, went with his sword drawn to the Lord Louis as he lay on the ground; but five other German knights falling on him with their spears bore him to the earth; but the goodness of his armour preserved his body, and he was taken prisoner without being hurt."

Froissart speaks of the lance-rest in the following instances: "Among the Cambressians was a young esquire of Gascony, named William Marchant, who came to the field of battle mounted on a good steed, his shield suspended from his neck, his lance in its rest, completely armed, and spurring on to the combat. When Sir Giles Manny, brother to Sir Walter, saw him approach, he spurred on to meet him most vigorously, and they met lance in hand without fear of each other. Sir Giles had his shield pierced through, as well as all the armour near his heart, and the iron blade passed quite through his body: thus he fell to the ground." Again: "The Lord of Potrelles was engaged against Albert of Cologne, a German, who, couching his lance, spurred his horse, and ran violently against Potrelles, but he struck him such a blow on his shield that his lance was shivered to pieces, the German squire however hit him strongly with a firm spear that broke not, but pierced through the plates of his shield and even his armour, passing straight to his heart, so that he knocked him off his horse, and gave him a mortal wound."

The mode of yielding prisoner at this time we learn from a memorandum inserted in the pedigree of the Pelham family, by John Philpot, Somerset herald in 1632. When John King of France yielded himself prisoner in the battle of Poictiers, he gave his right-hand gauntlet to the French knight in the service of the king of England, who advised him to yield; but he was taken, at that moment, by force from him by John de Pelham, (afterwards knighted,) who laid hold of his belt, while Sir Roger de la Warr got his sword. In memory of this the descendants of Sir John de Pelham constantly used the buckles of a belt as a badge in their seals, and the descendants of Sir Roger de la Warr the crampet or chape of a sword.[77]

So in the battle of Durham, in 1346, an esquire, named John Copland,

---

[76] The expression was" to couch," from the French coucher, " to go to bed," or " to lay," as the lance was then held tranquil; whence also the term" rest."

[77] Leigh's Accidence of Armoury, fol. 51.

called on David King of Scotland to yield himself, which so enraged him, that though wounded in two places, and having his weapons beat out of his hands, he struck him with his gauntlet, which beat out two of his teeth, saying that he would yield to none but a person of quality; but the esquire asserting he was a baron of England, the Scottish monarch delivered his gauntlet as a token that he was his prisoner.

At this time every man who took a captive might have for himself his ransom, provided it did not exceed 10,000 crowns, for, by the law of arms, those whose redemption exceeded that sum belonged to the king.[78]

When knights were desperately wounded it was the practice for their esquires to take them from the field, unarm and refresh them, and bind up their wounds. This was done to Lord James Audeley by his four esquires, after he began to faint from the wounds in his body and face at the battle of Poictiers.

We have a curious picture of the times in the pœtical Histoire de Jean IV de Bretagne, dit le Conquérant, from 1341 to 1351, by Guillaume de St. André, where the Bretons determined on defending themselves.

Les Bretons se vont aviser
Et leurs espées bien aguiser,
Pour soy deffendre, com que fust;
Chaicun gueroit et fer et fust;
Harnois de jambe et ganteletz;
Pou leur cbaloit de chappeletz.
Ains gueroit chaicun forte piece,
Que la poictrine ne se depece;
Bacinetz, aveque visieres.
Grand paour avoint d'estre en miseres;
Ne pensoint pas s'aler mucer;
Pour ce queroint plates d'acier,
Dagncs d'espreuve, ou mail, ou bâche
Et vandoint le bœuff et la vache
Pour quérir corsiers et chevaux,
Horczons,[79] et jacques tous nouveaux,
Canons et arcs, et arbalestres;
Trop doutoint avoir nouveaux maistres,
Salpêtre, canfre, souffre nouveau
Mettoit chaicun en son chasteau;
Garotz, saettes, et englaignes[80]

[78] Selden's Mare Clausum, c. 26, p. 171.
[79] Hourson d'estoffe, attaché au bacinet, says Lacombe.
[80] Englaines, enguegne, a kind of arrow: see Glossary sub voce Carellus.

Vouloint avoir en leurs enseignes,
Engins, bridolles, et mangonneaux
Faisoit on moult bons et moult beaux,
Martinetz,[81] arbalestres à tour
Mettoit l'en en chacune tour;
Barrières, palitz, et murs refaire;
Grands fossez de moult bel affaire
Reparer et mettre en estât,
Aux Bretons estoit bel esbat;
Dardes, javelotz, lances gayes
Sçavoint jetter et faire playes,
Goulfours, et fondres pour jetter pierres
Avoint en gros batons à quierre
Et si pensoint delfendre fort
Leurs libertez jusqu'à la mort.

"The Bretons choose to take warning,
And their swords well to sharpen
To defend themselves, and as it was
Each sought for iron and staves,
Leg-harness and gauntlets;
Few cared for head coverings,
But each sought a strong piece
That might defence his chest and
Basinets with visors.
Great dread had they of being wretched,
Not thinking of going to conceal themselves.
Therefore they sought plates of steel,
Proof daggers or mail, or axe,
And sold their oxen and cows
To procure coursers and horses,
Gorgets and jacks quite new,
Cannons, bows, and cross-bows;
Much fearing to have new masters;
Saltpetre, camphor and fresh sulphur
Each put in his castle.
Quarrels, arrows, and enguines.
They wish to have within their own limits.
Of engines, bridolles, and magonels
They made many good and fine.
Of martinets arbalètes a tour
Some were put in each tower,
Barriers, palisadœs, and walls to re-make
Great fosses very handsomely to form
To repair and put in a proper state

---

[81] Small cross-bows.

To the Bretons was fine diversion.
Darts, javelins, lance-gays
They knew how to throw, and wound with
Gouffours, and slings to throw stones
They had in great staves with slits in them;
And thus they determined bravely to defend
Their liberties until death.

Cuirasses have been spoken of, and the name occurs during this reign. Thus in a deed, dated 1355,[82] they are thus mentioned: Armaturas etiam in dictis galeis infra scriptas habebant, scilicet in qualibet ipsarum curacias CXXX, gorgalia CXXX. "Also they had the underwritten armour in the said galleys, that is, in each of them 130 cuirasses, 130 gorgets."

Again, in the year 1362, an author[83] speaks of double ones, the prototype of the breastplate with placcate, and such as were worn in Henry the Fifth's time, saying: Nullus in Caluxeno erat, qui armatus non esset sicut miles; et multi duabus coraciis erant præmuniti. "There was no one in Caluxeno who was not armed like a knight, and many were still more strongly protected with two cuirasses." The Italians called it corazza.

The monumental effigies of Sir Robert Wingfield and Sir John de Montague are perfect specimens of the plate-armour of this period, and the latter exhibits the jupon as laced down the side. The representation of Sir John Berdwell, in stained glass, in the window of Berdwell church, not only displays the chain collar as in the equestrian figure of Bernabo Visconti, but shews that the camail was sometimes flaccid, that is, when made of chain-mail instead of wire-mail, as it is there exhibited hanging from the basinet, which is supported on a ragged staff.

It has been observed, that Edward the Black Prince does not appear to have worn black armour, but that black armour was worn during this period from the paintings of Eustace and Mercure, found on the walls of St. Stephen's chapel. Their short surcoats are also black, but both these and their armour are ornamented with gilding. The visored basinet of Eustace de Ribemont is indeed altogether gilt, and as there are tasseled cords which come from underneath, he has probably a cervel-liere of mail attached to his camail. That this was worn at this time we have the authority of a statute, passed in the year 1351,[84] in which are the words . Armé de plates, de

---

[82] Ex Cod. Reg. Paris, 5956. A. fol. 1. v°.
[83] Pet. Azar. de Bell. Canepic.
[84] Tom. IV, Ordinat. Reg. Franc. p. 69, Art. 8.

crevelliere,[85] de gorgerette, &c. "Armed with plates, with cervelliere, with gorget," &c.

The Black Prince's monument is in Canterbury cathedral, but does not materially differ from other specimens of plate at this period, except in the gauntlets, which are given at the foot of Plate xxxv, and the ornaments of the sword-slieath, which are represented at the bottom of Plate xxxiv. He died in 1360. On his jousting helmet is a knight's cap surmounted by his crest, a lion crowned and standing; nor does he appear ever to have worn feathers in his helmet, a fashion which was first introduced in the reign of Henry V. The inscriptions on the walls of St. Mary's hall, in Coventry, seem at first to contradict this assertion, but they do not appear to be older than the time of Henry VI. That on the west side runs thus:

> "Edward the flowre of chevalre, whilom the Black Prince hyglit
> Who prisoner took the French King John in claime of Grandames ryght,
> And slew the Kyng of Beame in lielde, whereby the ostrych pen
> He won and ware in crest here first, which Price bare Ich dien
> Amid this martial feates of arms, wherein he had no peere
> His countie eke to shew this seate he chose and lov'd full deere
> The former state he gat confirm'd, and freedom did encrease
> A president of knyghthood rare as well for warre as peace."

That on the east side is in Latin, of which the following is a literal translation:

Edward III, in the 11th year of his reign, created the Black Prince Duke of Cornwall, and settled upon him the manor of Cheylesmore for life, after the decease of Queen Isabel, John of Eltham Earl of Cornwall, the tenant in remainder, having died without issue. It was not, however, till seven years after this, that the king made Coventiy a corporate town, nor did the citizens think of walling it in till eleven years subsequent to their incorporation. The Black Prince, moreover, did not enjoy his interest there till eight years later, just before his death. These circumstances, together with the false representation that the king of Bohemia wore the feathers together in his helmet instead of separately in his banner, are sufficient to shew that no reliance can be placed on the tradition recorded in these inscriptions.

The monument of Thomas Beauchamp Earl of Warwick only differs from this in having sleeves of mail to the elbows, which are guarded by demi-brassarts, or external plates of steel, buckled round them. On this account it has been selected for Plate xxxv. At the battle of Poictiers this

---

[85] For cervelliere.

nobleman is said to have fought so long and with such fury, that his hand was galled with the exercise of his sword and pole-axe.[86] As he was marshal of the army he is here represented with his staff of office.

The pole-axe seems to have been much used at this time, and Froissart says,[87] the French king was allowed by all to have performed the part of a valiant knight. He was on foot in the battle defending himself, and offending his enemies with a weighty axe of steel in his hands which he used with much praise.

The following circumstance will let us into the mode of etiquette, as well as the weapons used on some occasions. The French thought by treachery to surprise the castle and town of Calais, which, being reported to Edward, he desired the governor to keep up the pretence of delivering the fortress, while he and some troops should be concealed within. He then told Sir Walter Manny, that "he had a mind to grace him with the honour of the enterprize, for both he and his son (the prince) intended to fight under his banner." With a select body of 8,000 men at arms and 1000 archers, they sailed from Dover, and arrived at Calais in the evening, where their landing was effected with the utmost secresy, and they were placed in concealment. As the French entered they fell upon them with swords and battle-axes, crying out "A Manny! a Manny to the rescue![88] What! do the Frenchmen imagine with so few men to take the castle of Calais?" After this the mounted archers galloped after those who were without, and galled them with their arrows. The enemy, however, perceiving how few attacked them, rallied, on which the king of England threw away the scabbard of his sword, and drew up his foot archers on the elevated ground, which was protected by morasses from the charges of the enemy's cavalry. He then removed the visor of his helmet, and exposing his face, said: "Archers! do your duty; play them smartly, and know that I am Edward of Windsor;" —and victory declared for the English."[89]

We also learn the mode of fighting at sea from the account of an engagement that took place between the English and Spanish fleets, on the 29th of August, 1350, off Rye, in Sussex. The Spaniards in their huge carracks, overlooking the English vessels, attacked them with quarrels from their cross-bows, stones, timber, and bars of iron, with a view of overwhelming

---

[86] Dugdale's Warwickshire, p. 3]7, from a MS. in the Bodleian library, marked Cant. K. 84, 123.

[87] C. 164.

[88] Alluding to Sir Waltel'.

[89] Froissart, c. 15l.

PLATE XXXV

THOMAS BEAUCHAMP EARL OF WARWICK,

A.D. 1370.

them at once. The English archers, however, pierced their arbalisters at a greater range than their cross-bows would carry, frequently clearing the decks, obliging those who fought in the hatchways to cover themselves with planks, and bringing down with their arrows such as threw stones from the tops of their ships. After a long and doubtful fight, however, the English men at arms with great courage boarded the Spanish ships, and with their swords, lances, and battle-axes, gained the victory.[90]

A previous engagement with the French fleet, in 1340, further illustrates the subject of naval warfare.

On Midsummer eve Edward approached their station in the Swyn; and the next day, as the sun was rising, he beheld their fleet with the sails down arranged in four lines, and fastened together with ropes and great iron chains, that they might not be penetrated. They had wooden castles erected on the top of their masts, and small skiffs, full of stones, suspended half way down.[91] Edward drew up all his

ships, placing the strongest in front, and on the wings those containing his archers. Between every two vessels with bowmen there was one of men at arms. Detached ships, with archers, were posted in reserve, to assist such as might be damaged.[92] The sails being set they stretched out a little to gain the wind and get the sun behind them,[93] a circumstance of some importance in the style of fighting at this period. A gallant veteran began by attacking one of the ships of their front line; the Earl of Huntingdon selected another; the Earl of Northampton a third; Sir Walter Manny[94] a fourth; and others in succession engaged with individual antagonists. The trumpets sounded, and the battle became general. The archers and cross-bowmen shot with all their might; the men at arms engaged hand to hand. The English threw out their grappling irons to link themselves to their enemies, and their determined bravery after a long resistance mastered the first line. The French king's flag was torn down, and the English standard was mounted in its stead.[95]

The two next lines, dismayed by the capture of the first, which had been rendered a floating fortification, and had been thought invincible, attempt-

---

[90] Mattb. Villani, c. 99; Walsing. Hist. p. 160; Knighton, p. 2602; Fabian, p. 228; Hollingshed, p. 945; and Stowe, p.250.

[91] Avesbury, 55; Hemingford, 320.

[92] Froissart, c. 51.

[93] Ibid.

[94] This gentleman had come over in the suite of the queen, and became one of the greatest warriors of his time.

[95] Hem. 320; Froiss: 209.

ed to escape. The English surrounded them before they could separate. The crews threw down their arms, and jumped into their boats: most of these, being thus overladen, sank, and two thousand men perished. Three lines subdued, the English assaulted the fourth, consisting of sixty ships: and here the severest part of the conflict occurred. Some of the bravest defenders of the other lines rallied in these. Night came on in the midst of the struggle, and the impossibility of relief but from success produced a desperate courage. Two English ships with their defenders were overwhelmed by discharged stones, the rest were in proportionate peril. The king and his nobility were examples to all of undaunted and indefatigable valour. The conflict continued in the horrors of darkness, beyond the time of midnight, thousands perishing every hour before the victory was decided. The French had outnumbered their assailants four to one, with the additional advantage of being more experienced mariners. But the English resolution triumphed. The whole of the hostile fleet was captured, and thirty thousand of its fighting men perished in the action.[96]

This decisive achievement, observes Mr. Turner, gave a superiority of spirit and strength to the English navy, which was displayed on other occasions during this reign, and which has since become the inseparable character of the British islanders.

We may judge liow high in esteem the chivalric prowess and justice of King Edward were held from his being frequently made the arbiter in judicial combats. In September, 1350, there arrived in England Sir John de Vesconti, on the part of Hugh the Valiant, king of Cyprus, and Sir Thomas de la Marche, on that of the king of France, for this purpose. Sir John, therefore, openly, in presence of King Edward, accused the other of treason, challenging to prove it on his body: in token of this he threw down his gauntlet, which Sir Thomas as boldly took up, to shew his acceptance of the challenge. The 14th of October, being the Monday after St. Michael, was appointed for deciding this quarrel in close field, within the lists at the Palace of Westminster.

On that day they came armed at all points on horseback, the king, the prince of Wales, and the whole court of England, being spectators. On the sound of trumpet the combat began. At the tilt both their spears broke on each other's shield, without either of them being moved from their saddles, wherefore they both, alighted at one instant, and renewed the conflict on foot, till, having with equal valour and conduct fought a considerable time,

---

[96] Hem. 322; Froiss. 210; Avesbury, 58.

both then weapons were rendered useless: and coming to close grapple, wrestling for victoiy, both fell locked together. The visors of both their helmets were defended with small distant bars of steel, through which they might see and breathe more freely, all the rest of their bodies being covered with armour. Rising together, Sir Thomas de la Marche got the advantage of his antagonist by having sharp pricks of steel, called gadlings, fastened between the joints of his right gauntlet, and therewith struck at the visor of Sir John de Vesconti, (who had no gadlings on his gauntlets). Striking as often as opportunity offered, he grievously hurt him in the face, so that he exclaimed that he was unable to help himself. At this King Edward threw down his wardour, the marshal cried "Ho!" and the combat ceased.

The king adjudged the victory to the French knight, and that the vanquished should be at his mercy, according to the laws of arms. Sir Thomas de la Marche generously waived his right to punish, and presented his prisoner to the prince of Wales to do with him as he pleased. The prince gave him his liberty; and Sir Thomas dedicated his own suit of armour to the English patron St. George, with great devotion, in the cathedral church of St. Paul, in London.[97]

This French fashion of fixing upon the gauntlets the gadelins, or gadlings, was adopted by the English, and appear on the monument of Edward the Black Prince, from whence they are copied at the bottom of Plate XXXV. From this representation, it appears they were used on both gauntlets, but only between the knuckles and first joint of the fingers. The gads themselves, which are the semi-cylindrical pieces of plate that covered the fingers, are still used as heraldic bearings, and particularly in the arms of the armourers' company.[98]

The following account of jousts and tournaments in this reign is extracted from Stowe.[99] "Without the north side of Bow church towards West Cheape standith one fair building of stone, called in record Sildam; a shed which greatly darkneth the said church: for by mean thereof all the windows and doors on that side are stopped up. This building was made by King Edward III upon this occasion. In the reign of the said king, divers justings were made in London, betwixt Sopars lane, and the cross in Cheape; (for the standard stood not then in the place where now it is,) namely, one great justing was there in the year 1330, the fourth of Edward III, whereof is not-

---

[97] Walsingham, p. 160.
[98] See them figured in Edmondson's Heraldry, who can give no explanation of them.
[99] Survey of London, book III, p. 23.

ed thus: About the feast of St. Michael there was a great and solemn justing of all the stout earls, barons, and nobles of the realm; at London, in West Cheape, betwixt the great cross and the great conduit, nigh Sopar's lane. Which justing lasted three days, where Queen Philip, with many ladies, fell from a stage of timber, notwithstanding they were not hurt at all. Wherefore the Queen took great care to save the carpenters from punishment. And through her prayer (which she made on her knees) she pacified the king and council. And thereby purchased great love of the people."

"This took place in the year 1331 about the 21st of Sept[r]. The stone pavement was covered with sand (say divers writers of the time) that the horses might not slide when they strongly set their feet to the ground. And to the end that the beholders might with the better ease see the same, there was a wooden scaffold erected across the street, like unto a tower, wherein Queen Philip and many other ladies richly attired, and assembled from all parts of the realm, did stand to behold the justs; but the higher frame in which the ladies were placed brake in sunder, whereby they were (with some shame,) forced to fall down. By reason whereof the knights and such as were underneath, were grievously hurt. After this the king caused a shed to be strongly made of stone for himself, the queen and other states to stand on, and there to behold the justing and other shows at their pleasure."[100]

"Smithfield was antiently appropriated not only to markets of horses and cattle, but military exercises as justings, turnings, and great triumphs, which have been there performed before the princes and nobility, both of this realm and foreign countries. Fabian mentions that in the year 1357 the 31st Edw III. great and royal justs were then holden in Smithfield, there being present the kings of England, France, and Scotland, with many other nobles, and great estates of divers lands. In the year 1362 the 36th Edw III. on the first five days of May in Smithfield, were justs holden, the king and queen being present, with the most part of the chivalry of England and of France, and of other nations: to the which came Spaniards, Cyprians, and Armenians, knightly requesting aid of the King of England against the Pagans that invaded their confines. The 48th Edwd III, Dame Alice Perrers or Pierce (the king's concubine) as lady of the sun, rode from the Tower of London through Cheap accompanied of many lords and ladies, every lady leading a lord by his horse's bridle till they came into West Smithfield; and then began a great just which endured seven days after."[101]

---

[100] Book III, p. 36.
[101] Book III, p, 239.

To these extracts from Stowe may be added the following from a MS. at Cambridge.[102]

"In the year 1359, about the latter end of May, to honour the citizens of London King Edwd III caused a solemn just to be proclaimed to be held in that city for three days together, in which John Loufkin, mayor, John Barnes and John Bury the sheriffs, with their brethren the aldermen to the number of 21 as challengers, were to hold the field against all comers. But at the time appointed, in their stead but in their name, came the king privily with his four sons, Edward Prince of Wales, Lionel, John, and Edmund, with nineteen other great barons of England, the king representing the mayor, the prince the senior sheriff and so on, in presence of the kings of France and Scotland, and an infinite number of spectators. They all bore on their shields and surcoats the city arms, and maintaining the honour of the city so valiantly during the whole time gave the greatest pleasure to the citizens when they were made acquainted with the truth."

There is still extant an antient poem, entitled "Rychard Cœr de Lion,"[103] which, as it cites Ogier le Danois, composed in the year 1261, must have been written subsequently; and, from the description of the armour, appears to be of the time of Edward III. The following passages are extracted from it:

> " The fyrsle yere that he was kyng
> At Salybury he made a justing
> And coraaunded every man to be there
> Bothe with shelde and with spere."

The places where Richard I permitted jousts to be held have been before mentioned, but Salisbury does not occur in them.

> "The partyes were sonder set
> Togyder they ranne without let.
> Kyng Rychard gan hym dysgnyse
> In a ful strange queyntyse.[104]
> He cam out of a valaye
> For to se of theyr playe
> As a knyght aventurous
> Hys atyre was orgulous
> Al togyder cole black

---

102 Bibl. CCC, c. 230.
103 See Weber's Metrical Romances:
104 Cointisse.

Was hys horse without lacke,
Upon hys crest a raven stode
That yaned as he were wode,
And aboute hys necke a bell
Wherefore the resoun I shall you tell."

It appears from this and other pœms that, on the three days, during which the jousts generally lasted, the knights used frequently to appear differently habited.

"He bare a schafte that was grete and strong,
It was fourteen foot long;[105]
And it was grete and stout
One and twenty inches about.[106]
The fyrst knyght that he there mette
Ful egyrly he hym grette,
With a dente amyd the schelde,
His hors he bare down in the felde:
And the knyght fel to the grounde
Ful nygh ded in that stound.[107]
The next that he mette thare
A grete stroke he hym bare
Hys gorgette with his Cornell[108] tho
Hys necke he brak there atwo.
Hys hors and he fel to grounde,
And dyed bothe in that stounde.
Kyng Rychard gan hove and abyde
If any mo wolde to hym ryde."

In these extracts we have had the description of a joust; in the following the author describes a tournament:

"Trumpettes began for to blowe,
Knyghtes justed in a rowe,
Another knyght, hardy and good,
Sate on a stede red as blood.
He dydde hym aime, and well dyght
In all that longed to a knyght.
A shafte he toke grete and stronge
That was so hevy and longe

---

[105] This must be considered as more than the ordinary length of the jousting lance.
[106] That must be at tbe swell just above the gripe.
[107] Shock.
[108] The coronel at tbe end of the lance.

This knight determined to attack the king; but the author adds:

"Kyng Rychard of hym was ware
And a spere to hym he bare,
And encountryd hym in the felde,
He bare away halfe hys schelde,
Hys pusen therewith gan gon
And also his braudellet bon,
Hys vyser and his gorgere
Hym repented that he cam there."

I have not been able to discover the meaning of the word pusen, which, according to Mr. Weber, is the same as pesens, mentioned in another place, nor brandellet, unless the latter signifies the sword, and the pusen the chain, which attached it to the mamilliere. A blow of the lance might, after splitting the shield, carry away these, and enter the gorget and visor.

"Kyng Rychard, &c.
And in another tyre he hym dyght
Upon a stede rede as blode
With al the tyre that on hym stode,
Horse and schelde, armure and man,
That no man scholde knowe hym than,
Upon hys creste a rede hounde
he taylc henge to the grounde."

Having entered the field:

"A baroun he sawgli hym besyde,
Towarde hym he gan to ryde.
To a squyer he toke hys spere
To hym he wolde not it here
Forth he toke a mansell[109]
A stroke he thought to be set well
On hys helme that was so stronge
Of that dente the fyr outspronge."

The mace and massuelle were favourite weapons at this period, as well as the battle-axe. Thus at the time Lord Chandos received his death,[110] he was in Spain pursuing his enemy with a massive battle-axe in his hand, when, it being frosty, his foot slipped, and his surcoat, which was of the long kind,

[109] Probably an error for masuell, as the line would read the better.
[110] In the 43d of Edward III.

entangling his legs, he fell down. On rising again a lance was thrust into his face, under his left eye, between the nose and forehead: it entered, as was thought, into his brain, so that he fell again, and twice rolled upside down with the pain. Though he did not die on the spot, he never spoke after. His visor was up, and he was blind on that side where he was wounded, having lost his eye five years before in hunting a hart near Bourdeaux. Probably this accident occasioned the entire disuse of long surcoats. The author of the poem thus goes on to speak of King Richard

> "In his stirope up he stode
> And smote to hym with irefull mode,
> He set his stroke on his yren hat,[111]
> But that other in hys sadell sat.
> Hastely, without words mo
> Hys mase he toke in hys hande tho,
> That was made of yoten brass
> He wondryd who that it was.
> Suche a stroke he hym lente
> That Rychard's feet out of hys styropes wente,
> For plate ne for acketon
> For hauberk ne for campeson
> Such a stroke he had none ore
> That dydde hym halfe so moche sore.'

In this we see enumerated the breastplate, the hauketon, the hauberk, and gambeson. The author next speaks of the king in another change of habit:

> "In the thyrde atyre, &c.
> Alle his atyre whyte as mylke;
> His cropere was of sylke."

This is the croupierc, or covering for the hinder part of the horse. The king makes then an attack on "another noble knyglit," thus:

> "He smote hym on hys bacinet
> A grete dente withouten let."

After this:

> "And another stroke he hym brayde
> Hys mase upon his hed he layde."

---

[111] Chapel de fer.

The knight acted in the same manner:

> "And with hys hevy mace of stele
> There he galf the kyng hys dele,
> That his helme al to rove
> And hym over his sadell drove
> And hys styropes he forebare," &c.

What the swyre was I have not discovered, but it again occurs in the following line:

> "My swyr hadde gon in tweg."

The attack is thus described:

> "So harde to onr knyght he droff
> Hys schelde in twoo peses roff
> His schuldre with hys schafft he brak,
> And bar hym over hys hors bak
> That he fel doun and brak hys arme."

The author describes the king's expedition to the Holy Land, and speaks of troops—

> "On hors and foot wel aparaylyd; ·
> Two hundred schypps ben well vytailid,
> With force hawberks, swerdes and knyvys."

Relating the attack, he says:

> "And the Englishmen defended them well
> With good swerdes of brown stele."

The king was successful:

> "Portcules and gates up he won
> And let come in every man."

He himself is described as—

> "Well armed in armure bright."

We are then told—

> "Of silk, cendale, and syglatoun
> Was the emperour's pavyloun."

To carry on the siege—

> "The mynours ganne to myne faste
> The gynours sond and stones caste."

The following passage is remarkable, because it contains probably the earliest mention of splints:

> "Now speke we of Rychard out kyng
> How he cam to batayle with hys gyng
> He was armed in splentes of steel."

defended the inner part of the arm, and introduced in Henry the Eighth's time.[112] Probably, however, in this case, the whole armour is described, and therefore I conjecture that kind is referred to which is represented in Plate xxx. From the resemblance to this of the contrivance for the inside the arms, it is most likely the name was revived. Richard was mounted and

> "Hys ax on his fore-arsoun hyng."

From which we learn that antiently the battle-axe was often appended to the bow of the saddle, instead of the short sword, called estoc.

The gynours do not mean gunners, as they made no use of cannon, but engineers, and hence we are told:

> "The gynours mangeneles hente,
> And stones to the cyte they sente."

Several machines are mentioned as used at the siege, thus:

> "Arweblast[113] off weys with quarel
> With staff-slynges that smyte well
> With trepiettes[114] they slungen alsoo
> That wroughte hem ful mckyl woo;

---

[112] In the armoury of Llewelyn Meyrick, Esq. are several specimens, from the year 1536 to 1620, which seems to have comprised the whole period of their existence.

[113] Arbaleste.

[114] Such as in Plate xxvi, Fig. 5.

And blewe wylde-fyr in trumpes of gynne
To mekyl sorwe to hem withinne."

This shews that the Greek fire and not gunpowder was used at the time
this pœm was written.

But we have an express account of its composition in the "Practica" of
J. Arderne, an eminent surgeon of his day, in the service of Edward III. He
says: Si volueris domos inimicorum tempore guerrre cremarej fac unam
instrumentum caneanum interius de ferro vel ere ad modum fistule et
impleate de aqua turbentine et illud instrumentum ligetur uni sagitte vel
querale et igne accensum cum area vel balista mittatur ubicunque volueris
malefacere et non extinguetur in aere, et cremabit quicquid tetigit quod
ignis poterit consumere pro certo.

Ecce modum faciendi *ignem Græcum* inextinguibilem omnia combu-
rentem et precipue naves in mare et quicquid fuerit combustibile quod tan-
gere poterit. Accipe sulphuris vivi libram 1, colofonie libram 1, picis navalis
classe ante quaterium 1, ... opofanarum ante quateriam 1, de fino colum-
barum bene siccato quaterium 1; oinne predicta bene pulverate et post resolve in aqua terbentine vel oleo sulphuris vivi predicti, et tunc ponantur
omnia simul in vase vitreo forti cujus orificium bene claudatur, et ponatur
illud vas per xv dies in calido furno equinb, postea distilletur illud totum in
distillore vitreo ad modum aque ardentis et usui reservetur. Istud jactatum
cum area vel balista vel cum aliqua ave portata, cremat et inflammat quicquid teligerit in loco quo ceciderit sive in terra vel in aqua pro certo.[115]

"If you wish to burn the houses of the enemy, in time of war, make an
instrument hollow like a cane, within of iron or brass, in form of a tube,
and fill it with water of turpentine, and bind that instrument to an arrow
or quarrel, when, being set on fire, it may be ejected by a bow or cross-bow,
wherever you wish to do an injury, and it will not be extinguished in air, but
will burn whatever it touches, that can be consumed by fire for a certainty.

"This is the mode of making the Greek fire inextinguishable, and burning every thing, particularly ships in the sea, and whatever is combustible
that it may touch: Take of sulphur vivum 1ib, of colofony[116] 1ib, of pitch
used for naval purposes 1 quarter, of . . . . . of opoponax[117] 1 quarter, of pi-
geons' dung well dried 1 quarter: let all the before-mentioned be well pul-

---

[115] Sloane MSS. in the British Museum, No. 56.

[116] Common rosin, being the common residuum after distilling turpentine.

[117] Probably, extract opoponax. This is a gum resin obtained by wounding the roots of
the pastinaca opoponax, a plant which is a native of the Levant.

verized, and then resolve them in turpentine water or oil of sulphur vivum aforesaid, [118] and then put them altogether into a strong glass vessel, the mouth of which should be well closed, and put that vessel for fifteen days in a hot oven; afterwards distil the whole in a distilling vessel, in the manner of spirit of wine, and keep it for use. This may be thrown by a bow, a cross-bow, or carried by any bird. It will burn and inflame whatsoever it hath touched in the place where it shall fall, whether on land or water, for a certainty."

In another place the same writer states, that the Greek fire chiefly consisted of turpentine water slowly distilled with turpentine gum, and that it was ignited by throwing water upon it.

A warrior is afterwards said in the poem to have received such a blow, and the effect of a blow on the head gives us another term in antient armour.

"That hys helme al to cleff
And al to brosyd hys heme-panne."

The herne-panne is stated by Mr. Weber to be the scullcap, and I am of the same opinion, conceiving it to be a corruption of iron-pan, and worn under the helmet. We next meet with the following description of armour:

"Other festnynge none ther was,
Then yryne cheyncs for alle cas;
And thos were i-wrought ful wel
Both in gcrthes and peytral
A queyntyse off the kynges owen
Upon his horse was i-thrown:
Before his arsoun his ax off steel
By that other syde his masnel
Hymsclf was rychely begoo
From the crest unto the too,
He was armyd wondyr weel,
And al with plates off good steel
And there abovcn an hawberk.
A schafft wrought off trusty werk.
On his schuldre a scheeld of steel
With three lupardes wrought ful weel,

---

[118] It is not very clear how one of these could be substituted for the other. The former is of an inflammable nature, while the oil of sulphur vivum, usually termed oil of vitriol, is an acid and not inflammable. Perhaps it was some preparation from sulphur differing from that of modern chemists, and which retained its inflammable properties. Naptha might be used instead of oil of turpentine as that is a light spirit which floats on the mineral tar and is of a very inflammable nature.

An helmelie hadde off ryche entayle,
Trusty and trewe hys ventayle
On his crest a douve whyte," &c.

From this we learn that the caparison of silk, which was thrown over the poitral and croupiere of mail, was called cointisse; also that the breastplate, as before remarked, was worn under the hauberk; and that the cylindrical helmet is here alluded to with its ventaile over the face. There are two seals of Edward III with this kind of helmet, but it dœs not appear to have lasted much longer than this reign. The shield is mentioned as of steel, which was not a usual material, though a broad band of iron was frequently laid on near the edge, as may be seen on the shield of state in Westminster Abbey. It was generally of wood covered with a skin called paune, pane, penne, and penna. Thus the Roman de Partonopex has:

Vait ferir Gaudins durement
Halt tres parml l'escu l'asene
De soz la bouche lez la penne.

"He made a thrust violently at Gaudins,
Very high its direction, near the shield,
Below the mouth,[119] but near the penne."

Again:

De lez la penne de l'escu.
Parmi l'espaule l'a feru.

"From off the skin of the shield
Near tbe middle of the shoulder he struck him."

So likewise the Roman de la Violette:

Et le jayant parmi la pane
Do l'escu 1c fiert de la macbe.

"And the giant, near the skin
Of the shield, struck him with his club."

And the Roman d'Athis:

---

[119] That hollow in the upper angle on the fight side of the shield made for the lance, first in general use in the time of Richard II. The shield in Westminster Abbey, as well as the sword, is of the time of Henry VI.

> De fort escus fait Tarevene
> Lui perce la premiere peunc.

> "Of the strong shield made for Tarevenne
> He pierced the first pcnne.

By which it appears that they were sometimes covered with more than one skin. The belt by which the shield was suspended was called giga, by the Italians guiggia, and by the French guige. The Roman de Flore describes a warrior thus:

> Et l'en li aporte un escu....
> La guiche fu d'un paile frois
> Bien taillé d'or Sarrazinois.

> "And besides he bore a shield....
> The guiche was of embroidered drapery,
> Handsomely ornamented with Saracennec gold."

Again:

> Li cox est aval descendu
> Coupe la guiche de l'escu.

> "The cuckow going down in it's descent
> Cut the guiche of the shield."

So also the Roman d'Alexandre:

> Si fiert Emenidas sus la targe florie,
> Que dessous la boucle li a francò et percié
> La guige, en est routé et l'en arme saillie.

> "The proud Emenidas under his target fleury[120]
> Of which below the buckle he had penetrated and pierced
> The guige, is routed and with his arms put to flight."

And in the Roman de Garin:

> Escu et d'or a un lioncel bis
> Parmi la guige h son col le pandi.

---

[120] This is an heraldic term and implies any ornament terminating in a fleur-dé-lis.

> "On his shield was a lioncel divided of gold:
> Which by the guige hung from his neck."

The old pœm of Rychard proceeds thus:

> The spere-hed forgatt lie nought
> Upon hys spere he wolde it have
> Goddes hygh name thereon was grave.

The perversion of our mild religion to weapons of deadly warfare is most strange, but continued to the time of Henry VIII, as in the armoury of Llewelyn Meyrick, Esq. is a German sword, dated 1533, on which is engraved a passage from the 18th Psalm,[121] destined to be run through a man's body.

The pœm next gives us the description of a Saracen warrior, and thus mentions the furniture of his horse:

> Therefore as the booke telles
> Hys crouper hung all full of belles
> And hys peytrel, and hys arsoun;
> Three myle myghte men here the soun.

This Asiatic fashion of hanging bells upon the horse furniture was introduced into Europe at the close of the fifteenth century. The pœm also speaks of the Greeks under the term Griffouns, which accounts for one of Richard's machines having been called Mate-Griffoun.

On a brass-plate affixed to the monument of Bishop Wivil,[122] in Salisbury Cathedral, is represented the champion who had maintained his cause against William Montacute, Earl of Salisbury. In 1355, the bishop brought a writ of right against him for the Castle of Sherborne, in Dorsetshire. The claims of the respective parties were so complicated,[123] that it was thought impossible to determine them by legal issue, and they were consequently referred to single combat. At the time appointed, the bishop brought his champion to the lists, cloathed in white, with his lordship's arms on his sur-

---

[121] Noch lebt er, i. e_ he liveth.

[122] He died in the year 1376.

[123] It had been seized by King Stephen, and with others in 1134 was committed to the care of twenty-four barons. In the year 1258, being the 42nd of Henry 111, it was delivered to Stephen Longespee, Earl of Salisbury; and in 1337, Edward III. granted it to W. Montacute and Catherine his wife, for his services against Mortimer.

coat.[124] The earl's champion was habited in the same manner. Both were preparing to engage, when an order was brought from the king to defer the dispute to another day. In the meantime matters were compromised, the earl ceding the castle to the bishop and his successors, on payment of 2500 marks.[125]

The practice of tilting at the quintain had been continued ever since the reign of Henry II, but with improvements. In these the object seems to have been some slight punishment, arising from the machine, to those who attempted to strike it unskilfully. In a MS. in the Bodleian library at Oxford, which is dated 1343, three boys are represented as tilting jointly with one pointless lance at a tub full of water, which is to be struck in such a manner as not to throw it over them. They are probably learners only, and therefore depicted without their cloathes, having undressed themselves in order to save their garments from being wetted in case the attempt should prove unsuccessful. This farcical pastime, according to Menestrier,[126] was practised occasionally in Italy, where, says he, a large bucket filled with water is set up, against which they tilt with lances; and if the stroke be not made with great dexterity, the bucket is overset, and the lance-man thoroughly drenched with the contents. Matthew Paris mentions the quintain by name;[127] but he speaks of it in a cursory manner as a well known pastime, and probably would have said nothing about it, had not the following circumstance given him the occasion. In the thirty-eighth year of the reign of Henry III the young Londoners, who, he tells us, were expert horsemen, assembled together to run at the quintain, and set up a peacock as a reward for the best performer. The king then keeping his court at Westminster, some of his domestics came into the city to see the pastime, where they behaved in a very disorderly manner, and treated the Londoners with much insolence, calling them cowardly knaves, and rascally clowns. Some have thought these fellows were sent thither purposely to promote a quarrel, it being known that the king was angry with the citizens for refusing to join in the crusade.[128] Be this as it may, they resented this conduct by soundly beating the domestics. The

---

[124] In the brass-plate, however, he appears in a jack.

[125] In the inscription on the Monument it is said of the bishop: Inter enim alia beneficia sua minima castrum dicte ecclesie de Schireburn per ducentos annos et amplius manu militari violenter occupatum eidem ecclesie ut pugil intrepidus recupavit, &c.

[126] Traité de Tournois, published in 1669, p. 347.

[127] Sub. an. 1253.

[128] Strype's edit. of Stowe's Survey of London.

king, however, was so incensed at what he declared to be an indignity put upon his servants, that, not taking into consideration the provocation on their parts, he fined the city one thousand marks.

When the youths had learned to strike the tub of water in the exact part, they next were permitted to try their skill at the human quintain. This was a man completely armed, whose business it was to act upon the defensive, and parry their blows with his shield.

Another manuscript in the Bodleian library, dated 1344, exhibits a representation of this exercise, and the painting is justified by the concurrent testimony of the Roman de Giron le Courtois. The author of this romance introduces one knight speaking to another in this manner: Je ne vous tiens mie a si bons chevalier, que je daigne prendre lance pour jouster a vous, ains vous dy, que vous eloignez de moy, et me venez fern· de toute vostre force, et je vous feray quintaine. "I do not by any means esteem you a sufficiently good knight for me to take a lance and just with you; therefore, I desire you to retire some distance from me, and then run at me with all your force, and I will be your quintain." The satirist Hall, who wrote in the time of Elizabeth,[129] evidently alludes to a custom of this kind, when he says:

> Pawne thou no glove for challange of the deed
> Nor make thy quintaine other's armed head.

The living quintain, which occurs in the manuscript, is seated upon a stool with three legs without any support behind, and the business of the filter was, probably, to overthrow him; while, on his part, he was to turn the stroke of the pole or lance on one side with his shield, by doing which with adroitness he might occasion the fall of his adversary. He is represented in complete plate armour except his feet, having on his head a tilting helmet, differing but little from those of the time of Edward I, and wearing a surcoat. The living quintain seems to have been succeeded by a representation of a human figure carved in wood. To render the appearance of this figure more formidable, it was generally made in the likeness of a Turk or Saracen, in allusion to the crusades, bearing a shield upon his left arm, and brandishing a club or a sabre with his right. The quintain thus fashioned was placed upon a pivot, and so contrived as to move round with facility. In running at this figure it was necessary for the horseman to direct his lance with great adroitness, and make his stroke upon the forehead between the

---

[129] See his works printed in 1599, Lib. IV. Sat. 3.

eyes or upon the nose;[130] for if he struck wide of those parts, and especially upon the shield, the quintain turned about with much velocity, and, in case he was not exceedingly careful, would give him a severe blow upon the back with the wooden sabre held in the right hand, which was considered as highly disgraceful to the performer, while it excited the laughter and ridicule of the spectators.

To answer the same purpose, but at the same time to lessen the expence, the yeomen made use of a moveable quintain which was very simply constructed. It consisted merely of a cross bar which turned upon a pivot, or nail driven into a post, with a broad part to tilt against on one side, and a bag of earth or sand depending from the other, which, by the rotatory motion of the bar, after the board was struck, would hit the tilter on the head if he did not move on with the greatest activity.[131] In a manuscript in the Bodleian library, dated 1344, is a representation of the exercise with this quintain, on the board of which is painted a horseshœ.

The post-quintain was retained, however, for the practice of warriors on foot, in order to acquire strength and skill in assaulting an enemy with their swords and battle axes.

Froissart mentions[132] a trick used by Reynaud de Roye, at a justing-match between him and John de Holland. He fastened his helmet so slightly upon his head that it gave way, and was beaten off by every stroke that was made upon the vizor with the lance of John de Holland, and of course the shock he received was not so great as it would have been, had he made the helmet fast to the cuirass. This artifice was objected to by the English on the part of de Holland, but John of Gaunt, Duke of Lancaster, who was present, permitted Roye to use his pleasure, declaring at the same time that, for his part, he should prefer a contrary practice, and have his helmet fastened as strongly as possible. The trick, however, seems to have become more common after this, as the same historian speaking of a justing between Thomas Harpingliam and Sir John de Barres, says: f(As methought the usage was

---

[130] This shows us that the face was generally aimed at in charging with a lance, and probably on occount of the perforations and divisions of the helmet affording more prospect of striking- the wearer than any other part of the armour. It was, indeed, on this account, that the knights bent down their heads, when tilting, in order to leave the face as little exposed as possible. My friend Sir Walter Scott has beautifully described this custom in these lines:

> "He stoop'd his head, and couch'd his spear,
> "And spurr'd his steed to full career."

[131] See one of these at the foot of plate xxv,

[132] Chrono vol. III. C. 59.

tlianne, their lielmes were tied but with lace, to the entente the spere should take no hold."[133]

To this account of tournaments may be added the following extract from Gibbon's Roman Empire.[134] "The abolition at Rome of the antient games must be understood with some latitude; the carnival sports of the Testacean Mount and Circus Agonalis were regulated by the law or custom of. the city. The senator presided with dignity and pomp to adjudge and distribute the prizes, the gold ring, or the pallium, as it was styled, of cloth or silk. A tribute on the Jews supplied the annual expence, and the races, on foot, on horseback, or in chariots, were ennobled by a tilt and tournament of seventy-two of the Roman youth. In the year 1332 a bull feast, after the fashion of the Moors and Spaniards was celebrated in the Coliseum itself; and the living manners are painted in a diary of the times: a convenient order of benches was restored; and a general proclamation, as far as Rimini and Ravenna, invited the nobles to exercise their skill and courage in this perilous adventure. The Roman ladies were marshalled in three squadrons, and seated in three balconies, which, on this day, the 3rd of September, were lined with scarlet cloth. The fair Jacova di Rovere led the matrons from beyond the Tyber, a pure and native race, who still represented the features and character of antiquity. The remainder of the city was divided as usual between the Colonna and Ursini: the two factions were proud of the number and beauty of their female bands: the charms of Savella Ursini are mentioned with praise; and the Colonna regretted the absence of the youngest of their house, who had sprained her ancle in the garden of Nero's tower. The lots of the champions were drawn by an old and respectable citizen; and they descended in the arena or pit to encounter the wild bulls, on foot, as it should seem, with a single spear. Amidst the crowd, our annalist, (Ludovico Buonconte Monaldesco), has selected the names, colours and devices, of twenty of the most conspicuous knights. Several of the names are the most illustrious of Rome and the ecclesiastical state; Malatesta, Polenta, della Valle, Cafarello, Savelli, Capoccio, Conti, Annabaldi, Altieri, Corsi; the colours were adapted to their taste and situation; the devices are expressive of hope or despair, and breathe the spirit of gallantry and arms: "I am alone like the youngest of the Horatii," the confidence of an intrepid stranger: "I live disconsolate," a weeping widower: "I burn under the ashes," a discreet lover: "I adore Lavinia or Lucretia," the ambiguous declaration

[133] Ibid, C. cxxxiii, folio 148, Lord' Berners' translation.
[134] C. lxxi.

of a modern passion: "My faith is pure," the motto of a white livery: "Who is stronger than myself," of a lion's hide "If I am. drowned in blood, what a pleasant death," the wish of ferocious courage. The pride or prudence of the Ursini restrained them from the field, which was occupied by three of their hereditary rivals, whose inscriptions denoted the lofty greatness of the Colonna name: "Though sad I am strong," "Strong as I am great" "If I fall," adressing himself to the spectators, "you fall with me," intimating, says the contemporary writer, that, while the other families were the subjects of the Vatican, they alone were the supporters of the Capitol. The combats of the amphitheatre were dangerous and bloody. Every champion successively encountered a wild bull; and the victory may be ascribed to the quadru-peds, since no more than eleven were left on the field, with the loss of nine wounded, and eighteen killed on the side of their adversaries."

There was a particular kind of hastilude in the Low Countries called l'Espinette,[135] which seems to have taken its name from the religious cere-mony of gathering thorns on the Sunday before that called Quadrigesima. It was practised by the principal citizens of Lisle, who elected a chief from among themselves, on whom they bestowed the title of king. The first of these was Sir John le Grand, Knight, Lord de Joye, in the year 1283, and the last Jacques de le Cambe, surnamed Ganthois in the year 1485, when it was relinquished in consequence of the expence attending the dignity. Jacques de Tenemonde however undertook it the following year on condition that the cost should be defrayed by the state. The hastitudes of this society are recorded in the chamber of accounts in Paris up to the year 1328, and in that of Brussells[136] to that of 1382. Thomas Arthus, King of the Espinette, is thus spoken of under the year 1360. Il se présenta aux joustes à cheval, armé et pardessus aussi accoustré de samit blanc, son cheval armé, et houssé jusqu'en terre de mesme, entretaillé avec houppes et sonnettes dorées, mo-rillon doré, bien empannachié; ses valets à cheval et à pied et ses halbardiers tous accoustrés aussi de juppons de soie verte. "He presented himself for the justs on horseback, armed and also wholly accoutred in white samit, his horse armed and caparisoned to the ground with the same, intermixed with

---

[135] Some pretend that St. Louis was the institutor of this fête, but the history of the kings of the Espinette dœs not begin before 1283, thirteen years after the death of that monarch. It is not easy to discover the origin of the name, it is certain, however, that the king of this fête was presented with a little thorn or épinette, to mark his dignity, and that he went every year in state to honour the holy thorn, which was preserved in the church of the Dominicans, at Lisle.

[136] Marked Toison d'Or. See also on this subject Buzelin in Gallo. Pland.Jib. III, c.23.

tufts and round bells gilt, a gilt mo· rillion, and with a splendid panache; his
valets on horseback and on foot, and his halbardiers all clad in juppons of
green silk." The expence attendant upon the office of king was compensated
for by a title of nobility being conferred, if the person was not already of
that rank, and if a nobleman, by the investiture of the military girdle with
other privileges.

At the hastilude à l'Espinette, the Earls of Flanders were often present
with a numerous retinue. Sometimes they contended in it, as in 1464, when
Louis XI fought with Baldwin Gommer, then King of the Espinette.

The following statute, preserved among the public archives at Lisle,
was passed in tlie year 1489, and affords much explanation on tlie subject.
S'ensuit la forme et la conclusion prinse en la halle de la ville de Lille pour
et au nom de tout le corps et communauté de la ville de Lille par ceux qui
cy après sont dénommez et qui dores-navant à toujours seront à entretenir
pour le fait, réglé et conduite de la feste de l'Espinette, de grande anclii-
enneté maintenu en la ville, ainsi que a plust et plaist à mon très-redoubté
seigneur et prince Monseigneur le Duc de Bourgougne par vertu et teneur
de ses lettres patentes cy enregistrées.

Pour celui qui sera roy, sera tenu prendre l'Espinette au Riez de Los, et
de faire soupper en la manière accoustumée.

Le roy sera tenu faire une colasse le jeudy, second jour de caresme, pour
illecq terminer et décider les difficultez, qui souvent sourdent entre les jousteurs en diverses maniérés.

On fera le voyage de S. George à Templemars le vendredy ensuivant, et
le disner au retour, sans y appeller dames ne damoiselles quelconques; et ce
aux despens du roy.

Seront esleus quatre jousteurs du moings pour jouster avecq le nouveau
et le vieu rois de behour: lesquels seront tenus eulx houschiers lionnorable-
ment selon leur estât, à l'entendement des maistres de la feste, qui seront
esluz en la maniéré cy après déclarée. Le samedy veille du dit behourt, on
fera le disner, les monstres en robes pareilles, avec la colasse au soir en la
maniéré accoustumée.

Le dimence les deux rois et les jousteurs seront tenuz de faire chascun
une feste au disner, et illecq auront damoiselles, pour après disner accom-
pagner les roines.

On fera le soupper en halle, et puis le bancquet en la maniéré accoustumée.

Celui qui gaignera le pris de dedens, et aussi le roy, sera tenu de jouster le lundy aux joustes qui seront publiées, ou livrer jousteurs pour eux: et s'il advenoit que le roy nouvel gaigneroit le dit pris de dedens, le viez roi sera tenu de l'accompaigner et jouster ou livrer hommes pour lui.

Et se les mardy, mercquedy et aultres jours ensuivant en la sepmaine dudit behourt, on faisoit joustes, le dit roy nouvel sera tenu de monter à cheval et aller sur les rengs tous les jours qu'on joustera, et de assembler dames et damoiselles, et livrer vin et espices, avec allumerie en son liostel ou ailleurs.

Que au voyage de Bruges, les jousteurs pour le dit lieu de Bruges seront tenuz avoir robbes de parure, et y sera tenu le viez roy de jousteurs avecq le nouvel, et de faire le soupper et honneurs accoustumés.

Au jour du gras dimence sera le roy tenu faire danser aux dames et damoiselles chevaliers, escuiers pour espincer l'Espinette, et traitter par les viez roys de l'election du roy de la ditte Espinette, comme l'on le souloit faire le jour de caresmeaulx, et faire le soupper de six plats de viande ou de huit au plus.

Le mardy ensuivant sera tenu de faire disner pour illecq prendre conclusion de aller au riez en délaissant le don de roy et menestriers.

Et si les roys et jousteurs se veullent, oultre ce que dit est, mesler ou esbatre en aultres joustes, si alcune se faisoit en la ville ou ailleurs es pays de Monseigneur, on se rapporte à leurs voulontez et discrétion, sans les contraindre.

Et pour ce que dessus est dit, auront iceux roy et jousteurs la somme de douze cent livres Parisis monnoye de Flandres, qui leur seront distribuez des deniers de la ville comme s'enfuit, assavoir quatre cent livres au roy et jousteurs à payer le jour du behort. Au roy seul huit cent livres, si comme deux cent au jour du beliort, deux cent pour son premier voyage et jouste de Bruges, deux cent à son yssue du royaume et feste de l'Espinette, et deux cent livres à son second voyage de Bruges avecq son successeur roy de l'Espinette.

Et au regard de commettre les maistres, tant pour la feste de Bruges, comme celles de la ville, ils seront eslus au nombre des anchiens roys en la maniéré accoustumée; lesquels feront rendre compte de la dépense aux roys et compaignons jousteurs en dedens quinze jours, après les festes du behourt et de Bruges, en telle maniéré que si sur ces comptes y eclieroit contredit, ce sera décidé par Messieurs de la loy; et s'il y avait reliqua, oultre la despence ou charge, ce sera à partir également au roy et jousteurs.

A laquelle conclusion prendre furent le bailly de Lille, les lieutenans de la gouvernance, deux maistres des comptes, rewart, maieur et eschevins, neuf anchiens roys de l'Espinette, deux conseillers et deux clercqs de la ville dénommez au registre et livre cy dessus.

"Here follows the form and conclusion taken in the town-hall of Lille for and in the name of all the corporation and community of the town of Lille by those, who are hereafter named, and who, from henceforth for ever, shall be, to understand it for the fact, rule and conduct of the feast of the Espinette, of great antiquity established in the town, as it has pleased, and doth please my very redoubted Lord and Prince, Monseigneur the Duke of Burgundy by virtue and tenor of his letters patent here registred.

"For him who shall be king, he shall be held to take the Espinette at Riez de Los[137] and to give a supper after the accustomed manner.[138]

"The king shall be held to make an assembly on Thursday the second day of Lent, there to determine and decide the difficulties which often arise between the justers in various ways.

"The journey to St. George at Templemars shall be made on the following Friday, and the dinner on the return, without inviting to it any ladies or young ladies: and this is to be done at the expence of the king.

"Four justers at least, shall be chosen to just with the new and old king of the behort;[139] who shall be held to equip[140] themselves honorably according to their condition, to the satisfaction of the masters of the feast, who shall be elected in the manner hereafter declared. On Saturday, the eve of the said behort,[141] a dinner is to be given, the parties in the shew being apparelled like the assembly in the evening, after the accustomed manner.

"On the Sunday the two kings and the justers shall be held each to give a dinner feast, and there they shall have ladies, who after dinner may accompany the queens.

"They shall give a supper in the hall, and afterwards the banquet in the usual style.

"He who gains the prize of the dedans,[142] and also the king shall be held to just on the Monday at the justs that shall be proclaimed, or to find justers as substitutes for them; and if it happens that the new king gains the said prize of the dedans, the old king shall be held to accompany him, and just

---

[137] The brook of the Monastery of our Lady of Praise.
[138] At this entertainment the number of guests was usually 208.
[139] A name for a tournament derived from the nature of the lances which were hollow.
[140] The word principally applies to their draperies and those of their horses.
[141] The first Sunday in Lent.
[142] The dedans was probably like that of a racket-court. There were two prizes, the principal was a golden bawk with two leaves of green silk; the other a silver collar of the arms of the town.

or find substitutes for that purpose.

"And if on the Tuesday, Wednesday and other following days in the week, justs are given, the said new king shall be held to mount his horse, and go into the ranks all the days on which there is justing, and to assemble ladies and young ladies, and to distribute wine and spices with illuminations, in his hotel or elsewhere.

"As to the journey to Bruges, the justers for the said place of Bruges, shall be held to have robes of splendour, and the old king shall be held to just there with the new one, and to give the supper with its accustomed honours.

"On Sunday the day of grace the king shall be obliged to give a dance to the ladies and young ladies, the knights and the esquires to drive the Espinette, and to treat by the old kings on the election of the king of the said Espinette, as is the custom to be done on the day of carnivals, and to give a supper of six plates of meat or eight at most.

"The ensuing Tuesday he shall be held to give a dinner in order to make a conclusion there, for going to the brook to refresh the gift of the king and his guides.

"And if the kings and justers wish, besides what is said, to mix or contend in other justs, should any be held in the town or any where else in the country of my Lord, they shall act according to their wishes and discretion without hindrance.

"And for what is above said, the said king and justers shall have the sum of 1200 livres of Parisian money of Flanders, which shall be distributed to them by the paymasters of the town as follows: viz. 400 livres to the king and justers to pay the day of behort. To the king alone 800 livres, of which 200 to be paid on the day of behort; 200 for his first journey and just at Bruges; 200 at his quitting the kingdom and the feast of the Espinette; and 200 livres on his second journey to Bruges with his successor king of the Espinette.

"The conclusion of this matter shall be taken by the bailly of Lille, the lieutenants of the government, two masters of accounts, the rewart, the mayor and aldermen, nine former kings of the Espinette, two counsellors and two town clerks, named in the registers and delivered as above."

The Espinette was formally excepted in all the laws of the Kings of France against tournaments, as of Philip de Valois in 1328, etc.

As the practice of the sword and buckler had been prohibited by Edward I, a shield and club were substituted in their place. Two combatants, thus armed, are represented in an illumination in a manuscript in the Bodleian library at Oxford, marked 264, and dated 1344. The shields are rounded at the bottom, have a convex receptacle in the middle for the hand, and a diagonal bar for holding, being therefore modifications of the buckler.

When men of rank were slain in battle it was usual to have them carried off on their shields. Thus at the battle of Poictiers the Black Prince ordered the dead body of Sir Robert Duras to be taken up and borne away on a shield.

Part of Windsor Castle and that of Harewood in Yorkshire, will give us some idea of the military architecture of this period; and what where considered necessary stores for the defence of castles, we may collect from what was done in the instance of Norwich. In 1342 the gates and towers of that city were furnished by Richard Spynk, a citizen, with thirty espringolds for casting great stones, and to every espringold a hundred gogions or balls fastened up in a box, with ropes and other accoutrements belonging to them; also four great arbalests or large cross-bows, and to each of them a hundred gogions or balls, and two pairs of grapples to draw up the bows, besides other armour.[143] In the watch-towers it was usual to have a bell, on which the sentinel struck the alarm in case of danger.[144] Thus in the Chronicle of Bertrand du Guesclin we read:

> Y avoit une gaite toute jour à journée
> Qui sonnoit un bacin, quant la piere est levée.

> "He had a sentinel all day during the battle,
> Who sounded a bell, when the stone was raised."

Glaives and gisarmes continued to be used during this reign, for in a letter of Charles V, King of France, in 1369, the former is mentioned to signify the troops that carried them: Plusieurs gensd'armes jusqu'à quarente glaives ou environ, estoient venus devers les parties de Lorraine. "Many men at arms, and nearly forty glaives were come into the parts of Lorraine." The size of the glaive-blade we learn from an account of the year 1356. Unum glave de decern palinis. "A glaive ten palms long." There was also the half glaive, called glaviolus or glaviotus. It is spoken of in letters remissory of the year 1378: Icellui Picart prist en sa main une fourchefiere et son fils un demi-glaive ou glavelot. "That same Picart took in his hand a strong-fork

---

[143] LeI. Introd. civicum 1, p. 3,5.

[144] On this account he was called Bachinator.

and his son a demi-glave or glavelot."

So was the hand gisarme[145] common at this time. In a letter remissory of the year 1389, it is said: Icellui Jehan saicha une vielle guisarme qu'il avoit pendue à sa sainture. "That John seized an old guisarme which he had hanging from his girdle."

The Order of the Garter is, by historians, generally reported to have been established by King Edward III, as an honorary reward for valour and military prowess. The origin is variously attributed: some alledging that he picked up the countess of Salisbury's garter while at a dance, when his courtiers smiling, he said: Honi soit qui mal y pense. "Evil be to them that evil think," which was afterwards the motto. Others have said it was the queen's garter that he took up. But Grafton tells us[146] he writes from an old chronicle, that "King Richard I, before his departure to the Holy Land, called all the lordes and knightes unto him, and did swere them for evermore to be true unto him, and to take his part: and in token thereof he gave to every of them a blewe lace or ribband to be knowen by; and hereof, (sayth that olde chronicle) began the first occasion of the Order of the Garter."

This, however, never appears to be represented on monumental military effigies before the time of Edward III, nor, indeed, till some time after that, and the names of the knights are known from their establishment in this last monarch's time. Aslnnole says[147] that the Prince of Wales was the first knight of those illustrious companions, and that the institution took place in the 23rd of Edward III, but the garter is not on his monumental effigies. It seems, in reality, to have been merely a symbol of union.

The mode of degrading a knight was by hewing off his spurs, thus Mezeray relates, that the French King having taken prisoner, in the year 1350, Sir Emerci de Pavia, had him degraded of his knighthood on account of his deceit, which ceremony was performed by hewing off his spurs.[148]

The Black Prince's cry at the battle of Poictiers was: "Advance banner in the name of God and St. George," which was answered by the men at arms, who accompanied his standard-bearer, exclaiming: "St. George Guienne." The French cry was: "Mon Joye St. Dennis."

When the Black Prince, in the 29th of Edward III, led an army into France, he caused a proclamation to be made, that every one should bear

---

[145] See one at the foot of Plate xxviii.
[146] Chrono Vol. II, p. 86.
[147] P. 670.
[148] See also Stowe, p. 249.

the arms of St. George, he himself having a double-antient or ensign.[149] The difference between the guidon and banner is illustrated by the following anecdote.[150] " As the two armies (before the battle of Nagera) approached near together, the Prince went over a little hill, in the descending where-of he saw plainly his enemies marching towards him; wherefore, when the whole army was come over this mountain, he commanded that they should make an halt, and so fit themselves for fight. At that instant the Lord John Chandos brought his ensign folded up, and offered it to the prince, saying: "Sir, here is my guidon; I request your highness to display it abroad, and to give me leave to raise it this day as my banner; for I thank God, and your highness, I have lands and possessions sufficient to maintain it witliall." Then the prince took the pennon, and having cut off the tail,[151] made it a square banner, and this done, both he and King Don Pedro, for the greater honour, holding it between their hands displayed it abroad, it being Or, a sharp pile gules: and then the prince delivered it unto the Lord Chandos again, saying: "Sir John, behold here is your banner. God send you much joy and honour with it." And thus being made a knight banneret, the Lord Chandos returned to the head of his men, and said: " Here, gentlemen, be-hold my banner and yours. Take and keep it to your honour and mine." And so they took it with a shout, and said by the grace of God and St. George they would defend it to the best of their powers: but the banner remained in the hands of a gallant English esquire, named William Allestry, who bore it all that day, and acquitted himself in the service right honourably."

---

[149] Thomas de la More's journal printed in Stowe's Chronicle, p. 256.

[150] Joshua Barnes.

[151] This tail was by the French called fanon, whence the English word fane, to. imply a weather-cock,

Richard the Second.

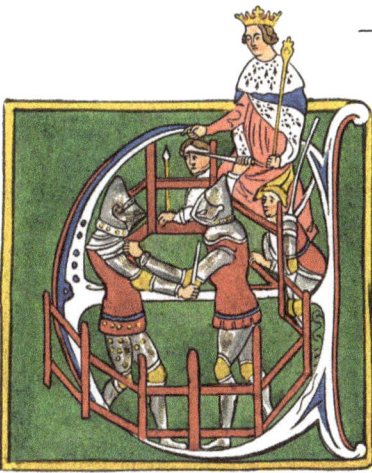

DWARD was succeeded by this young prince, his grandson, in the year 1377, who reigned till 1399. For some time after his succession the armour continued much the same as at the close of Edward III. Of this period is that military statue, found under the old stairs leading into the Receipt of the Exchequer, engraved in Carter's specimens of antient sculpture. The helmet is incomplete, wanting a stone at top to finish its conical form, and for which reason alone it has been noticed here. Of this period, too, is the brass effigy of Sir Miles Stapleton, in Ingham Church, Norfolk, whose armour is much ornamented. On his thighs is a covering of pourpointed silk. This is also to be seen of a red hue, spotted with yellow, on the effigy of Sir Robert Wingfield, his brassarts and vambraces being covered with the same colour.

The monument of Sir John Harsick affords a good specimen of the armour towards the middle of this reign, and has therefore been selected for Plate XXXVI. He is here, however, represented writh his helmet on over his basinet, so as to display the mode of wearing the crest and the cointisse, which latter ends in two tassels. This is the tilting helmet, and below the crest, which is a collection of turkey's feathers, is the wreath, which was formed of two pieces of silk of the colours of his armorial bearings, and twisted together by the lady who chose him for her knight. It is the earliest specimen of the wreath I have been able to discover, which took place of the cointisse, and left that a mere ornamental appendage. The helmet, ordinarily used in battle, is given at the foot of the plate, being taken from the monument of Lord Hastings.

In old Kilcullen Church, in the County of Kildare, is a curious specimen of the armour worn in Ireland during this reign. It is the monument of a knight of the Eustace family. He wears an haubergeon, in shape like those used in the time of William the Conqueror, but of chain-mail. His legs and arms, however, are protected by jambs and vambraces of plate, his feet by demi-sollerets, his knees by genouilliers, and his elbows by caps. His head is wrapped up in a cloth, tied at the top, such as worn in the reign of King John, and called cargan, over which was placed his conical vizored basinet, of the form of Edward the Ist's time; and he wears, attached by a cord round his waist, a large scymitar at his left side. The monument of Humphrey de Bohun, Earl of Hereford, in 1.367, is the earliest specimen of plate armour with taces, or overlapping plates to envelope the abdomen, at the bottom of the breast-plate, without any sur-coat. It was not till the reign of Henry V that this practice became general. He wears plate over the insteps, but the rest of his feet is covered with chain.

The monument of John Lord Montacute, in Salisbury Cathedral, is of the middle of this reign, and gives a good specimen of highly ornamented gauntlets, of a contrivance for the easier bending of the body, at the bottom of the breastplate, and of the elegant manner of twisting the hanging sword-belt, pendant from the military girdle, round the upper part of the sword. Indeed the detail of this figure is well worthy a minute attention.

We have a fine specimen, too, of ornamented armour in the monument of Sir Hugh Calvely, in Bunbury Church, Cheshire. Besides the foliated border running round the lower edge of the basinet, the conical part of it is encircled by a diadem of most splendid jewellery. Pendant from his military girdle is his sword on the left side, and his dagger on the right, which are attached by chains made in a tasteful manner. Like the armour on the monument of the Black Prince, he has a large plate over the jamb just below the genouilliere.

PLATE XXXVI

SIR JOHN  HARSICH,

A.D. 1384.

About the same period is one of those monumental effigies,[1] in the chancel of St. David's Cathedral, falsely said to be Welsh Princes, and the time is chiefly marked by the cord which attaches the camail to the basinet, being protected by an ornamented cover.

The artists of Milan were famous, even at this period, for their skill in making armour, which superiority they retained till its final disuse. Hence Froissart, in the account which he gives of the preparations made by Henry Earl of Derby,[2] and Thomas Duke of Norfolk, Earl Marshall, for their proposed combat in the lists at Coventry, says: "These two lords made ample provision of all things necessary for the combat; and the Earl of Derby sent off messengers to Lombardy, to have armour from Sir Galeas, Duke of Milan. The Duke complied with joy and gave the knight, called Sir Francis, who had brought the message, the choice of all his armour for the Earl of Derby. When he had selected what he wished for, in plated and mail armour, the Lord of Milan, out of his abundant love for the earl, ordered four of the best armourers in Milan to accompany the knight to England that the Earl of Derby might be more completely armed."[3]

This extract does not tend to exalt our opinion of the English armourers, and yet there was at this time a company of them in London, for they presented a petition to parliament[4] against the oppressions of Nicholas Brambre, a confidential partisan of government; as did also the company of bladesmiths, and the spurriers. Probably, therefore, the armour of Sir Hugh Calvely, and other splendid suits that decorate several monumental effigies at this period were manufactured at Milan.

It was a considerable time after the establishment of justs and tournaments, before the combatants thought of making either lists or barriers. They contented themselves, says Menestrier,[5] with being stationed at the four angles of an open place, whence they run in parties one against another.

The first lists consisted of cords stretched before the different companies, previous to the commencement of the tournaments, as we learn from

---

[1]   That wrongly attributed to Rhys Grûg. The other of the time of Edward III, Sir Richard Hoare has supposed to be Rhys Prince of South Wales. They are probably both of the Tudor family.

[2]   Afterwards Henry IV.

[3]   Johnes's Froissart, Vol. I, p. 597.

[4]   Parl. Plac. p. 227.

[5]   Traité de Tournois, printed in 1669.

the following passage in an old English romance:[6] "All these thinges donne, thei were embatailed eclie ageynste the otliir, and the corde drawen before eche partie, and whan the tyme was, the cordes were cutt, and the truinpettes blew up for every man to do his devoir. And for to assertayne the more of the tourney, there was on each side a stake, and at eaclie stake two kyngs of armes, with penne and inke, and paper, to write the names of all them that were yolden, for they shold no more tour nay."

But as these pastimes were accompanied with much danger,[7] they invented in France the double lists, which, besides the cords above mentioned, consisted of a paling put up in the centre, so that the knights might run from one end to the other without coming in contact, except with their lances. Other nations followed the example of the French, and the usage of lists and barriers soon became universal.

The lists for the tilts and tournaments, no doubt, resembled those appointed for the ordeal combats, which, according to the rules established by Thomas Duke of Glocester, uncle to Richard II, were as follows: "The king shall find the field to fight in, and the lists shall be made and devised by the constable; and it is to be observed, that the lists must be sixty paces long, and forty paces broad, set up in good order, and the ground within hard, stable, and level, without any great stones or other impediments; also that the lists must be made with good bars seven feet high or more, so that a horse may not be able to leap over them."[8]

The following ordinance for the conducting of the justs and tournaments, made about this period, occurs in one of the Harleian manuscripts.[9] It is preceded by a proclamation that was to be previously made, which is couched in these terms: "Be it known,[10] lords, knights, and esquires, ladies and gentlemen; you are hereby acquainted that a superb achievement at

---

[6] MS. Harl. 326.

[7] Thus at a justing held. on London Bridge, A. D. 1395, between David Earl of Crawford, and Lord Wells, the latter. was at the third course cast from his saddle to the ground and much hurt; and Caxton in his Addit. to Polychron, c. 7, fol. 399, tells us that in the 17th of Richard II: "The Erie of Moreyf, a Scotch Lord, cbalenged the Erle Marchal of England, to juste with hym on horsback, with sharpe speres, and soo they roode together certayne courses, but not the full chalenge, for the Scottyssh Erie was caste both horse and man, and two of hys rybbes broken with the same falle, and soo borne home into his inn, and anone after was caryed homewarde in a lityer, and at Yorke he dyed."

[8] MS. in Cotto Lib. marked Nero, D. VI, and MS. Harl. 69.

[9] Ibid.

[10] The words are Or ovez "hear now."

arms, and a grand and noble tournament will be held in the parade,[11] of Clarencieux, king at arms, on the part of the most noble baron, the Lord of T. C. B. and on the part of the most noble baron, the Lord of C. B. D. in the parade of Norrais, king at arms."

The regulations that follow are these: "the two barons on whose parts the tournament is undertaken, shall be at tlieir pavilions,[12] two days before the commencement of the sports, when each of them shall cause his arms to be nailed up to his pavilion, and set up his banner in the front of his parade; and all those who wish to be admitted as combattants on either side, must in like manner set up their arms and banners before the parades allotted to them. Upon the evening of the same day they shall show themselves in their stations, and expose their helmets to view at the windows of their pavilions, and then they may depart to make merry, dance, and live well. On the morrow the champions shall be at their parades by the hour of ten in the morning, to await the commands of the lord of the parade and the governor, who are the speakers of the tournament; at this meeting the prizes of honour shall be determined." In the document before us it is said: "that he who shall best resist the strokes of his adversary, and return them with most adroitness on the part of Clarencieux, shall receive a very rich sword, and he who shall perform in like manner the best on the part of Norroys, shall be rewarded with an helmet equally valuable."

It may be as well to remark here that the sword was the reward of the challengers, and the helmet that of the acceptors of such challenge, which will account for a herald being frequently represented in antient delineations of tournaments holding in his right hand a sword and in his left a helmet. But to proceed with this document,

"On the morning of the day appointed for the tournament, the arms, banners, and helmets of all the combatants shall be exposed at their stations, and the speakers present at the place of combat by ten of the clock, where they shall examine the arms and approve or reject them at their pleasure; the examination being finished, and the arms returned to the owners, the baron, who is the challenger, shall then cause his banner to be placed at the beginning of the parade, and the blazon of his arms to be nailed to the bottom of the roof of the pavilion outside; his example is to be followed by the baron on the opposite side, and all the knights of either party who are not in their stations before the nailing up of the arms, shall forfeit their

---

[11] Marche, i. e. the limit or part of the lists appropriated to him.

[12] The tents pitched on the occasion. In the original the word is loges. i, e. stations.

privileges, and not be permitted to tourney.

"The kings at arms and the heralds are then commanded by the speakers to go from pavilion to pavilion, crying aloud: A l'aclievier, chevaliers, &c. "To achievement, knights and esquires, to achievement;"[13] and soon after the company of heralds shall repeat the former ceremony, having the same authority, saying: Hors chevaliers, &c. "Come forth, knights and esquires, come forth," and when the two barons have taken their places in the lists, each of them facing his own parade, the champions on both parties shall arrange themselves, every one by the side of his banner; and then two cords shall be stretched, between them, and remain in that position until it shall please the speakers to command the commencement of the sports. The combatants shall each of them be armed with a pointless sword, having the edges rebated,[14] and with a baston[15] hanging from their saddles, and they may use either the one or the other so long as the speakers shall give them permission, by repeating the sentence: Lasseir les aler, "Let them go on." After they have sufficiently performed their exercises, the speakers are to call to the heralds, and order them to fold up the banners, saying: "Ployer vos baniers," which is the signal for the conclusion of the tournament. The banners being rolled up, the knights and esquires are permitted to return to their dwellings.

Every knight or esquire, performing in the tournament, was permitted to have one page armed, within the lists, but without a baston or any other defensive weapon, to wait upon him and give him his sword or baston as occasion might require; and also in case of any accident happening to his armour, to amend the same. In after times, three servitors were allowed for this purpose.

The laws of the tournament permitted any one of the combatants to unhelm himself at pleasure, if he was incommoded by the heat; none being suffered to assault him in any way, until he had replaced his helmet at the command of the speakers.

The kings at arms and the heralds who proclaimed the tournament had now[16] the privilege of wearing the blazon of arms of those by whom the

---

[13] This being the notice for them to arm.

[14] Bent or turned on one side, as "abated" signified taken off.

[15] This truncheon or small club was instead of the mace used in regular fight. Its form may be.seen under Pl. LXX.

[16] This was not the case in the time of Edward I, as in the MS. of St. Graal, the king at arms wears merely a party coloured dalmatie of blue and yellow.

sport was instituted;[17] besides which, they were entitled to six ells of scarlet cloth as their fee,[18] and had all their expences defrayed during the continuation of the tournament. By the law of arms they had a right to the helmet of every knight when he made his first assay at the tournament, which became their perquisite as soon as the sports were concluded. They also claimed six crowns a piece as nail-money, for affixing the blazon of arms to the pavilions. The kings at arms held the banners of the two chief barons on the day of the tournament, and the other heralds those of their confederates according to their rank.

After the conclusion of the tournament, the combatants, as we have seen above, returned to their dwellings; but in the evening they met again in some place appropriated for the purpose, where they were joined by the ladies, and others of the nobility, who had been spectators of the sports; and the time, we are told, was passed in feasting, dancing, singing, and making merry. But, "after the noble supper and dancing," according to the ordinance, "the speakers of the tournament called together the heralds appointed for both parties, and demanded from them alternately, the names of those who had best performed upon the opposite sides; the double list of names was then presented to the ladies who had been present at the pastime, and the decision was referred to them respecting the awardment of the prizes. They selected one name for each party, and as a peculiar mark of their esteem, the favorite champions received the rewards of their merits from the hands of two young virgins of quality." Neither is this the only deference paid to the fair sex by the laws of the tournament, for we are told, that if a knight conducted himself with any impropriety, or transgressed the ordinances of the sport, he was excluded from the lists avec une grele de coups "with a sound beating;" which was liberally bestowed upon him by the other knights with their bastons. This was to punish his temerity, and to teach him to respect the honor of the ladies, and the rights of chivalry. The unfortunate culprit had no other resource in such case for escaping without mischief, but by supplicating the mercy of the fair sex, and humbly intreating them to interpose their authority on his behalf, because the suspension of his punishment depended entirely upon their intercession.

Upon some particular occasions the strokes with the sword were per-

---

[17] Hence in Edward the IVth's time the Earl of Warwick bad a herald of bis own. See Dugdale's Warwickshire, and be is depicted in the curious drawing of John Rous.

[18] They wore a long scarlet robe under their tabards reaching to the feet, and with long sleeves.

formed on foot, and so were the combats with the axes, having generally a barrier of wood breast-high between the champions.

Caxton tells us[19] that Richard II himself attended the royal justs held at Smith-field; and all "of his hous were of one sute, theyr cotys, theyr armys, theyr slieldes, and theyr trappours were embrowdred all with white her-tis[20] with crownes of gold about their necks and cheynes of gold hanging thereon; whiche liertys were the kings lyveray,[21] that he gaf to lordes, ladyes, knyghtes, and squyers, to know his lioushold peple from other; then four and twenty ladyes comynge to the justys ladde four and twenty lordes with cheynes of gold, and alle in the same sute of hertes as is aforesayd, from the Tour on horsbak thrugh the cyte of London into Smythfield."

One of the rules at tournaments was to strike only the body or head; and he who hit the arms or thighs was excluded from receiving the reward. This was observed also at single combats, and challenges in war. Froissart[22] speaks of a duel between a French and English esquire in presence of the Earl of Buckingham which affords an example. "The French esquire," says he, "justed extremely well to the satisfaction of the earl, but the English one struck too low so that he thrust the point of his lance right into the Frenchman's thigh. The Earl of Buckingham and all the other noblemen were greatly vexed at this, and said that this was dishonourable justing."

Previous to the justing at Smithfield, the noblemen rode from the Tower to this spot. Stowe who tells us that this took place in the 9th of Richard II, adds: "that every lord led a lady's horse by its bridle. On the morrow began the justs, in Smithfield, which lasted three days. There bare them well Henry of Darby the Duke of Lancaster's son, the Lord of Beaumont, Sir Simon Burley, and Sir Paris Courtney."[23] The same author informs us that, at those royal justs noticed by Froissart as having taken place at Smithfield, "many strangers came out of other countries: viz. Valerian, Earl of St. Paul, who had married King Richard's sister the Lady Maud Courtney, and William the young Earl of Ostrevant, son to Albert of Baviere, Earl of Holland and Henault. At the day appointed there issued forth from the Tower, about the 3rd hour of the day, sixty coursers apparelled for the justs, and upon every one an esquire of honour riding a soft pace. Then came forth sixty ladies of

---

[19] Addit. to Polychron. c. 6, fol, 397.

[20] Harts.

[21] Being a badge of the House of York.

[22] Chrono Tom. II, c. 55.

Stowe's Survey of London, Book 3, p. 2.39.

honour mounted upon palfries, riding on the one side;[24] richly apparelled, and every lady led a knight with a chain of gold. Those knights being of the king's party had their armour and apparel garnished with white harts, and crowns of gold about the hart's neck; and so they came riding through the streets of London to Smithfield with a great number of trumpets and other instruments of music before them. The king and queen, who were lodged in the Bishop's Palace of London, were come from thence, with many great estates, and placed in the chamber to see the justs. The ladies that led the knights, were taken down from their palfreys, and went up to chambers prepared for them. Then alighted the esquires of honour from their coursers and the knights in good order mounted upon them. And after the helmets were set on then heads and being ready in all points, proclamation made by the heralds, the justs began, and many commendable courses were run, to the great pleasure of the beholders. These justs continued many days with great feasting."[25]

Sir David de Lindsay, first Earl of Crawford, was at this time[26] on a visit in London. He was attended by several gentlemen of quality, among whom was Sir William Dalzell, a man of lively wit and extremely clever. Chancing to be at the court he there saw Sir Piers Courtenay, an English knight, renowned for his skill in justing as well as for the beauty of his person. He was with much vanity parading the palace arrayed in a new mantle, bearing for device an embroidered falcon with this rhyme.

> I beare a falcon, fairest of flight
> Who so pinches at her, his death is dight.
> In graith.[27]

The Scottish knight appeared next day in a dress exactly similar to that of Courtenay, but bearing a magpie instead of the falcon, with a motto ingeniously contrived to rhyme to the vaunting inscription of Sir Piers.

> I beare a pie picking at a piece
> Who so picks at her, I shall pick at his ncse.[28]
> In faith.

---

[24] Probably it was this expression that induced Grainger in his Biog. Hist. to observe that ladies first rode on side saddles during this reign. It was however a practice in the time of the Anglo-Saxons.

[25] Stowe's Survey, Book 3, p.239. Froissart, Vol. IV, c.22.

[26] A. D. 1390.

[27] In armour, according to Sir Walter Scott.

[28] Nose.

This affront could only be expiated by a just a outrance, that is with sharp lances. In the course, Dalzell left his helmet unlaced, so that it gave way at the touch of his antagonist's lance, and he thus avoided the shock of the encounter. This happened twice. In the third encounter the handsome Courtney lost two of his front teeth. As the Englishman complained bitterly of Dalzell's fraud in not fastening his helmet, the Scottishman agreed to running six courses more, each champion staking in the hand of the king two hundred pounds to be forfeited if, on entering the lists, any unequal advantage should be detected. This being agreed to, the wily Scot demanded that Sir Piers in addition to the loss of his teeth should consent to the extinction of one of his eyes, he himself having lost an eye at the fight of Otterburn. As Courtenay demurred, Dalzell demanded the forfeit which, after much altercation, the king appointed to be paid to him, saying, He surpassed the English both in wit and valour.[29]

Stowe relates[30] that, "in the year 1393, the 17th Richard II, certain lords of Scotland came into England to get worship by force of arms; the Earl of Man· challenged the Earl of Nottingham to just with him; and so they rode together certain courses, but not the full challenge; for the Earl of Marr was cast both horse and man, and two of his ribs broken with the fall; so that he was conveyed out of Smithfield, and so towards Scotland, but died by the way at York. Sir William Darell knight, the king's banner bearer of Scotland challenged Sir Piercy Courtney knight, the king's banner bearer of England; and when they had run certain courses, gave over without conclusion of victory.[31] Then Cookborne, esquire of Scotland, challenged Sir Nicholas Hawberke knight, and rode five courses, but Cookborne was born over horse and man, &c."

Mention has been made of the form of duel in judicial combats, drawn up during this reign by Thomas of Woodstock sixth son of Edward III, who died on the 3rd of October, 1399; it is as follows:

Vere excellentissimo et vere potentissimo, ligio domino suo Richardo Dei gratia regi Angliæ et Franciæ, domino Hibernise, Duci Aquitanise.

Vere excellentissimo et vere potentissimo, ligio domino suo Richardo Dei gratia regi Angliæ et Franciæ, domino Hibernise, Duci Aquitanise.

Vobis, si placeat dicto domino suo, indicat homo vester ligius Thomas,

---

[29] Bower, quoted by Sir Walter- Scott.
[30] Survey, Book III, p.239.
[31] If Stowe .here alludes to the anecdote related by Bower, he has placed it three years later.

Dux Glocestriæ, plura admodum duella armata infra listas nuper fuisse in hoc regno vestro Anglise, tempore et prsesentia reverendi domini et patris mei, avi vestri, cujus animse mesereatur Deus, etiam tempore et prsesentia vestra, quam longo jam antea; multosque inde summum commodum, ut compertum est assequutos esse.

Cum vero nihil hoc sublimius fit inter conamina militaria: ad vos etiam celsissi-mamque, regalissimamque vestram Majestatem attineat suprema ejusdem jurisdictio et cognitio, ut secundum justitiam et æquitatem gloriosi vestri nominis, quo omni-modo habitaret justitia moderetur: sintque præterca diversa constitutionum, rituum et ordinationum genera in diversis regionibus et locis, turn vestræ ditionis in hoc regno vestro, quam aliorum alibi: nec tamen redactse sunt in scripta hujusmodi constitutiones, ritus, seu ordinationes duelli infra listas armati, aut vestro eevo, aut ævo illustrium progenitorum vestrorum omni magnanimitate refertissimorum. Itaque ut vos et posteri, et successores vestri, rectius justitiam et æquitatem omnibus distribuatis, tam ligiis et subditis vestris, quam alienigenis qui liujusmodi armorum negotia coram vobis sunt unquam aggressuri; ego dictus humilis vester ligius et conestabularius dietæ vestræ regali majestati libellum liunc ordinationum, modum continentem, quo pugna intra listas ab armatis per-agenda sit, offero: non ideo quòd prudenter et consulte sit compositus, sed quòd facile emendari queat: vestram nobilitatem qua possum liumilitate obtestans, ut benignæ vestræ gratiæ placeat, ipsum liunc libellum perlustra-re, corrigere, et emendare, eidemque addere et subtrahere ut vobis justum videbitur, adhibita matura deliberatione et eonsilio prudentissimorum, fortissimorum, et expertissimorum magnatum et equitum aura-torum regni vestri, qui armorum scientia maxime sunt imbuti. Quandoquidem vero banc in me provinciam suscepi, non me tamen eo ingenio aut facilitate præditum censeo, ut idoneus habear ad liujusmodi molimina: sed quòd at-tinet ad munus meum; licet sapientiores illi qui eodem prius fungebantur, scriptum nihil in hoc genere reliquerunt. Oro igitur regiam vestram majes-tatem, sociosque meos omnes et amicos, qui dictum hunc librum viderint, seti audierint, ut excusatum me habeant, si quid in eo fuerit vel plus vel minus quam justum est; nani juxta exiguam facultatem et ingenium meum eundem composui, obtestans vere excellen-tem et reverendum dominum meum ut dicto libro perlustrato, examinato, correcto, et emendato, aucto etiam, vel contracto, ut opus fuerit, juxta maturam delibera-tionem et con-silium vestrum, et eorum regni vestri qui armorum scientia maxime sunt imbuti, ut supra dictum est, eundem dignemini stabilire, approbare, ordinare, et confirmare, per vos hæredes et successores vestros in regno vestro Aligliæ retinendum.

In primis, ut querelæ et billæ appellantis et defendentis, piacitentur coram constabulario et marescallo in curià suà, et cum nequeant causam testibus alitervè comprobare, quin derimenda sit querela viribus; sic ut alter smini institutum super altero probare nitatur, alter vero se eodem modo defendere: constabularius potestatem habeat pangendi duellum illud, utì vicarius generahs sub deo et rege. Pacto autem duello per constabularium, ipse diem assignabit et locum: ita tamen ut dies non sit intra dies 40 post duellum compactum, nisi consensu dictorum appellantis et defendentis.

Tunc constituet eis armorum species, alias dictorum weapenes, quibus uterque utetur: viz: gladium longum, gladium brevem, et pugionem: dum tamen appellans et defendens invenerint sufficientem securitatem et vades, quòd ad diem ipsis assignatam comparuerint: appellans nempe ad effundendum vires suas super defendente: et defendens ad tuendun se similiter adversus appellantem. Hoc ut fiat, dabitur appellanti bora et terminus et sol certus, ad probationem suam facien-dam, et ut primus sit infra listas ad exonerandum vades suos. Nec non similiter et defendenti. Interea neuter eorum alteri inferat angorem, malum, damnum, insidias, insultimi, aliudvè gravamen seu invidiam, vel per se ipsos, vel per arnicos suos, benevolos, vel quoslibet alios.

Rex præstabit campum in quo pugnabitur: listæ autem composite et ordinaiæ fuerint à constabulario. Considerandum etiam est, ut listæ sint 60 passus in longitudine et 40 in latitudine bene constitutæ, et ut terra sit firma, stabilis, dura, et in planum redacta, sine magnis lapidibus, et jaceiis. Item ut listæ finniter claudantur circumquaque repagulis, januam liabentes ex parte orientali, et aliam in parte occidentali, sintque repagula bona et valida, ad altitudinem vii pedum vel eò amplius.

Tunc postulabuntur vades appellantis et defendentis, ut listas intrœant coram rege, et præsentabuntur in curiam uti prisonarii i. e. captivi, donee appellans et defendens intra listas pervenerint, et sacramenta sua præstiterint.

Quando appellans ad iter suum venerit: ad januam listarum orientalem veniet, iis accinctus arinis et telis quæ a curia sunt illi assignata; ibidemque morabitur donee introducatur per constabularium. Tunc autem constabularius et marescallus illue proficescentur, et interrogabit eum constabularius: quisnam ipse sit homo, qui armatus venit ad januam listarum, quod sibi nomen, et quæ causa veniendi? Et respondebit appellans: ego tabs sum, A de K, appellans, qui venio ad hoc iter, &c. ad faciendum, &c. Tunc constabularius aperiet buculum galeæ, ut vultum ejus perspicue intueatur, et si idem sit qui est appellans, aperiri faciet listaruam januas, ipsumque intromittet una cum armis, telis, cibariis, aliisque legitimis necessariis, et consiliariis suis. Tunc conducet eum coram rege, et dein-ceps in tentorium suum, ubi manebit usque dictus defendens advenerit.

Eodem modo fiet de defendente, sed is per occidentalem listarum januam ingredietur.

Clericus constabularii scribet, et in registrimi digeret adventum appellantis, et horam qua intravit, et quod pedibus listas intravit. Etiam armaturam ejus; et quomodo armatur; et quotis telis, ingressus est listas; quæ cibaria, et alia legitima necessaria secum introduxit. Eodem modo defendente fiet.

Curabit etiam constabularius, ut nemo præcedens vel subsequens appellantem sive defendentem, plura adducat tela sive cibaria quam assignata fuere per curiam.

Et si ita contigerit ut defendens non veniat ad iter suum, hora et termino à curia constitutis: constabularius imperabit marescallo, ut exigi eum faciat ad quatuor angidos listarum, modo qui sequitur, "Oyez, oyez, oyez, C de B. Defendens, venite ad iter vestrum, quod ad lianc diem suscepistis ab exonerandos vades vestros, coram rege. Constabulario et marescallo, in defensione vestra contra A de B, super hoc quod vobis imposuit."

Citius autem si non venerit, secundò exigetur eodem modo, et subjunget in fine "Venite, dies transit ocyor." Si vero nec tunc venerit, exigetur etiam tertiò. Sed hoc esto inter horam diei piene tertiam et nonam, eodem modo quo supra, at tunc subnectens dicet: "Dies transit ocyor, et hora nome appropinquat: veniatis igitur ad dictam horam nonæ, nec tardius, sub periculo incumbenti."

Licet autem constabularius horam et terminimi defendenti prsefixerit veniendi ad iter suum: nihilominus si usque horam nonæ moratus fuerit, judicium tamen adversus eum jure non est proferendum, sive sit causa proditionis, sive non. Aliter autum est ex parte appellantis, eum enim oportet horam et terminimi observare per curiam definitos, absque aliqua cunctatione sive excusatione quacunque etiamsi in causa proditionis.

Ingressis infra listas appellante et defendente, cum armatura, telis cibariis, et legitimis necessariis consiliariisque; ut supra dictum est, modo per curiam assignato: constabularius regiam percontabitur voluntatem, utrum ex honoratis magnatibus, venerabilibusque equitibus, quospiam partibus assignaverit, et an velit sacramenta prestari coram se ipso, vel coram con-stabulario et marescallo.

Scrutabuntur etiam appellans et defendens à constabulario, et mares-callo, quoad armorum species, alias dictorum weapenes, ut legales sint, et absque omni fraude super iis. Et si alise fuerint quàm ratio postulai, aufer-entur. Nam et ratio, et fides candida, et lex armorum, nullam fraudem nec astutiam in tanta actione patientur. Et intelli gentium est, quoti appellans et defendens, ita secure arina-buntur super corporibus suis ut ipsi voluerint.

Tunc constabularius primùm, deinde marescallus appellantem cum con-siliariis suis accersent ad prsestandum sacramentum suum. Constabularius interrogabit eum si quid ultra protestali velit: et ut omnes protestationes suas in scriptis edat, nam ex ilio tempore plures non faciet protestationes.

Constabularius liabebit clerium suum in procinctu paratura, qui mis-sale apertura proponet, et tunc mandabit constabularius dicto suo clerico, ut legat billam appellantis, integre et clara voce. Perlecta bilia, constabulari-us dicet appellanti "A de K, bene nostri hanc billam, et sponsionem istam et pignus, quee dedisti in curia nostra. Pones hie manum tuam dextram super sanctis istis, et jurabis modo sequenti. Tu A de K. Hsec tua bilia vera est omnibus clausulis et articulis ab exordio usque in finem in eadem contentis: atque id tui institui est liodiè probare super prædicto C de B ita te Deus adjuvet et ista sancta." Pacto hoc sacramento, reducetur ille ad locum suum: mandabitque constabularius marescallo, uti defendentem vocet; cui eodem modo fiet ut supra appellanti.

Constabularius iterimi per marescallum appellantem vocabit, faci-etque, ut manum sicut priùs, super missale ponat, et dicet: "A de K. Tujuras quod nec habes nec liabebis rem seu res alias super te aut super corpore tuo infra has listas nisi eas quse tibi assignatse sunt per curiam, viz: gladi-um longum, gladium brevum, et pugionem: nec cultura alium vel majorem vel minorem, nec aliud instrumentum, nec machinam cuspidatam aliamve, nec lapiderai potentem, nec herbam, nec carmen, nec experimentum, nec characterem, nec ullam aliam incantationem juxta te aut pro te, per quam speres quod facilius vincas C de B adversarium tuum, qui hodie intra listas istas contra te venturus est in sui ipsius defensionem, nec quod fiduciam habes in ullà re alia quam in Deo tantummodo, et in corpore tuo, et in justa tua querela, ita Deus te adjuvet et sancta illa." Peracto sacramento ad locum suum iterum reducetur, ipsoque eodem modo defendenti fiet.

Præstitis his sacramentis, remotisque ab utroque cubiculariis et servi-entibus suis, constabularius per marescallum vocari faciet et appellantem et defendentem, qui educentur et custodientur per famulos constabularii et marescalli coralli seipsis, et constabularius partem utramque alloquetur, dicens: "Tu A de K, appellator, accipies C de B. defensorem per manum dextram, atque ille te. Et prohibemus vobis et utrique vestrum nomine regis et sub periculo incumbenti, ut qui in his culpabilis deprehensus fuerit litem amittat; ut neuter vestrum adeo sit pertinax alteri malum aut gravamen, aut appugnationem, aut damnum manu inferre."

Tradito hoc mandato, jubebit constabularius ut dextras jungant, sinistrasque ponant super missale, dicetque appellatori "A de K appellator, tu juras per fidem quam tradis in manum adversari tui C de B defensoris et per omnia sancta quæ tangis manu tua sinistra, quòd hodie infra diem, omnem veram operam tuam et intentionem præstabis modis omnibus quibus melius poteris aut noveris at proban-dum intentionem tuam super C de B adversarium tuum et defensorem, ut eum cogas semet dedere in manum tuam et palinodiam canere, seu alioqui ut manu tua moriatur priusquam de bis listis exieris infra tempus et solem tibi assignatum à curia. per fidem tuam et ut Deus te adjuvet et sanctæ illa."

"C de B defensor, tu juras per fidem quam tu tradis in manum adversarii tui A de K appellatoris, et per omnia sancta quæ manu tua sinistra tangis, quòd hodie intra diem, omnum verum operam tuam et intentionem modis omnibus quibus poteris aut noveris intentionem tuam defendere in ornili quod tibi imponitur per A de K adversarium tuum appellatorem; per fidem tuam et ut Deus te adjuret, et omnia sancta ista."

Time constabularius mandabit marescallo ut ad 4 angulos listarum in hunc modum proclamet: "Oyez, oyez, oyez, decernimus et mandamus nomine con-stabularii régis, et marescalli, ut nemo vel grandioris præstantiæ vel minoris status aut æstimationis cujuscunque ordinis vel nationis fuerit, adeo sit pertinax ut ad listas appropinquare andeat per quatuor pedes, nec loqui, nec clamare, nec nutum edere, nec indiculum, nec speciem, nec sommi aliquem quo alterutri partium, A de K, appellatori, sive C de B, defensori in melius cedat versus alternili sub periculo vitæ, et membrorum et bonorum juxta placitum Regis."

Post hæc constabularius et marescallus, omnes quoscunque è listis sub-movebunt, exceptis locum tenentibus suis, et duobus militibus ex parte consta-bularii et marescalli, qui integra armatura induti erunt. Sed nec cultrum ferent, nec gladium, nec telum aliud, quo, negligenter conservato, appellans seu defen-dens in suum fruatur beneficium. Sed duo locumtenentes constabularii et marescalli habebunt uterque in manibus suis liastam sine ferro, ad separandum eos si rex mandaverit ut à pugna désistant: sive respirandi gratia, sive ex aha quavis occasione quam ipse probaverit.

Sciendum etiam est, quòd si vel cibus vel potus, vel aliqua alia légitimé necessaria, administranda fuerint appellanti seu defendenti, postquam consiliarii, amici et famuli ipsorum appellantis et defendentis semoti sunt, ut dictum est, ipsa administratio ad heraldos pertinet, ac etiam proclamationes quæ in curia fiunt: qui heraldi régis et prosequutores ad arma, locum habebunt ipsis assignatum à constabulario et marescallo, tain prope à listis quàm commodè fieri poterit. Sic ut omnem intueantur actionem, et præsto sint ad faciendum id ad quod vocati fuerint.

Custodito apellante in loco suo per quosdam assignatos à constabulario seu marescallo, et defendente similiter in loco suo, et utroque parato et induto, ministerio comitum et custodum suorum supradictorum, marescallo apud alterum existente, apud alterum vero locumtenente constabularii, constabulario etiam ipso, in loco suo coram rege sedente uti vicario ejus generali, et partibus, ut dictum est ad pugnam accinctis, constabularius sonora voce dicet, "Laissez les aller," id est "Dimittite eos moratusque paululum, "Laissez les aller." Etiam iterum moratus paulisper "Laissez les aller et faire leur avoir au nom de Dieu," i.e. "Dimittite eos ut faciant officium suuin in nomine Dei."

Hoc dicto, unusquisque discedet ab utrisque partibus, ut congrediantur et faciant quod ipsis optimum videbitur. Nec appellans deinceps aut defendens vel edat, vel bibat sine venia et licentia regis sub periculo incumbente, ne id fecerint ex consensu inter se.

Dehinc in posterum, res à constabulario diligenter animadvertenda est: ut-pote, si rex mandaverit partes pugnantes separari, acquiescere, vel morari ex quacunque occasione, is caute observât quo statu separati sunt: nempe et resti-tuantur eisdem statui et gradui in omnibus, si rex voluerit eos iterum adjungi et congredi. Etiam ut accurate eos auscultet et intueatur, si forte alteruter alterum alloquatur de deditione, vel aliter: ad illuni enim attinet verborum testimonium, recordumque ferre ex ilio tempore, et ad nullum alium.

Si prædictum duellum sit in causa læsæ majestatis, is qui victus est annis exuetur intra listas, jubente hoc conestabulario: effractoque in vituperami ejus aliquo listarum ángulo, equis per eundem extralietur à loco ubi exarmatus fuit ad locum supplicii, ibidemque decollatus et suspensus erit, juxta consuetudinem curiæ. Hoc ad marescallum pertinet, cujus muneris est, rem inspicere, supplicium inferre, ambulare, equitare, et juxta reum semper

consistere, donee exequutio fiat, omniaque adhnpleta, tam adversus appellantem quam defendentem. Recta enim fides et æquitas, et jus armorum
volunt ut appellans eandem incurrat pcenam quam defendens, si is victus
fuerit et subactus.

Si verò ita contigerit ut rex litem in manus suas susceperit, ipsosque ad
concordiam redegerit absque ulteriori pugna: conestabularius unum eorum
ac-cipiet et marescallus alterum, et aducunt eos coralli rege, interlectaque
illius volúntate, constabularius et marescallus eos conducent ad partem listarum alteram, eis telis eodemque armorum habitu instructos, quo depre-
hensi sunt, cum rex litem in suas manus suscepit. Eodemque modo educentur per januam listarum gressu æquali, ut neuter alteri aliqualiter prsecedat.
Cum enim rex litem sus-ceperit in manus suas, inbonestum fuerit ut major indignitas uni inferatur quam alteri. Grandævorum autem testimonio
proditum est, quod qui listis primus egreditur, indignitatem contrahit, tarn
in causa proditionis quam rei alterius cujuscunque.

Heraldis feodo cedunt tela omnia et armaturæ diruptse, et quæ vel ar-
ripit vel deserit tarn appellans quam defendens, postquam intra listas in-
gressi sunt. Tela etiam omnia et armatura ejus qui victus est sive appellantis
sive defendentis.

Marescalli feodum sunt listæ et repagula, quæ barras vocant, et ipsorum
postes

Tbe following which is extracted from a MS. book, vin the library of
the College of Arms, written about tbe commencement of tbe reign of
James I, appears to be a translation of tbe foregoing.

"To his right liighe and mightie Lorde and Leige Rychard by tbe Grace
of God Kinge of Englande and France, Lord of Ireland and Acquytaine,
Thomas Duke of Gloster your Conestable of England, shewethe that whereas many batteyles within listes have been in this your realme of England as
well as late in the tyme, and presence of my right worthie lorde and father,
your grandfather, whom God pardon, as in this your tyme and presence,
more then hatlie ben longe tyme before, and it is very apparaunte that many
oughte to have been. And for that yt is the greateste arte that may be in
armes and that to your righte excellente royall majestie,[32] appertaynetli the
sovereigntye, jurisdicion and knowledge so that yt be grounded by justice
and equitie to Yo honorable re-nowne in whom all justice ought to remayne
and be; Wherfore for that there are dyvers maners, costomes and orders

---

[32] The mention of majestas, and equites aurati, proves these not to be original, the
former not being earlier than Henry VIII, the latter than that of his successors.

establyslied in dyvers partes and contries as well within your subjection as otherwhere whersoever, howbeit this your said realme had never any establishmente, costomes or ordynance of armed batteyles within listes in your tyme nor yet in the tyme of your noble progenytors, olbeyt they were wise, valyant and juste. Nevertlieles becawse that Yo, your heirs, and successors may the bettar do justice and equytie to all suche as in lyke feates of armes shall have to do before you as well your lieges and subjects as others whatsoever, I your said humble liege and constable do offer unto your

royall majestie this little booke of the order and maner of combatinge in listes not denyenge, but that it is not so wisely nor with so good advisement and discretion made but that yt maye easily be amended, requyreng your noblesse as humbly as I maye or can that of your bengnytie yt might please your Grace to survey, exa-myne, correcte, and amend the said booke, sliewenge your opinyon as yt shall seeme good with the delyberation and advisement of the wiseste, most valyant and sufficient lordes and knightes of your realme who in feates of armes have the greateste knowledge, albeit I have enterprised this worke, I have not don the same to take upon me suclie knowledge or skill, that I ame liable to accomplyshe suche a matter but for that yt belongeth to my office. Although that those which were in the same office before me did never write the same, howbeit they were wise and discreete, ye farre more than I am, wherefore I requyre your royall majestie and all my companyons and friendes, wch the said book shall see or lieare, that you and they will hold me xcused if there be any thinge more or lesse added to the same then ought to be, for accordinge to the litle power and knowledge that I have I have made the same, beseechinge your higlines my right excellent and right worthie lorde that the saide booke may be xained, corrected, and amended of you your Grace, and valyant and sufficient lordes and knightes of your realme who in feates of armes have the greatest knowledge, as aforesaid, further maye yt please you to establyshe, approve, ordeyne and confirme the said booke to be kept in your said realme of England for you, your heirs and successors being kinges of England as to whome of right it appertayneth.

Firste, the quarrells and billes of the challenger and defendante shalbe pleaded in the cowrte[33] before the conestable and marshall, and if they cannot prove their cawse neyther by witnes nor otherwise, but discide their

[33] At the College of Arms still exists the court of the earl marshall. as it did when the last causes were tried. The advocates at Doctors Commons pleaded therein, and the form of such pleadings is yet preserved in their library.

quarrell by force the one to prove his entent uppon the other, and t'other in like case to defende, the conestable bathe power to appointe the battaile as chief vycaire or captaine under God and the kinge. The battaile being appoynted the conestable shall assigne them the daye and place in sorte that yt be not within xl daies after the battaile appointed unlest yt be by the consent of the challenger and defendante awardinge them how many weapons thei shall have, that is to saye, glayve,[34] longesword, short sworde, and dagar. Also the said challenger and defendante shall finde sufficient sureties and pledges that every of them shall come at their saide daye, the challenger to trie his proofe uppon the défendante, and the défendante in his defence uppon the challenger. And that the howre be appointed to the challenger, and that he be in the listes at leaste by the howre of pryme to make his proofe and discharge his sureties, and the defendant to do in lyke case and that neyther of them do liurte, damage, laye in waiglit nor do the other any grevance or annoyance by them or any of their frendes, well willers, or others whatsoever before the howre appointed to the battaile.

The kinge shall find the feelde to fight in and the listes slialbe made and devised by the conestable, and yt is to be considered that the listes must be 60 pace long and 40 pace brode in good order, and that the grownde be harde, stable and firme, and equally made without great stones, the grownde flatt, and that the listes be strongly barred abowte with one dore in the este, an other in the weaste, with good and strong barres vij foot hyglie or more, that a horse cannot leape over them.

The following part between the parentheses, translated from the Latin,
is wanted in this document.

(Also it must be understood that subaltern lists[35] should be formed without the principal lists, where the servants of the constable and marshall, and the royal serjeants at arms shall be placed, in order that they may hinder and forbid any one from making any squabble or tumult against the bann or proclamation of the court, in such as advert to the royal prince's majesty, or the rights of arms; and those ministers themselves shall be in complete armour.

The constable may have there as many of these armed ministers as he pleases, but the marshall only so many as the constable shall assign him; nor

---

[34] The glaive consists of a large blade at the end of a pole, and differs from the bill in having' its edge on the outside curve, but in the Latin text tbis weapon is not mentioned.
[35] Called faux listes.

more; but in all these care shall be taken as above said.

The king's serjeants at arms shall have the custody of the gates of the lists, and the arrests, if any shall be, at the command of the constable and marshall.)

The daye of the battaile the kinge slialbe in a state upon a higlie skaffolde and a place slialbe made for the conestable and marshall at the foote of the stears of the said skaffolde were they shall sit, and then the surities of the challenger and défendante slialbe called into the listes and present in the cowrte before the kinge as prisonars, untill the challenger and defendant be come into the listes and have made their assurance.

When the challenger comethe in his torneye he shall come to the easte gate of the listes in suclie manner as he will fight, with his armour and weapons, as is appoynted by the cowrte and there he shall remayne untill that he be led awaye by the conestable in sorte that when he is com to the gate the conestable and marshall shall go thetlier, and the conestable shall aske him what man he is that is come, armed to the doore of the listes, what is his name, and wherefore he is come, and the challenger shall answer, "I am suclie a one A de F the challenger that is com hether, etc. for to accomplishe, etc." Then the conestable openynge the umbrell[36] of his heaulmet, and perceavinge him to be the same man which is the challenger shall cawse the doore of the listes to be opened and suffer him to enter with his said armour, weapons, victualls, and other lowable necessaries abowte him, and also his counsaill with him, and then he shall bringe him before the hinge, and to his state wlieere he shall attend untill the defendant be come.

In the lyke sorte shalbe donne to the défendante, but that he shall enter in at the weste dore of the listes.

The conestable's clarke shall write and put in regester the comynge of and the liowre of the entrance of the challenger, and how he entered into the listes a foote, or on horsebacke, with the coolor of the horse and how the horse is armed leste anye thinge sliolde happen by weaknes of the horse or harnes; and also the liâmes of the challenger, and liowe he is armed, and with how many weapons he entrithe the listes and what victualls or other lowable necessaries he bringethe into the listes withe him. In like sorte shall be donne to the défendante.

Further that the constable cawse goode heede to be taken that no man neyther before nor behinde the challenger or défendante shall bringe any

---

[36] The part which projected and shaded the eyes, called sometimes umber, but here it also implies the cover for tbe face -attached to it.

more weapons or victualls than are appointed by the cowrte.

If so be that the defendant come not in tyme at the daye, howre, and tyme lymeted by the cowrte, the conestable shall comande the marshall to cawse him to be called at the fower cornars of the listes, the whiche crie shalbe made there in manner and forme followenge, "Oies, oies, oies, E de B défendante come to the tourneye the which yow have enterprised this daye to discharge the surities before the kinge, the conestable and marshall, do encounter in your defence A de F the challenger in that he hathe surmysed the same." And if that he com not then in tyme he shalbe caled the seconde tyme in the lyke manner, and in the ende he shall saye "come the daye passethe to moche," and if he come not at that tyme, he shalbe caled agayne the thirde tyme, but yt shalbe betwen the highe third and middaye in the same manner as before, and in the ende he shall saye "the daye passeth to moche, and the howre of middaye is at hand, see that you come at that howre of middaye at the farthest uppon perill that may ensue."

Albeit that the conestable have appointed the howre and tyme unto the defendant to com to his torney, nevertlieles though he tarry untill middaye the judgment ought not to pass against him whether yt be in case of treason or otherwise, but yt is not so with the challenger, for yt behoveth him to kepe his howre and tyme lymeted by the cowrte without any prlonginge or excuse whatsoever, whether yt be in case of treason or otherwise.

The challenger and the defendant beinge entred into the listes with their armour, weapons, victualls, other lowable necessaries and cownsailes, as they are assigned by the cowrte, the conestable shall knowe the hinge's pleasure, whether he will appointe any of the lordes or kniglites of honor to the saide parties to lieare their otlie, or whether he will that the said otlie be made before him or before the conestable and marshall within the listes, the which thinge beinge donne the conestable and marshall shall veue the speares of the said challenger and defendant, and shall cawse them to be cut and sliarpned of equal measure as shalbe after rehersed.

Then the challenger and defendant beinge by the constable serched for their weapons that thei be allowable without any manner of engyne in them disallowable, and if they be otherwise then reason requyreth, then thei shalbe taken awaye clearly for reason good faitlie nor lawe of annes ought not to suffer any false engyne or treachery in so greate a deede, further yt is to be noted that the challenger or defendant may arme themselves as surely upon their bodies as shall seeme good to them, and to have a targe or pavis in the listes, becawst yt is but armure, so that it be withowt any engyne in hit disallowable, if the one have yt, and th'other not, and if yt fortune that the one of them wolde make his glave sliorte within the mesure of the standard, yt nevertheless the other maye have yt of the measure of the standard if he will demand yt of the cowrte, but as towcliinge the speares which has the measure of the standard, the one shalbe made of equall measure after the other.

And then the conestable shall sende by the marshall furste for the challenger and his cownsaile to make his othe, and before the said otlie, the conestable shall aske him whether he will proteste any more, and if he will, that then he put yt in writinge for from thence foortlie he shall not make any other protestation.

The conestable shall have his clarke redie in his presence, and shall laye before him a booke open, and then the constable shall cawse his saide clarke to reade the saide bill of the challenger alowde, and the bill beinge redde the conestable shall saye to the challenger "A de F tliow knowest this bill well and this the warrante and gage that thou gavest into owr cowrte, so shall thow laye thi righte liande upon these saincts and shall sware in manner and form followenge.

"Thou A de F slialt sware that this tliei bill is trewe in all poynts and articles conteyned in the same from the begynyng to the ende, and that thow entendest to prove the same this daye uppon the said E de B defendant, so God the liealpe and all the saincts." This beinge ended the marshall shall cawse him to be led backe into his place and the conestable shall cawse the defendant to be caled by the marshall and the lyke slialbe don to the defendant as before to the challenger.

Afterwardes the constable shall cawse the challenger to be caled agayne by the marshall and shall cawse him to laye his hande as before uppon the booke, and shall saye " A de F, thow shalt sweare that thow ne haste nor slialt have more weapons abowte the, ne on thie bodie nor within these listes, other then are assigned the by the cowrte, that is to saye, glave, long sworde, short sworde and dagger, nor any other knyfe smale or greate, ne stone of vertue, ne lierbe, ne charme, experience carrecte, or enchantment by the, ne for the, by the whiche thow trusteste the bettar to vanquyshe the said E de B, thine adversarie whiche shall com agaynst the within the listes this daye in his defence, and that thow trusteste in no other thinge but only in God, in thi bodie and in thi riglitfull quarrel, so God the liealpe and all sainctsafter the said otlie being ended he slialbe led agayne to his place.

In the like sorte slialbe don to the defendant:

The whiche otlies being ended, and their chamberlains and pages beinge taken awaye, the conestable shall cawse by the marshall bothe the challenger and defendant to be called, who shalbe brought and garded by the conestable and marshall's men before them, and the conestable shall saye to bothe parties "thowe A de F, the shalt take E de B defendant by the right hand and he the in lyke case, charginge you and every of you in the kinge's name upon perill that maye ensue, and upon perill to lose your quarell, that whosoever yt is that is fownde in defawte, that neyther of you be so hardie to do to the other any hurte, troble or grevance nor to thretten any other myschef at this tyme by the hand uppon perill beforesaid." This charge beinge ended, the conestable shall cawse them to claspe their handes together and to laye their leffce handes upon the booke, sayeing to the challenger "A de F challenger, thow sweareste by the faitlie that thow geveste in the hande of thine adversarie E de B defendant, and by all the saincts that you touche withe youre lefte hand, that this present daye you shall do all your power, by all meanes that you can devise to prove your entente againste E de B defendant your adversa-rie to make him yelde into your liandes, and so he to crie or speake, or ells to make him die by your liande before you depart owte of these listes by the tyme, and sonne appoynted you by this cowrte, by your faith, and so God you liealpe and all his saincts."

Then he shall saye to the defendant "E de B defendant, you sweare by the faithe that you give into the hand of your adversarie A de F, the challenger, and by all the saincts that you touche with your lefte liande, that this present daye you shall use your strenght, pollycie, and connynge in the beste sorte that you maye or can to defend your selfe againste A de F the challenger your adversarie in that he hathe sunnysed, the so God the healpe and all his saincts."

Then he shall saye to the defendant " E de B defendant, you sweare by the faithe that you give into the hand of your adversarie A de F, the challenger, and by all the saincts that you touche with your lefte liande, that this present daye you shall use your strenght, pollycie, and connynge in the beste sorte that you maye or can to defend your selfe againste A de F the challenger your adversarie in that he hathe sunnysed, the so God the healpe and all his saincts."

The othes being ended and every of them led to his place, their cownselors and frendes beinge taken awaye from them, there shalbe certaine gardes appoynted by the conestable and marshall to garde them, and yt is to be noted that then the sureties of botlie parties ought to be discharged of their suretiesliip if they will requyre yt of the cowrte.

Then afterwardes, the conestable shall comand the marshall to make a proclamation at the 4 cornars of the listes, in manner and forme followenge, "Oies, oies, oies, we charge and commande you in the behalf of the kinge, the conestable, and marshall that no man weyther of great or small estat of what condition or nation soever he be, be so hardie from hencefoorthe, to approclie the listes by 4 foote nor to speake one worde, to make any cowntenance, signe, likelehood, or noyse wherby any of the parties A de F, challenger and E de B defendant maye take advantage of eclie other, upon perill to lose their life and goods at the hinge's pleasure." That done the conestable and marshall shall cawse the listes to be voyded of all manner of persons except their lieutenante and two knights for the conestable, and one for the marshall, who shalbe armed uppon their bodies, but they shall have no knyves or swordes abowt them nor any other weapons wherby the challenger or defendante maye have any advantage whether yt be by negligence or otherwise by not kepinge thcm, but the two lieutenants of the conestable and marshall ought to have in their liandes, eyther of them, a speare without iron, for to parte them if the kinge wolde cawse them to staye in their fightinge, whether it be to rest or otherwise howsoer it be.

The challenger beinge in this place garded and accompanied by suche as be appoynted by the conestable and marshall, and the defendante in lyke manner, botlie parties being made redie, appareiled and accompanied by their kepers, aforesaid, the marshall with the one partie and the conestable's lieutenant with th'other, the conestable sittinge in his place before the kinge as his generall vicayre, and the parties beinge redie to fight as ys said, the conestable shall by comandement of the kinge saye with a lowde voyce " let them go and reste awhile, let them go agayne and reste awhile, let them go and do their indevoir in Godes name." That beinge saide every man shall departe frome bothe parties, so they maye encownter, and do what shall seeme to them beste.

The clialenger nor defendant maye not eate nor drinke from thenceforthe without leave or lycence of the kinge for any thinge that myght happen, albeit they wolde agree to hit by assent within themselves.

Thencefoorth yt is to be considered diligently of the conestable that if the kinge will cawse the parties fightinge, to be parted, to reste or tarrye for what cause soever it be, that he take good regard how theye are parted, that they be bothe in one estate and degree in all things if the kinges pleasure would suffer or cawse them to go together agayne, and also that he harken well and have good regard to them whether they speake to eache other to render or otherwise, for the witnessinge and reporte of the wordes from thenseforthe appertaynethe unto him, and unto none other.

And if the batayle be in case of treason of whiche he that is convicte shalbe unarmed in the listes by the comandement of the conestable, and a pese of the listes broken in reproche of him, uppon the whiche he shalbe drawen owt with horses from the same place where he is unarmed throughe the listes, unto the place of execution, where he shalbe heded or hanged accordinge to the manner of the country the whiche thinge aperteynethe to the marshall to surveue and perform by his ofice, and to put the same in execution and to be by untill yt be donne and fully ended, as well for the challenger as defendant, for good faithe, righte, and lawe of armes will that the challenger ensure the lyke danger that the defendant should if he be vanquisht, and overcome.

If so be that, the case be for any other cryme he whiche is convicte or overcome shalbe unarmed without the listes at the place of execution, whether yt be to be hanged or hedded as well as the challenger as the defendant, as yt is said accordinge unto the usage of the contry, but he shall not be drawen unlesse yt be in case of treason.

Also yf yt be for any facte or action of armes he that is convicte and overcome shalbe unarmed as ys aforesaid and put forthe of the listes withowte any execution.

And yf it fortune that the kinge will take the quarrell in hande and cawse them to agree withowt sufferinge them any more to fighte, then the conestable taking the one partie, and the marshall th'other oughte to bringe them before the kinge, and he shewing them his mynde the conestable and marshall shall leade them to one of the doores of the listes in suche sorte with their weapons, horse and armour as they were fownd when the kinge toke the quarrell in hande. And so they shall be ledde owte of the doore equally so that the one go not owte before the other in no wise, for after that the kinge liathe taken up the quarrell yt were dislioneste that the one partie sliolde receave more dys-lionor than th'other for yt hatlie ben sayd by dyvers auncient wryters that he whiclie goetlie first owte of the listes hatlie the dyshonor, the same as ys as well in case of treason as otherwise.

Also ther oughte to be false listes withowte the principall listes, between the which the conest, and marshall sarvantes, and the king's sargeants at armes oughte to be to kepe and defende, if any man sliold make any offence or troble contrary to the proclamation made in the cowrte, or any thinge that might be contrary to the kinge's roiall majestie, or lawe of armes, and those people ought to be armed at all points.

The conestable shall have there so many men of armes as are needfull and the marshall shall have also by the assignment of the conestable so many as are requysite, wliiche people shall have the garde as is aforesaid, and the kinge's sargeante of armes shall have the kepinge of the dore of the listes and the arests yf any be made by the comandement of the said conest, and marshall.[37]

Farther if there be any meate or drinke mynestred to the challenger or def* or any other lawfull necessaryes, after the cownselors, frendes, and pages of the challenger and def*· are taken awaye as afore ys saide, the saide admynistration dothe belonge to the herehaults and also the proclamation made within the cowrte and listes.

The wch kinges, herehaults and pursuyvants shall have a place appointed for them by the conestable and marshall as nere to the listes as tliei maye well be made, so that tlicyc maye se all the deede and be redy if thei be caled to do any thinge.

The fees of the kinge of armes of the province and the other officers of armes is all the weapons, horses, and armour, the wch they had medled w*1' all and let fall to the grownde after thei are entred into the listes as well of the challenger as deft., and also all horses, weapons and armour of him that is convict whether yt be the challenger or def^t, wth the listes, scaffold, and tymber used at the said battaile."

"The fees of the marshall are the lists and railing which are called barriers and their posts."

The initial to this reign is taken from a MS. in the Cotton lib. marked Nero D. 17, and represents the combat near the Palace of Westminster, between a French esquire of Navarre, and John Welsh, whom he had accused of treason, in presence of Richard II. The armour of the two fighting figures is silver, and consists of hauberks held from the chest by globular breastplates underneath, the plates at their elbows and their girdles are gilt, and on their thighs may be observed the ouvrage de pourpointerie. The first figure to the right is the same. The king is in high pink, with a blue robe lined with ermine; the figure next the king is in silver armour, the body of which is purple. The back ground is red flowered, the ground of the lists is green, and the rails are red; the letter is blue and red, on a purple ground with a gilt edge.

---

[37] These two paragraphs are the same as what have been inserted at p. 74, ànd are, therefore, evidently misplaced according to the Latin document.

In January 1398, the Duke of Hereford accused the Duke of Norfolk before Richard, in parliament at Shrewsbury, of treason. That noblemen had not thought proper to attend his duty in parliament, but surrendered on proclamation, and was introduced to the king at Oswestry. He loudly maintained his innocence against his accuser; and bending his knee said: "My dear Lord, with your leave, if I may answer your cousin, I say that Henry of Lancaster is a liar, and in what he has said and would say of me, lieth like a false traitor, as he is." Richard ordered both parties into custody, and proceeding to Bristol, determined, with the consent of his committee of parliament, that the controversy between the two dukes should be referred to a high court of chivalry.[38] For this purpose the barons, bannerets, and knights of England were summoned to assemble at Windsor, and by award of the court wager of battle was joined to be fought at Coventry, on the 16th of September.[39] On the appointed day the combatants entered the lists, in presence of the king, the committee of parliament, and an immense assemblage of people. Hereford made with solemnity the sign of the cross; Norfolk exclaimed: "God speed the right." The former drawing forward his shield so as to get it over his arm, and fixing his lance in its rest with the point towards his adversary, advanced a few paces, the latter remained motionless at his station; and the king throwing down his warder, took, in the language of the age, the battle into his own hands.

Remnants of the antient popular military sports may still be traced in different parts of this island, though now degenerated into mere contentions for the mastery with fists or clubs. Thus at Longthorpe, in Gloucestershire, on the 1st of May, the inhabitants of that and the adjoining parishes assemble on the top of Yarleton Hill to fight for the possession of it, and on Whitsunday a similar battle takes place between the Fulham boys and those of the hamlet of Hammersmith. Of the like nature was the Giuoco del ponte di Pisa, which took place every three years. The numbers engaged amounted to four hundred and eighty, divided into six troops, each consisting of eighty persons, of whom two and thirty acted solely on the defensive, having narrow kite-shaped shields for that purpose, and were called giocat.ori de targona; twenty-four to attack with clubs, called ruffiani; and twenty-four unarmed whose business it was to creep by the side of the last mentioned and suddenly catching the shield bearers by the legs to throw

---

[38] Rot. Parl. iii. 372.

[39] This is represented in an illuminated MS. in the Harleian library, marked 4380, and engraved in Pennant's Tour to Chester, p. 167.

them down, these were appropriately called celatini. The combat took place on the several bridges of Pisa, three troops being drawn up on one side of the river and three on the other, and all were armed with cuirasses and close helmets, delivered from the arsenal for that purpose. It was a gala day for the town's-people, who covered the water with their gondolas and decorated their houses with flags and banners. The last exhibition took place in 1806, when Bonaparte put an end to the custom, as although the combat lasted but three quarters of an hour, it generally occasioned three or four deaths. The antient Greek figures of the Ægina marbles, as they were disposed in the pediment of the temple from whence they were brought, are arranged in fight with a very close resemblance to this Pisan performance, the celatini in that are very evident,[40] and as the ruffiani were also called pugiani, we may fairly conjecture, that, instead of clubs, their antient weapons of attack were poignards.

We learn from Froissart that John Tycle a pourpointer of London, assisted the insurgents under Wat Tyler and Jack Straw in the year 1381 with sixty pourpoints, for which he demanded thirty marks. As this sum is equal to twenty pounds, of course it appears that they wrere valued at six shillings and eight pence each.

When the same rioters plundered and burnt the palace of the Duke of Lancaster in the Savoy, they took his jacke which Walsingham calls vestimentum precio-sissimum ipsius "his most precious garment," and stuck it upon a spear to shoot at, but finding their arrows could not damage it sufficiently, they chopped it to pieces with their swords and axes. This anecdote shews that the jacke was composed of very tough materials, and as Strutt conjectures, with its facing or exterior surface of leather. Indeed Coquellart describes the jaque d'Anglois as made of sha-mois leather, much like a pourpoint and reaching to the knees.

It seems to have been generally used at this period as armour itself, for Walsingham, under the year 1379, has: Quod mille loricas vel tunicas, quas vulgojackes vocant, redemerit de manibus creditorum. "In order that he might redeem from the hands of his creditors a thousand loricæ or tunics which are commonly called jackes."

And in a letter remissory, dated Paris, 1374, it is thus mentioned: Prædictus monachus monachal! habitu abjecto se armavit, et indutus quodam indumento, vulgariter jacque nuncupato. "The aforesaid monk having put off his mo· nastical habit, armed himself, putting on a certain garment vul-

---

[40] See the representation in No. 12. of the Journal of Science of the British Institution.

garly called a jacke."

It was, however, sometimes stuffed with silk, as Froissart describes that to have been which belonged to Sir John Lawrence, who was slain at the siege of Lyxbone in Castile. The same is asserted in the Chronicle of Bertrand du Guesclin:

> Car il fut bien armez de ce qu'il luy failli
> S'ot un jacque moult fort de bonne soie empli,
> Le baccinct au chief, &c.

> "For lie would bave been well armed with that which he wanted,
> If he had a very strong jacque well stuffed with silk,
> His bascinet on his head, &c·"

This passage accounts for Walsingham's expression *preciosissimum*. But the length and facing of the English jacke seem to have distinguished it from that of Germany, which, in the year 1399, is described in an account of a warrior: Vestu un court jaques d'un drap d'or à la façon d'Alemagne, "Clad in a short jacke of cloth of gold in the German fashion."

The tabard was an upper military garment which seems to have become more general during this reign, and which continued in fashion till the time of Henry VIII. It was a species of tunic which covered the front and back of the body, but was generally open at the sides, from under the shoulders downwards From the time of its first introduction it was used by the military, hence Henry de Knyghton relates that in a meeting appointed between the English and Scots, in the year 1295, the latter: Dederant signum inter se ut sic suos mutuo cog-noscerunt in congressu cum Anglicis, ut Scotus diceret Anglice tabart, alter res-ponderet surcote, et e converso. "Gave a sign among themselves by which they might be mutually known to each other in their meeting with the English, that a Scot should say the English word tabard to which another should reply surcoat, and vice versa."[41]

An English origin is, therefore, here given to this garment. It was soon emblazoned like the surcoat with armorial bearings, and called also tabarum. Long tabards were assumed by the nobility on state occasions, and we see that such was worn by King Richard II when a boy, he being thus depicted in a psalter, which formerly belonged to him, and is now in the Cotton library.[42] These long tabards were peculiar to the English, being called midlags, because as they were made in imitation of the surcoat, they reached

---

[41] We see in this an early instance of what is now called the sign and countersign.

[42] In the British Museum, marked Dom. A. XVII.

to the middle of the legs. On the continent they were shorter, being called renones. Hence in a Latin and French glossary, composed in the year 1348, this word is explained: Renones a renibus dicuntur, gallice tabart, quia usque ad renes contingunt. "The renos are so called from the reins, in French tabart, because they reach to the reins." Instead of a sleeve they latterly had a large flap which hung over the shoulder.[43] Their amplitude concealed the dagger worn underneath, though the lenghth of the sword-hilt occasioned that to protrude through the side opening. Thus in a letter remissory, dated 1445, we are told: Icellui Nicaise tira son coustel hors de sa gaigne, qu'il avoit mis dessus son tabart, &c. "That Nicaise drew his knife out of its sheath, which he had concealed under his tabart, &c."

Doublets were also worn at this time from the following lines of Richard Ireleffe, clerk of the green cloth to Richard II, and preserved in Harding's Chronicle:

> "Yeomen and groomesin cloth of silk arrayed
> Sattin and damask, in doublettes and gownes
> In cloth of grene and scarlet, for unpayed."

Froissart describes the men at arms of this period as homines armez de pied en cap de toute piece et armeures de fer, "men armed from foot to head with all pieces, and in suits of plate armour."

As we approach the close of this reign we find the armour undergoing a slight change. The first figure in which this is remarkable is that monumental effigy in Tewkesbury Abbey Church, Gloucestershire, falsely attributed to Lord Wenlock. In the first place the form of his bascinet is a little more pressed in at bottom. His hauberk is of chain-mail, but his camail if not of rings hooked into brass wires, is pourpointed in the manner of Sir John d'Aubernoun. His jupon is made to open a little at the sides and then fastened by small clasps, and his brassarts and vam-braces covered with silk connected at intervals underneath. But the protection of the bends of the arm by gussets of mail is managed in a curious manner. Over his thighs is pourpointed work, and his feet, instead of being guarded by solerets, are in a kind of stocking, which displays the shape of the toes. As the jamb extends but just to the instep perhaps he had footed stirrups when on horseback, and if so, this is the earliest instance of that contrivance in armour.[44]

---

[43] Of this form they are' still worn by the heralds.

[44] There is a pair of very ancient footed stirrups guarded on both sides with ankle-plates but with merely the stirrup bars at bottom, at Warwick Castle, called the ladies slippers.

The next figure is that selected for Plate XXXVII, and is taken from the monument of a knight of the Blanchefront family.[45] The first thing curious is the visored bascinet, and the camail covered with silk and ornamented at bottom with a fringe. The next is the mamillieres which are highly ornamented, and from one of which is a chain having its end fastened to the pommel of the sword, and from the other one to that of the scabbard. Then the complete round-cuffed gauntlets which are here only covered with plate on the hands and fingers, but are each ornamented with a tassel. Next the military garments which, though seen in the monument, from being of the same length can only be so drawn in an upright figure as to shew the uppermost. These are the hoqueton, the hauberk tipped with an ornamented fringe like that to the camail, and the exterior garment. This last seems to be a kind of jacke. It fits close to the body being laced down the side, but has at the lower part a large puckered skirt which buttons down the middle. The shield belt and that for the sword are ornamented with elegant rosettes, the shoulders and elbows with roundels. The monument of Sir Bernard Brocas,[46] who died in 1399, shows that invention on the edge of the bascinet for covering the cord of the camail, which was not introduced till this reign. It is remarkable too that his gauntlets though fingered, do not extend to the last joint. A very curious visor and beevor united, probably the uniber, was at this time worn by the soldiery. It is. of a conical shape and greatly perforated, and is given at the foot of Plate XXXVII.

Of this period is the monumental effigy of John IV, Duke of Brittany,[47] the short chain sleeves of whose hauberk hang over his shoulders and are rolled up round them.

The Duke of Lancaster is depicted in an illuminated MS.[48] of this period with a purple velvet tunic upon which is placed his cuirass, the termination of the chain from the taces being seen below and invecked. Its wide sleeves are tucked up at the elbows. All his armour is gilt.

From the following circumstance mentioned by Stowe,[49] we find Richard II to have had a very numerous guard of archers. In the year 1397, as

---

[45] In Alvechurch Worcestershire .. The arms of the Blanchefront family were ermine, on an escutcheon of pretence, the arms of Mortimer, viz. barry of six or and azure, on a chief or two palcets between two squires dexter and sinister, an escutcheon of pretence argent.

[46] In Westminster Abbey.

[47] See Lobineau's Hist. de Bretagne. He died in 1399.

[48] The Journal of Francis de la Marque in the British Museum.

[49] P.3l6.

PLATE XXXVII

A KNIGHT OF THE BLANCHFRONT FAMILY,

A.D. 1397.

one day the members were leaving the Parliament-house "a great stir was made as was usual; whereupon the king's archers, in number four thousand, compassed the Parliament-house, thinking there had been some broil or fighting, with their bows bent, their arrows notched, and drawing, ready to shoot, to the terror of all that were there: but the king coming pacified them." Little else is recorded of the bow during this reign except that a number of archers were sent at the request of the Genoese to assist them against the Turks on the coast of Barbary; and that they performed some meritorious exploits with their long-bows.[50]

An act of parliament, however, passed in this reign to compel all servants to shoot on Sundays and holidays.

The English archers were accustomed to draw the arrow to the eye or ear, which every one who understands the nature of archery well knows is a method that has greatly the advantage of drawing to the breast.[51]

From an illumination in the historical account of the last years of Richard II by Francis de la Marque in the British Museum, we find that the Irish archers, during this period, were habited in tunics, with their heads guarded by conical skull-caps, and had round quivers of arrows at their right hips which were confined by a broad belt that went round the body.

Froissart says that the French army, sent to assist the Scots in 1385, complained that there were no banquets, no balls, no tournaments. The quarto register of Robert II, quoted by Pinkerton, History of Scotland, Vol. I, p. 165, contains the agreement between the Scots and their auxiliaries before they began then· expedition. From it we learn that all were to wear a white cross of St. Andrew before and behind. The punishment for a riot was to be

---

[50] Hollinshed Chrono Vol. III, p. 473.

[51] From having been formerly a member of the Toxopholite Society, I know this fact from experience. Drawing to to the breast, however, had been long the practice with the antients, and it was èsteemèd a great improvement when the Roman auxiliaries were instructed to draw the right hand to the ear. Hence Procopius describing them says: "They ride with ease and shoot their arrows in every direction; to the right, the left, behind, or in the front while at full speed; and as they draw the bow-string to the right ear they drive their arrows with such rapidity, that is certain death to him on whom they fall, nor can. the stoutest shield or helmét resist the violence of the stroke." Mr. Barrington too, in the Archreologia says: "That several years ago there was a man named Topham, who exhibited most surprising feats of strength and who happened to be at Islington, to which the Finsbury archers resorted after their exercise. Topham considered the long-bow as a play-thing only fit for a child; upon which one of the archers laid him a bowl of punch. that he could not draw the arrow two thirds of its length. Topham accepted this bett, with the greatest confidence of winning, but bringing

the loss of horse and armour, if the offender be a knight; of a hand or an ear, if he be not. The same punishment to be incurred by the man who shall set fire to a church in England, kill a woman or child, or commit a rape. Prisoners to belong to such as first receive their hands.

When a regular siege was made upon a town or castle, the first care was, to stop up all the avenues, as well to prevent the sallying forth of those within, as to hinder all assistance that might be given from without. Thus Edward III when he laid siege to the town of Calais built strong towers of wood between the town and haven; and another tower behind the town to guard the passage towards the downs.[52]

The next thing was to fill up the ditches in order to move forward the engines. Thus the Scots in the reign of Edward III, at the assault of a castle belonging to the Earl of Salisbury, carried wood and timber for this purpose, and also for a firm foundation on which to place the scaling ladders.[53]

Froissart, speaking[54] of the town d'Aurene, besieged by John a Gaunt Duke of Lancaster, says: Il ne avoit point d'eaue au fosses, mais il y avoit bons pallis de boys audevant des murs, et y avoit de bonnes espines et de ronces ou gensd'armes ne se pouvoient jamais embatre. "There was no water in the ditches, but they had strong palisadoes before the wall, besides great piles and sharp stakes, where the men at arms could never come to fight." It further appears that this town was surrounded with a double ditch: the first next the wall was occupied by the palisadoes, and the outermost by the sharp stakes and the piles. The method the duke took to assault it was this: he sent men well armed to advance to the ditch, being well provided with axes, and other necessary implements, who thus began by cutting down the sharp stakes; meantime the archers of the duke's army plyed the besieged so fast with their arrows, that they scarcely dared to look over the wall. Notwithstanding, however, all these necessary precautions the piles being but newly put down, they met with the greatest difficulty to cut and break them off; and many of the soldiers were killed by the darts of the enemy; but, encouraged by the presence of the duke, they cleared the passage over the first fosse, up to the palisadoes; and thus ended the first assault. To make the second, they went well provided with large axes "des haches a grans fer, longs, et larges" up to the second ditch, which was full as large as the first, and set with palisadoes. Impatient, however, at the thought of these diffi-

---

[52] Grafton's Chrono 'p. 277.
[53] Ibid, p. 251.
[54] In vitâ Rie. II^di.

culties, they leaped into the ditch, broke up the palisadoes, and proceeded close to the wall; notwithstanding those above sent down showers of darts, of stones and other offensive weapons which made great carnage. The next step of the undaunted Englishmen was to apply their scaling ladders to the wall, which had been already prepared by the carpenters of the army; then the valiant knights and esquires mounted the ladders covering their heads with their shields, and with their swords in their hands, came hand to hand in fight with the besieged; who, notwithstanding a long and valiant resist--ance, at last were overcome and forced to yield up the town.[55]

The same author describing the siege of Reole, in the same reign,[56] says the English made use of a wooden tower on wheels, so that it might be moved by the soldiers wherever they desired; within it would easily contain a hundred knights and as many archers. When they had filled the ditch, this engine was brought to the walls. Its frame was of strong timber, covered over with boiled leather to prevent its being set on fire.[57] From this tower the archers annoyed the besieged with their arrows; while the rest, with pickaxes and hammers, beat down part of the wall in spite of all the resistance of the besieged, who were by no means sparing of their darts. Thus they entered the town and took possession of it.

Hollinshed tells us[58] the means which the besieged adopted to defend themselves. He says when the English had taken the city of Caen in the 20th year of Edward III, as they entered therein, the French went into their houses, and cast down upon the Englishmen below in the streets, great stones, timber, hot water and bars of iron; so that they hurt and slew more than five hundred persons.

Some authors have supposed that the invention of gunpowder was about the year 1381 made public,[59] it having been discovered by a German monk; but as Camden justly observes it must have been much earlier, "For," says he, "the very time of the first invention of guns is uncertaine, but certaine it is that King Edward III used them at the siege of Calice, 1347, for gunnarii had their pay there as appears by record."[60] About thirty three

---

[55] Froissart's Chrono Vol. III.

[56] Ibid, Vol. IV.

[57] Towers of wood were sometimes called "Bastelles" hence the Bastile, formerly in Paris, derived its name.

[58] Chron p, 930.

[59] Fifth of Richard II.

[60] Remains, p. 241. Spelman, however, conjectures that these were machinists, or engineers, and in the original document they are called "gynours."

years before they were seen in Italy, and about that time they seem to have been used in Spain, where they were known by the name of dolía igninoma or fire-flashing vessels; yet if we can believe Polydore Virgil, the French were not acquainted with them till the year 1425. But an original document, dated 1368, in the chamber of accounts at Paris falsifies this completely. It is entitled: "an Account of auxiliaries collected together for the liberation of John King of France," and among other items is the following: Guillaume l'Escuier, maistre des canons du roy, que icelui seigneur lui a ordonné estre baillé pour quérir cent livres d'estoffe à faire poudre pour quatre grans canons, qu'il doit faire pour mettre en la garnison de Harefleur. "William l'Escuier, master of the king's canons, whom that lord has ordained to be delivered to him for seeking a hundred pounds of stuff to make powder for four great canons, which he ought to make to put in the garrison of Harfleur."

In the year 1377, being the 1st of Richard II, Thomas Norbury was directed to buy and provide of Thomas Restwold of London, two great and two less engines called cannons; 600 stone shot for the same and other engines, and a great quantity of bows and arrows, iron, steel, saltpetre, sulphur, charcoal and other amunition for stores, to be sent to the Castle of Brest.[61]

In 1380 the Venetians used cannons against the Genoese boats attacking their city, which Guicciardini erroneously considers their first appearance in Italy.

When the Bishop of Norwich besieged Ypres in the year 1383, the garrison is said by Walsingham[62] to have defended themselves so well with stones, arrows, lances, Greek fire, and certain engines called guns, that they obliged the English to raise the siege with such precipitation, that they left behind them their great guns, which were of inestimable value.

The same author further relates that in three years after certain English ships met with two French ships sailing towards Sluys, which they took and brought into Sandwich; there was found on board those ships a master-gunner who before had served in the English army at Calais under Sir Hugh Calveley, and also divers great guns and engines to beat down walls, with a great quantity of powder that was worth more than all the rest.[63]

In the account of Bartholomew de Drach, treasurer of war in France for the year 1388, there is a charge to Henry de Faumechon, for powder and

---

[61] Rot. Franc. 8, Ric. II, p. 2, m.1ô.

[62] P.303.

[63] Gonnæ plures cum magna quantitate pulveris cujus precium prrevaluit omnibus manubiis supra dictis, p. 323. These gunnoe at p. 398, he says were what Galli canones vocant " the French call cannons."

other things necessary for the canons which were before Puy Guillaume in Auvergne. In the Chronicle of Bertrand du Guesclin is this expression: Pour la ville assaillir ordonnèrent canons. "They ordered canons to attack the town."

Froissart,[64] in the life of Richard II, speaking of a naval engagement, tells us, that John Bucq, the Flemish admiral, was in a ship that carried three canons, which cast forth darts or quarrels (carrieaux) so large and heavy, that they did great damage wheresoever they fell.

Certain it is that, at the first invention of cannons, darts and bolts were shot from them; and thus in an old MS. Chronicle, said to have been written by Douglas, a monk of Glastonbury, we are told that, in the 9th year of Henry IV, the Earl of Kent was smote upon the head with a quarrel shot from a gonne of which wound he died. But twenty years before this, stones were used instead, for, in the year 1388, at the siege of Chiosa, the renowned Peter Doria was killed by a stone bullet which weighed 195lbs, and was discharged from a bombard called the trevisan.[65]

The French, in this reign, intending to invade England, made a wall of wood.[66] It was twenty feet high and at every twelve feet was a tower large enough to hold ten men. These towers were built ten feet higher than the rest. To this account Hollinslied adds[67] that, when set up, the whole contained full 3000 paces, and was to have been brought over in their ships to defend their men from the arrows of the English archers. But, their ships being taken by the English, the wall according to Lambard,[68] was brought to Sandwich, and there set up "to our great safety and the repulse of the Frenchmen."

The French had been very sanguine as to the success of this attempt, and prepared for it with a splendid gaiety. They had their arms painted on their vessels; many had then· masts covered with leaf gold, as indications of their riches and power, and their banners, penons and streamers were as handsome as art could render them.[69]

---

[64] This author so minute in all his circumstances does not mention that Edward used cannon at the battle of Cressy iand tbe more recent author, Villani, who notices them, is not sufficient authority.

[65] Chrono della Guerra di Chioza.

[66] Walsingham, p. 315.

[67] Chrono p. 1053.

[68] Peramb. of Kent, p. 129.

[69] Froissart, p. 113. It took place in the year 1386 .

Henry the Fourth.

1399.

ANY particulars have already been brought under consideration, but soon after the succession of this monarch we have a very curious account of the armour worn by the European cavalry. This is from the pen of Chere-feddin, a Persian, the cotemporary and historian of Timour Bee. Describing his battle with Bajazet, the Ottoman Sultan, in 1401, he tells us that "The Tartar ordered several ranks of elephants to be posted at the head of the whole army, as well to intimidate the enemy as to display his Indian successes. They were covered with the most splendid trappings, and, as usual, armed with towers on their backs in which were placed archers and castors of wild-fire, (the feu gregois) to spread terror and disorder wherever they should go. Bajazet also took care to draw up his army in order of battle. The right wing was commanded by Pesir Laus, an European, his wife's brother, *with 20,000 cavalry of Europe, all armed in steel, from head to foot, so that nothing could be seen but their eyes. Their armour was fastened below*

the foot by a padlock, which except they open, their cuirass and helmet cannot he taken off. About ten o'clock the infantry of the Tartars, with their bucklers before them, posted themselves on the neighbouring hills."

It is very difficult to comprehend how this armour could be fastened, and of what kind it was, since no existing monuments of that period seem at all to correspond with such a description. Yet Froissart's expression: armez de pied en cap, "from foot to head," instead of from head to foot, in some degree gives countenance to it. Certain it is that the author here describes plate-armour[1] and alludes to the troops of Greece.

The armour at this period was certainly very splendid. That may be observed in the monumental brass of Sir Nicholas Dagworth, whose jupón also terminates in elegant foliage. In this we perceive the first approach towards making pauldrons, in the several overlapping shoulder-plates or epaulieres being extended greatly in front. The plate below the genouilliere likewise occurs. These things are also observable in that of Sir George Felbridge, which has been selected for Plate xxxviii, But the plates below the knees in both these specimens are much larger than those worn by the Black Prince, and, therefore, there was a necessity to have them fastened by a strap which passed round the jamb. This is shewn in the leg at the bottom of Plate xxxviii, taken from a French serjeant at arms during this period, and which will be more fully noticed presently. Sir George Felbridge besides these plates below his genouillieres has others which hang over his thighs. These were called tuiles, from their resemblance to a tile. This is the earliest instance in which they occur, and it is singular that they come from under the hauberk.[2] In the rhyme of Sir Thopas in Chaucer's Canterbury Tales, we have the following account of a knight arming himself:

> And next his shert an baketon
> And over that an habergeon
> For percing of his herte,
> And over that a fine hauherke.

By habergeon he seems here to mean the breast and back plates under the hauberk. Whether, however, the tuiles of Sir George Felbridge were attached to the bottom of his hauketon, or whether they were merely

---

[1] Because he mentions it by way of contrast with that of the Asiatics. Froissart bears in mind the manner in which armour was put on, when he begins with the foot, and the Persian may have been misled by a similar statement which he did not rightly comprehend.

[2] Such was sometimes tbe case as late as the time of Henry VIII, as appears from a brass-plate found in Netley Abbey and eng-raved in the Archreologia.

strapped on the upper part of his jambs we have nothing whereby to determine, though I am inclined to imagine the former.[3]

The monument of Louis le Mai, or as he is there stiled Luys le Male,
Earl of Flanders, in the collegiate Church of St. Peter's at Lisle,[4] furnishes
an example during this reign of the omission of sollerets, so that he must
have had footed stirrups, which we have seen[5] had been previously invented.
The chain-mail is also observable above and below the jambs, and though
he wears vambraces, the sleeves of his hauberk cover the upper parts of his
arms, while his shoulders are protected by shield-like plates buckled round
the arm and fastened at top with ribbons called points. His shield, too, is
not quite so sharply pointed as during the two last reigns.

The bas-reliefs on the under part of the seats of the choir of Worcester
Cathedral afford good specimens of the armour of this period. On one of
these is a warrior who holds a curved sword in his hand, while a straight
one is pendant from his girdle. His shield, which resembles that of Louis
le Mai in being wider at the lower part than in the preceeding reigns, is deprived of the point, being rounded at the bottom. In the centre of the top,
too, appears the bouclie or excavation through which the lance was thrust.
Another of these represents a just, wherein the shields at bottom instead of
being rounded are formed by three lines, but the mouth at top is nearer the
left corner.[6] The horses are handsomely trapped, and the combatants are attended by a man playing on the kettle drums and another with a large horn.

In the year 1400, Manuel Emperor of Constantinople visited England
in the hope of procuring succours from Henry IV. Laonicus Chalcondyles,
who accompanied him, has left us a description of the countries through
which he passed, and in that of Britain he says: "The natives are bold and
hardy, renowned in arms, and victorious in war. The form of their shields
or targets is taken from that of the Italians, and that of the swords from the
Greeks. The use of the long bow is the peculiar and decisive advantage of the
English."

In an inventory taken at Holy Island in the year 1401, we have the
following enumeration of arms and armour of the period: In camera, iii
bacinetts cum eventill, ibrestplat, i hawbirion, iiii jakkys antiqˢ, i awblast'an-

---

[3] Indeed in the directions how a knight should be armed, in the time of Henry VI, we
are told that they are to be attached to the doublet that was worn underneath the breast-
plate.

[4] See Millin's Antiq. Nationales.

[5] Page 85.

[6] These figures are represented in the initial letter of this reign.

tiq⁵, iiii gonnys, ii lancee. "In the chamber, three bascinets with avantailes, one breast-plate, one haubergeon, four old jacks, one old cross-bow, four guns (or cannons,) two lances."

In another, taken eight years afterwards, are these: iii basinetts cum ii eventall, i brest-plate, i liabirion antiquum, ii jackks nullius valoris, ii lancee, iii gunnes. "Three bascinets with two avantailes, one breast-plate, one old haubergeon, two jacks of no value, two lances, three guns (or cannons.")

As Chaucer was an eye witness to the tournaments and justs which took place during this reign, the following description from his Knight's Tale cannot but he interesting:

> "There mayst thou sen devysing of harneys
> So uncouth,[7] and so ryche, and wrought so wel,
> Of goldsmithrye, of brodynge.[8] and of stel;
> The scheldis bright, the testers,[9] and trapurys,
> Gold hewen[10] helmys, hauberkys, cote armourys,
> Lords in paramentis[11] on ther courserys;
> Knyghtis of retenue, and eke squyerys;
> Rayinge[12] of sperys, and helmys bokclynge;
> Gigginge[13] of scheldys, with lanyeris[14] lacynge;
> There as nede is, they weren nothing idle;
> The fomy stedys on the golden bridle
> Gnawing, and fasti the armureisjt also,
> With file and hammer prickinge to and fro:
> Knavysi[15] on fote, and commonys many on,
> With schort stavys, as thikke as they may gon:
> Pypis and trumpis,[16] nakerys,[17] and clariounys,
> That in battayle blowen bloody sounys."

In another place Chaucer speaks of the lance-rest thus:

---

[7] Uncommon.

[8] Embroidery.

[9] Testieres.

[10] Not gilt but ornamented with solid gold.

[11] Robes of state.

[12] Arraying.

[13] Fastening on the giga, guige, or shield-belt.

[14] Armourers who closed the rivets.

[15] Young men or servants.

[16] Large brazen horns, such as exhibited carved under the seats at Worcester Cathedral.

[17] Kettle drums called by the Asiatics nacaires. These are also on the carving under tbe seat at 'Worcester.

PLATE XXXVIII

SIR GEORGE FELBRIDGE,

A.D. 1400.

"In gon the sperys ful gladly in at rest."

This ample description is fully illustrated by an illumination in a copy of Froissart,[18] representing a joust given on the public entry of Queen Isabel[19] of Bavaria into Paris, in the champ de Sainte Catherine, in June 1389, but drawn at this period. The king and queen with their courtiers and ladies are in a gallery covered with cloth of gold of a splendid pattern, and are all in the costume of the reign of Henry the IVth of England. There are four combatants on each side. The first on the right has his housing, which is merely the croupiere, fretty, with fleur-de-lis and roses alternately within the spaces, which, as Mont-faucon observes, seems to indicate that the warrior is of the House of France. On his helmet is a bouquet, consisting of three boughs with their leaves on; the second on the same side has as his crest two wings joined, the third an owl, the fourth a covered vase. On the left side the first combattant has on his croupiere a number of suns, and on his helmet a bouquet of three feathers, the second a pelican for his crest, the third a cap such as ordinarily worn, and the fourth something like a lantern. Persons who are to pick up the broken spears for the heralds are in the area. On the faces of the horses are placed the testieres, or as they have since been called champfreins. These are of a very peculiar construction, and being the earliest I have seen represented, demand particular notice. Instead of fitting close round the cheeks as in later specimens or bending back over the top of the head, each consists of a plate, having the indications of the subsequent form but only bent a little longitudinally, so as to form two sides. At the bottom it is made to curve up from the nose, while it extends greatly on each side, appertures are made for the eyes, and what is extremely curious, others for the ears, through which they are drawn while the testiere rises much higher than the head.[20] The breasts of the horses are protected by a large plate called the poitral, which is highly ornamented, and the thighs of the warrior by another on the saddle, extending from the abdomen downwards on each side to the middle of the legs. The spears have coronels at their ends, and very large vamplates, also the earliest known specimens. The warriors are in plate armour, while from their shoulders hangs a long robe slit up behind, and highly ornamented. This seems to be what Chaucer calls the parament or parement.

---

[18] Engraved for Montfaucon's Mon. Fr. Pl. CXLII.

[19] Wife of Charles VI, King of France.

[20] There is in the round tower of Windsor Castle a chanfron of the flat kind, which, though of later date than this described, is an early specimen.

The tilting helmets, however, take a new form, the upper part is no longer a truncated cone, but is convex over the head, and the face covering,
antiently called the ventail, is made to project considerably beyond the ocularium or aperture for the eyes, while the shields remain the same as in
the last reign. In close conformity with both these is the seal of Robert III,
King of Scotland,[21] who ascended the throne in the year 1400. It has been
observed that, from the apex of one of the helmets of the knights in this
illumination of Froissart, there is a plume of feathers. This however, must
rather be considered as what lead to the panache or plume on the top of
the helmet, than what became afterwards so denominated; as feathers thus
worn do not occur till the next reign.

There is a deed, however, of the time of Richard II,[22] that would incline
one to think that the pennache had been adopted even then. It runs: Jeo
Gervais de Clifton chevalier aye donnée, grantee, et par Cette ma présente
chartre confirmée à mon bien aimé Richard de Bevercotes, un heaume, c'est
à sçavoir une tuife de plumes, la moitié, c'est à dire par amont de plumes
noires et l'autre moitié, c'est à dire par aval de plumes blanches, à avoir, et
tenir l'adite heaume. "I Gervais de Clifton knight, have given, granted, and,
by this my present charter, confirmed to my well beloved Richard de Bevercotes, a helmet, that is to be understood, a tuft of feathers, the half, that is to
say, upwards of black feathers, and the other half, that is to say, downwards
of white feathers, to have and to hold the said helmet."

Still I consider this as only a crest of which many were formed of feathers, that of Sir Henry Percy in Edward the First's time is of this kind,[23] so is
that of Sir John Harsick in Richard the Second's,[24] which is of turkey's feathers, and in this illumination of Froissart all the other knights have crests.

Crests were distinguishing marks and had been particularly conferred
by sovereigns. Thus Edward III, in the year 1333, granted one to William
Montagu, Earl of Salisbury. Concessimus pro nobis et hæred. nostris W. de
Monte acuto tymbriam nostram de aquilâ.[25] "We grant for us and our heirs
to William de Montacute our crest of the eagle." And from a further grant
in the 13th of the same king, we find that the crests were to become hereditary. Et ut honorem dictæ tymbriæ posset decentius conservare concesser-
imus ei ut manerium de Wodeton, &c. remaneant prefato comiti et hæred.

---

[21] See Anderson's Diplo mata Scotiæ.
[22] Pere Daniel, Milice Françoise, Tome II.
[23] See bottom of Plate XXIV.
[24] See Plate XXXVI.
[25] Pat. Rot.9, Edward III. In the French translation, à porter nostre tymbrede l'egle.

suis in perpetuum.[26] "And in order that the honour of the said crest may be with more decency preserved, we have granted in addition to it the manor of Wodeton, &c., that it may remain to the said earl and his heirs for ever."

"In the year 1409 the 10th of Henry IV," says Stowe,[27] "a great play was played at Skinner's Well which lasted eight days; where were to see the same, the most part of the nobles and gentles of England. And forthwith began a royal justing in Smithfield, between the Earl of Somerset and the Seneschall of Henault, Sir John Cornwall, Sir Richard Arundell and the son of Sir John Cheney against certain Frenchmen. And the same year a battle was fought in Smithfield, the one called Gloucester appellant, and the other Arthure defendant, they fought valiantly, but the king took up the quarrel into his hands and pardoned them both."

This last circumstance refers to the trial by wager of battle which was granted upon petition to the king. Of this kind the most curious was the ceremony performed by the king's champion at the coronation. Froissart, who was present at that of Henry IV, gives us the following account: En la moitié de ce disner vint un chevalier qui se nommoit Dimeth tout armé, monte sur un cheval tout couvert de mailles de vermeil, chevalier et cheval, et estoit armé pour gage de bataille, et avoit un chevalier devant lui, qui portoit sa lance, et avoit le dit chevalier à son costé l'espée tout nuë, et sa dague à l'autre costé, et bailla le dit chevalier un libelle au roy, qui fut leu; lequel libelle contenoit, que s'il estoit chevalier, escuier, ou gentilhomme, qui vousist dire ne maintenir, que le Roy Henry ne fust vray roy; il estoit tout preste de le combattre present le roy, quand il plairoit au roy assigner journée, et là fit le roy crier par un heraud d'armes par six lieux en la dite ville, et aussi en la sale. "In the middle of this dinner[28] came a knight who was named Dimeth[29] completely armed, mounted on a horse all covered with mail of a vermillion colour, both knight and horse; and he was armed as for wager of battle, and had a knight to proceed him, who carried his lance. The first mentioned knight had at one side of him his sword quite naked, and at the other his dagger, and the said knight delivered a paper-writing to the king which was read; which paper-writing stated that, if there was any knight, esquire, or gentleman who chose to say or maintain that King Henry was not the true king, he was quite ready to combat him in the king's presence, whenever it might please the king to assign a day, and thereupon the king

---

[26] Rot. Vase. 13, Edward III, m. 4.
[27] Survey of London, Book 3, p.239.
[28] In Westminster Hall on the day of the coronation.
[29] Dymock.

caused the same to be proclaimed by a herald at arms in six places within the said city, as well as in the hall."

An instance occurs during this reign which shews the warlike character of the age. The Lady Spenser, a widow, accused the Duke of York of treason, and in proof of her assertion produced her champion, William Maidstone, and offered to be burnt, (the usual punishment) if he should be vanquished. The duke accepted tlie challenge, but Henry imprisoned him and thus prevented the fight.[30]

Henry IV, soon after he came to the throne,[31] found it necessary to revive the prohibiting statutes established by his predecessor relating to apparel, which however was done with several considerable alterations and additions. Among other things it was ordained "that no person should use baselards, girdles, daggers or horns decorated with silver, nor any other trappings of silver, unless he be possessed of the yearly income, in lands and tenements, to the amount of twenty pounds, or of goods and chattels to the value of two hundred pounds. An exception was made in favour of the heirs to estates of the yearly value of fifty marks, or to the possession in goods and chattels to the amount of five hundred pounds. This exception was four years afterwards[32] restricted to such as had the full sum of five hundred yearly in reversion; and it was at the same time ordained, that no man, let his condition be what it might, should be permitted to wear a gown or garment cut, or slashed into pieces in the form of letters, rose leaves, or posies of various kinds, or any such like devices under the penalty of forfeiting the same.

But in all cases of formal ceremony the sword was still considered not only as allowable but indispensable. So in all those legal instruments which issue under the title of, "Trial by grand assise," for the recovery of seisin of lands and tenements, there is always inserted the following: "Therefore it is commanded the sheriff, that he summon by good summoners four lawful knights of his county, *girt with swords*, that they be here on . . . . to make election of the assise aforesaid."

Chaucer reproaches his compatriots with "wasting cloth in indenting or barring, or oundying,[33] palying or bending and such like." The lower ends of the juppons, of this period we may frequently observe, are made to terminate in various kinds of leaves, ànd the cloaks and sleeves are so peculiarly marked by their waved or indented edges as to be distinctive characteristics

---

[30] Otterb. p. 250.
[31] In the year 1403, the 4th of his reign.
[32] In the 8th of Henry IV.
[33] All these are heraldic terms, but for "oundy" is now generally used "wavy."

of this and the next reign. Perhaps one of the most decisive specimens of
this time are the two sculptured stones over the entrance of the Church of
St. Catherine des chanoines réguliers de Ste. Genevieve, which gives us the
costume of the serjeant at arms.[34] Two of them are in armour, and two in
tlieir ordinary dresses. One of those in armour has on his head that piece
of cloth wrapped round it which had formerly been a hood, as in the monumental effigy of a knight of the Eustace family in Ireland, before noticed,
and in King John's time was called the cargan. It is, however, worn in the
manner usual with Henry IV himself, and such as is often met with in this
reign. Both those in armour and those without, have swords and very large
maces resembling such as are still carried by the beadles of the English universities.[35] The inscription on these stones is as follows: A la prière des sergens d'armes, Monsieur Saint Louis fonda cette Eglise, et y mit la première
pierre; et fut pour la joye de la victoire qui fut au pont de Bouvines l'an
1214, les sergens d'armes pour le temps, gardoient le dit pont, et vouèrent
que si Dieu leur donnoit victoire ils fonderoient l'Eglise de Sainte Catherine, et ainsi fut il. "On the petition of the serjeants at arms Monsieur Saint
Louis founded this church and laid the first stone of it. This was done in
testimony of joy for the victoiy obtained at the battle of the bridge of Bouvines in the year 1214, the serjeants at arms for the time, guarded the said
bridge, and vowed that if God would give them victory, they would found
the Church of Saint Catherine, and so it was."

All the French authors have hitherto considered these stones as put up
at the time of the foundation of the church, and hence supposed the armour
to be that of the year 1214, but the wording of the inscription shews it must
have been subsequent, and the costume places it in the reign of our fourth
Henry.

This guard, as a military body, lasted no longer than the reign of the
French King John. Philippe de Valois, his successor, reformed it, and reduced it to the number of one hundred men. It is easily accounted for,
therefore, that on the repair of this church the serjeants at arms should thus
endeavour to point out the prowess of their predecessors.

The same kind of sleeves is observable on a figure of St. George in the
Church of St. Peter at Lisle,[36] which also affords us a specimen of the war
helmet that became so prevalent in the next reign. It is higher in the apex,

---

[34] See an engraving of them in Père Daniel's Milice Françoise, Pl. II, Tome II.

[35] It is the leg of one of these figures that is at the bottom of Plate xxxviii.

[36] See Millin's Antiq. Nation.

and shews the intermediate form of the uniber[37] between the conical one of the early part of this reign and the convex one of the next. His shield is nearly oblong in shape, but rounded at the bottom like that before described at Worcester Cathedral.

Chaucer in his Canterbury Tales, speaks of the priests appearing with:

> "Bucklers brode and sweardes longe
> Baudryke with baselards kcne."

We have seen that the statute of Henry IV prohibited expensive belts, except to persons of a certain rank. But, with respect to the baudrick, which was properly the belt that went over the shoulder rather than the girdle, it may be observed that baltlieus aureus gennnatus continually occurs in antient inventories. Still it was the girdle that we see so very highly ornamented in the monumental effigies and illuminations of this period, and that seems here to be meant by the term baudrick. So the author of the Roman de Garin describes his hero as habited in a bliaut of samit and with a baudrick embellished with great fillets of fine gold and precious gems that were attached to it:

> Et ot vesti un bliaut dc samiz
> Un baudre ot a grant bandes d'or fin,
> A chiere pierres sont attaches et mis.

Froissart speaks of the bascinets of this period as being fastened behind. Thus: Il meit son bacinet en sa teste, et son escuyer le luy laça par derrière.[38] "He put his bascinet on his head and then his esquire laced it behind." He also speaks of a kind of chapelle de fer, which he calls chapelet de Montauban. Thus describing the page of Charles VI, King of France, when riding with his master, he tells us that he wore un chapelet de Montauban fin cler et net, tout d'acier, "a Montauban hat fine, clear and shining all of steel."

Chaucer in his Canterbury Tales thus describes a squire's yeoman: He "bore a mighty bow," and beneath his girdle appeared a bundle of sharp bright arrows, plumed with peacock's feathers, and upon his arm he wore "a gay bracer," that is an ornamented one. To his baudrick, or sash of green, was appended a horn. Besides this he had hanging on one side of him a sword and buckler, and on the other

---

[37] That which contains both beavor and vizor.
[38] Tome I, Ch. 288.

"A gay daggere
Harneysed well, and sharpe as poynte of spere."

From his dress, says the poet, I should have taken him for a forrester. Besides the dagger, Chaucer, in his Canterbury Tales, mentions the anelace[39] which was broad bladed, but lessening from the hilt to a sharp point, and having a sharp edge on each side.

The most memorable circumstance, with respect to the bow, which occurred in the reign of Henry IV, was the victory gained over the Scots near Halidown-hill, in the year 1402, "Where," in the words of an old historian, "the Lord Percies archers did withall deliver their deadly arrows so lively, so couragiously, so grievously, that they ranne through the men of armes, bored the helmets, pierced their very swords, beat their lances to the earth, and easily shot those who were more slightly armed, through and through;" and according to Otter-bourne,[40] "rendered it unnecessary for the men at arms to draw a sword."

In the 7th year of his reign, however, it was found necessary to pass a law relative to fletcliers or arrow-makers. This act complains of the arrow-smith, and ordains that the heads of arrows shall in future be well boiled and brazed, and hardened at the points with steel; under the pain of the forfeiture of all such heads otherwise manufactured, and imprisonment to the makers. All arrow-lieads to be marked with the maker's name.

Arrows, as well as other missile weapons were considered as artillery, and hence the mistaken assertion that artillery antiently signified archery. Thus in a letter, dated 1397, it is said: Le suppliant comme leur ami et complice en icellui cas se fust armé comme eulx de haubergeon, cliappeline, gardebras, arc, artillerie, et autres armeures invasibles. "The suppliant, as their friend and accomplice in that business, was armed like them in an haubergeon and cliappe-line (on his head) with a gardebras (or bracer to protect his arm from the effect of the bow string) a bow, artillery (arrows) and other missile arms."

From a letter dated 1405, in Rymer's Fœdera,[41] the baudrick seems to have been worn by the cross-bow men as well as the archers, for the enumeration there made is in these words: Quatuor cophinos cum quarellis, tria bauderikes, et quindecim pavisses, &c. "Four boxes of quarrels, three

---

[39] Several of these of the time of Henry VII and later are in the armoury of Llewelyn Meyrick, Esq.

[40] P. 237.

[41] Vol. VIII, p, 384.

baudericks and fifteen pavises, &c." The capelline mentioned under the year 1397, also occurs in a letter dated 1403. Thus: Armé d'une coiffette sur la teste et d'un grand coustel, le dit Thevenin lui osta ses diz grant coustel et capeline. "Armed with a coiffette on his head, and a great knife, the said Thevenin took from him his said great knife and capeline." By the coiffette was meant the bascinet, for in another letter remissory of the year 1400, it is said: Le dit Jaquet fery d'un plançon sur la teste du dit vassel, dont il lui fist cheoir un bascinet ou une coiffette de fer, dont il estoit armé. "The said Jaquet struck the said vassal on the head with a stick, by which he made him drop a bascinet or coiffette of steel with which he was armed."

There is some reason for thinking that the weapon which at this time was called besagiie, was more used for throwing than for close combat. Thus in a letter remissory, of the year 1380, it is said: Le dit Hue d'un gran martel qu'il portoit, appelle besagiie, getta au dit Colart, et l'en euida ferir. "The said Hue threw a large martel which he carried, called besagiie, at the said Colart, with an intention of striking him.[42]

In a letter dated 1414, we have a weapon called harsegaye, which is explained to be a kind of demi-lance: Le suppliant d'une harsegaye ou demi-lance frappa par la poitrine icellui cavalier. "The supplant with a harsegaye or demilance, struck that knight in the chest." It was the same as the archegaye the favourite weapon of the Greek troops at this time, and its name is of Asiatic origin.[43]

The custom of ornamenting the necks and bridles of horses with bells had been introduced from Asia at this time, for Chaucer, in the Tale of the Monk, tells us that:

——When he rode men might hys bridel here
Gyngelyng in a wys'tling winde as clere
And eke as loude as dothe the chapel bel.

Swords were reckoned among defensive arms at this period, for in a letter dated 1408, it is said: Cum dictus Bernardus gladium vel aliud deffensiorum non haberet, accessit ad domum suam et gladio balasardo accepto, dictum Guillelmum tribus vel quatuor ictibus de dicto balasardo percussit. "When the said Bernard had not a sword or any other defensive weapon, he

---

[42] The natives of India often practice throwing their battle-axes, and for that purpose hold them at the thick part opposite the blade, between their fore-finger and thumb.

[43] The name, sometimes merely zagaye has travelled to the remotest parts of Africa, having been introduced by the Mahomeddans, and applied by the Hottentots to their lances.

went home, and took his balasard sword, and struck the said William three or four blows with the said balasard."[44]

Froissart who wrote in the time of Henry IV, has been very particular in his account of the forty-six knights, made by this king the day before his coronation, and observes that before their creation: Et eurent tous ces esquires chascun sa cliambre, et chascun son baing ou ils se baignerent cette nuit. "And all these esquires had each his chamber, and each his bath, where they bathed that night."[45]

Bathing, however, before knighthood was an antient custom, for John the Monk of Mairemonstier says that when Geoffry of Anjou was made a knight at Rouen, by Henry I, he with twenty-five esquires who attended him, were bathed according to custom. He adds that when he first came from the bath, he was clothed in fine linen, over that a gown of gold tissue, with a tunic of purple upon that furred with furs of a blood colour, with velvet hose, and shoes wrought with gold upon his feet, and the edges of his garments were also ornamented witli gold; and when he was to be created, he was uncloathed, and cloathed again in fine linen and purple garments ornamented with gold, like those before mentioned.

Dr. Percy[46] has justly remarked that: "A collar was antiently used in the ceremony of conferring knighthood," but I do not conceive this could have been introduced sooner than the time of Henry IV, as collars do not appear earlier on the military monumental effigies. That which was used was called the collar of SS, according to Camden,[47] "because it is composed of a rep-etition of that letter which was the initial of Sanctus Simo Simplicius, an eminent Roman lawyer, and that it was particularly worn by persons of that profession." It is, however, more consistent with the practise of this period to consider it as the initial of Henry's motto, which, while he was Earl of Derby, had been "Souveraine,"[48] and which, as he afterwards became sov-ereign, appeared auspicious. The Queen of Henry IV is sculptured on her monument with this collar, nor does it occur in any instance before this reign.

In the acts of the French parliament at Paris, in the year 1415, is the following description of the making a knight: Et print d'un des ses gens son espee et le dit seigner mis a genoux pres du Greffier, frappa trois grans coups

---

[44] The same as basilard.
[45] Vol. IV.
[46] Reliques of English Poetry, Vol. II, p. 79.
[47] Remains, p. 193.
[48] He is thus typified by Chaucer, where he describes the nobility by their mottos.

le dit roy sur le dos du dit seigner. Puis fit decliausser l'un de ses esperons dorez, et lui fit chausser par l'un de ses gens et l'y ceindre une ceinture oil estoit pendu un cousteau long pour espee. "And one of his people took his sword, and the said nobleman placed himself on his knees near the registrar, when the said king struck the said nobleman three great blows with it on his back. Then he caused to be taken off one of his gilt spurs, and made one of his people fasten it on the heel of this lord, and had him girded with a girdle from which was suspended a long knife instead of a sword." Though this event took place in the time of Henry V, it shews the practice at this period.

In the Church of St. Audoen at Dublin there is a monumetal effigy which exhibits a knight in plate armour, with a large gorget of chain-mail, reaching much below his shoulders, and on it are placed two circular plates just over the shoulder. To the last of the tassets or successive plates, which cover the abdomen and which received their names from being over the pockets,[49] is an apron of chain. He also wears a collar round his neck, and the date of the monument is 1402. These circular plates seem to be the clavengi, mentioned by Radulphus Cadomensis in his Gestis Tancredi thus: Benedictus quoque infelix archiepiscopus captus trahebatur imposita humeris geminorum sarcina claven-gorum. "Also Benedict, the unfortunate archbishop being taken, he was dragged about having put on each of his shoulders the burthen of the clavengi." And again: Primo in congressu lancet viget, lancet perfodit, lancea dejicit, qua? mox tanto sub onere fatiscens, ut penetrare peltas, pectora clavengos nequet integra. "At first, in the assembly he flourished the lance, then pierced with it, and then cast it down, being very soon rendered unable to proceed from its weight, so that he could not completely penetrate targets, breast-plates, or clavengi."

In Italy the back and breast-plates continued to be called cuirasses or curazzi, and the hauberks, panceroni, for in the Chronicon Bergem. under the year 1404, is the following passage: Guelplii dimiserunt de eorum armis plus-quain scutos cccc, balistas 1, et multas curazias et panceronos. "The Guelphs dispatched from their armoury more than four hundred shields, one of balistee, and many cuirasses and pancerons."   ,

In Thornton Church, Hampshire, is the effigy of Sir John Lysle on a brass plate, who died in 1407. This is the earliest specimen of the armour which distinguished the next reign. No juppon is worn over it, nor any chain apron at the bottom of the tassets, but these are increased in number, and therefore extend lower. Not only are there the plates below the knee

---

[49] The word is of German origin.

caps, but corresponding ones are placed above. There is no mail at all used, but instead of the gussets to protect the armpits, circular plates are attached by points which are tied at their centre. The bascinet has nothing to protect the face, from which we may conclude that the uniber was put on and taken off at pleasure.[50] To the elbow-pieces, but on the inside, are attached large fan-like ornaments, to protect the arm when straightened. The girdle is not used, but instead a baudrick or ornamented belt, coming from the right hip to the left thigh diagonally, and to this is appended the sword; a curious circumstance, as it shews the shape of the baudrick at this time.

The circular plates on the shoulders, which, in the next reign, took a variety of forms, appear to have been called palettes;[51] for in a deed of Henry IV, dated 1405, and, therefore, only two years preceeding the date of Sir John Lysle's monument, are enumerated: 11 palettes, 23 paria circotecarum de plate, 13 loricas. "Eleven palettes, twenty-three pairs of gauntlets of plate, and thirteen hauberks."

In after times the points were variously disposed in fastening on the plate armour. On the monument of Neville at Coverham, they appear near the ears, on that of one of the Rythers, at Ryther, at the elbows; one of the knights at Harwood has them on his elbows and shoulders, and a Middleton in the chancel of Ilkley Church at his wrists. James Lord Berkely, who died in 1463, and the figure by his side, at Berkeley, have them on and above each elbow, and Sir Richard Harcourt, buried in the year 1470, has them at his elbow's and wrists.

Among the military instruments of war used at this period we meet with one called coullart. In the account of expences for munitions provided for a castle in 1391,[52] is the following: Item, pour la feczon des dous engins, un angin et un coillart pour la defense doudit chautel. "For the making of two engines, one engine and one coillart for the defence of the said castle." So again in the history of Charles VI, King of France, under the year 1405: Laquelle (place de Mortaing) les François delibererent d'assiéger, et de faict y mirent le siege, et y assortirent canons et coullars et au très engins, et si endommageoient fort ceux de dedans les coullars, par où on jettoit grosses pierres et pesantes. "Which place the French determined on deliberation to besiege, and thereupon they laid siege to it, and brought up against it can-

---

[50] A vizored beaver made so to do, of the time of Edward VI, is in the armoury of Llewelyn Meyrick, Esq.

[51] Whence, probably, or from a similar origin, the flat circular pieces of wood or ivory used by artists had their name.

[52] In the library of St. Germain de Pré.

PLATE XXXIX

RICHᴰ. DE VERE   EARL ᴏꜰ OXFORD,

A.D. 1416.

nons and coullars and other engines, and so did great damage to those within, especially from the coullars, from which they cast great heavy stones."

From this we perceive that the introduction of cannon did not at once occasion the disuse of other warlike machines. The form of the cannon used at this period may be seen in an illuminated manuscript in the Slonian library, at the British Museum, entitled Chronique de St. Denis,[53] from which it has been copied by Strutt in his Dresses and Habits of England. It exhibits a bombard on a carriage, slight in proportion to the bulk of the piece; its trail consists of a prolongation of the cascable, which rests on the ground, a block of wood serving as a quoin for the purpose of depression. The bombard was so called from the Greek word βὸμβος, which expressed the noise made by it in firing; and which seems to point out what country first invented this kind of cannon.

We have also the dress of the artillery-man, which seems to have been a jacke, and those of the archers and cross-bow men of the same period.

Froissart describes a very extraordinary bombard, used at the siege of Oude-narde, made by the people of Ghent, under the direction of d'Arteville. He says it was "Fifty feet long, and threw great heavy stones of a wonderful bigness; when it was discharged it might be heard five leagues by day, and ten at night, making so great a noise in going off that it seemed as if all the devils in hell were abroad."

As the bombard was a Greek invention, so is there some reason to conceive that gunpowder owed its origin to the same nation. It seems to have been first applied merely to recreative fire works, whence, probably, its discovery is involved in obscurity, as it did not obtain celebrity till applied to the purposes of war.[54] It was from a treatise on pyrotechny, by Marcus Graecus, that Friar Bacon, in 1270, learnt that its composition was two pounds of charcoal, one of sulphur, and six of saltpetre, well powdered and mixt together.

---

[53] Marked 2433.

[54] This, on a due consideration of all the notices.left us, appears to have been about the commencement of the fourteenth century, as guns are mentioned in the metrical romance of Sir Tryamour, written in the time of Edward 11.

Henry the Fifth.

1413.

HE complete armour of plate, worn by Sir John Lysle in the last reign, was the general fashion of this, and, therefore, a specimen is given of it in Plate XXXIX, which represents Richard de Vere, Earl of Oxford. In this specimen the pallettes are very small, but the greatest novelty is the wreath on the bascinet and the inscription on the forehead plate; a custom which was afterwards extended to other parts of the armour as well as the weapons. The tilting-helmet with the knight's cap and crest are depicted near the warrior, the whole being taken from his monumental effigy.

Henry V on his great seal is also represented in complete plate-armour, and this further affords us the earliest specimen of the manefaire or protection for the horse's neck. Only three plates of this, however, which appear overlapping each other, are visible, and these seem to envelope the throat. Whether the manefaire extended all the way of the neck, though in all probability it did so, does not appear, as that part is covered by the housing,

underneath which, at the chest, is seen the poitral of chain-mail. The chanfron or cliampfrein takes a different form from what we observed in the last
reign and not only wraps round the nose, but has likewise cheek-plates. It,
however, reaches only to just above the nostrils. On the top of the chanfron,
or rather on that part of it which now acquired the exclusive appellation of
testiere, are placed the fore legs of the lion, the king's crest, and on the third
plate of the manefaire appear his hind ones. In all preceeding instances the
crest had been fixed on the head stall. The bow of the saddle is protected by
a plate of steel reaching below the knees.

From several contracts in Rymer's Fœdera[1] we learn the terms and manner in which the English army was raised, in 1415, for the expedition to
France.

1. Contracts were made by the keeper of the privy seal with different
lords and gentlemen, who bound themselves to serve with a certain number
of men for a year, from the day on which they were first mustered.

		s.	d.	
2. The pay of a Duke was to be		13	4	per day.
An Earl.		6	8	. . . . .
A Baron or Banneret.		4	0	. . . . .
A Knight.		2	0	. . . . .
An Esquire.		1	0	. . . . .
An Archer		0	6	. . . . .

3. The pay or security for its amount, was to be delivered by the treasurer a quarter of a year in advance; and if the money were not actually paid at
the beginning of the fourth quarter, the engagement was to be at an end. As
an additional remuneration, each contractor received "the usual regard," or
douceur of one hundred marks for every thirty men at arms.

4. A Duke was to have	50	horses.
An Earl.	24	. . . . .
A Baron or Banneret.	16	. . . . .
A Knight.	6	. . . . .
An Esquire.	4	. . . . .
An Archer	1	. . . . .

The horses were to be furnished by the contractor, the equipment by
the king.

5. All prisoners were to belong to the captors; but if they were kings,
the sons of kings, or officers high in command, bearing commissions from

---

[1] Tom. IX, 223, 227, 239.

kings, they were to belong to the crown on the payment of a reasonable recompence to the captors.[2]

6. The booty taken was to be divided into three parts, of which the leader took two and left the third to the king.

Under the last reign notice has been taken of the sleeves worn with the armour, with undulated edges. In an illuminated manuscript in the British Museum,[3] is a specimen of these where they appear very ample and slit up in front for the arm to be more easily used. This drawing is curious, however, on another account, and that is from its giving us a representation of the first step towards ornamenting the breast-plate, as there appear two curved fines ending in scrolls for that purpose. The figure on which this occurs has also the globose beaver not projecting quite so much as in other specimens. The knight thus armed is introduced into Plate xli, and is the tallest figure of the two. Perhaps, however, no specimen affords a more correct idea of the helmet and pennache,[4] than that of Robert Chamberleyn, who was esquire to King Henry V, on which account, therefore, it has been placed at the bottom of Plate XXXIX.[5]

In the Livres des Hommages du Comté de Clermont en Beauvoisis is a painting representing Louis II, Duke of Bourbon, who distinguished himself in the reign of Charles VI, King of France, and his esquire Le Sire de Beaujeu. These figures shew the complete armour of the time, the ordinary helmets or vizored bascinets with feathers at top, like that of Robert Chainberlayn, the heaume or justing-hehnet, which the squire carries in his hand, and the caparisons of the horses. It may be remarked that the knight has three feathers issuing from the charnel or apex of his bascinet, while the squire has but one.[6]

The vizors of the bascinets were frequently at this time termed ventailes, thus in an inventory taken at Holy Island, in the year 1416, are enumerated: ii basnetts cum ventells, ii basnetts sine ventells, i antiquum basenet cum le ventell, ii paria cerotecarum de plat, i par de wainbras, ii lancee, i jacke, iiii can ones. "Two basnets with ventailes, two ditto without ventailes, one old ditto with the ventaile, two pairs of gauntlets of plate, one pair of vambrac-

---

[2] This practice had been introduced by Edward III.

[3] Royal library, marked 15, D. III.

[4] The proper distinction between the pennache and plume is that the former is fixed on the top of the helmet, while the latter is placed behind, in front, or on the side.

[5] It is taken from a painting in the Cotton library in the British Museum, among the founders of St Alban's Abbey, dated 1417, and marked Nero. D. VII.

[6] An engraving of this may be seen in Montfaucon's Mon. Franç. p. CLI.

es, two lances, one jack and four cannons."

In the beginning of this reign, we are told,[7] "a memorable encounter happened in Smithfield between Robert Carey of the West, son of Sir John Carey, knight, and a foreign kniglit called Arragonese, one of the kingdom of Arragon, who having performed many noble atchievements in other countries, at last visited England, where he challenged many persons of his rank and quality to make trial of his skill in arms. The said Robert Carey accepted this challenge; between them was waged a cruel encounter, and a long and doubtful combat. But at last he was vanquished by the English gentleman; who was, therefore, knighted by the king and restored to part of his father's inheritance, having been Lord Chief Baron of the Exchequer in King Richard the Second his time, and taking part with him had forfeited his estate. And whereas by the law of heraldry, whosoever fairly in the field conquered his adversary might justify the wearing and bearing of his arms whom he overcame; he accordingly took on him the coat-armour of this Arragonese; being argent on a bend sable three roses of the first; which is ever since borne by the name of Carey; whose antient coat of arms was gules a chevron argent between three swans proper, one whereof they still retain in their crest."

A statute was enacted in this reign, said to have been made and established by parliament at the request of all the nobility of England,[8] which contains the following regulations relative to tournaments.

It prohibits any combatant from entering the lists with more than three esquires to bear his arms, and wait upon him for that day. It further specifies that no knight or esquire, who was appointed to attend in the lists as a servitor, should wear a sword, or a coutel,[9] or carry a baston or any other weapon excepting a large sword used in the tournament:[10] and that all combatants who bore lances should be armed with breast-plates, tliigli-pieces, shoulder-pieces and bascinets without any other kind of armour.

---

[7] Isaacke's Remarks on Exeter.

[8] MS. in the Harleian library, marked 69.

[9] This answered the purpose of a knife as well as dagger, and, therefore, has been frequently called a knife in this work. One of this description, of about this period is in the armoury of Llewelyn Meyrick, Esq. The blade has a sharp edge on one side, and the point forms somewhat less than a right angle. It has a handle of stag's horn, below which is a fox or .squirrel, the cognizance of the owner, and it was found on digging a well near Rochester Castle. The coutel was generally worn behind, just over the right hip.

[10] The swords as well as lances were larger and heavier for the tournaments .than for war. The baston was, of a peculiar shape, being composed of a handle and cross bar, with the striking part made to swell out at the sides. See at the foot of Plate LXX.

Another clause, which probably refers to such as were not combatants for the day, runs thus: "No one, except the great lords, that is to say, earls or barons, shall be armed otherwise than above expressed; nor bear a sword, pointed knife, mace or other weapon, except the sword for the tournament."

No earl, baron or knight might presume to infringe the regulations of this statute under the penalty of forfeiting his horse and arms, and the pain of imprisonment for a certain space of time, at the pleasure of the governors of the tournament; but if an esquire transgressed the law in any point, he not only lost his horse and his arms, but was sent to prison for three years.

If, however, the knights or esquires were possessed of lands, and appeared in arms for the service of their lords, they might recover their horses.

The kings at arms, who are called les roys des harnois, the heralds and the minstrels were commanded not to wear any kind of sharp weapons, but to have the swords which belonged to them without points. Respecting those who came as spectators on horseback, they were strictly forbidden to be armed with any kind of armour, or to bear any offensive weapons, under the penalty that was appointed for the esquires; and no boy or man on foot, coming for the same purpose, might appear with a sword, dagger, baston or lance; and, in case of disobedience to the statute, to be punished with one year's imprisonment.

The cessation of the round-table game occasioned little or no alteration respecting the justs, which had been practised by the knights belonging to it; they continued to be fashionable throughout the annals of chivalry, and ultimately superseded the tournaments, which is by no means surprising, when we recollect that the one was a confused engagement of many knights together, and the other a succession of combats between two only at a time, which gave each of the performers an equal opportunity of shewing his individual dexterity, and thus attracting general notice.

We have seen that the privilege of distributing prizes and remitting the punishment of offenders, were, by the laws of the tournament, invested in the fair sex, but at the justs their authority was much more extensive. The justs themselves indeed, were usually made in honour of the ladies, who presided as judges paramount over the sports, and whose determinations were in all cases decisive. Hence in the spirit of romance arose the necessity for every "true knight" to have a favourite fair one, who was not only esteemed by him as the paragon of beauty and virtue, but supplied the place of a tutelar saint, to whom he made his vows and addressed himself in the day of peril; for it seems to have been an established doctrine, that love made valour perfect, and incited the heroes to undertake great enterprizes.

Indeed, at the termination of a just with lances, the last course was made in honour of the female sex, and was called the "lance of the ladies;" the same deference was also paid to them in single combats with the sword, the axe and the dagger.

Mr. St. Foix[11] observes: "It is astonishing that no author has remarked the origin of this devotion in the manner of the Germans, our ancestors, as drawn by Tacitus who, he tells us, attributed somewhat of divinity to the fair sex."

This sentiment was not confined to the military pastimes, it animated the warriors in the day of battle. "Oh that my lady saw me," said one of them as he was mounting a breach at the head of his troops and driving the enemy before him.[12]

At the celebration of justs and tournaments the lists were superbly decorated, and enclosed at each end by the pavilions belonging to the champions, ornamented with their arms, banners, and banerolls; the scaffolds for the reception of the nobility of both sexes who came as spectators, and those especially appointed for the royal family, were hung with tapestry and embroderies of gold and silver. Every person, upon such occasions appeared to the greatest advantage, decked in sumptuous array, and every part of the field presented to the eye a rich display of magnificence. We may also add the splendid appearance of the knights engaged in the sports; themselves and their horses most gorgeously arrayed, as well as their esquires and pages. The heralds and minstrels, who attended the ceremonies, were all cloathed in costly and glittering apparel.

Such a show of pomp, where wealth, beauty and grandeur were concentred must have made a strong impression on the mind, which was further heightened by the cries of the heralds, the clangor of the trumpets, the clashing of the arms, the rushing on of the combatants and the shouts of beholders. Hence the popularity of these exhibitions may be easily accounted for.

The victory gained at Agincourt, in the year 1415, is in great measure ascribed to the English archers, and that there might be no want of arrows, Henry V ordered the sheriffs of several counties to procure feathers from the wings of geese, picking six from each goose.

An archer of this time was clad in a cuirass[13] or a hauberk of chain-mail,

---

[11] Essais Hist. Paris, Tome I, p. 327.
[12] Ibid, Tome III, p. 263.
[13] According to some illuminations.

with a salade on his head, which was a kind of bascinet but projecting much behind, and upon which was a moveable visor; he also had a sabre suspended at his side. Fabian, however,[14] thus describes the dress of the archers at the battle of Agincourt: "The yomen liadde at those dayes theyr lymmes at lybertye, for their hosyn were than fastened wyth one point, and theyr jackes were longe and easy to shote in, so that they myghte drawe bowes of great strength and shote arrowes of a yerde longe besides the liedde." Caxton also says:[15] "The yeomanry hadde theyr liosen terven or bounden bynethe the knee, having long jackys. But every man hade a good bowe, a shefe of arowys, and a swerd."

The Rev. Mr. Lingard, in his History of England adopting the authority of Monstrellet, says: "The archers by their savage appearance struck terror into their enemies. Many had stripped themselves naked: others had bared their arms and breasts, that they might exercise their limbs with more ease and execution." But he forgot that the Frenchman had to account for the defeat of his countrymen, and therefore fabricated this tale, so unlike the coolness of the English character, that of Henry the Fifth himself, and the mode in which this battle of all others was brought about. The English writers,[16] indeed so far from representing such foolhardiness in the archers, tell us that, besides the bows, arrows, swords and battle-axes, each bore on his shoulder a long stake sharpened at both extremities, which he was instructed to fix obliquely before him in the ground, and thus oppose a rampart of pikes to the charge of the French cavalry.

The cross-bows at this time were made powerful enough to send the quarrels forty rods, for in the Dunstable Chronicle[17] we read, that "Henry V came near to the city of Roan, by 40 rodes of length, within sliotte of quarrell."

As the cross-bow men were stationed on the tops of besieged castles, behind the crena or crenelles, which were the turrets that were pierced for them to shoot through, they were frequently called crenequiniers and their cross-bows crene-quins. Thus in a letter remissory dated 1420, it is said: Lequel Haquinet a chevauchié tendu crenequins et arbalestes à croq. "Which Haquinet rode along with crenequins bent and arbalestes on the hook." By the former the large arbalest, called by the English latch, is meant, and by the latter the prodd which was bent by a hook that was caught in the

---

[14] Vol. II, p.172.
[15] Addit. to Polychron. book VIII, ch. 13.
[16] Elmham, p. 61. Titus Livius Forojul, p. 19.
[17] Harl. lib. marked 24.

trigger. In another letter dated 1422 occurs: Icellui Bauduin prist un arbalestre nommée cranequin et la monta. "That Bauduin took an arbalest called
cranequin and drew it up." We are also told that the expression "bande ton
crennequin" implied "arbalestre à pie," arbalest to the foot, by which we
see that the crenequin was the large stirruped cross-bow. That by the croc
or crook was meant the hook into which the trigger caught, we learn from
Sanutus,[18] whose words are: Expedit etiain dari tendentibus balistas val-
idas crochorum bonorum auxilium et largorum; præsertim quod à parte
posteriori sint ampla crocha præfata, et quod prædictas balistas tendentes,
utantur prædicis crochis tarn tendendo, quam etiam balistando, &c. "It was
necessary, therefore, to give to those who bent strong cross-bows, the assistance of good and large crooks, especially as the aforesaid large crooks may
be placed on the posterior part of the stock, and because those who bend
the aforesaid cross-bows may use the aforesaid crooks not only in drawing
the bow, but also in shooting." In describing the armour of the last reign,
mention was made of an Irish knight who, on his ample cainail or gorget,
wore the clavengi. The monumental effigy of a knight of the Birmingham
family, affords another specimen of it, and also of that kind of cuirass which
was flexible, being formed of overlapping bands of steel. It has, therefore,
supplied a subject for Plate XL, and exhibits the form of the salade worn at
this period which, if not for a certainty of German, was of Italian origin, as
I shall hereafter have occasion to remark. There is something curious too, in
the genouillieres or knee-caps which he wears. At the bottom of this plate
is given the hood of Sir John de Wydevill taken from his monumental brass
plate. It is pointed and seems studded round the bottom with nails. In the
monument the figure has a huge helmet for tournaments to cover it, on
which is the crest. This specimen seems properly assignable to the close of
this reign: the chain apron is seen below the tasses, and, what is curious and
worthy of remark, has the same form as the tuiles of the next reign, and,
therefore, appears to have been their prototype.

In the Bedford Missal, late in the possession of the Duke of Marl-
borough, is an illumination representing Henry V being armed by his esquires.[19] It was done immediately after his death, and is curious on many
accounts. The king is in a suit of gilt armour. He has attached to his left
shoulder his tilting shield? which is bent forward in the upper part so as to
acquire a perpendicular situation when the arm is lifted to the bridle, and

---

[18] Lib. II, pars 4.
[19] See Gough's Sepulch. Monts. Vol. n.

PLATE XL

A KNIGHT OF THE BIRMINGHAM FAMILY,

(A.D. 1420.)

was contrived for the better putting off the thrust of the lance. At the under part it is a little lower on the outer side than that which goes over the saddle, and it has on it a large round boss in the centre to prevent its being pierced. As this is very curious and under certain modifications became prevalent in the next reign, it has been placed under Plate xlii. One esquire is employed in fixing this, having taken off the fighting shield which much resembles in shape those of Edward the Third's time; the other esquire is fixing on the spurs, and both are habited in their tabards. The helmet with its uniber is completely globular and is surmounted by a crown; the breast-plate is extremely convex, and consists of two pieces, the lower of which may be denominated a demi-placcate or placard, rising up towards a point in the centre and fastened there by a buckle and strap to the upper one. These globose breast-plates were introduced from the Lower Countries, and first occur in the paintings of the Earls of Holland which appear to have been done at this time and are now at Utrecht. The lance-rest, in this delineation of Henry V, is represented simply as a hook placed just below the right breast; the pauldrons or coverings for the shoulders are turned up a little at the top for the convenience of raising the arm, and the brassarts consist of several overlapping plates extending to the elbows.[20]

Black armour seems not only to have been worn in battle but used as mourning, for Hollinshed in the account he gives[21] of the funeral of King Henry V, tells us that "round about the chariot (on which was the corpse) rode five hundred men at arms, all in black armour, their horses barbed blacke, and they with the but ends of their spears upwards."[22]

A delineation representing a pilgrim delivering his book to Thomas Montacute Earl of Salisbury,[23] exhibits that nobleman in armour with a large fur cap on his head. In this drawing, although the breast-plate is not of the globose form, yet it is made of two pieces, and the buckle is fully shewn and appears highly ornamented. This figure also shews us that, as the undulated sleeves were sometimes worn without the cloak so was the cloak without the sleeves: it has therefore been introduced into Plate XLI. The palettes or plates over the armpits, in this specimen, have the shape of shields reversed and are highly ornamented. The earl holds in his hand one of those pole-axes carried by commanders from this period to that of

---

[20] This curious subject has been introduced into the initial letter.
[21] Cbron. Vol. III, p. 584.
[22] See also Elmham, p. 386, Wals. 407, Monstrel. Tome I, p. 325, 326.
[23] Drawn by Lydgate, in the HarI. lib. of the British Museum, marked 4826.

Edward IV inclusive without any variation. The buckle on the breast-plates just noticed was called by the French boucliete. Thus in a letter remissory, dated so early as 1386, we may read: Icellui Jehan en soy jouan, frappa de son badelaire, à l'endroit d'une fendace, qui estoit en la ditte cote de fer près de la gorge, et n'estoit pas fermée aux bouchettes qui y estoient ne close ainsi qu'il appartenoit. "That John, in lus transport of joy, struck with his badelaire on the place of a fendace which was on that coat of mail near the throat, and was not fastened to the buckles that were there, nor close, as it ought to have been."

Although this happens too early to be strictly applicable to the armour of Henry the Fifth's time, yet it shews that the gorget or camail, which is here termed the fendace or protector, was fastened with buckles to the breast-plate, and that the same was the case with the back one, the figure of Bernabo Visconti in Plate XXXIV has shewn us.

The monumental effigy of Thomas Plantagenet Duke of Clarence, who died in 1421, gives us the earliest specimen of the beavor, being so constructed of several overlapping pieces as when wanted for covering the face to be drawn up from the chin: it has been, therefore, placed below Plate XLI.

It is a helmet of this kind which is referred to by Shakespear, in his play of King Richard the Third when he introduces the question, "But had you seen him with his beavor up?" and they were worn so late as the reign of Edward VI.

The gauntlets of the Duke of Clarence, like those of the Earl of Salisbury, are without fingers, being formed of overlapping plates, the lowest of which is made somewhat pointed. These are the earliest specimens; but such gauntlets were used till the close of the reign of Henry VIII. The duke has a curious tabard formed much like a short surcoat, and the dagger is so placed at his side as to hang with its hilt downwards.

Mention has been made of the badelaire: a letter remissory dated 1415, informs us that, un petit coustel portatif appellé baudelaire, "a little portative knife was called baudelaire."

Two-handed swords with flaming blades, though never common, first occur in this reign. In the series of whole-length portraits of the Earls of Flanders at Ypres and of the Earls of Holland at Utrecht, both executed about the close of the reign of Henry V, or copied from authorities of that time; there are several specimens of that weapon, but they were probably intended for state rather than war. In the great collection of wood cuts, by

Hans Burgmaier about 1490, there is not one and yet he has introduced warriors armed with them into his triumph of Maximilian, and, though certainly not with flaming blades, yet such, and of that time are in the armoury of Llewelyn Meyrick, Esq. There are many authorities to shew that such were used in fight, as we shall subsequently find; and Guillaume le Breton tells us that so early as the battle of Bovines the Emperor Otlio weilded with both hands a one edged sword. Indeed, it had long been a favourite weapon of the Switzers.

A grant by Henry V, King of England, for performing the following service,[24] shews how early existed the custom of arming one arm differently from that of the other, a difference which we afterwards meet with in many specimens of military figures. Reddendo nobis, et eisdem heredibus nostris unam cerotecam de plate pro dextra manu, et unuin vantbras pro dextro bracliio. "Rendering to us and those our hews one gauntlet of plate for the right hand and one vantbras for the right arm."

We have some accounts of the Irish forces at this time from Speed, who thus speaks of them when raised for the battle of Agincourt:[25] "With the English sixteen hundred Irish kernes were enrolled from the Prior of Kilmainham, able men but almost naked; their arms were targets, darts and swords, their horses little and bare no saddle, yet, nevertheless, nimble, on which upon every advantage they plaied with the French in spoiling the country, rifeling the houses, and carrying away children with their baggage upon their cowes backs."

From this description the common Irish appear to have remained in the same state as in the reign of Henry II.

With respect to the modes of attack and defence at this time, in which cannons[26] had come into somewhat more general use, we may gather the following. Hollinshed tells us that,[27] when Henry V came before the town of Caen,[28] he caused forthwith a high mount and deep trenches to be made to keep those within from issuing out; from which we learn that the first thing done in besieging a town, was to draw round it lines of circumvallation. "Then studying all ways possible to dammage their enemies, some shot

[24] In the Hist. Harem'. Vol. II,
[25] Chrono p. 638.
[26] Thus Chaleondyles, lib. v, p. 128, mentions the Turkish cannon at the siege of Constantinople in 1422, and the Earl of Salisbury, introduced into Plate XLI, was shot by a cannon ball at the siege of Orleans.
[27] Chrono p. 1187.
[28] In the fifth year of his reign.

PLATE XLI

THOMAS MONTACUTE EARL OF SALISBURY,
AND A KNIGHT,

A.D. 1422.

arrowes, some set scaleing ladders to the walls, others shot gonnes, some brake the walles with engines, and others cast wild fire; every man endeavouring to come hand to hand in engagement with his enemies."[29]

Besides these methods of assault, it was usual at this time to undermine the walls: the miners supported their work with wooden pillars rubbed over with rosin, pitch and other combustible matters, so that, when the work was finished, the pillars were set on fire, and they giving way, the part that was undermined generally fell down. Thus, says Hollinslied,[30] while the king was besieging Caen, "and seeing that he lost more than he wonne by his dayly assaultes, he determined to undermyne the walles, wherefore the pioners cast trenches, and made mines, and brought tymber; so that within a few dayes the walles stood only on postes, ready to fall when fire should be put to them." The mode of defence adopted by those within we learn from Grafton[31] who, speaking of the same siege, says: "The Normans seeing themselves closely besieged threwe downe great stones, barres of yron, dartes, hot pitch, brennyng brimstone, and boyling lead." Harding, writing of the acts of Henry V, speaks of the effects of this wild fire thus:

> With his gunnes castyng, they made the towrr to fal
> And their bulwerke hrcut with shot of wild fire.

It has been before observed that stones succeeded bolts and quarrels as charges for cannon. Thus it is related of Henry V that, having received a taunting message from the Dauphin of France and a ton of tennis balls by way of derision; "He anoone lette make tenes balles for the Dolfin, in alle the haste, that he myght, and they were great gönne stones, for the Dolfin to playe with alle; and there (before Hareflete) he (Henry V) playede at the tenys with his harde gonnestones, that were shot into the towne, and whenne they begänne to pleye, they within the towne sänge welle awaye, and seyde, alias that evir suche tenes balles were made, and cursede alle those that the warre byganne, and the tyme that they evir were borne.[32] The same authority tells us that, when in the fourth year of his reign, the king "prepared to go over sea into France, he stocked himself with all maner of ordinyance, that is to say, armoure, gonnes, tripgettis, engines, scales, bastelles, brugges of le-

[29] Grafton's Chrono p. 357.
[30] Ut supra.
[31] Chrono p. 465.
[32] Chrono of Dunstable MS. HarI. lib. marked 24, folio 170,

ther, pavysses, bowe and arrowes; and thither come unto hym shippes laden with gonnes and gonnepowder." By scales the writer means scaling-ladders, bastelles were wooden castles, brugges were small boats of leather, pavysses were large shields used by those who protected the archers, and tripgettis were engines for throwing stones.

In the year 1414, Henry V commanded the collectors of the port of London and other ports, not to suffer any gunpowder to be carried out of the kingdom without the king's special licence.[33]

In 1418, he ordered the clerk of the works of his ordnance to procure labourers for the making seven thousand stones for guns of different sorts in the quarries of Maidstone, in Kent.[34]

In the same year, he further commanded him to prepare twelve great carriages for large guns, twenty pipes of powder made of charcoal of willows, and various other articles for the use of the guns.[35]

Polydore Virgil is therefore wrong when he says[36] that it was at the siege of Mans, which was taken by bombardment in the year 1421, that the English first used large battering cannon.

Mr. de Boucicaut says[37] that the King of England, at the battle of Agincourt, placed some pieces of cannon on an eminence, which did not kill many men, but threw a panic into the French army who where strangers to them. This, however, was not the case, as they had known of and used them prior to the English, and both Livius Forojuliensis and Elmliam positively assert that the French were drawn up thirty deep, and had within their lines a number of military engines or cannons, "saxivoma" to cast stones into the midst of the English.

Hand guns, according to Montfaucon,[38] were first used in the year 1414, at the siege of Arras, but his authority is wanting. It was, however, most probably Juvenal des Ursins, an author cotemporary with Charles VI, as under the year 1414, he calls them hand canons.

the walls and gave the assaults."[39] And at the town of Eme, "Many Englishmen were hurt with quarrells shot from the loopes and walles of the

---

[33] Claus.2, Henry V, m, 16.

[34] Pat. 5, Henry V, m. 4.

[35] Ibid, m. 3.

[36] Hist. Ang. p, 591.

[37] Hist. p. 264, published in 1699.

[38] Mon. Franç.

[39] Cron. p. 1214.

town."[40]

At the battle of Agincourt, having chosen a convenient spot on which to martial his men, the king sent privately two hundred archers into a low meadow, which was on one of his flanks, where they were so well secured by a deep ditch and marsh, that the enemy could not come near them. Then he divided his infantry into three squadrons or battles, the vawarde or avant-guard, composed entirely of archers; the middle-warde, of bill-men only; and the rere-ward of bill-men and archers mixed together; the horsemen as wings went on the flanks of each of the battles.[41] He also caused, as before mentioned, stakes to be made of wood, about five or six feet long, head-ed with sharp iron. These were fastened in the ground, and the archers so placed before them that they were entirely hid from the sight of the ene-my. When, therefore, their heavy cavalry charged, which was done with the utmost impetuosity, under the idea of cutting down, and riding over the archers, these shrunk at once behind the stakes, and the Frenchmen unable to stop their horses, rode full upon them, so that they overthrew their rid-ers, and caused the utmost confusion. The infantry, who were to follow up* and support this charge, were so lost in amazement that they hesitated, and by this were lost; for during the panic the English archers threw back their bows, and with axes, bills, glaives, and swords slew the French till they met the middle-warde.[42]

The king himself, according to Speed,[43] rode in the main battle com-pletely armed; his shield quartering the royal atchievements[44] of England and France; upon his helme he wore a coronet circled with pearls and pre-cious stones, and after the victory, although it had been cut and bruised, he would not suffer it to be ostentatiously exhibited to the people, but ordered all his men to give the glory to God alone. His horse was one of fierce cour-age, and had a bridle and furniture of goldsmith's work, and the caparisons were most richly embroidered with the victorious ensigns of the English monarchy. Thus is he represented on liis great seal, with the substitution of

---

[40] Ibid, p. 1176.

[41] Grafton, Hollinshed, Stowe, &c.

[42] "This device," says Hall in his Union, p. 49, "of fortefiyng of an arrnie with stakes, was at this tyme first devised and practised, but since that tyme they have devysed caltrop-pes, harrowes, and other new trickes."

[43] P.779.

[44] Armorial bearings were thus called because they were originally granted to com-memorate military atchievements.

the knight's cap and crest for the chaplet. Elmham's[45] account, from which this is amplified, is more particular in some of the details. He says: "The king appeared on a palfrey followed by a train of led horses ornamented with the most gorgeous trappings; his helmet was of polished steel surmounted with a coronet sparkling with jewels, and on his surcoat, or rather jupon, were emblazoned the arms of France and England, viz. three fleurs de lis or, and gules three lions passant gardant or.[46] The nobles in like manner were, with their horses, decorated with their proper armorial bearings."

Before him was borne the royal standard, which was ornamented with gold and splendid colours.

The light cavalry at this period were still called hobilers, as the heavy were men at arms, for in a deed of Henry V, we read:[47] Pro munitione et apparatibus hominum ad anna, hobelariorum, sagittariorum seu peditum quorumcunque pro obsequio nostro vel hseredum nqstrorum in posterum eligendorum. "For amunition and apparatus of men at arms, hobilers, archers, or infantry of whatsoever kind, for the service of us or our heirs to be chosen for the future.

A species of infantry arose in France called maillotins, from being armed with mallets.[48] The rebels, however, in 1413, were the first to obtain this name, and from the same cause. They are thus spoken of: Eodem fere contextu quo et prsemissa invaluerunt eis similia cives Parisienses macliinati sunt attentare: quorum directores et promotores esse decreverant illos aui malleatores seu malleti vulgariter nominantur: sed eis deductis ad notitiam regis quotquot ex eis culpabiles inventi sunt, morte damnati, aut bonis spoliati, aut in exilio damnati fuerunt. "Nearly of the same kind as those

---

[45] P. 61. His words are: Persona vero regia induta secura et lucidissima armatura, caput etiam immensi jubaris claritate circumamicta resplendenti galea, quam coronal aureoe fulgurantis gemmarum preciosa correa circulus circumcinxit, armorum Anglioe et Francire circumornatur tunica: in quâ istac trium florum aureorum in agro plantatorum azureo, splendor sydereus emicabat; illac vero tres leopardi aurei, in agro lascivientes purpureo apparatum regium non modicum solenni' zant, Ipse eciam princeps nivei coloris manno nobili insidens, equos eciam habens sequaces ditissimis trappaturis modo regio decoratos, festivis choruscationis sure radiis arvi perfundens planitiem suis non modicum consolationis Inferons ad actus Marelos exercitum mirificè invitabat. Proceres eciam ex parte regis armorum suorum tunicis prout tales conflicturos decuit sunt induti. T. Livius Forojul. writes nearly in the same words.

[46] See note in Vol. I, p. 36.

[47] Mon. Ang.

[48] When these had spikes fixed into them they were called holy-water sprinkles by the English. Such a one is in the armoury of Llewelyn Meyrick, Esq.

which, on former occasions, were rendered invalid, was an enterprize which the citizens of Paris contrived to attempt, the directors and promoters of it were discerned to be those who are commonly called malleators or malletors, but of these as many were brought to the notice of the king as were found guilty, and they were either condemned to death, or to the forfeiture of their goods, or to be sent into banishment." Rabelais relates the same fact in the following words:[49] Et à bon droit estjusques à présent de prudence grandement loué Charles Roy de France sixième de ce nom, lequel retournant victorieux des Flamans et Gantois en sa bonne ville de Paris, et au Bourget en France, entendant que les Parisiens avec leurs maillets, dont furent surnommez maillotins, estoient hors la ville issus en bataille, jusques au nombre de vingt mille combattans, n'y voulut entrer. "And with good reason is Charles the Sixth, King of France, still greatly praised for his prudence, who returning victorious over the Flemings and people of Ghent, to his good city of Paris, and having heard at Bourget, in France, that the Parisians with their mallets, whence they were surnamed maillotins, had issued from the city in manner of battle, to the number of twenty thousand combatants, would not enter it."

The reign of Henry V may fairly enough be closed with an account of the memorable battle of Azincour or Agincourt fought on the 25th of October, 1415. It is thus related by Mr. Turner.[50] "At dawn the King of England had mattins and the mass chaunted in his army. He stationed all the horses and baggage in the village under such small guard as he could spare, having resolved to fight the battle on foot. He sagaciously perceived that his only chance of victory rested in the superiority of the personal fortitude and activity of his countrymen; and to bring them face to face and arm to arm with their opponents, was the simple object of his tactical dispositions. He formed his troops into three divisions with two wings.

The centre in which he stationed himself, he planted to act against the main body of the French; and he placed the right and left divisions, with their wings, at a small distance only from himself. He so chose his ground, that the village protected his rear, and hedges and briars defended his flanks. Determined to shun no danger, but to be a conspicious example to his troops, on a day when no individual exertions could be spared, he put on a neat and shining armour, with a large and brilliant helmet, and on this he placed a crown radiant with its jewels, and he put over him a tunic

[49] Liv. IV, c. 36.
[50] Hist. Eng. Vol. II, p. 192.

adorned with the arms of France and England. [51] He mounted his horse and proceded to address his troops.

The French were commanded by the Constable of France; and with him were the Dukes of Orleans, Burgundy, Berry, and Alençon; the Marshal and Admiral of France, and a great assemblage of French nobility. Their force was divided into three great battalions, and. continued formed till ten o'clock, not advancing to the attack. They were so numerous as to be able to draw up thirty deep, the English but four. A thousand speared horsemen skirmished from each of the horns of the enemy's line and it appeared crowed with balistæ for the projection of stones of all sizes on Henry's little army.

Henry sent a part of his force behind the village of Agincourt, where the French had placed no men at arms. He moved from the rear of his army unperceived two hundred archers, to hide themselves in a meadow on the flank of the French advanced line. And old and experienced knight, Sir Thomas Erpingham, formed the rest into battle-array for an attack, putting the archers in front and the men at arms behind. The archers had each a sharp stake pointed at both ends to use against the French horse. Sir Thomas having completed his formation, threw up his truncheon in the air and dismounted. The English began the attack, which the French had awaited not choosing to give the advantage as at Poictiers, but when they saw them advance, they put themselves in motion and their cavalry charged; these were destroyed by the English archers; the French frightened by the effect of the arrows, bent their heads to prevent them from entering the vizors of their helmets, and pressing forward became so wedged together as to be unable to strike. The archers threw back their bows, and grasping their swords, battle-axes, and other weapons cut their way to the second line. At this period the ambushed archers rushed out and poured their impetuous and irresistible arrows into the centre of the assailed force, which fell in like manner with the first line. In short every part successively gave way, and the English had only to kill and take prisoners."

---

51 Tit. Liv. 16, Elm. 60, 61. The arms are thus described by Elmbam. Tbree gold flowers planted in an azure field, and three gold *leopards* in a purple one. These leopards we well know, from existing specimens of tbe royal arms at that period, were lions.

𝕳enry the 𝕾ixth.

1422.

HE frieze of the screen to the monument of Henry V has sculptured on it the equestrian figure of his successor. It may therefore be considered as the earliest specimen of armour during this reign, and has accordingly been selected for Plate XLII.

The shield is the most distinguishing feature, and is an improvement on that of the last reign which is given underneath. Not only is it made to bend forward at top, but a similar piece is put at the bottom to prevent the lance, when struck against it, from slipping downwards and so injuring the thigh. The splendid caparison of the horse, and the projection of the chanfron so as to cover the horse's nose, being, as well as the eye-caps, perforated to allow for sight and breathing, are worthy of remark. One of these clianfrons, on a similar plan but of immense size, is in the collection at Warwick Castle, and is represented in Grose's Treatise on Antient Armour.[1] This specimen falsely attributed to Guy Earl of Warwick, is thus proved to

[1] Plate XLII

be of a date not earlier than the commencement of this reign. It is, however, very curious, and in all probability the oldest piece of horse-armour in Europe. The figure of Henry VI exhibits the close tabard covered with armorial bearings, and those insignia are on the bridle cloths, bit ornaments, and stirrup leathers.

There is an oaken chest preserved in York Cathedral on which is a carving done at the commencement of this reign: it represents Henry the Fifth in the character of St. George delivering Catherine of France, his wife, from the dragon.[2] In the upper part the king is standing in front of his horse with his shield at his back. He is next seen mounted, thrusting the spear into the mouth of the dragon;[3] and he is then represented on his horse with his shield again thrown behind, and following the dragon, which is led home in triumph by the lady. In all these situations he is sculptured in a conical bascinet with either a camail or gorget,[4] attached to the part near where it passes under his chin: a close tunic which laces down the front reaches almost to the chain apron which is attached to the doublet, and seen below the lowest tasset, and has very large sleeves with undulated edges.[5] The plates above and below the genouillieres are on the armour,' which, in other respects, is well defined. This carving is very curious for the female costume and the architecture of the period, but the above description is confined to the armour. The coronation of Henry VI, at Paris, accomplished by the arms of his father, will account for the subject of this sculpture, as well as that in the Bedford Missal, as it was the policy of the day by every means to uphold the English title to the throne of France.

Notice has been taken of the chanfron. The French nobility piqued themselves much on the magnificence they could display on this part of horse-armour. Thus in the history of Charles VII,[6] the Count de St. Pol at the siege of Harfleur, in the year 1449, had a chanfron on his clieval d'armes, or charger, valued at twenty thousand crowns. It must, therefore, not only have been of gold but of most astonishing workmanship. Again, in the same year, after the capture of Bayonne by the army of this king, we are informed that the Comte de Foix on entering the place had the head of his horse covered with a chanfron of steel, ornamented with gold and precious stones,

---

[2] See it etched in Carter's Specimens of Antient Sculpture, &c. But I could not discover it on enquiring at York Cathedral.

[3] This figure has been introduced into the initial letter of this reign.

[4] This is Ilot very clear in the carving.

[5] This kind of vest is on all the Earls of Holland, painted just antecedent to this time.

[6] Page 188.

PLATE XLII

HENRY THE SIXTH KING OF ENGLAND,

A.D.1422.

which was valued at fifteen thousand gold crowns.

The principal reason for arming the horse in plate, as well as his rider, was to preserve his life, on which depended the life or liberty of the man at arms himself; for when he was unhorsed, the weight of his own armour prevented him from speedily recovering himself, or getting out of the way, when under the animal. Besides this, by thus preserving the horse, the expence of another one was prevented.

In Lowich Church, Northamptonshire, is a monumental effigy attributed to one of the Grene family, and dated 1426. The bascinet, and indeed the whole upper part of the armour is like that of the Earl of Oxford in Plate xxxix, while that of the thighs and legs is still earlier. It may therefore be considered as one of the latest specimens of this stile. Very similar to it is a monumental figure, falsely attributed to Sir William Fitzwilliam, in Marholm Church, in the same county, and which cannot, therefore, be later than the commencement of this reign, though the fashion of the armour more properly belongs to the proceeding one. Both these effigies have the tilting helmets placed under their heads surmounted by their crests.

It is said[7] that at the entry of Charles VII, King of France, into the city of Rouen: Il estoit armé de toutes pieces, monté sur ung coursier couvert jusqu'aux pieds de veloux azure, semé de fleur-de-lys d'or de brodure. En sa teste ung chapel de veloux vermeil, et avoit un lioupe de fil d'or et après lui les paiges vestus de vermeil, leurs manches toutes couvertes d'orfèvrerie blanche, portant ses har-nois de teste couverts de fin or de diverses façons d'orfevrerie, et de plumes d'austruclies de plusieurs couleurs. "He was armed at all pieces, mounted on a courser,[8] covered to the feet with blue velvet, powdered with golden fleurs de lis embroidered on it; on his head he wore a cap of scarlet velvet, which had a tuft of gold thread on it. After him came his pages clad in scarlet, their sleeves all covered with goldsmith's work white, carrying his head harness covered with fine gold in various fashions of goldsmith's work, with a plume of ostrich feathers of different colours."

The following arms and armour are enumerated in an inventory taken at Holy Island in the year 1437. Anna in primis v galee cum v umbrell8 et iiii ventells. Item i steilhatt. Item ii shelles de basenetts. Item iii pectoralia. Item i bryne. Item i pettycote de mayll. Item i paunce. Item ii par de reirbrace. Item ii paria de vaumbrace et dimidium. Item ii paria cerotecarum. Item iii lancee. Item iii batelaxes. Item iiii gunnse bene reparatse cum pul-

---

[7] In the Hist. d'Alain Chartier.
[8] The borse was so called from being used in the justs to run courses.

PLATE XLIII

TWO  CROSS-BOW MEN.

A.D. 1425.

vere. Item i alblast. "Arms, in the first place five helmets with five umbrells (or projecting pieces to shade the eyes) and four ventailes. Item, one steel hat. Item, two shells of basenetts. Item, three poitrals. Item, one broigne. Item, one petticoat of mail. Item, one paunce (the panzirone). Item, two pairs of rearbraces (for the upper arm). Item, two pairs and a half of vambraces (for the lower arm). Item, two pairs of gauntlets. Item, three lances. Item, three battle-axes. Item, four guns in good repair with powder. Item, one cross-bow."

Plate XLIII represents two cross-bow men being taken from two copies of Froissart, one written and illuminated in the early part of this reign and the other at its close. The earliest represents a man stringing the arcubalista grossa ad stapham, or great stirruped cross-bow.[9] This operation he performs by placing his foot in the stirrup, while he winds up the string by means of a moulinet and pulleys. His armour consists simply of a leathern jacket, with mamellieres or plates on the breast, and round elbow-plates, and he is armed with a cut and thrust sword. Other arbalisters, in this manuscript, wear helmets and are represented with large heart-shaped pavises[10] hanging at their backs, and a case of quarrels at their right hips, or attended by a paviser whose duty it was to ward off the missile weapons of the enemy. This large cross-bow being so complicated and consequently expensive a weapon, was often carried by the sons of knights who were attended by one of their father's retainers who carried the pavise. Hence in Spain, during the reign of its King James I, a cross-bow man was regarded as on a level with a knight, a distinction in those days of great importance. Statuimus quod nullus filius militis qui non sit miles vel balistarius, sedeat ad mensain militis, vel domiiue alicujus. "We enact that no knight's son who is not a knight himself or a cross-bow man, shall sit at table with knights or their ladies."

The other figure exhibits one when not about to prepare for battle.[11] The only armour he has is the genouilieres and a helmet he holds in his hand, but, as the illumination is not intended to represent a regular soldier, but one of the mob who broke into the royal arsenal and armed himself, this cannot be taken for the correct costume of a cross-bow man. This will account too for the small shield hanging at his back, which seems to belong to the cavalry. It is curious, however, as shewing the progress towards

[9] From a drawing in-a copy at Havod library in Cardiganshire.
[10] A pavise constructed of osiers is represented in an illumination copied by Montfaucon, and is given at the foot of the Plate.
[11] From Plate CXL of Montfaucon's Mon. Fr.; both these figures are in the attitudes in which are drawn the originals.

those of the next reign. At the beginning of this we see the flat shield has a piece at top and bottom placed at half right angles. In this specimen we find those angles rounded but to an excess which was afterwards contracted. The circumstance worthy of remark is, that this figure is represented with the moulinet and pulleys taken off and hung to his girdle.

The following Plate, Fig. 1, represents one of these large stirruped cross-bows.[12] It consists of a large stock made of some veiy hard wood stained and curiously though rudely inlaid with ivory, three feet three inches in length, one inch three quarters in the thickest part, and five inches three quarters in the deepest; and of a steel bow about two feet eight inches from end to end, two inches in the deepest part, and nearly three quarters of an inch thick, weighing fifteen pounds. The bow is fitted into the stock at the distance of four inches and a half from the end, at which place projects a stirrup seven inches and a half in length by five inches and a quarter in the widest part of the span. The length of the groove for the quarrel is one foot four inches including that of the nut, which is above half an inch wide. The nut is of ivory and about two inches in diameter, but, that it might not obstruct the sight, the stock is hollowed out accordingly from about four inches and a half above it. At the distance of eleven inches from the butt-end is an ivory sight which being brought with the head of the quarrel in the same straight line as the object, or a little above it, as elevation may or not be requisite, enabled the marksman to shoot with certainty. The spring of the trigger, which is within side the stock, is eight inches long; and the trigger itself, which projects from the under part of the stock, is protected by a bar of iron which serves, not only as a guard and to steady the hand, but also as a handle by which to take off the lock.

It is furnished with the moulinet and pulleys, which, after the bow has been bent, may be removed for the discharge. These consist qf an iron cylinder in a frame of the same metal, made to turn by two moveable handles in opposite directions, and having a cap likewise of iron to fit on the butt end of the stock. On each side of this cap is a small pulley the wheel of which is one inch and a half in diameter, having attached to one of its arms a strong cord that passes thence round another equal-sized wheel, returns over the first and then goes round one double in diameter, situated beyond the second described, and so passes to the cylinder of the moulinet, by winding which the power required to bend the bow is lessened to a fourth. Attached to the arms of the greater wheels is a double claw made to slide on the plane of the stock, which, catching hold of the bow-string, draws it up to the

---

[12] In the armoury of Llewelyn Meyriëk, Esq.

nut. No. 3, at the bottom of the plate, is a quarrel made of bone found in an antient camp at Danbury in Essex.[13] In the point of its pyramidal head is a notch in which a piece of steel had been inserted, and which was still adhering to it, but in a corroded state when first discovered. The upper end has affixed to it a small truncated cone which accounts for the great width in the cleft of the nut in the arbalest just described.

No. 4 is a variety of quarrels, bolts and viretons from the armoury of Llewelyn Meyrick, Esq. some with feathers, others feathered with wood or leather. The name of bolt was given from their great resemblance to those used for doors, but in the expression *bolt upright* and the word *thunder-bolt* we still retain the original meaning. The species of quarrel, however, which was called by the French vireton, has its name from spinning round as it passed through the air.[14] This was made like other arrows, but with the feathers set on a little curved, and such are some of those in the plate from my son's armoury. But this mode of placing them does not seem common in the fifteenth century, the period in which the vireton was most in use; they are, however, mentioned before this time. In a deed, dated 1345, occurs: xx caissiie viretonorum in quarum qualibet ad minus sint d viretoni. "Twenty cases of viretons, in each of which are at least five hundred viretonsand, in a charter dated 1377: Dedit balistas, viratonos, pavesia, &c. "He gave crossbows, viretons, pavises, &c." It is thus mentioned in a French deed, dated 1461: Vireton garni de ses fers, "a vireton furnished with its iron appendages." The armour of the Bretagne archers and pavisers at this period, we learn from an ordonnance of John, fifth Duke of Brittany,[15] published in the year 1425,[16] they are to be equipped in the following manner: Sçavoir est ceux qui sçauront tirer de l'arc, qu'ils ayent arc, trousse, cappelline, coustille, hache, ou mail de plon, et soient armez de forts jaques garnies de laisches, chaisnes ou mailles pour couvrir les bras: et ceux qui ne savent tirer de l'arc, qu'ils soient armez de jacques et aient cappelines, coustilles, haches, ou bouges, et avec ce aient paniers de tramble ou autre bois plus convenable qu'ils pourront trouver, et soient les paniers longs a couvrir liaut et bas, &c. "That is to say, those who understand archery shall have a bow, quiver, cappeline,[17] coustille,[18] axe, or maul of lead, and be armed with strong jacks,

---

[13] In the possession of William Bray, Esq.
[14] Du Cange says that it is only the diminutive of veru, a dart..
[15] He was also Earl of Montfort and Richmond.
[16] Lobinean Hist. de Bretagne, Tome II, p. 999
[17] Skull-cap.
[18] The coustille or cultellus served the purpose of knife and dagger.

PLATE XLIV

Fig. 1.

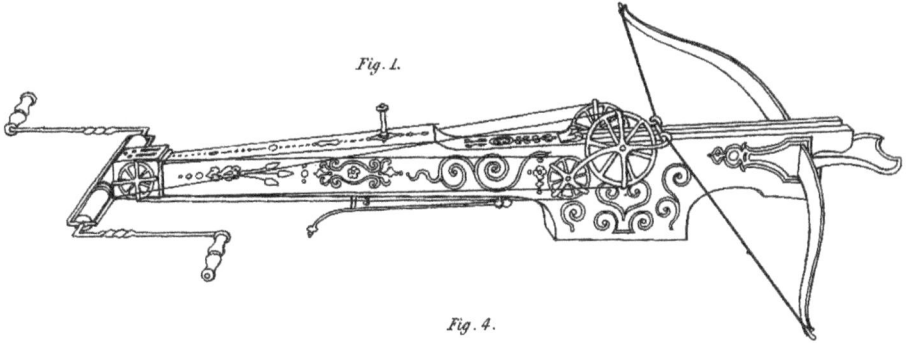

Fig. 4.

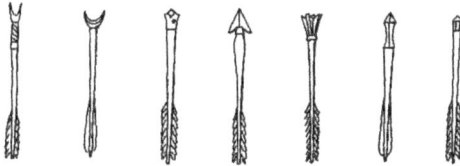

Fig. 2.

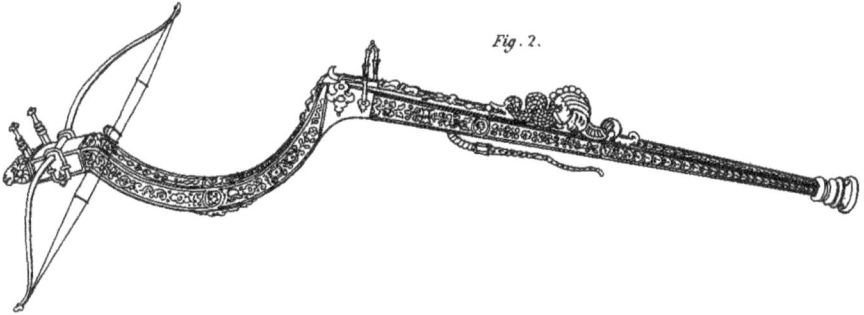

Fig. 3.

S. R. Meyrick. del.ᵗ

Etched by R. Bridgens.

CROSS BOWS AND QUARRELS.

furnished with little plates of iron, chain or mail to cover their arms. And those, who do not understand how to shoot, shall be armed with jacks and have cappelines, coustilles, axes or bouges,[19] and, with this paniers of aspin tree or other wood the most suitable they can find, and that these paniers should be long, so as to cover them above and below, &c." These paniers were large shields of an oblong shape curving inwards, and may therefore be considered as pavises. They were called paniers on account of their construction, which was this: The interior was formed of osiers, over which was placed a cover of aspin wood, or the black poplar, the wood of which is white and very light. Sometimes, indeed, this exterior surface was wanting, and then the osiers were more closely interwoven. Montfaucon, from a MS. of this period, has given examples of them in Plate clx of his Monarchie Françoise, which have been copied by Strutt without either knowing what they particularly represented. For the satisfaction of the reader they may be found at the bottom of Plate XLIII.

Père Daniel says that the voulge or bouge was a large two handed sword with a leaf-shaped point, and that there is some reason to conclude that it is the same as the gisarme.[20] There was certainly such a two handed sword, but not quite so early as this period, and that was used in boar hunting. He is more correct in considering the voulge somewhat like the gisarme, and we shall hereafter see that it was used much in the same manner being a long blade at the end of a pole. Two voulges are in the armoury of Llewelyn Meyrick, Esq. and these have blades wider than those of a sword which swell a little in the middle of each side, and have the leaves as an ornamental termination at the bottom. As far as the swell they are made sharp on both sides, and the top is cut off to a point. Twohanded swords were certainly introduced generally among the European nations at this period, being first adopted by Charles the Bold, King of France, from the Switzers. These people had made use of them from a very early period, but having become renowned by their victory over the Burgundians at the battle of Moret, their weapons were thus brought into notice.

In Lidgate's MS. poem, entitled the Pilgrim,[21] among the delineations of soldiers one appears with wliat Strutt calls a hand gun, which is certainly without any lock, but, as the barrel is made to curve, this must be impossible. Another soldier has a large axe, the blade of which is at least three feet

---

[19] These are the same as the voulges which will be explained hereafter, and may be seen under Plate LXX.

[20] Mil. Franç, Tome I, p. 243.

[21] HarI. library, in British Museum, 2278.

long and the handle rather more. Axes somewhat of this kind are in the collection of Llewelyn Meyriek, Esq.

During this reign after the victories obtained by the French arms under the Maid of Orleans, the warlike genius of the English began to decline, no longer animated by a monarch with heroic spirit; and a greater taste for dress than war, readily received the fantastic Lombard fashions which the expeditions of the house of Anjou to Naples brought into use.

Charles VII, aware of the great service done by the archers in the English armies, instituted, in his own kingdom, what were called the Francs-arcliiers. He ordered every parish to provide the best bow-men, and to them he granted the privilege of freedom from all subsidies. His ordonnance was as follows:

"We ordain that in each parish of our kingdom there shall be an archer, who shall keep himself ready with sufficient and suitable liabilliinent with salade, dagger, sword, bow, quiver, jack or liuque of brigandine, and that these shall be called Francs-archers; who shall be elected and chosen by our electors in each election, from being most skillful and practised in archery that can be found in each parish, without having regard to riches or any request that may be made to them; and who shall be held to attend in the aforesaid liabilliinent, and to shoot with the long bow, and particularly to go thus equipped on all feastdays and liolydays, in order that they may be as skillful and practised in the aforesaid exercise as possible, to serve us whenever called upon. And we will cause them to be paid four francs each man per month during such their time of service. We ordain that they and each of them should be free and quit, and we grant them exemption from all tallages and other charges whatsoever which shall be established by us in our kingdom, as well from being enrolled as men at arms, for Avatch and ward, or duty at the gates, as from all other subventions whatsoever; except in those absolute and requisite for war and the salt-duty. We forbid all those who are commissioned to assess the tallages and other imposts ordered by us, to assess them; and the captains castellans of castelanies to constrain them henceforth to make the said watch and ward. We will that the same validity shall be allowed to the lettres of affranchisement given by our electors as if they had been immediately obtained from us. We ordain that they shall take the oath before the said electors to serve us Avell and loyally in their habilliment towards all and against all, and to repair with all due diligence for the service of our wars as affairs may induce us to order, and not, on any account, to serve any one making war, nor in the said habilliment without an ordonnance from us. We will that the said Francs-archers should be enregistered by our said electors by their names and surnames, and the parishes where they dwell, and that from this should be made a register for the court. Given at Montils les Tours in the year 1448, and in the twenty-sixth year of our reign."

Montfaucon has given the effigy of Guillaume de May[22] who was captain of the king's archers and died about thirty years[23] after the date of the above ordonnance. He wears a brigandine jacket terminated with an indented skirt of mail, probably a petticoat attached to his under garment, and a gorget of the same. He has a close helmet, with plate armour on his legs and arms, the latter having pauldrons attached by points; also a sword, dagger, bow and quiver of arrows.

Philippe de Comines, in the first book of his Memoirs, gives some interesting particulars relative to the military customs of this reign, and, as his English translator has added equally curious comments on them, the following have been extracted from the edition of 1596. The commentator, in a note on the IInd chapter, says: "Every Frenchman of arms is allowed three men to accompanie him in the wars, one to beare his head-piece, called in latin ferentarius, and two archers. La March—but the Burgundians had here some 5 some 6. These archers were bow-men mounted on liorsebacke, as liarquebusiers on horsebacke are now."

In the IIIrd chapter of the text we are told: "The Earle of Charolois company set themselves in order of battell as they marched, and at their arrivall found the Earle of St. Paul on foot, and all the archers dismounted, ech man having a pale pitched before him. Order was given at the first that we should all lighte on foote, none excepted, but that order was afterwards altered. For almost all the men of armes mounted againe on horseback, save certain valiant knights and esquiers appointed to fighte among the foot men, namely Monsieur de Cordes, and Master Philip of Lalain, with divers others: for at that time among the Burgundians, the honourablest personages fought on foote among the archers, to the end the infanterie might be the better assured, and fight the more courageously, which order they learned of the Englishmen with whom Duke Philip (being confederate in his youth), &c." Again: "The king's bands were lead by Poncet of Riviere, being all archers of his ordinary retinue, glistening in gilt,[24] and very well ap pointed." Again: "Of the Burgundian men of armes I thinke hardly fifty

---

[22] Mon. Franç. Plate CLXXXVII.
[23] A.D. 1480.
[24] The gilt studs of the brigandines or j azerine jackets.

knew how to charge a launce, there were not foure hundred of them armed with quiracies."

The editor has the following notes to this chapter: "Vawarde, battel, and rerewarde are now the terms for the three (lines or) battails. Brezey had changed armor with the king, which caused his death; for those that slew him supposed it had been the king—Annal. Aquitanᵉ. The Burgundians dismounted so suddenly, that laying downe their complete armor, they had not leasure to buckle their lighter armor about them, which was the cause of Lalain's death—Annal. Burgund.

In chapter IV it is said: "The Earle of Charolois was there in great danger and received many hurts, especially one in the throte with a sword the marke whereof stuck by him as long as he lived, by reason that his beavor being evill fastened in the morning was fallen away, and I myselfe saw when it fell."

In chapter V: "Of archers and other soldiers armed with good brigandines they had great force."

In chapter VI: "The Burgundians had great store of artillerie under the charge of a notable gunner named Master Girald." Again: "John Duke of Calabria had in his pay five hundred Switzers foote men, which were the first that ever came into this realine." Afterwards: "The Dukes of Berry and Britaine were mounted upon small ambling nags, and armed with slight brigandines; light and thin, yea and some said they were not plated, but studded only with a few gilt nailes upon the sattin for the lesse weight; but I will not affinne it for a truth." What the translator calls brigandines were the jazerine jackets,²⁵ composed of overlapping plates of steel within, and studded without with gilt studs. One such, in the armoury of Llewelyn Meyrick, Esq. is represented in Plate LVI.

In chapter VIII we are informed that "The Earle of Charolois was armed at all peeces, save the head-peece and vantbraces, and wearing upon his quirage (cuirass) a short cloke marvellous rich."

The following note of the commentator on chapter XI is also worthy of remark: "By the expression to measure with the long ell, he meaneth the pike, werewith souldiers at the sacke of a towne use to measure velvets, silks, and cloths."

In the Record Office in the Tower of London is an indenture of retainer whereby Sir James Ormond knight retains Mr. James Skidmore,²⁶ a Here-

---

²⁵ In the Rist. Caroli VII, p. 514, it is termed a jesseran, whence any thing worked in this manner was said to be jazequené.

²⁶ Or Scudamore, a grandson of Owain Glyndyvr,

fordshire gentleman, to serve under him in the expedition against France under Richard Duke of York, in the 19th of King Henry VI, which is as follows:

"This indenture, made bitwene Sir James of Ormond knyght, son and heir to the Erl of Ormond, on the one part, and James Skidmore esquier of the countee of Hereford on the other part, witnesseth that the seid James Skidmore is belast[27] and w'holden toward the seid Sir James for an hole yeer to do him service of werre in the perties of France and of Normandie, in all places whereas it shall like the seid Sir James to ordeyn and comaunde him, as a man of armes with vj archers in his company, all on horsebak, and wele chosen men, and likly persones wele and sufficiently armed, horsed and arayed, ev'y man aft[r] his degree; that is to say that the seid James Skidmore have harneis complete, w[t] basnet or salade, with viser, spere, axe, swerd and dagg[r]; and all the seid archers specially to have good jakks of defence, salades, swerdes, and sheves of xl arwes atte lest: and the seid James Skidmore shall take wages of the seid Sir James in the man[r] followyng, that is to sey, for himself xij[d] st'ling the day, w[t] the reward accustumed, and for ev'y of the seid archers vj[d] st'ling the day, of the which wages and reward he shall be paied before the hand for a quartr of a yeer by way of p'st, and for the second q[u]rt[r] the day that he shall make first his moustres of himself and his seid archers on the see side; or Avhere as the seid Sir James will ordeyne him to do, and for the other half yeer, he shall be content and paied for himself and his seid archers in France and in Normandye, aft[r] the wages of France, and aft[r] their moustres and reviewes, in money of France, or upon appatice of the cuntres désobéissant, or in provisions, in such wise as by raison he ought to hold him content the yeer of his seid s'vice, and w[t]holding; begynning the seid day of his first moustres; the which moustres shall be made at the day and place therefore to be appoynted by the hiegli and inyghte Prince Richard Duk of York, and the seid James shall take for himself and his seid archers huk'[28] of my seid lord the duk' liv'e,[29] paying for theym like as othr souldiers of their degrees do: and the seid James Skidmore byndeth liym by these p'sent lr~es to make moustres of him and his seid archers at all tymes when he shall be comaunded or required by the seid Sir James, during the seid terme, and before any persone or persones that him shall like to comytte thereunto. And the seid Sir James shall have as wele the thirde part

---

[27] From the verb "belay" to make fast.
[28] Huques or cloaks, see before p. 131.
[29] The duke's livery.

of the wynnings of werre of the seid James Skidmore, as the thirde p' of the thirddes of the seid archers duryng the seid tyme, and the seid James Skidmore shall have all the persons of werre yf any be taken by him or by any of his seid archers during the seid tyme except kyngs, kyngesones, princes, and oth' capitains and men of kyngs blode or oth' havyng their power, the which all shall be res'ved prison's to the seid Sir James, for the which he shall reasonably content him or theym that shall fortune to take any such prisoners.

"And except also rebelles and traitors which heretofore have ben the kyng's liegemen and dwelled in the kyng's obéissance the which shall semblably[30] be reserved to my seid lord the duk and to the seid Sir James, for to have the punycyon that they have deserved. And the seid James Skidmore byndeth him by thise p'sent lr~es to serve duely and truly w^t his seid archers the seid Sir James duryng all the seid tyme and to make w^{t}hem wacche and warde[31] in all places and at all tymes when he shall be resonably required, and to kepe them in justice and from robbyng and pillyng[32] of the cuntrees of the king's obéissance, and of his trewe people and subgetts there w^{t}ynn; and for to obeye at all tymes to such cries as shall be published and proclaimed by the ordenance and comaundement of my seid lord the duk.

"And in cas the seid James Skidmore on his ptie wele and truly kepe, observe, and fulfille all man^r of covenants and condicions afor seid in the forme above-seid, the seid Sir James granteth by this indenture that than an obligacion of an c. mark,[33] in which the seid James Skidmore is bound to the seid Sir James, be voide and of no strength. And els the said obligacion abide in his full force and virtue. In witness wherof the parties aforseid chaungeably to these indentures ban sette ther seals the, xiiijth day of Januer the xixth year of the reigne of Kyng Henry the Sixt."

Several suits of armour have been attributed, in France, to Joan of Arc, the celebrated Maid of Orleans. One of these, formerly at Chantilly, is evidently of Henry the Eight's time, or more correctly speaking that of François I; being furnished with pass-guards and cod-piece. There is also a breast-plate in my son's collection, in which is a written certificate on paper in French, asserting that it belonged to this celebrated personage, with a reservation with respect to the casque which accompanies it and seems to have been worn with it. Both, however, are of a form at least sixty years later.

---

[30] From the French semblablement, "probably."
[31] Watch 'and Ward.
[32] Pillaging.
[33] A hundred marks.

As, however, the breast-plate has on it the fleur de lis, it is most probably French, that mark not having been granted to the Medici family till a later period. It has been placed at the bottom of Plate XLV.

This plate represents Charles VII, King of France, and the Maid of Orleans. The armour of both is remarkable, because it affords us a very early and fine instance of the use of the tuiles or toiles as they were called. These were flaps of plate appended to the lowest tasset, by straps and buckles, and which hung over the thighs in the manner of tiles. They are here in great numbers and of different sizes, but it must be confessed that, as the figures from which these were taken, were not made till after the death of the Maid, some doubt may exist whether this style of armour was in fashion during her life. The monumental effigy, however, of Sir Bryan Stapleton in Ingham Church, Norfolk, who died in the year 1432, exhibits him with two small ones called tuilettes; and that of William Lord Bardolph very large ones. The plates above and below the kneecaps, of this last, form vandyked ornaments. Being a knight of the garter he wears that appendage, and like Sir Bryan Stapleton, has palettes or plates to cover the arm-pits, but his are flutted; he died in the year 1435. Besides the two over the thighs, King Charles and the Maid of Orleans have small ones at their hips, and the king has one coming from under his espauliere or shoulder plate. The genouilliers are very large as well as the swords, and the Maid is armed with a ponderous lance. The spurs are screwed on outside the armour, and the helmets are of a form which continued till the close of Elizabeth's reign.

These figures were taken from a monument erected by King Charles VII, in the year 1458, which represents that king and the Maid kneeling, one on each side of a cross. It was placed on the antient bridge of the City of Orleans, to commemorate her patriotic services. At the foot of the cross was represented the virgin holding in her lap the dead Christ, and, therefore, it gave offence to the protestants, who regarded it as a relic of superstition: the consequence was that, in the troubles which took place in the year 1567, they broke all the figures except that of the king. The pieces, however, were afterwards collected, and on the 9tli of October, 1570, they were recast, at the expence of the town, by Hector Lescot, called Jacquinot, and replaced on their bases the 15th of March in the following year. This monument was again removed from the old bridge, in the year 1745, for the sake of protection during the alterations that took place, and erected on the modern pedestal, where it now stands, in the year 1771, by the municipal officers. The figures are of bronze almost the size of life, and nothing has been intro-

PLATE XLV

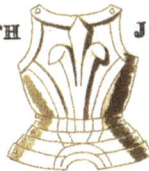

CHARLES THE SEVENTH   JOAN OF ARC, THE

KING OF FRANCE AND   MAID OF ORLEANS,

A.D. 1430.

duced into this plate but what occurs in the originals.

The Maid of Orleans appears here in man's armour, and that she wore such is clear from it having been urged as one of the charges against her. When in the hands of the English, and had engaged no more to assume man's apparel; she was, contrary to the terms proposed, again thrown fettered into a dungeon, and when she was once more summoned to appear before the Bishop of Beauvais, this prelate had the perfidy to contrive that she should be furnished with none but male attire; on her appearing in which, he condemned her as relapsed and incorrigible, and, therefore, to be delivered over to the secular arm. She was burnt on the 29th of May, 1430.

While at the stake preparing for death, she asked for a crucifix, but as such was not at hand, an Englishman made one of two sticks. Probably she had refused to consider the hilt of his sword, called by the French croix de l'épée, as such, but this was a frequent practice, and gave occasion for the name of Jesus to be inscribed on some part of it; an instance of which occurs on the monument of a knight in the vestry-room of the church at Winchelsea. This also will account for the pommel often having the cross stamped on it.

The Earl of Talbot, who commanded the English forces at this time, had engraved on the blade of his sword: Sum Talboti pro vincere inimicos suos· "I am Talbot's to conquer his enemies." "A sword," says Fuller, "with bad Latin upon it, but good steel within it."

The family of Joan of Arc was ennobled by Charles, and on the 8th of May, the epoch of the deliverance of France, an annual fête is still held at Orleans. But it should not be forgotten in the history of this monarch that, in the hour of misfortune, he abandoned to her fate the woman who had saved his kingdom.

From a Flemish illuminated manuscript life of Christ, in the possession of my worthy friend F. Douce, Esq. and some other authorities, it appears that, at the commencement of this reign, the helmet was very different from that held by the Pucelle. The perforated projecting cone of Richard the Second's and Henry the Fourth's time, as represented at the foot of Plate XXXVII, was, after being elongated and considerably lessened in its base, placed on the uniber of the last reign, the helmet of which is at the bottom of Plate XXXIX.

The ordonnance to cause the nobles and archers of the parishes in Brittany to arm themselves, which was issued, in the year 1450, by Peter Duke of Bretagne, in order to be prepared against the enterprises, invasions, and descents of the English, directs that each of the nobles should be equipped in the following manner: *Que de chascun des dits nobles que trouverez estre de richesses et revenu du montement de vii ving 1. de revenu soit en estât et appareil d'homme d'armes pour sa personne, bien armé son corps, et bon cheval, avec son coustilleur et un page montez, les chevaux competants comme en tel cas appartient, prests de nous servir ez armes toutes fois que les manderons. Item, que les nobles tenant des richesses entre cxl 1. et lx 1. en descendant, se tiennent en habilement d'archer en brigandine, s'ils se savent aider de traits; ou autrement soient garnis de bons juzarmes et bon salades et harnois de jambes et aient chacun un coustilleur et deux bons chevaux competants ainsi qu'au cas appartient: et si aucuns desdits nobles qui n'aient la richesse desdits cxl 1. de rents, ains soient au dessous veuillent se mettre en habillement d'homme d'armes, ils le pourront faire, et pour tels seront soudoiez passant aux monstres. Item, que les nobles tenant au dessous de lx 1. de rente aient brigandines, bonnes salades, ou à tout le moins bons paletocques armez de nouvelle façon sans manches, à laisches de fer, ou mailles sur le bras, avec bons juzarmes, ou arcs s'ils s'en savent aider. Item, que les nobles estant entre ce 1. de rente et ccc 1. soient en appareil d'hommes d'armes, garnis chacun d'un archer ou juzarmier avec brigandines, un coustilleur et un page, en bons habillement. Item, ceux d'entre ccc et cccc 1. de rente soient en appareil d'homme d'armes, garais chacun de deux archers, et un desdits archers juzarmier en brigandine, avec un coustilleur et un page. Item, ceux d'entre cccc et d 1. de rente soient en appareil d'homme d'armes, garnis chacun de trois archers, et au moins de deux archers, un juzarmier, un coustilleur, et un page, en bons et suffisans habillemens. Item, ceux d'entre d dc et dcc 1. de rente soient en appareil d'homme d'armes, garnis chacun de iv archers, ou m archers et un juzarmier, un coustilleur, et un page, en bons habillemens.*

"That each of the said nobles that you shall find possessing riches and revenue, reckoning upwards, amounting to one hundred and forty livres of rent and revenue, and between this sum and two hundred livres of revenue, shall be in the state and apparel of a man-at-arms in person, his body well armed and a good horse, attended by a coustiller and a page mounted on competent horses, as to such case appertain, ready to serve us with arms, whenever commanded. Item, that nobles possessing riches between one hundred and forty livres, and sixty livres, descending, shall furnish themselves with the accoutrements of archers in brigandines, if they know how to make use of arrows, or otherwise shall be furnished with good girsames and good salades with leg-harness, and shall each have a coustiller and two good competent horses, as to such case appertain. And if any of the said nobles, who have not riches amounting to one hundred and forty livres of rente but less, are willing to put themselves in the equipments of men at arms they may do it, and for such they shall be paid, passing at musters. Item, that nobles having less than sixty livres of rent, have brigandines, good salades, or at least good paletocques,[34] armed in the new fashion without sleeves, Avith overlapping plates of iron, or mail on their arms, with good gisarmes or bows, if they know how to use them. Item, that the nobles having from two hundred livres to three hundred livres of rent, be apparaled as men at arms, furnished each with an archer or gisarmier with brigandines, a coustiller and a page in good dresses. Item, those from three hundred livres to four hundred livres of rent, be in the apparel of men at arms, attended each by two archers, and one of the said archers a gisarmier, in brigandines, with a coustiller and a page. Item, those from four hundred fiA^res to five hundred livres of rent, be in the apparel of men at arms, attended each by three archers, or at least two archers, a gisarmier, a coustiller and a page, in good and sufficient dresses. Item, those from five hundred, six hundred livres to seven hundred livres of rent, be in the apparel of men at arms, attended each by four archers, or three archers and a gisarmier, a coustiller and a page in good habiliments."

The English were not backward in the encouragement of archery, and in 1453, the parliament voted an army of twenty thousand bomen for service in France. The battle of St. Alban's, in 1455, seems, indeed, to have been won entirely by the archers, as the men at anns never once engaged.

The Honourable Miss Grimstone is in possession of an archer's black leather brace, found at Bolton Hall, in Yorkshire, Avliere it Avas left by one of the attendants of Henry VI, after the disastrous battle of Hexham. It is a semicylinder; the half of which received the rub of the bow-string plain, the other carved having on it a rose with other ornaments, and the words 𝔍𝔢𝔰𝔲𝔰 𝔥𝔢𝔩𝔭𝔢 on a gilt ground.

Plate xlvi represents a cross-bow man and liis paviser, shewing in what manner the former was protected hy the latter, and underneath is a collection of quarrels, taken from Mr. Douce's wood engravings to his Illustrations of Shakespear.

The paviser is clad in the monstrous jacque so much used at the early part of this reign, while the man with the arbalest wears the jacket and par-

---

[34] Coria, or leathern jacks, literally skin-cloaks, from pellis.

ty-coloured cloatlies. The first of these is from a Chronique d'Engleterre,[35] while the paviser is from a copy of the Roman de la Rose.[36] Under the great jacque are seen sleeves of mail, and a gorget of the same protects his throat.

The lioketon was generally white, whence the proverb: Plus blanc d'un auketon, "Whiter than a hoketon." This, however, was not always the. case, for Matthew de Couci, in his History of Charles VII, says: Portoient auctons rouges, recoupez dessous, sans croix, "They wore red hoketon's, slit up from below, without any cross," which was probably their usual ornament.

Besides the pavois, there was used at this time a large thick kind of shield called talevas or talvas, and as this is said to have differed merely in shape, being of French origin, it was probably applied to those which were of an oblong form. It is supposed to have derived its name from a resemblance to a table, and being of wood. Thus the Academy della Crusca have defined: Tavolaccio, as spezie di targa di legno. It w'as called also tavolace and tavel. Hence in a letter remissory, dated 1445, it is said: Icellui Anthoine de Segaler ayant en sa main ung liaiz vulgarement appelle tavel, &c. "That Anthony de Segaler having in his hand a portable protection[37] commonly called a tavel, &c."

It is curious that the word targe, at this time, signified a dagger or small sword; thus Monstrellet says: Les autres gens avoient targes et semitarges, qui sont espees de Turquie. "The others had targes and scymitars, which are Turkish swords." And in a letter remissory, dated 1451, we read: Le suppliant tira une targe ou dague qu'il avoit, et en frappa icellui Seguin. "The suppliant drew a targe or dagger which he had-and struck that same Seguin."

Mention has been made, under the last reign, of that kind of skull-cap called a salade, and it may here be noticed that that worn by the paviser, in Plate XLVI, is of this kind. The Italians called it celata, thus we read:[38] Vidit tres vel quatuor celatis vel saladis supra eorum capita, et aliis armis ante dictam ecclesiam transeúntes. "He saw three or four with celâtes or salades on their heads, and with other arms passing before the aforesaid church."

It has been falsely supposed that the salade was so called from its concealing the head, whereas the reverse was precisely the case, as it only covered the upper part of the head. Its origin is probably, therefore, from the German word schale a saucer, as bascinet is from basin a bason. Three spec-

---

[35] In the British Museum, Royal library, 15, E. IV.
[36] In the Harl. marked 4425.
[37] Lacombe explains halse by porte faite en forme de claie ou de grille.
[38] Proces. Egid. de Rayo, anno 1440.

imens are in the armoury of Llewelyn Meyrick, Esq. the first Italian, and like that on the paviser in Plate XLVI, and on the billman's head in Plate LVI, where it differs from the morían, which it otherwise much resembles, in having its rim inclining downwards: the second is a German one, having an ocularium or transvere slit for the sight: and the third an English one, which is furnished with a moveable visor.

All were worn on horseback, and the two last as often as on foot; and at the tournament, as some illuminations of this period and this following doument[39] shew.

A Mery Baudet, plumasseur, deinourant à Tours, pour avoir garni d'or clinquant XXIX jacques de bougram blanches et noires; XXIII plumeaux de mesme, pour mettre sur les salades de partie des gens du duc qu'il avoit fait armer pour combattre au bouhourdeix que le roy faisoit faire le ix dudit mois à la feste des roix, qui avoit esté laissé pour sa maladie.

A Jacquemin Herode pour le louage de XVII corsets et autres liarnois pour armer partie de gens du duc audit bouhourdeix.

A Thomas le Brun pour le louaige de vii brigandines, n avantbras, et une salade pour semblable cause.

"To Amery Baudet, feather dresser, living at Tours, for having ornamented with gold tinsel nineteen white and black buckram jacks, twenty-eight plumes of the like to put on the salades of a party of the duke's people, that he had caused to arm to combat at the bouhourdeix which the king had directed to be held the ninth of the said month, at the fête of the kings, which had been deferred on account of his illness.

"To Jacquemin Herode for the hire of seventeen corsets and other harness to arm a party of the duke's people at the said bouhourdeix.

"To Thomas le Brun for the hire of seven brigandines, two vambraces, and a salade for the like cause."

The monument of John Fitz-Alan Earl of Arundel, who died in 1434, exhibits him with a bever which lifted up, or put down under the chin. He has also the straps to fasten the pieces below the knee, but his tuilles are hid by the front flap of his tabard. At the side opening, however, of this, we perceive the tassets, and similar ones behind called culettes, which buckle to the former with straps at the right side, having hinges corresponding at the other. He has also an additional plate put on the upper part of the left gauntlet, and which buckles round it. The guard of the misericorde is com-

---

[39] Extracted from tbe account of Olivier de Roux, treasurer and receiver-general under Arthur, third Duke of Bretagne, in 1458.

PLATE XLVI

A CROSS-BOW-MAN AND HIS PAVISER,

A.D. 1433.

posed merely of two round knobs, and such a one, of the same period, is in the collection of Llewelyn Meyrick, Esq.

The sheath of the misericorde is also made to hold a knife. The shape of the armour, particularly what covers the body and legs, is very much like that of Richard Beauchamp, Earl of Warwick, who died in 1439. The monumental effigy of the Earl of Warwick is all brass, exactly like a suit of armour, and laid on his sepulchre; his breast and back plates have each placates or placards rising up with scalloped edges to points before and behind, and on the front one appears the screw holes which held the lance rest. Each of these placards is fastened at top with a strap and buckle. The elbow pieces, particularly that part of them within the bends of the arms, are very large, that on the bridle arm being the greatest of the two, and are so ridged as to look like several successive plates. For such they were mistaken by my friend Major Smith, and so represented in his Antient Costume of England.

I have, therefore, copied and corrected the engraving he has given of this earl, and it forms Plate XLVII.[40] Upon the espaulieres are placed pauldrons, also ridged with the edges turned up so as to form the prototypes of pass-guards. Pendant from the last tasset is the apron of chain, which is continued all round being likewise behind appended to the last culette, which, from the appearance of two buckles and straps, might, it seems, be removed at pleasure. Besides the two large tuiles over the thighs, there are two tuillettes at the hips, as in the figures of Charles VII, and the Maid of Orleans, and these are elegantly ridged. The cuisses are also ridged all the way up so as to resemble so many distinct pieces, and in this specimen we have a distinct display of those latteral pieces attached by hinges to the cuisses, from which we learn that they did not envellope completely the under part of the thigh, but only reached to where the saddle could meet, allowing the rider a better seat on his horse. These pieces were held in their places by a buckle and strap. This warrior has the garter round his left leg a little below his knee.

It is somewhat curious, too, that the pauldrons, though covering the armpits in the front, the right one having its excavation supplied by a palette, should in reality extend only to the outsides of the shoulders where they terminate with scallopped edges, and that the espaulieres form the coverings for the blade-bones, the pauldrons being strapped to them. The tilting helmet is placed in the monument under his head, but is here re-

---

[40] At the foot of the plate is part of the armour enlarged as it appears on the monumental effigy.

PLATE XLVII

RICHARD BEAUCHAMP   EARL OF WARWICK,

(A.D. 1439.)

moved to his side.

Palettes are spoken of as used in this reign in a charter of Henry VI, in the year 1450,[41] the words being: Quod nullus de caetero palettos, loricas, gladios, seu aliqua alia arma invasiva. "That none of the rest have pallettes, cuirasses, swords or any other invasive arms." And so early as the reign of Henry V, a single one, as in the Earl of Warwick's armour, was considered sufficient, the sword arm only requiring to be more at liberty. Thus in the will of Sir William Langford,[42] knight, dated the 24th of August, 1411, is the following item: "Also I bequeyth to William my son a haberion of steele wyth a palet covrd wyth rede velvet, a payre of gloves or plate black. Also to Harry my son a haberion, a ketill hatte,[43] &c.

In the seal of this earl, he is represented on horseback, and his helmet more globular over the face. He has also over his armour the same kind of vest as that described on the carved coffer at York, and the same kind of scalloped sleeves but rather shorter. Two appendages of a similar form hang from his helmet instead of the cointisse. The chanfron of his horse is, however, without cheek-pieces, but larger on that account, and just where it terminates above the nostrils is a kind of proboscis rising upwards.

This proboscis which, after being turned up as high as between the eyes, was then bent forward, was, at the close of this reign, superseded by the invention of a spike made to rise at once from between the eyes, a fashion that continued as long as this species of armour lasted; namely, till the end of the reign of Queen Elizabeth.

Besides the salade there was another covering for the head called huvette, which had been known ever since the time of Edward III. Thus in a letter remissory, dated 1421, some persons are spoken of: Lesquelz entrèrent en la maison d'un armoiseur, et la prindrent chacun une huvette ou capeline. "Who entered the house of an armourer, when each took therefrom a huvette or capeline." Perhaps it was the same as the steel-hat, or ketill hatte mentioned above.

The flayel or flail, called by the French flayau or fleau, from the Latin flagellum, was used at this time as well as in that of Henry III and his son. Hence in an account at Abbeville, dated 1450, one of the items is: for money paid, Dicto Petro pro qua dam ferrura nova, cum cramponibus ad bendas. flagello apposita vii sol. "To the said Peter for a certain new piece of

---

[41] Rymer's Fœdera.
[42] In the Halam Register at Salisbury Cathedral.
[43] Probably sucb a one as the squire wears in Plate XLVIII.

iron, and with its cramps to the bends applied to the flail, vii sous."

The following is an inventory of certain articles delivered out of the armoury at the Tower of London, contained in the schedule to a writ of privy seal, in the thirty-third of Henry VI, A. D. 1455, preserved among the records in the tower.

"This is a parte of the goods that been delivered out of the armore by the king's comaundement sythen the tyme that John Stanley,[44] hath been serjeant of the armoyre as it apperith hereafter mor playnly by the pcells that here folowen.

"Furst viij swerds and a long blade of a swerde made in waiters,[45] some gretter and some smaller for to leme the king to play in his tendre age.

"It'm a lytyl barneys that the Erie of Warwyk made for the kyng, or that he went over the see, garnysshed with gold which was delivered to Due of Suif for his sone.

"It'm xiiij li' delyvered by John Merston, clerc of the jewells to the said sergeant for to pay to certain armurers which is doon as it apperith by en-dentures and the said money paied at the tymes, that is to say vij li' at a tyme.

"It'm a Scottysh swerde liylte and pomell covered with sylver, and a small corone aboute the pomell which was stollen oute of the king's chambr' and the blade broken and cast into Tempse.[46]

"It'm j banner of Satyn of enter-taille[47] of the armes of England and Fraunce.

"It'm ij banners beten of the armes of England and Fraunce.

"It'm iij banners of Satyn of en-tertain of the armes of Fraunce.

"It'm iij banners beten of the armes of Fraunce.

"It'm vj banners of entertaille of Seint George armes.

"Of the which banners, ij were delyv'ed to John Chete wyn, and ij to Thom~s Boulde and ij to John Seynlov that tyme squiers for ye kings body and ij nowe late to my Lord of Shrewsbury and all the remanent were delyv'ed for ye en-tierments of the iij queenes that is to say, Quene Kat^rine, the Quene

---

[44] Of Wyrall, in the County of Chester, esquire.

[45] With the flat of the blade placed in the usual direction of the edge, and hence waft-ing the wind at every blow.

[46] Probably the river Thames. Here is nothing to sanction the 'idea that tbe Scottish sword had then a. basket-hilt. The figures sculptured at Ilay bave simple cross-bars bent down like the general fashion in Europe in the time of Edward I.

[47] From the French entretailler, 'to cut one within the other,' wove-work.

"It'm vj banners beten of the Tri-nitee.

"It'm iiij banners beten of our Lady.

"It'm iij pennons of the feders, of entertaille.

"It'm v pennons beten of the feders.

"It'm cccix pensells of the feders.

of Fraunce, and Quene Johan, my Lord of Bedford and my Lady his his wyf, and the pennons and ye pensell were delyv'ed in like wyse for to sett aboute ye herses of hem. And wher' that it liked him that had the rowel y^e of.

"It'm a breste with a boxe upon for the egle, and a pomell of a swerd with armes y^e in which was deliv'ed to Parker Annrrer for to make ye king's lierneys by which he hath loste.

"It'm iij lityll cote armurs which been the sergeant's fee of the armrye, and so delyv'ed by the king's comaundement to hym by cause that they were so lytyll, and wole serve no man for they wer made for hym when he was but vij year of age.[48]

"It'm xxxiij standards of worsted of y^c armes of England and Fraunce.

"It'm xxij standards of worsted of the armes of Fraunce.

"The which standards been woren and spendid in karying of the king's herneys in and oute in to his chambre for faulte of their stuffs.

"It'm v banners for trumpetts deliv'ed to ye trumpetts when the Due of Gloucestr went to the restowe of Calais.

"It'm viij habergdo~s some of Meleyn and some of Westewale[49] of the which v of Meleyn were delyv'ed to the College of Eyton and other iij broken to make slewys of woyders[50] and ye~s.   .

"It'm x gowers of sylke v white and hlewe and other iij pourpul and oye ij pourpul and gold which were delyvred into the king's chambr', to serve hym when he had nede.

"It'm vj tresses of sylke, iij white and blewe, and iij pourpul and xv smale poynts of silke for the king's briganders which were in . . . . in like deliv'ed

---

[48] That must have been in the year 14'29.

[49] Probably Milan and Westphalia.

[50] Sleeves of vuiders, that is with openings through which appeared the mail. as In those of the king's guard, Plate LXI. This cutting up and adapting old hauberks to plate .armour is one of the principal causes of their present very great scarcity. Yës is a contraction signifying "these."

in like wyse.

"It'm ij yerds, iij carters of corse
of' rede sylke.

"It'm d'yei-ds d'qrters of rede
velevet.

    "It'm iiij grosses of poynts.

    "It'm vj arinyng nayle.

"All spendid and moch more to
oon of the king's herneys.

"It'm ix olde picers, j olde paytrill brode of ledder, xj testures, iiij frounters of testures, iij olde justing sadells peynted of divers werks, x olde justing sadells pcell broken for the pese,[51] iij olde justing sadells for torne-ments, xiiij olde bastard sadyll some pcell broken, iiij smale olde sadylls, xij olde sheldes poynted,[52] xiij olde paveys peyntyd, x olde banner shafts bound with yren, v olde spere shafts for pese, j speresliaft, i long spere with a hed, j olde trapper of plat broken in divrse placs, ij olde grete coeffers bound with yren lacking keys which wer cast out of an olde house in the Touir of Lon-don, by Maistr. Willin~. Clyf, at yat tyme clerc of the werks by cause that they wold serve for no thing. And y* house poulled downe.

"It'm a hamer, j bequerne, j payr of pynsons iij pounde of wyre, which was sold by Maystr Wyllliam Fox armerer.

"It'm j bowestaffs worme eten delyvered by the king's comaundement to my Lorde of Gloucestr' when he went over to Caleys.

"It'm i peyre of trussing coeffers, and j payir of gardeviants,[53] spended long tyme agoo in the king's cariage.

"It'm a wyre liatt garnysslied ye bordour serkyll. And a sterr of sylver gylt lacking a point in ye sterre, w'oute bocle and pendant, delyv'ed to John Curson sometyme squier for the king's body.

"It'm a peyr of curasses delyvered to the Lord Powys that last died which yat the king comaunded to geve him."

To shew the form of the tabard at this period, and also that of the vi-sored capelline, or steel hat, Plate XLVIII contains the figure of Sir John Cornwall, afterwards Lord Fanliope, and his squire. He is here represented from a painting in glass at Ampthill Church, Bedfordshire. Before his ele-vation to the peerage he and James of Artois engaged in the lists at York, against a Frenchman and an Italian, in the year 1400, in presence of Henry

---

[51] For justs of the peace, or peaceable justs.

[52] The fashion of this reign was to have them square.

[53] Garde viande, French, to carry meat in, probably answering the purpose of the mod-ern havresack,

IV. Being victorious, the king created him a knight of the garter. He again signalized himself at the battle of Agincourt, where he took Louis de Bourbon, Count de Vendoine, prisoner. In this plate, therefore, he is seen trampling on the shield, and with the tattered banner of the French nobleman. On this account it was that Henry VI, in the eleventh year of his reign, made him Baron Fanliope and Milbrook. He died in 1443.

Underneath this plate is a tilting helmet, copied from an illumination in the British Museum, of this time, where it is represented as carried by an esquire on his left hand, while he holds the tilting-lance in his right. From that illumination we moreover learn that the vamplates were removed from one lance to another, as although the cronel is at the end, the shaft is without any vamplate.

In the year 1430, on the 14th of January, a battle was fought before the king, within the lists at Smitlifield, between two persons of Faversham, in the county of Kent. It was a trial by wager of battle, John Upton, a notary, being the appellant. He had accused John Downe, a gentleman of his own town and his compeer, says Stowe, of high treason, in having imagined the king's death on the day of his coronation. John Downe was, therefore, the defendant. The battle, however, did not last long, for the king, probably persuaded of the innocence of the one party, and the loyalty of the other, soon after the fight commenced, put a period to it, by forgiving both.

Another renowned champion was Sir John de Astley, knight, of Astley, in the county of Warwick. On the 29th of August, 1438, he maintained a duel on horseback, in the Rue St. Antoine at Paris, against Peter de Masse, a Frenchman, in the presence of Charles VII, King of France, "pierced the said Peter through the head, and had (as by the articles betwixt them was conditioned) the helmet of the said Peter, being so vanquish't, to present to his lady."[54]

Again on the 30th of January, 1441, another fight took place in Smitlifield, in the presence of Henry VI, King of England, between this hero and Sir Philip Boyle, an Arragonese knight. This person had been in France by the command of his king, "to look out some such hardy person, against whom he might try his skill in feats of armes, and missing there of his desires, repaired hither. After which combate ended (being gallantly performed on foot, with battail-axes, spears, swords and daggers) he was knighted by the king, and had an annuity of c marks given him during his life."[55]

---

[54] Dugdale's Warwickshire, p. 73.
[55] Ibid.

PLATE XLVIII

SIR JOHN CORNWALL  LORD FANHOPE,

A.D. 1442.

The original jacque which belonged to this renowned knight is, I am informed, still preserved in the armoury at Melton Constable, the seat of Sir Jacob Astley, Bart. There is also, at the same place, a painting of both these combats, but as an engraving of it is given in Dugdale's Warwickshire, we find by the costume that it was not done earlier than the time of Henry VIII, and, indeed, the inscription on it states that it was painted at the desire of Sir Isaac Astley, Bart.

In the very next year another combat was fought on the 30th of January at Smithfield, by an esquire of the king's household, who entered the lists against Sir Philip la Beause of Arragon, knight. This was also in the presence of the king, and the esquire was John Ansley or Antsley. Stowe says:[56] "They came into the field all armed, the knight with his sword drawn, and the esquire with his spear, which spear he cast against the knight, but the knight avoided it with his sword, and cast it to the ground. Then the esquire took his axe, and smote many blows on the knight, and made him let fall his axes,[57] and brake up his uniber[58] three times, and would have smit him on the face with his dagger, for to have slain him; but then the king cried "Hold," and so they were parted. The king made John Ansley knight, and the knight of Arragon offered his harness at Windsor."

The same author[59] relates that, in the year 1446, "John David appeaclied his master William Cater of treason; and, a day being appointed them to fight in Smithfiekl, the master being well beloved, was so cherished by his friends and plied with wine, that, being therewith overcome, was also unluckily slain by his servant. But that false servant lived not long unpunished, being after hanged at Tyborn for felony. From hence arose the word "If ye serve me so, I will call you Davy."

Grafton informs us that the master was an armourer, and the incident has been introduced by Shakspeare into his play of Henry VI.[60] The dramatist has, however, altered the names to Horner and Peter, probably from having had a glimpse or heard of the precept issued to the sheriffs whose names were Godfrey Bologne and Robert Horne, from which latter lie

---

[56] Survey of London, Book III, p. 239.

[57] By this it appears that, when the esquire laid aside his spear, the knight put up his sword and each fought with pole-axes.

[58] The face guard which contained both viser and beaver in one. I am, however, much inclined to think that this is a misprint for umber, though that was, strickly speaking, the shade for the eyes.

[59] Stowe's Survey, ut antea.

[60] Part II, act IJ, scene 3rd.

fabricated that for the armourer. The original document, in the exchequer, acquaints us that the real names of the combatants were John Daveys and William Catour, and the following is the last article of the record of expences:

"Also paid to officeres: for, watchyng of ye ded man in Smythfelde ye same day and ye nyghte after i ye batail was doon, and for hors hyre for yeofficeres at ye execucion doying, and for ye hangman's labor xj^s. vj^d.

"Also paid for ye cloth yat lay upon ye ded man in Smythfelde viij^d.

"Also paid for 1 pole and nayllis, and for settyng up of ye said mannys hed on London brigge, v^d.

"Sum xij^s. vij^d."

That defeat was considered proof of guilt has been already shewn in all the regulations upon the subject of trials by wager of battle, introduced into this work, but A. Murimuth giving an account, under the year 1380, of the Duellum inter Dominum Johannem Hannesly militem, et Robertum Kalenton armigerem, in which Robert was slain, gravely infers from thence that magna fuit evidentia quod militis causa erat vera, ex quo mors alterius sequebatur. "The death of the other party was strong evidence that the knight's cause was true." The case, however, of the armourer proves that the vanquished, even if killed in the battle, was adjudged to the punishment of a convicted traitor, and that his body, whether alive or dead, underwent the act of hanging, in order that his posterity might participate in his infamy. By the exchequer record it appears, that the erection of the barriers, the combat itself, the watching of the dead body, and the subsequent execution of the armourer occupied the space of six or seven days; that the barriers had been brought to Smithfield in a cart from Westminster; that a large quantity of sand and gravel was consumed on the occasion; that the place of battle was strewed with rushes, and that the total expence incurred was ten pounds, eighteen shillings and nine pence.

The most curious instance, of this kind, where the vanquished party was slain in the combat and still underwent degradation, is that of the jouste a outrance, in 1387, between Jaques le Gris and Jehan de Caronge. A lady was accused of treason and adultery and her cause espoused by her husband. Had he been conquered, his wrife would have been burnt and he would have been hanged, but it chanced that he was victorious. The account is very long, and, after what has been said above on the subject, would occupy too much space for insertion, but will be found in the Second Volume of Lord Berners' translation of Froissard.

Shakespeare arms his combatants with bâtons and sand-bags at the end of them, yet his is the only authority I have met with for the use of this latter appendage. Probably such were the weapons of the lower class of people, and were therefore, considered by him as appropriate to the parties. Hudibras, however, alludes to this custom in the following lines:

> "Engaged with money-bags, as bold
> As men with sand-hags did of old."

And the fool's bftton with the bladder at the end of it seems to bear some analogy.

The monument of John, Duke of Somerset, who died in 1444, affords a specimen of splendid armour, and has therefore been selected for Plate XLIX. The upper part of the helmet has a conical shape, but its apex bends backwards. The pauldrons are inimitably fine, and over the back is placed a piece of armour not very usual, unless it be the gorget, which, as well as the lower part of the helmet, has a handsome border. Borders also run along the arms and legs and cover the genouillieres. To the lowest tasset are four tuilles, under which is an apron, or rather petticoat of chain-mail as it hangs all round. In his hand is one of those pole-axes so generally used at this period, besides which he has a very long sword and large rowelled spurs.

It was not unusual to inscribe some motto upon the shanks of spurs at this time. One of this kind is engraved in the Archæologia,[61] which was found on digging in the field where the celebrated battle of Towton was fought. The neck is straight, the shanks curved, and the rowel consists of six spikes, each of which is in length three quarters of an inch. The inscription on the shanks is in the old characters used at that time, and is: 𝕰𝖓 𝖑𝖔𝖎𝖆𝖑 𝖆𝖒𝖔𝖚𝖗 𝖙𝖔𝖚𝖙 𝖒𝖔𝖙𝖙 𝖈𝖔𝖈𝖗. " In loyal love all my heart is absorbed." The date of this spur is not, however, quite so early as those of the Duke of Somerset being more consistant with the make of such as were used at the close of this

---

[61] Vol. XI. Plate xx.

PLATE XLIX

JOHN DUKE OF SOMERSET,

A.D. 1444.

reign. There is, however, in my son's collection a pair of the large rowelled spurs, and an engraving of one, found in St. George's Fields, may be seen in the Archæologia.[62]

Besides the pole-axe which was carried by leaders of forces, several of the weapons, used by the troops themselves, are noticed in different documents of this period. One of these was the espiet, espiot or espieu,[63] called by the Spaniards espetón; which seems to have been a kind of small glaive. Thus in a letter remissory, dated 1450, it is said: Le suppliant print ung bastón ferré, appellé espiot. Le navrerent au corps d'un espoit ou espée. "The suppliant took a staff furnished with iron called espiot. They pierced his body with an espiot or sword." It seems to have been the origin of that kind of sword called the espadón, and was probably a kind of sword blade fixed at the end of a short staff. What is called espriet in another letter of this date, gives some information, the words of which are: Pour ce que le suppliant n'avoit point d'aviron ou espriet á conduire le batelet. "For that the suppliant had no kind of oar or espriet, wherewith he might conduct the little boat." From which we leam that its shape somewhat resembled an oar. It is further shewn to have been of wood and iron from the following extract from a letter dated 1457: Les suppliants portans chascun ung bastón ferré c'est assavoir Hugonin du Plan ung espy.

The length of the glaives used at this time, we learn from a letter remissory dated in 1445, which says: Robin Duhamel qui tenoit en sa main une longue glave bien de xij á xiij piez de long, &c.

The word lance was sometimes used at this period to signify a banner. Thus in a letter remissory, dated 1451, it is said: Comme le suppliant nous a servi coinme archier soubz la lance de nostre amé et feal Jehan le Lezay chevalier, Seigneur des Maroys. "As the suppliant has served us in the situation of archer under the lance of our beloved and trusty John le Lezay knight, Lord of the Maroys." Javelins were also used at this time, for, in a letter dated 1455, it is said: Petrus de Fabro praemunitus una gevelina cum cúspide illius gevelime supplicantem in eolio percussit. "Peter de Fabre being armed previously with a javelin, ran the blade of that javelin through the neck of the suppliant." And, in another letter of the same date, are enumerated: Espiotz, lance-gayes, gevelines, &c. Again in another, dated 1454, occur the words: Couffort or javeline, the couffort being a kind of demi-glaive.

As an arrow, for a cross-bow, was by the English called a bolt, so by

---

[62] In a paper by Captain Grose, upon the express subject of spurs.
[63] Espieu, in authors of an earlier date, implies a lance.

the French was it termed trait. Hence in a letter, dated 1450, it is said: Le suppliant dist a ung sien nepveu qu'il prinst une crenequin et du traict, afin d'eulx deffendre. "The suppliant said to one of his nephews, take a crene-quin[64] and some traits, in order to defend us from them." They were also called by the French raillon or reillon, and by the Spaniards rejón. Thus in a letter remissory, dated 1442, it is said: Gaillardus Borii, qui suam balis-tam habebat oneratam quodam rallone, dictam suam balistam desseravit, et cum dicto rallone corpus dicti Bartas omnino perforavit, aliter quod dictus radio ab alia parte in terrain cecidit. "Gaillard de Bore who had his cross-bow drawn up loaded with a rallo, shot his said crossbow, and, with the said rallo, completely perforated the body of the said Bartas, insomuch that the said rallo came out at the opposite side and fell on the ground." In another of the same date: Jehan Conte remist le raillon sur l'arbaleste, et desbanda ledit raillon contre Caluet, et telement qu'il le attaigni par le bras, et lui per-sa tout oultre. Le suppliant garni d'une arbalestre de bois, viretons, raillons et autres liabillemens de guerre. "John Conte placed a raillon on his arbalest and shot the said raillon against Caluet, and, in such manner, that he struck him on the arm and pierced him quite through. The suppliant furnished with an arbalest of wood, viretons, raillons and other habillements of war." The vireton had its feathers placed diagonally to make it spin round in the air.

These raillons, traits and viretons were all carried in a case hung at the side as depicted in Plate XLIII. This case is called caexia in a document pre-served in the archives of the Convent of St. Victor at Marseilles, being an appeal to a general council in the year 1424. Thus: Considerantes expensas pro custodia Monasterii S. Victoris, necessarias tam in vallatis quam in eed-ificiis, bombardis, ballistis, tabucis, viratoniis, caexiis, lancéis et bombardis, curassiis et cassidilibus, loriéis, et aliis armorum generibus. "Considering the expences for guarding the Monastery of St. Victor, the necessaries as well in the fortifications as in the buildings, for bombards, ballistee, tabuc-es, (trabuchets) viratons, cases, lances and bombards, cuirasses and casques."

The monumental effigy of Robert Lord Hungerford, who died in the year 1455, shews us the still further approach to that splendid armour which was carried to its greatest perfection in the reign of Richard III. Besides the four tuilles he has, like Charles VII King of France, a smaller one on each side behind. These, as well as his pauldron and demi-pauldron, his fine el-bow-pieces and vambraces, his cuisses, genouilliers, and plates below them

---

[64] A cross-bow.

are most beautifully ridged, and much more closely than in the monument of the Earl of Warwick; and it is worthy of remark that this ridged armour became the origin of the fluted style so prevalent in the reign of Henry VII and for a short time after. No palette was used for the right armpit in this specimen, but the antient mode of a gusset of mail is introduced; the same circumstance also occurs in the bend of the foot; and, instead of a gorget or hausse-col, as the French called it, we observe a collar of mail. The fine foliated elbow-pieces are attached each by two points that are made of yellow cloth, but the foliated genouilliers are fastened by a strap and buckle.

A most splendid girdle filled with jewels and in the style of Edward the Third's time is put round the lower tasset, from which are suspended the sword and dagger also highly ornamented. The culettes are, as before, buckled on the right side to the tassets,[65] and his lordship wears the collar of SS. The solerets, at first sight, appear to have been square, but, on closer inspection, the pointed toes may be observed on the back of the dog which is placed at his feet.[66] The armour which covers the right arm has been copied and placed at the bottom of Plate of XLIX.

The monumental effigy of John Talbot the great Earl of Shrewsbury, at Whitchurch in Shropshire, is evidently not older than the latter part of the reign of Henry VII although he died in the year 1453.[67]

The hausse-col or gorget of plate is well represented in the monumental brass-plate of Sir Thomas Shernborne at Shernbome, which has therefore been selected to form Plate l. The pauldrons are so formed as to have, as it were, double pass-guards, by an upright plate at their termination near the neck, and a projecting ridge on the top of the shoulder. This specimen also shews the mode of wearing the sword in front now first introduced, the monument bearing date 1458, instead of the side as heretofore, and also the cropped hair, the wide locks observable in the monument of the Earl of Warwick being now cut off.

Underneath this Plate has been inserted a representation of an open helmet termed the casquetel which is furnished with an umbrel, and the hind flap of which is made flexible, in the armoury of Llewelyn Meyrick, Esq. This stile of flattened helmet was introduced about this period, and continued to be much worn in the next reign, and occasionally until the

[65] These together seem to have been termed brichettes.
[66] The armour of Arthur Duc de Bretagne, who died in 1458, as represented on his monument, greatly resembles this It is engraved in Lobineau's Histoire de Bretagne, Vol. I, p. 665.
[67] His sword, mentioned p. 173, was formerly hung up in the cathedral of St. Denis.

PLATE L

SIR THOMAS SHERNBORNE,

A.D. 1458.

close of that of Henry VII.

In the monument of an Irish knight of the Leinster family at Dublin, the tuillettes are exhibited and formed of successive pieces, each being composed of two and fluted. The date of this is in 1460 and, in the armoury of Llewelyn Meyrick, Esq. is a suit within a few years as old which has a pair very similar; one of which is engraved at the bottom of Plate LVIII. A manuscript of Lidgate's, in the British Museum, exhibits the fantastic Lombard fashions in armour and military attire at the commencement of this reign, and an illuminated History of the Bible in the possession of Mr. Ratclyffe, as well as many other MSS., shews those which had succeeded towards the close of it. From this and other cotemporary MSS. we find that the casquetels had many of them large ciraclar oreilets or ear-pieces, were sometimes furnished with moveable visors, sometimes with umbrils or shades for the eyes, as in the specimen at the foot of Plate L. and were sometimes without any; sometimes were flat at top like that last referred to, sometimes were conical, and sometimes terminated in a little point called the crenel or charnel. The breast and back plates were covered with silk of one colour, and the placards of another, and that from the bottom of these hung a drapery, open the whole way before and behind, but reaching to the ankles. The light cavalry, who wore loose boots, had merely slips of steel put over their hose or pantaloons terminating in ornamented knee-caps like Sir Guy Brian,[68] with their arms protected in a similar manner, and their shoulder-plates were so ornamented as to resemble the wings of a bird. The guard of the sword was turned up before and down behind, and two handed swords were used instead of axes for the purpose of beheading.[69] The shields were fancifully made in the shape of the heart as represented on cards, but longer, and targets or circular shields were also used. Maces, feathered javelins, poleaxes, glaives, bills, and spears of great variety are also depicted in this History of the Bible, and most splendid tents both circular and oblong. It is to be observed, too, that the knights invariably ride with long stirrups and their toes pointed down, a fashion that was introduced at the conquest and which continued until that of Henry VII, from which period the toe was elevated. The necks of the spurs too are uncommonly long, which is proved not to be an error in the drawing by two of this description being in the possession of Llewelyn Meyrick, Esq.

---

[68] See Plate XXXIV.

[69] These had often engraved on their bladesv representations of various punishments. One such, from Nuremberg, dated 1674, is in the armoury of Llewelyn Meyrick, Esq.

The men at arms used often to dismount and fight on foot. Thus, at the battle of Patay, Monstrellet tells us: Les François moult de pres mirent pied à terre, et descendirent la plus grand partie de leur chevaulx. "The French almost immediately dismounted, and the greater part got oif their horses."

In Plate VI there is a figure with a two-handed sword, but it is a curved one, the back three times escalloped. The warriors here represented have all casquetels with circular ear-pieces.

Plate VII exhibits a tournament. The knights here have double demi-placcates on their breast-plates, tuillettes and the breech of mail. Their helmets are flat at top, are ornamented with wreaths and long pendants, and have spurs so long as to equal half the length of the leg.[70] There are rings placed at their saddle-bows, and coronels at the ends of their lances.

In Plate IX the knights, who are on horseback, have oval shields or targets,[71] and on their shoulders, by way of pauldrons, circular plates with wide fan-shaped borders; their spears are ornamented in a spiral manner. This engraving represents Arthur crowned as best knight at the tournay, a curious fact as relating to antient manners.

Plate X exhibits two men within a tower, armed with flails, and another with an axe, the blade of which much resembles in shape some of the halberts of the reign of Henry VIII in the armoury of Llewelyn Meyrick, Esq.

In two or three copies of the illuminations the swords have flat circular guards; and Plate XIV represents a faulchion exactly like a scythe-blade.

Plate XIII shews the helme to be fastened to the breast-plate by a ring in front, and Plate XV by a ring to the back-plate behind.

When the town of Caen was besieged by the English in this reign, it was, according to Grafton,[72] strongly fortified, having placed at the tops of the battlements " great rolls of timber, so moving and unsteadfast, that neither scaleing ladders could catclie any holde, nor no person that should climb up could get any sure footing."

Æneas Sylvius says:[73] that, in the year 1453, the French had their entrenched camp defended by three hundred bombards, which had been brought on carriages, and discharged three hundred stones into the midst of the English.

---

[70] Such a pair is in the armoury of Llewelyn Meyrick, Esq.

[71] Probably it is from this period that we should date the introduction of the target, instead of a shield borne by an esquire of the champion at the coronations of the Kings of England.

[72] Chrono p. 604.

[73] Opera, p. 441.

Drayton enumerates the following English preparations for war, from what he had read and heard:

> "The engineer provided the petard,
> To break the strong portcullis and the balls
> Of wild-fire devised, to throw from far
> To burn to ground their palaces and halls."

And in another place he says:

> "Their brazen slings send in the wild-fire balls."

Where he speaks of wild-fire he alludes to the Greek fire, although he is speaking of the reign of Henry V. If, therefore, he had authority for this, it shews that this combustible was not laid aside for a long time after the invention of gunpowder. The petard is also of much later contrivance than this period, having, according to Pere Daniel, been invented but a short time before the year 1579, at which period it was used by Henry IV of France, then only King of Navarre.

This extract shews with how much caution we should receive the information of those authors who are not cotemporaries of the events they relate. The petard therefore, will be described at the proper time.

We, however, meet with the description of several pieces of artillery at this period.

Thus in a letter remissory, of the year 1432, are enumerated: "Canons, bombarders, vulgaires, poudre, trait et autre artillerie," and in another, dated 1434, "Canons, veuglaires, coulevrines, &c." The veuglaires, or more properly vulgaires, were the ordinary artillery. Thus in a letter, dated 1455, it is said: Les Anglois faisoient grans maniérés de getter, canons, culevrines, et autres vuglaires, icellui suppliant doubtant avoir le cop desdiz vuglaires ou culevrines. "The English made a gréât many kinds of projectiles, cannons, culevrines, and other vuglaires, that suppliant expecting to receive the blow of the said vuglaires or culevrines." In the year 1460, James II of Scotland was killed by the accidental bursting of the cannon. Another kind of cannon was called the scorpion, from a supposed resemblance in its effect to the sting of that insect. Thus we read:[74] Ubi cassidem posuisset, scorpionis cornu in caput percussus, interiit. "Where he had put on his casque, he was struck on the head by the horn of a scorpion and perished." So in the

---

[74] Hist Franc. Sfort. sub. anno 1428.

Annals of Placentia, under the year 1444, occurs: Scorpione seu balistra. "With a scorpion or a balistra." It does not, however, appear by these quotations to have, at this time, been applied to the cannon, as it certainly was at a later period; and the Annals of Placentia also speak of troops armed with this weapon in this enumeration: "Scorpionistas sive balistrarios," and again: Alios levis annaturæ, stipendarios, vastatores, scorpionistas, et pilularios. "Others more lightly armed, soldiers, artillery-men, those armed with scorpios, and those with darts."

From this, however, it seems that the scorpio was, at this time, a tube for firing the gunpowder from, held in the hand, and called by the English hand cannons, and which became frequent in the next reign. If so, the origin of the musket, or rather its prototype, would be of as early a date as the close of this reign, but we shall presently see that it was soon after its commencement.

In a roll of purchases made for Holy Island, occur the following:

"A. D. 1440, bought ii handgunnes de ere," from whence we learn that they were made of brass, "iiii^s. and i crossebow, iii^s. and gonepowder iiii^s. . xi^s.

"1450 I^m, xi shafe sagittarium emptis x^s. yiii^d.

"1452 I^m, i brestplat, iii crosbowys and gonpowder empt^s. x^s."

Billius, a noble and learned Milanese, and who lived at the time speaks, in his history, of hand-guns as first used at the siege of Lucca, in 1430. The Florentines were provided with artillery, which, by the force of gunpowder, discharged large stones; but the Lucquese perceiving that they did very little execution, came at last to despise them, and every day renewed their sallies to the great slaughter of their enemies, by the help of small fire-arms, to which the Florentines were strangers, and which, before this reign, were not known in Italy. The following is the curious description which Billius gives of them: Præter jacula, et sagittarum balistas, novum quoque teli genus invenerunt: ge-rebant manibus fustem cubiti et alterius dimidii longum; huic suffixee erant cannse ferreæ, quibus item sulphure, ac nitro oppletis, glóbulos férreos vi ignis emittebant. Certa erat in ictu, si tetigisset, pernicies, nec arma aut scuta satis tegebant, quin saepe duos aut et tertium, si per ordinem eccurrerent, una glande transfoderent.[75] " Besides darts and what projected arrows: they invented a new kind of weapon also; in their hands they held a (sort of) club about a cubit and a half in length: to this were affixed iron

---

[75] Hist. p. 127, The author speaks as if to one stock were several barrels, but I imagine that not to his intention, but to the looseness of his Latin that appearance should be attributed.

tubes, which being filled with sulphur and nitre by the force of fire, emitted iron balls. The blow, if it struck, was certain destruction, neither armour nor shields were sufficient protection; for often two or three deep, if fired upon, would be transpierced by a single ball."

Badges to distinguish the troops of different leaders were much used at this time.

On a blank leaf of parchment at the beginning of the Digby Manuscript, no. 82, in the Bodleian library at Oxford, is an enumeration and explanation of the devices borne as badges of cognizance by Richard Duke of York, the father of King Edward the Fourth, written in a contemporary hand, evidently in the duke's fife time, as follows .

"Thes ben the names of the lordesliippes with the bages that perteynyth to the Duke of Yorke.

"Furste, the Dukeshyp of Yorke with the badges ben the fawcon and the feturlocke.

"The bages that he beryth by Conysbrow ys the fawcon wyth a mayden, ys liedde and hur here hangyng abowte here shuldris with a crowne abowte hir nekke.

"The bages that he beryth by the Castle of ClyfFord is a white roose.[76]

"The bages that he beryth by the Erldom of the March ys a white lyon.

"The bages that he beryth by the Erldom of Wolst^r. ys a blacke dragon.

"The bages that he beryth by King Edwarde[77] is a blewe bore with his tuskis, and his cleis, and his membrys of golde.

"The bages that he beryth by Kyng Richard[78] ys a whyte herte, and the sonne sliyning.

"The bages that he beryth by the honor of Clare ys a blacke bolle, rowgh, his homes, and his cleys and membrys of gold.

"The bages that he beryth by the fayre mayde of Kent[79] is a whyte liynde."

This reign may be properly closed with Gibbon's spirited account of the siege of Constantinople, in 1463,[80] as it was distinguished, to use his own

---

[76] This is that which became, in after times, the distinguished badge of the House of York. It was, perhaps, originally nothing but a tenure, and the red rose of Lancaster had probably a similar origin; though Shakespeare, in the first part of Henry IV, has represented the Temple Garden as the place whence those roses were plucked. If he be right, then they were so plucked to represent the antient badges.

[77] Edward III.

[78] Richard II, see p. 65 of this volume.

[79] The wife of the Black Prince and mother of Richard II.

[80] Vol. IX, p, 144.

words, "by the reunion of the antient and modern artillery."

"Of the triangle which composes the figure of Constantinople, the two sides along the sea were made inaccessible to an enemy; the Propontis by nature, and the harbour by art. Between the two waters, the basis of the triangle, the land side was protected by a double wall, and a deep ditch of the depth of one hundred feet. Against this line of fortification, which Phranza, an eye witness, prolongs to the measure of six miles, the Ottomans directed their principal attack; and the emperor, after distributing the service and command of the most perilous stations, undertook the defence of the external war.

"In the first days of the siege, the Greek soldiers descended into the ditch, or sallied into the field; but they soon discovered, that in the proportion of their numbers, one Christian was of more value than twenty Turks: and after those bold preludes, they were prudently content to maintain the rampart with their missile weapons. Nor should this prudence be accused of pusillanimity. The nation was indeed pusillanimous and base; but the last Constantine deserves the name of an hero; his noble band of volunteers was inspired with Roman virtue, and the foreign auxiliaries supported the honour of the Western chivalry. The incessant vollies of lances and arrows were accompanied with the smoke, the sound, and the fire of their musketry and cannon. Their small arms discharged at the same time either five, or even ten, balls of lead of the size of a walnut; and according to the closeness of the ranks and the force of the powder several breast-plates and bodies were transpierced by the same shot. But the Turkish approaches were soon sunk in trenches, or covered with ruins. Each day added to the science of the Christians; but their inadequate stock of gunpowder was wasted in the operations of each day. Their ordnance was not powerful, either in size or number; and if they possessed some heavy cannon, they feared to plant them on the walls, lest the aged structure should be shaken and overthrown by the explosion.

"The same destructive secret had been revealed to the Moslems; by whom it was employed with the superior energy of zeal, riches, and despotism. Among the implements of destruction, Mahomet the Second studied with peculiar care the recent and tremendous discovery of the Latins; and his artillery surpassed whatever had yet appeared in the world. A founder of cannon, a Dane or Hungarian, who had been almost starved in the Greek service, deserted to the Moslems, and was liberally entertained by the Turkish Sultan. Mahomet was satisfied with the answer to his first question, which he eagerly pressed on the artist. 'Am I able to cast a cannon capable of throwing a ball or stone of sufficient size to batter the walls of Constantinople.' 'I am not ignorant of their strength, but were they more solid than those of Babylon I could oppose an engine of superior power; the position and management of that engine must be left to your engineers.' On this assurance, a foundry was established at Adrianople: the metal was prepared, and at the end of three months Urban produced a piece of brass ordnance of stupendous, and almost incredible magnitude; a measure of twelve palms was assigned to the bore; and the stone bullet weighed above six hundred pounds. This enormous engine," having been brought with great difficulty before Constantinople, "was flanked by two fellows almost of equal magnitude; the long order of the Turkish artillery was pointed against the walls; fourteen batteries thundered at once on the most accessible places; and of one of these it is ambiguously expressed, that it was mounted with a hundred and thirty guns, or that it discharged one hundred and thirty bullets. Yet, in the power and activity of the Sultan, we may discern the infancy of the new science.

"Under a master who counted the moments, the great cannon could be loaded and fired no more than seven times in one day. The heated metal unfortunately burst; several workmen were destroyed; and the skill of an artist was admired, who bethought himself of preventing the danger and the accident, by pouring oil, after each explosion into the mouth of the cannon.

"The first random shots were productive of more sound than effect; and it was by the advice of a Christian, that the engineers were taught to level their aim against the two opposite sides of the salient angles of a bastion. However imperfect, the weight and repetition of the fire made some impression on the walls; and the Turks, pushing their approaches to the edge of the ditch, attempted to fill the enormous chasm, and to build a road to the assault. Innumerable fascines and hogsheads and trunks of trees were heaped on each other; and such was the impetuosity of the throng, that the foremost and the weakest were pushed headlong down the precipice, and instantly buried under the accumulated mass. To fill the ditch was the toil of the besiegers; to clear away the rubbish was the safety of the besieged; and, after a long and bloody conflict, the web that had been woven in the day was still unravelled in the night.

"The next resource of Mahomet was the practice of mines; but the soil was rocky; in every attempt he was stopped and undermined by the Christian engineers , nor had the art been yet invented of replenishing those subterraneous passages with gunpowder, and blowing whole towers and cities into the air.[81] A circumstance that distinguishes the siege of Constantinople, is the reunion of the antient and modern artillery. The cannon were intermingled with the mechanical engines for casting stones and darts, the bullet and the battering-ram were directed against the same walls, nor had the discovery of gunpowder, superseded the use of the liquid and unextinguishable fire. A wooden turret of the largest size was advanced on rollers; this portable magazine of ammunition and fascines was protected by a threefold covering of bulls' hides; incessant vollies were securely discharged from the loop-holes; in the front, three doors were contrived for the alternate sally and retreat of the soldiers and workmen. They ascended by a stair-case to the upper platform, and as high as the level of that platform, a scaling ladder could be raised by pullies to form a bridge, and grapple with the adverse rampart. By these various arts of annoyance, some as new as they were pernicious to the Greeks, the tower of St. Romanus was at length overturned. After a severe struggle, the Turks were repulsed from the breach, and interrupted by darkness; but they trusted that, with the return of light, they should renew the attack with fresh vigour and decisive success. Of this pause of action, this interval of hope, each moment was improved by the activity of the emperor and Justiniani,[82] who passed the night on the spot, and urged the labours which involved the safety of the church and city. At the dawn of day the impatient sultan perceived, with astonishment and grief, that his wooden turret had been reduced to ashes; the ditch was cleared and restored; and the Tower of St. Romanus was again strong and entire. He deplored the failure of his design; and uttered a profane exclamation that the word of the thirty-seven thousand prophets should not have compelled him to believe that such a work, in so short a time, could have been accomplished by the infidels.

"One ship, bearing the imperial flag, and four belonging to „the Genoese, laden with troops and provisions, at length came to the relief of the Greeks: but the city was already invested by sea and land; and the Turkish fleet, at the entrance of the Bosphorus, was stretched from shore to shore, in the form of a crescent, to intercept, or at least to repel, these bold auxiliaries. The reader, who has present to his mind the geographical picture

---

[81] The first theory of mines with gunpowder appears in 1480, in a MS. of George of Sienna, (Tiraboschi, Tome VI, part I, page 324.) Tbey were first practised at Sarzanella, in [1487; but the honour and improvement in 1503, is ascribed to Peter of Navarre, who used them with success in the wars of Italy, (Hist, de la Ligue de Cambray, Tome II, p.93-97.)

[82] He commanded the Genoese.

of Constantinople, will conceive and admire the greatness of the specta-
cle. The fire ships were guided by skilful pilots, and manned with veterans
of Italy and Greece, long practised in the arts and perils of the sea. Their
weight was directed to sink or scatter the weak obstacles that impeded
their passage; their artillery swept the waters their liquid fire was poured on
the heads of the adversaries, who, with the design of boarding, presumed
to approach them; and the winds and waves are always on the side of the
ablest navigators. In this conflict the imperial vessel, which had been almost
overpowered, was rescued by the Genoese; but the Turks, in a distant and
closer attack, were twice repulsed with considerable loss. Mahomet himself
sat on horseback on the beach, to encourage their valour by his voice and
presence, by the promise of reward, and by fear, more potent than the fear
of the enemy." But finally "the Christian squadron triumphant and unhurt,
steered along the Bosphorus, and securely anchored within the chain of the
harbour." "The introduction of this supply revived the hopes of the Greeks,
and accused the supineness of their Western allies."

"In this perplexity the genius of Mahomet conceived and executed a
plan of a bold and marvellous cast, of transporting by land his lighter vessels
and military stores, from the Bosphorus into the higher part of the harbour."
This was effected "by the strength of obedient myriads; and the real importance of the operation was magnified by the consternation and confidence
which it inspired." "Here the Turkish fleet was far above the molestation of
the deeper vessels of the Greeks, and the sultan next constructed a floating
battery. On this he planted one of his largest cannons, while the four-score
gallies with troops and scaling ladders approached the most accessible side
which had formerly been stormed by the Latin conquerors. The indolence
of the Christians has been accused for not destroying these unfinished
works, but their fire, by a superior fire, was controlled and silenced, nor
were they wanting in a nocturnal attempt to burn the vessels as well as the
bridge of the sultan. His vigilance prevented their approach; their foremost
galliots were sunk or taken; forty youths, the bravest of Italy and Greece,
were inhumanly massacred at his command; nor could the emperor's grief
be assuaged by the just though cruel retaliation, of exposing from the walls
the heads of two hundred and sixty Musulman captives. After a siege of forty days, the fate of Constantinople could no longer be averted. The diminutive garrison was exhausted by a double attack; the fortifications, which
had stood for ages against hostile violence, were dismantled on all sides by
the Ottoman cannon, many breaches were opened; and near the gate of

St. Romanus, four towers had been levelled with the ground." "A spirit of discord impaired the remnant of the Christian strength: the Genoese and Venetian auxiliaries asserted the pre-eminence of their respective service; and Justiniani, and the great duke, whose ambition was not extinguished by the common danger, accused each other of treachery and cowardice.

"During the siege the words of peace and capitulation had been some-times pronounced, and several embassies had passed between the camp and the city "but after some fruitless treaties, Mahomet declared his resolution of finding either a throne or a grave under the walls of Constantinople." "On the evening of the 27th of May, he issued his final orders, and the sea and land, from Galata to the Seven Towers, were illuminated by the blaze of the Turkish nocturnal fires." "On the following night the troops, the can-non, and the fascines were advanced to the edge of the ditch, which, in many parts, presented a smooth and level passage to the breach; and his four-score gallies almost touched with their prows and their scaling ladders the less defensible walls of the harbour."

"At day break, without the customary signal of the morning-gun, the Turks assaulted the city by sea and land; and the similitude of a twined or twisted thread has been applied to the closeness and continuity of their line of attack. The foremost ranks consisted of the refuse of the host, a vol-untary crowd who fought without order or command; of the feebleness of age, or childhood, of peasants and vagrants, and of all who had joined the camp in the blind hope of plunder and martyrdom. The common impulse drove them onwards to the wall; the most audacious to climb were instantly precipitated; and not a dart, nor a bullet of the Christians, was idly wast-ed on the accumulated throng. But their strength and ammunition were exhausted in this laborious defence; the ditch was filled with the bodies of the slain; they supported the footsteps of their companions; and of this devoted vanguard, the death was more serviceable than the life. Under their respective bashaws and sanjacks, the troops of Anatolia and Romania were successively led to the charge: their progress was various and doubtful; but, after a conflict of two hours, the Greeks still maintained, and improved, their advantage; and the voice of the emperor was heard, encouraging his soldiers to achieve, by a last effort, the deliverance of their country. In that fatal moment the Janizaries arose fresh, vigourous, and invincible. The sul-tan, himself, on horseback, with an iron mace in his hand, was the spectator and judge of their valour; lie was surrounded by ten thousand of his domes-tic troops, whom he reserved for the decisive occasions; and the tide of battle was directed and impelled by his voice and eye. His numerous ministers of justice were posted behind the line, to urge, to restrain, and to punish; and if danger was in the front, shame and inevitable death were in the rear of the fugitives.

"The cries of fear and of pain were drowned in the martial music of drums, trumpets, and attaballs: and experience has proved that the mechanical operation of sounds, by quickening the circulation of the blood and spirits, will act on the human machine more forcibly than the eloquence of reason and honour. From the lines, the gallies, and the bridge, the Ottoman artillery thundered on all sides; and the camp and city, the Greeks and the Turks, were involved in a cloud of smoke, which could only be dispelled by the final deliverance or destruction of the Roman empire.

"The immediate loss of Constantinople may be ascribed to the bullet or arrow, which pierced the gauntlet of John Justiniani; he withdrew from the city, his example was imitated by the greatest part of the Latin auxiliaries, and the defence began to slacken, when the attack was pressed with redoubled vigour.

"The number of Ottomans was fifty, perhaps an hundred times superior to that of the Christians; the double walls were reduced by the cannon to a heap of ruins: in a circuit of several miles, some places must be found more easy of access, or more feebly guarded, and if the besiegers could penetrate in a single point, the whole city was irrecoverably lost. The first who deserved the sultan's reward was Hassan the Janizary, of gigantic stature and strength. With his scymetar in one hand and his buckler in the other, he ascended the outward fortification; of the thirty Janizaries, who were emulous of his valour, eighteen perished in the bold adventure. Hassan and his twelve companions had reached the summit, the giant was precipitated from the rampart, he rose on one knee, and was again oppressed by a shower of darts and stones. But his success had proved that the atchievement was possible: the Avails and towers were instantly covered with a SAvarm of Turks, and the Greeks now driven from the vantage ground, Avere overwhelmed by increasing multitudes.

" Amidst these multitudes the emperor, who accomplished all the duties of a general and a soldier, was long seen and finally lost." "The distress and fall of the last Constantine are more glorious than the long prosperity of the Byzantine Caesars." "The nobles, who fought round his person, sustained, till their last breath, the honourable names of Palaeologus and Canta-cuzane: his mournful exclamation was heard: 'Cannot there be found a Christian to cut off my head,' and his last fear was that of falling alive into the hands of the infidels. The prudent despair of Constantine cast away the purple: amidst the tumult he fell by an unknown hand, and his body was buried under a mountain of the slain. After his death, resistance and order was no more." "It was thus after a siege of fifty-three days, that Constantinople, which had defied the power of Chosroes, the Chagan, and the Caliphs, Avas irretrievably subdued by the arms of Mahomet the Second."

Edward the Fourth.

S the seal of this monarch must have been made at the commencement of his reign, it may be regarded as the truest specimen of the armour of the time, and represents him in a complete suit. Over it is his tabard, which is a close tunic girted round the waist and reaching to the bottom of the abdomen. The sleeves of it are wide, but short, and cut diagonally from just above to just below the elbows. On his helmet, besides the knight's cap, is the crown surmounted by a lion. His tabard is plain,[1] but his shield, which in shape greatly resembles those of Edward the Third's time, bears the qv.nr-terings of the royal arms.

His horse, too, is fully caparisoned with the armorial ensigns of England. His chanfron has cheek-pieces, and from between his ears arise three ostrich feathers. Behind the saddle, on the middle of the crupper, is a round ball apparently for ornament, but as we may observe in the tournament book of Munich, dated 1504,[2] for the purpose of catching the rider when

---

1 Tbe jupon, (or it may have been a tabard), of this monarch, enriched with rubies, was preserved at Windsor Castle, till the civil wars. See Walpole's note on Hentzner's Travels, p. 73.

[2] It has lately been published in tbe original German with fac-similies of the paintings.

pushed out of his saddle.

It had been found that, when this happened from the thrust of the lance, the knight frequently slipped off behind, and thus afforded an easy conquest. By this plan, therefore, he was enabled to recover his seat. This invention appears to have been what was called "a rerebrake," for such a thing is stated in one of the Paston manuscripts, as requisite for a tilter, and is described as made of, or accompanied "with a roule of leather well stuff-id." At a later period, a large bell was substituted for this at the tournament. There does not appear to be any spike projecting from the chanfron of the horse, but such was soon after adopted, as in a combat fought in Smithfield in the year 1467, between the Lord Scales and the Bastard of Burgoyne, "The Lord Scales' horse had on his chafron a long sharp pike of steele, and as the two champions coaped together, the same horse thrust his pike into the nostrils of the bastard's horse, so that for very paine, he mounted so high that he fell on the one side with his master."[3]

Edward the Fourth was a great warrior, and Philip de Comines gives of him the following character in that respect:

"King Edward was a man of no great forecast, but very valiant, and the beautifullest prince that lived in his time."[4] "Now you shall understand that the custom in England is, after the victorie obtained neither to kill nor raunsome any man, especially of the vulgar sort, knowing all men then to be ready to obey them, because of their good successe. Notwithstanding, King Edward himself told me, that in al battels that he wan, so soon as he had obtained the victory, he used to mount on horsebacke, and cry too: 'Save the people, and kill the nobles.' "[5]

This small degree of humanity, however, he afterwards sacrificed to his policy, as the same author afterwards tells us "King Edward at his departure out of Flanders, resolved no more to cry save the people and kill the nobles; but he had conceived extreme hatred against the communalty of England."[6]

In the celebrated battle which he fought at Towton against superior numbers, the only manoeuvre we can discover, from the confused accounts now extant, was the ordering his archers to shoot a volley of flight arrows, which were used for great distances, and then retire a little. The consequence was that when another was returned from the Lancastrians, in whose fac-

---

[3] Howes.

[4] English translation of " The History of Philip de Commines, knight, 1596," p. 93.

[5] Ibid, p. 96.

[6] Ibid, p. 100.

es the snow descended with great violence, they fell far short of the mark. Fauconbridge, who commanded Edward's archers that composed the van, then ordered them to throw back their bows and draw their swords, whereupon the armies met, and the battle became a furious conflict of personal strength and bravery, which was ultimately decided in favour of Edward, after a most excessive slaughter.[7]

The figure leaning on a pole-axe which has been introduced into the initial letter of this reign must be considered as referable to that part of it which preceded the restoration of Henry VI, as it is taken from the illuminated manuscript life of St. Edmund, by Lidgate, in the British Museum. The warrior's head is covered by the earliest specimen of the morian, with a turban wrapped round its base, but it should probably be regarded as shewing, in this respect, the costume of the Turks and the Moors of Spain; as the illuminator intending to represent pagans, seems to have thought that the infidels of his day were the best authorities for the purpose.

Mention was made in the last reign of hand cannons. There is in the Royal library, in the British Museum, a manuscript, entitled Croniques d'Engle-terre,[8] highly illuminated; and as it is embellished with the white rose we may conclude it to be of the time of Edward IV, agreeing, as it does, with other delineations of this time in point of costume. It seems to have been, illuminated in Flanders, as many of the figures have on their thighs the steel and sparks of fire, the badge of Burgundy. Among others are some soldiers with long tubes, which rest upon their shoulders, and which they hold up by both hands. These appear to be the hand cannons, or rather hand guns, and the men who are holding them seem to be taking their aim.[9] These tubes are bound round at different distances of their length, being probably composed of two or more pieces and thus held together. The helmets worn by the soldiers have the large circular or oval ear-pieces, which distinguish the early part of this reign.

Besides these are dismounted men at arms, archers and cross-bow men. The former are in complete armour, but instead of a helmet wear a capeline, the crown of which is convex, and the rim cut into angles before, behind,

---

[7] Some historians say upwards of thirty thousand. It was in this battle that the spur was lost, mentioned in the last reign.

[8] Marked 14, E. IV.

[9] As, however, they are without stocks, there is some reason to conceive that they- may have been for the Greek fire, as in the description of the siege of Constantinople, it may be seen that it had not altogether become disused.

and at the sides; their gorgets[10] and aprons of chain-mail are vandyked, and their breasts protected by two demi-placards over the plate and of different colours. The archers have black or purple pantaloons, shirts of mail with short sleeves, and over these close vests vandyked; and the tight sleeves of the under garment cover the rest of their arms. Some carry their arrows in a girdle at the right hip, and some have them in quivers. The cross-bow men are habited somewhat in the same stile, except that, instead of salettes with large oreillets, they have salades with moveable vizors; and wear their cases, containing their bolts or viretons, at their right hips. Their large arbalestes wind up somewhat in the same manner as those of the last reign, but the handles of the cylinder instead of being one up and the other down, are both in the same line.

In the description of the battle of Towton, it is said the archers took to their swords and bucklers, but though what have been just noticed are without the latter, yet those in the drawings of John Rouse of Warwick, which will be hereafter noticed, have them. Hence we learn that although the use of the sword and buckler was more antient, yet their being assigned to the archers, owes its origin to the time of Edward IV.

A very good idea may be formed of the costume of the archers and crossbow men at the commencement of this reign, from an illumination to a copy of Froissard made at this period, representing the naval battle of Grenesai, in 1343.[11] Besides this, the form of the vessels and mode of engaging may also be perceived, as well as the military habits of the glaive-men and other soldiery. Another illumination, in the same manuscript,f gives some further representations of the archers, by which we perceive that they, sometimes, had their knees guarded by genouillieres, as has been shewn in Plate xliii. From this delineation we also learn that the lances of the cavalry were of an excessive length; and when held out for charging scarce any part projected beyond the elbow, as heretofore had been the case and which so greatly tended to counterbalance the weight.

In the reign of this king an act passed, ordaining every Englishman to have a bow of his own height, and during the same reign butts were ordered to be put up in every township, for the inhabitants to shoot at on feast days, and if any neglected, the penalty of one half penny was incurred. By the

---

[10] The gorgets about this time were termed gorgerettes and gorgieres, as appears by a MS. in which is represented the ordination of a knight, by Charles Duke of Burgundy, in 1473.

[11] It has been engraved for Montfaucon's Monarchie Franç. Pl. cl.

twenty fourth also of Edward IV, c. 4, hows of yew were to be sold for three shillings and four pence.

Louis XI, King of France, who was cotemporary with Edward IV, issued the following memoire respecting the arms and armour of the Francs-archers, the guisarmiers, and the cross-bow men of his kingdom.

"Memoire of what the king wills respecting the Francs-archers of his kingdom, as they are to be from henceforth clad in jacks; and for which he has charged the Bailly of Mante to give in a projet. It, therefore, appears to the said Bailly of of Mante, that jacks are most suited for their cloatliing, as profitable and advantageous in time of war, seeing that they are infantry, and in having bri-gandines,[12] they are compelled to carry many things, that a man of himself and on foot cannot do.

"And first, they must have for the said jacks, thirty or at least twenty-five cloths, and a stag's skin at least; those of thirty with the stag's skin being the best. Secondhand and unravelled cloths are best for this purpose, and these jacks should be made in four quarters. The sleeves should be as strong as the body, with the exception of the leather, and the arm-holes[13] of the sleeves must be large, which arm-hole must be slooped close up to the collar, not on the back of the shoulder, that it may be broad under the arm-pit, and plaited under the arm, sufficiently ample[14] and large on the sides below. The collar should be like the rest of the jack, but not made too high behind, to allow room for the salade. These jacks must be laced in front, under which opening must be a lianging-piece[15] of the same strength as the jacks themselves. Thus the jacks will be sure and easy, provided that there be a pourpoint without sleeves or collar of two cloths only, that shall be only four fingers broad on the shoulder; to which pourpoint shall be attached the cliausses. Thus shall the wearer float, as it were, within his jack, and be at his ease; for never have been seen half a dozen men killed by stabs or arrow wounds in such jacks, particularly if they be troops who are accustomed to fighting.

"Item, it seems best to the Bailly that the Francs-archers should be divided into four kinds of armed troops. One armed with voulges,[16] another

---

[12] As had been the case under Charles VII.

[13] Assiéte,

[14] Faulce, tbis word appears to be used in opposition to juste, wbich signifies' close.'

[15] Porte-piece. Such are used at tbis day in tbe Marhatta war-dresses.

[16] The voulge or vouges were staves, on one end of which was a long blade pointed, but made to cut and broad in the middle, greatly, therefore, resembling glaives, except that tbey were double edged. Two of these are in the collection of Llewelyn Meyrick, Esq. one of wbich is engraved at the foot of Plate LXX.

with lances, a third archers, and the rest cross-bow men.

"Item, it seems to him that those who carry voulges, should have them suitably broad, and a little widened in the middle, and that they should be for cutting and thrusting; and that the said guisarmiers[17] should have salades with visors, gauntlets and large daggers, but not swords.

"Item, those who carry lances should have salades with vizors, gauntlets, and swords for thrusting,[18] suitably long, stiff and sharp for cutting. And their lances should be the length of arming lances,[19] that they be not so very thick, but all of a piece;[20] except that, at the bottom, they have a little cutting bit, and a small stopping piece about half a finger in height behind the cutter to give them a smart appearance. The blade should likewise be cutting and pretty long, and by all means strong and neat.

"Item, the archers should have salades without visors,[21] bows and pushing swords sufficiently long in the blades, stiff and cutting, which are called bastard swords.[22] If they choose to carry bucklers there is no harm, and they may have suitable daggers, but the rondelles[23] should not be of large diameter.

"Item, the cross-bow men should have salades with vizors, which they may raise sufficiently high when they choose; but the under part of the vizor must not be of such strong armour, as to obstruct their sight; and also the right side must not come so low down on the cheek as the left, in order that they may with ease close their arbrier[24] to their cheek. They should have pushing-swords, but not very long, stiff, and cutting. Their girdles, also, should hold up the sword a little behind, that it may not touch the ground. Their cross-bows should be about ten quarrels[25] and they should bend them with four pulleys, or indeed two, if they are good benders. They should also

[17] They are so called because the vouge differed froin tbe guisarme, merely in wanting the projecting spike at the back, and a little in the form of the blade, seebottom of Plate XXVIII.

[18] Espées de passot, cut and thrust swords.

[19] Lances d'armes, i. e. those used by the men at arms in battle, in contradiction to those for the tournament.

[20] Or.width, d'une venuë.

[21] Both kinds of salades occur in the illuminatio';s of this period, but particularly in Rouse's life of the Earl of Warwick, and are also in the armoury of Llewelyn Meyrick, Esq.

[22] Itdoes not appear why, unless they were made with only one edge.

[23] Either the circular shields, or the plates on the hilt of the dagger may be meant by this expression.

[24] The bow-stock.

[25] That is the stock and bow together should measure thus much.

have quivers,[26] pannelled[27] and waxed, containing eighteen bolts at least, and should not have daggers."

These Francs-archers were relinquished after this reign, and did not, therefore, continue in existence beyond the year 1480.

The mounted arbalesters, in the service of Louis XI, were called crane-quiniers. Thus Philippe de Comines speaks of them: Il avait quatre cens cranequiniers que lui avoit prête le Comte Palatin, gens fort bien montez et qui sembloient bien gens de guerre. "He had four hundred cranequiniers, whom the Count Palatine had lent to him, very warlike men."

Brigandines took their name from the troops called brigands, by whom they were first worn. These people were a kind of light armed irregular foot, much addicted to plunder, and frequently mentioned by Froissard. Owing to their irregularities, the appellation of brigands was used in common to signify all sorts of freebooters.[28] The brigandine jacket was composed of square iron plates, quilted within linen, and continued to be used by the archers, from the latter part of the reign of Henry VI to that of Queen Elizabeth inclusive, with some intermissions. They are mentioned in a statute, of the year 1476, in these words: In arnesiis, videlicet, arbalestis, bregantinis, colubrinis, &c. "In harness, namely: cross-bows, bregantines, culverines, &c."[29]

The crenequin or grenequin was a usual name for the cross-bow at this time. Thus in the will of Thomas de Failly, dated 1473, one of the clauses runs: Item, a legué, donné, et devisé à son frère Jehan de Failly son petit grenequin fourny. "Also he leaves, gives, and devises to his brother, John de Failly, his little grenequin with its furniture." And in a letter remissory, dated 1476, Michel de Commelanne, Alement, lors cranequinier de la compagnie, &c. Les arbalestriers ou crennequiniers auront brigandine ou corsset comme les coustilliers. "Michael de Commelanne, a German, then cranequinier of the company, &c. The arbalesters or crennequiniers shall have brigandine jackets or corsets, like the coustillers or cutlers."

These coustillers were men armed with long knives, some of whom are delineated in the before noticed representation of the battle of Grenesai.[30]

---

[26] Or more properly speaking, cases.

[27] Empanées,

[28] See Owen's Welsh and English dictionary in voce brigant.

[29] There is some reason, however, to conclude that the word brigandine, was applied, at this time, to the jazerine jacket. I have not, myself, seen any brigandine older than the time of Elizahetb; but their perishable construction may account for that.

[30] See Mont. Mon. Franç. PI. Cl.

They are mentioned in a letter remissory, dated 1455, thus: Le suppliant homme de guerre soubz l'ordonnance et compagnie du Mareschal de Loheac comme coustilleur. "The suppliant, a warrior, under the orders, and in the company of Marshall de Loheac, as a coustiller." Again in the military orders of Charles Duke of Burgundy, in 1473, it is ordained that: Les hommes d'armes seront montez de trois chevaux, dont l'un sera souffisant de courre et rompre lance. Les deux autres clievaux ne soient moindres du prix, l'un de xxx escus, et l'autre de xx escus pour porter leur paige, et coustillier. "The men at arms shall be mounted with three horses, of which one will be sufficient for the course and breaking the lance. The two other horses shall not be worth less, one than thirty crowns, the other than twenty crowns, to carry their page, and a coustillier." From this we perceive that they were provided by the men at arms, sometimes, instead of archers; at others they were their pages. Thus in a letter remissory, dated 1478, it is said: Ainsi que le suppliant archier de nostre ordonnance se pounnenoit sur le petit marchie d'Arras,—il vist deux ou trois coustilliers ou pages. "It was thus that the suppliant, an archer of our ordonnance, advanced towards the little market of Arras. He saw two or three coustilliers or pages."

A specimen of armour, not unlike that of this period, and particularly of the globular breast-plate, exists in a painting on glass at Trinity Hall, Cambridge. It represents Richard Duke of York, the father of Edward IV, but, has been inadvertently called Richard Duke of Gloucester, afterwards Richard III, in Plate li, for which it has been selected. The Duke of York played his most conspicuous part from the year 1452 to 1454, and was killed at the battle of Wakefield, in 1460. But although the date 1470, put under the plate, is at least ten years too late, scarce any mis-representation need be feared, whether it be considered the portrait of him or the Duke of Gloucester, for Dr. Shaw, in his sermon at St. Paul's Cross, in 1483, said to the populace: "Here, in the Duke of Gloucester, we have the very picture of that hero: (Richard Duke of York) here, every lineament reflects the features of the father."[31] Those parts of the suit which cover the arms and legs are engraved, but, what is not usual at this period, the gauntlets are fingered, and the military belt is used without any upper garment. The hand of the figure rests upon one of those large twohanded swords, used at this period, and until the close of the reign of Henry VIII. A great variety of these forms part of the collection of Llewelyn Meyrick, Esq. In the drawings of John Rouse, of Warwick, are

[31] Sir Thomas Moore's life of Richard III. Edward IV was also the son of the Duke of York, and scarce nineteen years of age when he mounted the throne.

PLATE LI

RICHARD DUKE OF GLOUCESTER,

A.D. 1470.

several delineations of shields used by the cavalry at this period, which were continued with scarce any alteration to the middle of Henry the Seventh's time. One of these made of wood, covered with a skin, and lined with leather, having on it a hook and rings for the guige, in the armoury of Llewelyn Meyrick, Esq. is given at the bottom of Plate LI. The skin, which is outside, is coated with white cement, and this is again painted black, and covered with intertwining gilt foliage. In the centre also is the motto in German, of the knight to whom it formerly belonged.[32] This shield is curved outwards for the convenience of the bridle arm, has three ridges down its front, and is wider at bottom than at top. The bouclie, or mouth for the lance to pass through, is at the left upper corner.

The monument of Sir Thomas Sellinger shews that, at the latter part of this reign, the tabard was made quite loose, and its sleeves the same.

The helmet of Henry Green, who died in the year 1467, has the vizor in the middle of the ventaile, with perforations above and below for the sight and breath.

Etienne de Vignoles, called la Hire, and Poton de Saintrailles, engraved Plate CLXXI of Montfaucon's Mon. Franç from an illuminated copy of Monstrellet's Chronicles of this period, in the Colbertine library, afford good specimens of the fantastic armour still continued in this reign.[33] The former has a casque terminating at top in the Phrygian stile, with oreillets like bird's wings. Both have ornamented circular plates with lambrequins attached on their shoulders, and Poton wears the salade of the infantry; he carries suspended from his neck by the guige a target; chain gorgets and petticoats of the same with ornamented genouillieres and long spurs are on both. The figures in the Manuscrit de Berri in Montfaucon's Mon. Franç Pl. CLXXIV, and the three following are also curious examples; they wear the

---

[32] About the year 1460, during the Neapolitan wars, the use of armorial bearings was in a great measure relinquished by the Italian chiefs, who caused certain emblems or symbolical devicès to be painted upon their shields, illustrated by short classical allusions and quotations, descriptive either of the particular enterprize, or of the general character of the bearer. See Le imprese illustre con espositioni e discorsi del S. Jeronimo Ruscelli, 4to. 1582.

From the Italian word "impresa," we have imprese or impress, the use of which, in England, arose in the reign of Henry VIII, when the English were so ambitious of acquiring the fantastic modes of that nation. Such were more common at public shows than armorial bearings. Dugdale has collected those used in a tournament between the Earls of Leicester and Oxford, in the reign of Elizabeth. By a statute of the 5th of her reign, c. 15, an. 1564, a severe penalty was laid on all fantastical prophecies upon, or by occasion of any arms, fields, beasts, badges, or like things accustomed in arms, cognizances, &c.

[33] That suit of armour at Castle Howard, falsely called La Hire's, is of the time of James I.

cappelline.

A statute passed in the third year of the reign of Edward IV, prevents "all knights under the estate of a lord, esquire, or gentleman, from wearing the pikes of their shoes exceeding two inches in length, under forfeiture of forty pence." The expression is: solers, &c. oveque ascun pike ou poleine, and it had been not only the custom with shoes but of the sollerets attached to the armour. Monstrellet tells us that, in the year 1467, even boys had poulaines at the toes of their shoes a quarter of an ell long and upwards, and Paradin[34] says: "the men wore shoes with a point before half a foot long, the richer and more eminent personages wore them a foot, and princes two feet long; which was the most ridiculous thing ever seen, and when men became tired of these pointed shoes, which were called poulaines,[35] they adopted others in their stead, denominated duck bills, &c."[36] In the fourth year of Edward IV, it was "enacted that no shoemaker or cobler in London, or within three miles of the same, shall make or cause to be made any shoes, guloches, or husens,[37] with pikes or poulaines exceeding the length of two inches, under the pain of forfeiting twenty shillings."

Feathers are mentioned as worn by the men at arms on their helmets, in the year 1473. Thus in a manuscript of that date in the king's library at Paris, where Charles the Bold, Duke of Burgundy is represented detailing the armour of his company of gens d'armes, he says: Les homines d'armes auront plumes sur leur habillement de teste. "The men at arms shall have plumes on their habillement for the head."

The representation of Pierre de Rohan, Seigneur de Gie, in Montfaucon's Mon. Franç Plate CCXV, exhibits him with a tremendous feather like a fox's brush, hanging from a pipe on the top of his helmet so low as almost to touch his horse behind. The ventaile projects like a cone. This further gives the form of the battle-axe, which has a spear-blade on its top and a curved one opposite the axe like a halbert.

The helmet of William Lord Hastings, on his seal[38] to a deed, dated 1469, has on it a scroll instead of a cointisse, and this is the earliest specimen I have met with. It has been conjectured that the scroll was an imitation of the cointisse after it had been torn in battle, and consequently a notion of

---

[34] Histoire de Lyons, p. 271.

[35] Care sbould be taken to distinguisb the poulaine, whicb was the long point at the toe, from poleyn, which was the knee cap in tbe reigns of Henry III and Edward I.

[36] Tbe pointed toes were also called crakoes.

[37] Buskins.

[38] See Archæol. Vol XV, p 400.

valour being attached to it, became a favourite with the military.

The cappeline has been noticed as worn by the men at arms of this reign, and its form described. In a letter remissory, dated 1463, troops are spoken of: enbastonnez de cappeligne guisarmes, &c. "armed with cappelines guisarms, &c.

It is further said, in the military orders of Charles Duke of Burgundy, that: Les homines d'armes seront armez, habillez, et montez ainsi qu'il est declairie cy apres; c'est assavoir de curache complette. "The men at arms shall be armed, dressed, and mounted, as in the manner here following is declared, that is to say, with cuirass complete."

The breast-plates of the men at arms have already been mentioned, as covered with several successive placards. Perhaps we cannot have a finer specimen of this kind of armour, than that afforded by the monumental effigy of Sir John Crosbie, Alderman of London, and which has, therefore, been selected to form one of the subjects of Plate LII. Sir John's breast-plate is covered with three placards, his elbow pieces are fastened by double points, like those of Lord Hungerford, and two very fine tuilles, are buckled to the lowest tace. His genouillieres are ornamented by handsome plates above and below. The serjeant at arms near him is taken from an illumination in the British Museum.[39] All the armour he wears is a skull-cap under his hat, a cuirass and large genouillieres; but the immense hilt of his sword is worth notice.

One of these long hilted swords is in the possession of Llewelyn Meyrick, Esq., but the wood and leather grasp are only half the lenghth of the hilt, extending from the cross bar upwards, the rest being merely a bar of iron, on which is the letter Ā, resembling that on the initial letter to the reign of Henry I, and terminated by a large flat circular pommel, in order to counterpoise the weight of the blade. The two-handed sword shewn at Dunbarton Castle, as that of Wallace, is of this period, as will be evident to any one who compares it with that of the earldom of Chester, in the British Museum. The guard of this undoubted original is a simple bar, a little inclined to curve downwards, with an inscription on each of its four sides; the pommel is a flat hexagon with an emblazoned shield on each side. The hilt has also three shields enamelled on copper on each of its sides; the centre one is the royal arms of England, with a label of three points, supported by two kneeling angels, and the corresponding one is those of Mortimer.

The sword blades, anterior to the middle of Henry the Eighth's reign,

---

[39] in the Harl. Lib, marked 4425.

PLATE LII

SIR JOHN CROSBIE & A SERJEANT AT ARMS,

A.D. 1475.

tapered from the guard gradually to a point; in the time of Edward IV they were nearly flat, but in earlier times a section of them would have presented the figure of a lozenge. In Henry the Seventh's they had a ridge on each side, and at the commencement of Henry the Eighth's instead of the ridge were thickened towards the point. The form before the middle of the fifteenth century may be seen in the sword of Hugh Lupus, Earl of Chester, also in the British Museum. On one side of its blade is stamped HUGO COMES, in characters like those on the seal of William the Conqueror, and on the other a wolf's head and CESTRIÆ. This kind of inscription and the shape of the blade authenticate it, but the hilt and pommel are not of earlier date than the middle of Henry the Eighth's time.

Below this plate is a visored salade taken from a figure in an illuminated MS. in the British Museum.[40] These salades became very common at this time, but the figure is otherwise curious, having on a globular breasted cuirass with a short petticoat of mail attached, and in the act of slipping over this a hauberk or shirt of mail. The legs are without any armour, being in pantaloons or hose, as they were then termed; the cuirass is beautifully flowered, and, therefore, may not be steel but pourpointed work, with merely a breast-plate underneath.

In an inventory taken at Holy Island, Durham in the year 1481, is the following enumeration: Anna, item, iii galee cum umbrell·, ii saletts, iii jakks, i jak lent to Robyn Vikar, i breste, i curas, i garbrase, i polronn, (pauldron) i par gardes, i par pipes, i par lambels, i par taces, ii speris, iii batell axes, iiii crosbowes, viii gunnes, i long bow, i shafe sagittarum.

The garde-bras was an additional piece laid on the upper part of the gauntlet, as in the monument of John Earl of Arundel, or screwed to the elbow-pieces as in Plate liii. The pair of gardes I take to be the double placate, as when the left side of the breast-plate was wholly protected by another plate, such was termed a grand-guard. The pipes may have been the vambraces, and the lambels, what were subsequently called lamboys, a corruption of lambeaux, the petticoat of velvet or ornamented stuff.

In the College of Arms is a folio book containing several entries, made apparently about the close of the reign of Queen Elizabeth, and subsequently. This book is marked M. 6; but as the entries are, in all probability, copies of original documents,[41] I have no hesitation in making use of them

---

[40] Entitled Boccace de cas des nobles hommes et femmes, in tbe Roy. Lib. 14, E. V.

[41] This seems to bave been taken from the manuscript in the Harleian Library, marked 69.

as such. One of them is as follows:

"The ordinances, statutes, and rules made and enacted by John[42] Erie of Worcestre, Constable of England, by the hinge's commandement at Windesore, the 14tli day of May, in the Vlth year of his noble reigne, to be observed and kepte in all manner of justes of peace royall, within this realme of England, before his highness or lieutenant by his commandement or licence, had from this time forth, reserving alwais to the Queen's highness, and to the ladies there present, the attribution and gifte of the price,[43] after the maner and forme accostoined, the menâtes and demerites attribute according to the articles fol-lowenge:

"Firste, whoso breaketh most speares, as they ought to be broken, shall have the price.

"Item, who so liitteth thre tymes in the heauhne shall have the price.

"Item, who so meteth two tymes coronoll to coronoll, shall have the price.

"Item, who so bearetli a man downe with stroke of speare, shall have the price.

How the price should he loste.

"Firste, who so striketh a horse shall have no price.

"Item, who so striketh a man his back turned, or disyarmyed of his speare, shall have no price.

"Item, who so hitteth the toyle or tilte[44] thrise, shall have no price.

"Item, who so unheaulmes himself twice shall have no price without his horse fade him.

How speares broken shall he allowed.

Firste, who so breaketh a speare between the saddell and the charnell[45] of the heaulme slialbe allowed for one.

"Item, who so breaketh a speare from the charnell upward shalbe al-

---

[42] John Tiptoft, Earl of Worcester.

[43] Pretium or reward.

[44] This we learn, from the regulations for the tournament, 1st Henry VIII, is below the waist or in the saddle.

[45] The pinnacle of the helmet, which was considered as resembling a turret. Hence in the Chronologia Augustinensis Cantuariensis there is a "Charta de Charnelle faciendis super muros Ecclesire."

lowed for two.

"Item, who so breaketh a speare so as he strike him down or put him out of his saddell or disarme him in such wise as he maye not runne the nexte cowrst after, shalbe allowed for three speares broken.

How speares broken shall be disallowed.

"Firste, who so breakethe on the saddell shalbe disallowed for a speare breakinge.

"Item, who so hites the toyle or tilte[46] once shalbe disallowed for two.

"Item, who so hitteth the toyle twice for the second tyme shalbe abased thre.

"Item, who so breaketh a speare within a foote of the coronoll shalbe judged as no speare broken, but a good attempte.

For the price.

"Firste, who so bearethe a man downe owte of the saddell or putteth him to the eartlie, horse and man, shall have the price, before him that striketh coronoll to coronoll two tymes.

"Item, he that striketh coronoll to coronoll two tymes shall have the price before him that striketh the sight[47] three tymes.

"Item, he that strikethe the sight three tymes shall have the price before him that breakethe moste speares.

"Item, yf there be any man that fortunetly in this wise shalbe demed he bode longest in the feeld lieaulmed and ranne the fairest cowrse, and gave the greatest strokes, helpinge himselfe best with his speare.

"Whereas your most noble grace haste moste habundantly given unto fowre maydens, of your moste honorable courte, the castell called Loyall, to dispose accordinge to their pleasures, they have most lyberallye given the garde and custodie of the same unto a captaine, and with him fifteen gentlemen, of whom I ame the officer of armes, and have by them in commandement to certifie unto your moste noble grace under their fourme,

---

[46] The toyle or tuile was the piece of armour which was buckled to the tasset, and hung over the cuishes. The-tilt was, perhaps, the same as the port, and consequently thé receptacle near the saddle bow for the butt end of a lance when held upright. The introduction of the word toyle is. a proof that this entry is copied from a document older than the time of Henry VIII.

[47] Those perforations in the helmet through which the wearer looks.

that wheres thei straungers evermore, servinge to ladies for the famous renown of this your noble courte, liathe departed their foren contries, for to
se that same youre cowrte therein to serve unto ladies accordinge to their
custome under your protection and favour. That yt might please your grace
. . . . they have undertaken the defence of the same to knowe and understand
the fourme and manner under the whiche, to the beste of their power, lyke
after the facion of their contrie, thei purpose, by your favorable suffrance,
to defend and keype the same against all comers, gentlemen of name and
of armes.

"Firste, in the place before the holde without shall stand an unycorne
white and with his fore legges sustaynenge iiij slieldes, the one white signy
fienge to the justes, that is to say, who toureth that to be answer'd . . . . .
. coursts at the tilte with hastinge harnoys,[48] and double pieces,[49] by one
of the castell, the ij zede signyfienge to the tourney, that is to saye, who
toürhethe that to be answer'd xij strokes with the sword edge and point
rebated,[50] the iij yellowe signyfyieng to the barriars that is to saye who toureth that to be answered at the barrière xij strokes with one hand sworde,
the poynte and edge rebated, the iiijth blowe signifienge to the assaulte, and
who toureth that to assaulte the said castell with suche weepons as the said
gentlemen shall occupie, that is to saye, sworde, target, and morrispike,[51]
with the edge and pointe rebated.

"Item, yt shall be lawfull for the assaulters to devise all manner of en-
gynes for the wynenge of the said castell engyn or tole to breake the grownd
or howse will all only xcepted.

"Item, that no man assaulte the castell with pike, sword, sliott, no throw
other than shalbe lefte by the unycorne a patrone and example.

"Item, none do meddell with fier, neyther within nor without, but to
fire there gunnes.

"Item, yf any of the approchers or defenders be taken to paye for his
ransom, thre yardes of right sattin to the taker, and every captayne thirteen
yardes.

---

[48] Armour used at hastiludes.

[49] That is with a placate over the breast-plate, sometimes called a pair of plates.

[50] Bent back, or beaten back, from the French "rebattre." Rebating the points of swords
gave origin to the buttons on the ends of fencing foils. Spears and swords in this state' were
called épées gracieuses, glaives courtois, armes courtoises.

[51] Probably in the original, pike, as the morris pike did not come into fashion till the
time of Henry VIII, or the specification of the weapon may have been added by the writer,
who copied, the document into the book.

"Item, in any day es that this enterprise shalbe don to begin at one of the cloke at afternone, and to continue until seven of the cloke at afternone.

"Moreover, yt is to be understood that the firste day of this enterprise shall begin on St. John's day, which is the xxvijth daye of Novembre, now next commynge and to end on new year's day at six of the clock at afternone.

"Whereas divers noble persons have enterprised and taken upon them to hold justes roiall and tourney, the iiijth and . . . . th daye of November, at Westend, as plainlie appeare by their articles, and at so noble a feaste dyverse and sondrie exercises of armes are used, therefore, and to thee intent that if there be any gentlemen or other men of armes that present not themselves at the said daies of justes or torneye there be vi gent, that will make them disporte the xiith day of Novembre, accordinge to these articles followenge yf yt so please the kinges highness for whose pleasure, the queens and all the ladies they undertake the said enterprice, as especially for the pleasure of their redoubted lady and fairest princesse the eldest daughter to our sovereigne lord the kinge.

"Firste, in the place appointed for the said justes and tourney there slialbe ordeyned, against the said xijth daye, a good nombre of speares and swordes, suclie as shall please the kinges grace, and the said vi gent sent in the same place in hastinge harnises to answer other vi gent in this nam'd wise.

"The vi comers shall take a speare and a sword every of them, in like wise the vi gent puttinge themselves in range directly against their fellowes, every man his speare on his thiglie and his sworde where yt shall please him, and then at the sownde of the trumpete to charge and runne together all at once every man to his fellowe that shall stande against him, and so pas throughe.

"Item, the cowrse with the spears passed, every man to take his sworde and do his beste, only the foyne[52] except, cliosinge his fellow by fortune as it shall happen, and so to continew untill the tyme that the kinge shall comand to reast.

"Item, yf any man of armes breake his sworde or lose yt by any fortune, he may retorne to the skaffold, where the hereliaults[53] be, and there receave an other, and so enter into the tourney againe. Also yt shall not neede that every man confyne to still in fightinge with him whome he shall firste encounter, but if he will maye also serche to and fro taking his advantage, and

---

[52] Thrust.
[53] Heralds.

helpinge his fellow if neede be, alwaies defended that no man lay hande on other, but only with his sworde to do his beste, nor twaine to sett uppon one alone, unlest yt be in aydinge of his fellow as above.

"Item, if yt hap that there com to answer this enterprise more than the nombre of vi, yt slialbe at the kinges pleasure if the said gent shall answer them at suche daies as shall please his grace, or ells to be divided, halfe with them and th'other halfe against them, alwaie observinge the said articles.

"Item, if any man be disarmed he maye withdrawe himselfe if he will, but once past the barres he may not com agayne into the torney for that daye. Also there shall no man have his servant within the barres, with any peeee of harnois, for no man slialbe within the said barres, but suche as shalbe assigned by the kinges grace.

"Item, who shall beste demeane himselfe at thee same arte of armes, shall have a sworde garnished,[54] to the valew of iij hundred crownes or under.

"Item, every man that will be at the said tourney shall delyver his name to one of the thre kinges of armes, by the laste daye of October, which shall declare to them if any doubte be made to the said articles.

"Item, if any man strike a horse with his speare, he shalbe put out of the itorneye withowt any favour incontinent, and if any slaye an horse he shall paye to the owner of the said horse, an hundred crownes in recompence, also yt is not to be thought that any man will strike an horse willingly, for if it do, it shalbe to his great dishonor.

"Therefore, the said vi gentlemen beseclie the kinges noble grace, that this bill of the saide articles, signed with his most noble hande may be a sufficient warrant, and comandement unto his officers of armes to make proclamation thereof, as well in his moste noble cowrte, as in all such other places as shalbe moste requysite."

Then follows this challenge:

"Ever in the cowrte of great kynges are wonte to com knights of dyvers nations, and more to this cowrte of England, where is mayntayned knyghthood and feats of armes valliantly for the service of ladies, in more higher degrees and estates then in any reahne of the worlde. It beseemeth well to Don Francisco de Mendoza, and Carflast de la Vega that here, better than in any place, thei may shew their great desire that they have to serve their ladies. They saye that they will mayntayne to fight on foote at the barriers, with footmen's harnois, iij pushes with a pike, and xii strokes with a sworde,

---

[54] That is "with its appurtenances," as scabbard, &c.

in the place appoynted before the cowrte gate, the Twesday being the iiij daye of Decembre, from xii of the clocke untill six at night to all noble men or knigliteth at will com to the said combates with the condicions that here followe, requyring these lordes, the Erie of Arrondell, the Lord Clynton, and Gar de Lopos de Padilla, and Don Pedro de Cordoua, that they wilbe judges of their triumplies.

"Firste, he that cometli raoste gallauntly fortlie, not bringinge any golde or silver tyne for counterfait woven or embroidered, nor no gold smythe's worke on him, shalbe given a brooclie of golde.

"Item, he that fightest best with the pike shall have a ringe of golde with a ruby in yt.

"Item, he that fightest best with a sword shall have a ringe of golde with a dyamonde.

"When they shall iointly fight together, accordinge to the appoyntment, he that then dothe moste valiantly shall have a ringe with a dyamonde.

"Item, he that giveth a stroke with a pike from the girdle downward, or under the barriar shall win no price.

"Item, he that shall have a close gauntlett,[55] or any tliinge to fasten his sword to his hande shall win no price.

"Item, he that his sword falleth out of his hand shall win no price.

"Item, he that stayeth his hand in fight on the barriars shall win no price.

"Item, whosoev. shall fight and sheweth not his sword to the judges shall win no price.

"Yet it is to be understood that the challengers maye wyn all these prises agaynste the firste comers, defandants, and more, the moste gallaunte as yt is afore expressed.

"The mayntenars may take ayde or assistance of the noble men and of suche as they shall thinke beste.

"Moreover, that all suche triumphes, as are agreed uppon by the challenger and allowed by the prince, shalbe puplished by the kinge of armes of the province, in suche places as shalbe appoynted by the prince. And also, that the next night after any triumphes is ended the gifte of the prises is to be p'claymed by the said king of armes in the psence chamber, after the second cowrse be served, the manner whereof hereafter followethe.

"Oyes, oyes, oyes, we lett to understand to all princes and princesses,

_____

[55] This was a gauntlet with immoveable fingers, with the exception of one joint; so that the sword once fixed in it the wearer could not be disarmed. One of these is in my son's collection.

lordes, ladies and gentlewomen of this noble cowrte, and to all others to whom yt

"Oyes, oyes, oyes, we lett to understand to all princes and princesses, lordes, ladies and gentlewomen of this noble cowrte, and to all others to whom yt appertaynethe, that the nobles, that this daye have exercised the feates of armes at the tilte, tornoy, and barriars, have every one behaved themselves moste val-lyaantly in showing their prowes and valour worthe of greate proise.

"And to begine, as towchinge the brave entre of the Lorde —— made by him very gallauntly, the kinge's majestie[56] more brave than he, and above all the Erie ——, unto whom the price of a very riche ring is given by the quenes majestie, by the advice of other princesses, ladies and gentlewomen of this noble cowrte.

"And as towchinge the valyantnes of the piques; the Duke M. liathe very well behaved himselfe, the Erie of P. bettar than he, and above all others the Erie of D. unto whome the price of a ringe of golde with a ruby is given, by the moste hige and mightie princes, the Quene of England, by the advice aforesaid.

"And as towchinge the valyantnes of the sworde; ——knight, hathe very well behaved himselfe, the Erie N. bettar than he, and Sir J. P. knight, above all the reste, unto whome is given the price of a ringe of golde with a dyamond, by the quenes most excellent majestie, by the advice of other princesses, ladies and gentlewomen.

"And as towchinge the valyantness of the sworde at the foyle; Sir W. R. knight, hathe very valyauntly behaved himselfe, the Marquis C. bettar than he, and above all others the kinge's majestie, unto whome was given the price of a ringe of golde with a dyamond, by the quenes majestie, by the advise of other princes, ladies and gentlewomen.

"Finally, towchinge the valiancie of the pique, the poynte abated;[57] Thomas P. hathe well and valyantly behaved himself, Charles C. bettar than he, and above all others Z. S. unto whom was given, by the quenes majestie, a ringe of gold, by the advise of other princes, ladies and gentlewomen.

---

[56] This expression puts this entry as late as the time of James I; the Emperor Charles V having been the first for whom the title of majesty was formed; highness was previously applied to the kings and quenes of Europe. Such date is further corroborated by the piece of armour noticed in the last note.

[57] Taken off.

Fees apperteyning to the officers of armes at all those triumphes aforesaide.

"Firste, yf any of the sayd challengers or défendante fall to the grounde, horse and all, the said horse ought to be the officers of armes.

"Item, at all justes with speares, or axes that is made in those fields, the covertures of the horses behinde the saddells, the cotes of armes of the challengers or défendante, with all the speares, axez and swordes broked and broken, the states whereon the said officers of armes sit, belonge unto them. And, furthermore, the kinge of armes or herehault, that pclameth the said justes, shall have vi elles of skarlett, and duringe the said justes their wages, and also all the banners, standards and cotes of armes, that be wome in that feeld that daye, belonge to the said officers.

"Also what nobleman so ever he be that entreth into the saide feelde or justes, the firste tyme, he ought to give the officers of armes six crownes of golde, for the marshallinge of his armes that tyme and no more."

In the Bibliothèque du Roi, at Paris, is a book of tournaments, of this period,[58] having the following curious contents:

Beneath a large illumination of Louis XI sitting on a throne are verses. Next, knights on horseback, heralds, &c. with coats of arms. On the ninth leaf, John Duke of Bretagne delivering a sword to a king at arms to carry to his cousin, the Duke of Bourbon, in order to break a lance with him. Next illumination, the Duke de Bourbon receiving the challenge. Then the herald offering the Duke de Bourbon the choice of eight suits of armour to put on. Then the process preceeding the combat in which several knights and their attendants appear. In the thirty-second and thirty-third leaves, the combat of the two dukes. The seats and benches of the spectators are then displayed. Next, a very large illumination of the procession of knights and their attendants to the place of contest. Then banners, coat armour, &c. suspended from buildings. The entry of the judges. Then the procession preparing for the combat. The cavalcade of judges, dames et damoiselles. Rencontre of the knights attendants, beneath a balcony of ladies, in the cauchoise cap; the judges being in balconies below, with sundry mottoes spread beneath. The baton seems to be the general instrument of attack and defence in the combat. Another more splendid tournament, throngs of combattants, and ladies above in boxes, and trumpeters. Last illumination, the ladies bring a white mantle to throw over the shoulders of the conquer-

---

[58] It is marked 8351. There is another of the year 1470, which describes a combat à outrance, in 1306, marked 8024.

or. In the whole there are seventy-four leaves.

The following is from Stowe's Survey of London.[59]

"In the year 1467, the seventh of Edward IV, the Bastard of Burgoine challenged the Lord Scales, brother to the queen, to fight with him, both on horseback and on foot. The king, therefore, caused- lists to be prepared in Smithfield, the length of 120 taylor's yards and 10 foot; and in breadth 80 yards and 20 feet, (one computes this 379 foot in length, 260 in breadth,) double barred, five foot between the bars, the timber work whereof cost 200 marks, besides the fair and costly galleries, prepared for the ladies and others. At which martial exercise the king and nobility were present.

"The first day they ran together with spears and departed with equal honour. The next day they turneyed on liorsebacke; the Lord Scales' horse having on his chafron a long spear-pike of steel,[60] and as the two champions coupled together, the same horse thrust his pike into the nostrils of the Bastard's horse; so that for very pain he mounted so high that he fell on one side with his master, and the Lord Scales rode about him with his sword drawn, till the king commanded the marshall to help up the Bastard, who said: ' I cannot hold by the clouds, for though my horse fail me, I will not fail an incounter companion.' But the king would not suffer them to do any more that day. The next morrow they came into the lists on foot with two pole-axes, and fought valiantly; but at last the point of the pole-axe of the Lord Scales, entered into the side of the Bastard's helm, and by force might have placed him on his knees; but the king cast down his warder and the marshall severed them. The Bastard required that he might perform his enterprize; but the king gave judgment, as the Bastard relinquished his challenge."

From the poem of Luca Pulci, on the tournament which took place at Florence, in the year 1468, we learn that the lances frequently produced sparks of fire when struck against the armour:

> Dettonsi colpi che pavon d'Achille
> E balza un mongibel fuori di faville.

---

[59] Book III, p. 239.

[60] This may probably be the first instance of a spike fixed on the middle of the chanfron. The seal of the Earl of Warwick, represents the chanfron of his horse as having a proboscis turned up from the lower' part of it, as before noticed, but those with spikes became general from the time of Henry VII. Such may be seen in Grose's Treatise on Armour, Pl. XXIV; and there are several different specimens in the armoury of Llewelyn Meyrick, Esq.

> "Achilles rage their meeting stroke inspires,
> Their sparkling armour rivals Etna's fires."

At this tournament Lorenzo de Medici greatly distinguished himself.

The peaceable justs or tiltings, that were performed for the amusement of the ladies and other spectators; and in which the successful knights received some prize or reward from the hand of a fair and courteous damsel, were called: Justes of Peaces Royall, Justes of Pecis, and Justes of Peirs. They were termed by the French Joutes a Plaisance, and in the Latin of the middle ages Hastiludia pacifica.

They were performed with pointless lances or coronels, and were used in opposition to the real and sanguinary justes or tournaments, denominated "Joutes a outrance," or, as Froissart calls them, "Joustes mortelles et a champ."

The ceremonials observed on these occasions, are contained in a volume, whicli belonged to Sir John Paston, knight, in the reign of Edward IV, and are now in the Lansdowne Collection of MSS. in the British Museum.

First, is the proclamation of the justs as follows:

To cry a Justes of Peas.

"Wee, herawldes of armes, beryng sheeldes of devise, here we yeve in knowlege unto all gentilmen of name and of armys, that there be vi gentilmen of name and of armes that for the grete desire and woorship that the seide vi gentilmen, have taken upon them to bee, the third day of May next coomyng, before the high and mighty redowted ladyes and gentlewoomen in this high and most honourable court. And in their presence the seide sixe gentilmen there to appeer at ix of the clok before noone, and to juste agenst all coomers without, the seide day, unto vi of the clok at aftir noone. And then, by the advyse of the seide ladyes and gentilwoomen, to yeve unto the best juster withoute a dyamaunde of xl li.

"And unto the next best juster a ruble of xx li. and to the thrid wele juster a saufir of x li. And on the seide cfaye there beyng officers of armys, sliewyng their mesure of theire speris garneste,[61] that is cornall,[62] vamplate,[63]

---

[61] Spears garnished or furnished as follows.

[62] Cornal or coronel, the head of a tilting lance, so called from its resemblance to a little crown.

[63] A round plate of iron fixed at the end of the tilting lance to guard the hand.

and grapers,[64] all of acise,[65] that they shall just with. And that the comers may take the lengthe of the seide speris with the avise of the seide officers of armes that shall be indifferent unto all parties unto the seide day."

Then we have the particulars of the armour for horse and man, and all its appurtenances, under the title of

Abilments[66] for the Justus of Pees.

"First, an helme wele stuffid, with a creste of his devise.

"A pair of plates,[67] and thritty gyders.[68]

"An haustement[69] for the body with sleevis.

"A botton with a tresse[70] in the plates.

"A shelde coovirde with his devise.

"A rerebrake[71] with a roule of lethir wele stuffid.

"A maynfere[72] with a ryngge.

"A rerebrace.[73]

"A moton.[74]

"A vambrace[75] and a gaynepayne,[76] and two brickettes.[77]

"And two dozen tresses and vi vamplates.

---

[64] Gripers or velvet coverings for the gripe or grasp.

[65] Assize, or due proportion as established.

[66] Habiliments or armour and accoutrements.

[67] The breast and demi-placate as on the figure of the Earl of Warwick.

[68] Guyders or Vuiders, straps to draw together the open parts.

[69] A stiff under garment to keep, the body straight and erect. Fr. Ajustement.

[70] Clasp, see the figure of the Earl of Warwick, PI. XLVII.

[71] As the mane fare follows next, this seems to r-efer to a part of the horse furniture, and probably to a guard fixed on the crupper .to break the fall of the rider when thrust out of his saddle.

[72] Armour to cover'the' horse's mane.

[73] An arriere bras; that which went on the fore arm was called avant bras, and consequently arrière bras would, signify a plate for the upper arm, such as may be seen in Plate xxxv, and its subsequent cylindrical form.

[74] A plate put on the right shoulder, see Plate LV.

[75] Avant bras, or armour for the fore arm.

[76] This was the antient name of the sword used at tournaments, from the French, gagnepain. The term continued in use to a late period, either for a sword or musket, as the symbol of the soldier's professsion, by which he got *his bread*,

[77] French Brichette. The pieces 'which covered the loins, and joined tbe tassets; probably both these and the tassets are included by the word "two."

"And xii grapers,[78] and xii cornallys,[79] and xl sperys.

"And an armerer with hamour und pynsons.[80]

"And nails with a bickorne.[81]

"A good courster[82] and new shodd, with a soft bitte.

"And a grete halter for the reyne of the bridell.

"A sadill wele stuffid, and a peire of jambus.[83]

"And iii double girthis with double bocles.

"And a double singull[84] with double bokuls.

"And a rayne of lethir hungry, tied fro the hors liede unto the girthis beeneth betwene the ferthir bouse[85] of the hors for renassyng.[86]

"A rynnyng patrel.[87]

"A croper of lethir Hungrye.

"A trapper[88] for the courster, and two servaunts on horsback wele be-seene.

"And vi servauntes on foote all in oone sute.[89]

Next follows a description of:

The Commynge into the Felde.

"The vi gentilmen must come into the felde unhernsyd, and their lielmys borne before them, and their servaunts on liorsbak, beryng aithir of them a spere garneste, that is the seide vi speris which the seid vi servaunts shall ride before them into the felde, and as the seide vi gentilmen be coomyn before the ladyes and gentilwomen.

"Then shall be sent an herowde of armys[90] up unto the ladyes and

---

[78] Holders for the gripe.

[79] Coronells.

[80] Pincers.

[81] Anvil with a double born.

[82] Courser.

[83] Armour for the legs.

[84] Cingle or horse girth.

[85] Boss, or round plate of metal, used to adorn the horse.

[86] Curbing or acting as a martingal.

[87] The poitral was armour for the horse's. chest, but the running poitral merely a breast leather. We still denominate breast-plate the leather strap, which passes from the. saddle round the horse's breast, and between his fore legs.

[88] Trappings.

[89] One livery.

[90] Herald of arms.

gentilwomen, seying in this wise: High and mightie redoutyd and right worchyfull ladyes and gentilwoomen, theis vi gentilmen ben com into your presence and recomaunde them all unto your gode grace in as lowly wise as they can, be-sechyng you for to yeve unto the iii best justers without, a diamonde, and a rubie, and a saufir unto them that ye thenk best can deserve it. Then this message is doon.

"Then the vi gentilmen goth into the tellws,[91] and doth on their helmys. And when the lierawldis krye a Tostell, a l'ostell,[92] then shall all the vi gentilmen within unhelme them before the seide ladyes, and make their obeisaunce and goo home unto their logging and change the . . . . . ."[93]

After this the justing is supposed to take place, and being concluded:

Nowe he coomyn the Gentilwoomen without into the presence of the Ladyes.

"Then cornys foorth a lady by the avise of all the ladyes and gentilwoomen, and yevis the diamonde unto the best juster withoute, saying on this wise, Sir, theis ladyes and gentilwomen thank you for your disporte and grete labour that ye have made this day in their presence. And the seide ladyes and gentilwoomen seyen that ye have best just this day. Therefor the seide ladyes and gentilwoomen geven you this diamounde and send you much worshup and joy of your lady. Thus shall be doon with the rubie, and with the saufre, unto the othir two next the best justers. This doon, then shall the lieraude of armys stonde up all an high, and shall say witliall an high voice, John hath wele justed, Richard hath justid bettir, and Thomas hath justkl best of all.

"Than shall hee, that the diamount is geve unto, take a lady by the hande and begynne the daunce. And whan the ladyes have daunced as long as them liketh, than spyce wyne and drynk, and than avoide."[94]

Here terminates the ceremonial that relates to the justs in question, and, in order to understand the armour specified in it, we should refer to some delineation of a just at the same period. The book of John Rous of Warwick furnishes us with six. They are engraved in the Second Volume of Strutt's Manners and Customs of England, Plate XI, XXVIII, XXXV, XXXVI,

[91] Tilt-house.
[92] A l'hôtel, the cry of the heralds to the combatants, that they should return to their dwellings .
[93] The transcriber seems to have left this part unfinished, but probably the conclusion of the sentence would have been "habiliments" or "apparel, for the dance."
[94] Clear away.

xxxvii, and xl.

The following documents from the same volume of Sir John Paston, knight, as connected with single combats, are not less curious in their way than the preceeding.

How a Man shall he armede at his ease when he shall fight on foote.

"He shall have none sherte upon him, but a doublet of ffustian, lynid with satin, kut full of holes; the doublet must be streightly bounde there, yᵉ poynts must be sett aboute the grete of the arme, and the best before and behynde, and the gussets of mail[95] must be sowid unto the doublet into the bought of the arme, and under the arme, the armyng points[96] must be made of fyne twyne, such as men make streengs for crossbowis, and they must be trussid small and poynted as points; also they must be waxed with cordeners wax, and then they will neither recche[97] ne breke; also a peir liosen of stamyn single, and a peir short bulworks[98] of thyn blanket, to put aboute his knees, for chawfyng of his leg harneis; also a peire of shone of thyk cordewayne, and they must be fret with small whipcorde, iii knotts upon a corde, and iii cordis must be fast sowed unto yᵉ . . . . of the shoo, and fyne cordis in the myddil of the sole of the same shoo, and that there bee betwene the frettis,[99] of the hele and the frettis of the myddil of the shoo the space of iii fyngers."

To arme a Man.

"First, ye must set on sabatynes,[100] and tye them upon the shoo with small poynts that will breke, and then griffus,[101] and then quysshews,[102] and

---

[95] Small lozenge-shaped pieces of chain mail to protect the arm-pits and bend of the arms; the hams, and insteps. They were fastened to the under garments by means of arming points. There is a set of them in the armoury of Llewelyn Meyriok, Esq.

[96] The arming points were short ends of strong twine with points like laces. See Pl. lii.

[97] Stretch.

[98] As the thigh piece's of the infantry terminated just above the knee, they were apt to chafe the wearer when in active motion; to prevent this the bulworks were used.

[99] Ornaments of cross-work, what the heralds call frets.

[100] Wide coverings for the shoes, made of several bands of steel, as won! by the figure in Pl. LX. That they were also used by the infantry, or those who fought with swords on foot, see the triumph of Maximilian. In one plate, however, they actually appear as clogs.

[101] Greaves or shin pieces.

[102] Cuisses or armour for the thighs.

than the breche of maile;[103] and than towletts,[104] than the breste, than the vambrace, than the rerebrace, than the cloovis,[105] and than hong his dagger upon the right side, than his short sworde on his left side in a rounde ring, all nakid to pull it out lightly; than put his cote upon his bak, and than his basenet pynned upon two grete staples before the breste,[106] with a double bocle behynde upon the bak for to make the bacenet sit juste; and than his long swerde in his liande, than his pensell[107] in his liande, poynted of Seynt George, or of our lady, to blisse him with as he goth towards the felde, and in the felde."

"The day the appellaunt and the defendaunt shall fight, what they shall have with them into the feelde.

"A tent must be piglit[108] in the felde.

"Also a chaire.

"Also a basyn.

"Also vi loves of bred.

"Also vi galons of wyne.

"Also a messe of mete, fleshe or fislie.

"Also a borde and a peir of trestils to ete on his mete and his drynk.

"Also a bord cloth.

"Also a knyf to kut his mete.

"Also a cupp to drynk in.

"Also a glass with a drynke made.

"Also a dosen trisses of annyng poyntes.

"Also an liamour, pynsons, and a bycorne.

"Also a dosen of smale nailes.

"Also a long swerd and a short and a dagger.

"Also a kerchief to hele[109] ye visour of his basnet.

"Also a pensel to here in his hande of his avowrye."[110]

Reference has been made to the book of John Rous. That work is, the Life of Richard Beauchamp, Earl of Warwick, who was born in 1381, and

---

[103] A piece of chain-mail which hung over the breech.

[104] Tuilettes or small tiles, sometimes called cuissarts, the flaps which hung on the thighs from the tasses.

[105] Gloves or gauntlets.

[106] These staples and the basenet will be seen in PI. LX.

[107] A pennonsell or small pennon.

[108] Pitched.

[109] Cover.

[110] Cognizance.

died in 1439. The original MS. is in the British Museum, in the Cotton Library, marked Julius, E. IV. and appears to have been written in the time of Edward IV. Although there are fifty-three drawings in this MS. it would be foreign to our purpose to notice any but those which throw light on antient armour.

The first of these is thus described: "Here shewes how atte coronacion of Quene Jane[111] Erie Richarde kept juste for the quene's part ageynst all other com-mers, where he so notably and so knyghtly behaved hymself, as redounded to his noble fame and perpetuall worship." The Earl of Warwick is in full armour, on a saddle of war, his visor closed, his crest the bear and ragged staff on the top, a tilting shield suspended from his neck, and hanging over his left arm, a small round plate to cover the right arm-pit; brichettes or tasses, from underneath which, behind, descends the breech of mail, and on his cuisses the tuillettes. He is thrusting with the lance, on which is placed a steel vamplate. His horse is armed with a chanfron of two pieces, a manefere, and a rerebrake, with its roll of leather, and fully caparisoned. His antagonist, on the other side the barrier,[112] is armed in a similar manner, having for his crest a wing. Each is attended by his squire. At the back, in a covered gallery, are the king, queen, and the lords and ladies. On their right, open galleries with spectators. In front, other seats for the same purpose. Boys are climbing the trees for a better view, while the clerk of the ground is disputing with a man who endeavours to take away the broken spears, which are his perquisites. Within the paling is an attendant with two ungarnished lances, that is, with their coronels on, but without vamplates. On the left of the royal personages is a gate-way, under which are seen advancing other comers, the first of whom is couching his lance, on which an attendant has just placed a vamplate, and about to take the place of the first who is discomfited.

The second "shewes howe at theis daies appeared a blasyng sterre, called Stella comata, which, after the seiyng of clerkys, signyfied great deth and blode-shede; and sone upon begänne the warre of Wales, by Owen of Glendour their chief capteyn; whom emonges other Erie Richard so sore sewed, that he hadde nere hande taken hym and put him to flyght, and toke his banner, and inoche of his people, and his banerer." The Welsh are exhibited in full retreat, with the English in pursuit. The Earl of Warwick is in full armour, but, instead of a helmet has a basnet, with a moveable visor. On the upper part of his right arm is a inoton. The apron of mail covers his belly, instead of

[111] Joan Duchess of Bretagne, wife of Henry IV.
[112] The paling.

the pair of plates, and below it is seen the breech, perhaps of leather, and also the tuillett.es. He is thrusting his lance into the Welsh standard-bearer, whose casque or open helmet is somewhat in the Phrygian form, and who appears to wear over his armour a shirt of mail, with wide sleeves, reaching not quite so low as the elbows; and over this a tabard, without sleeves. Behind the earl is a knight, habited like him, except that his basnet has no visor, and that below his breast are the plates. The rest are armed in like manner.

The third "shewes how at the battle of Shrewesbury, between King Henry the Fourth, and Sir Henry Percy, Erie Richard there beyng on the kynges party, ful, notably and manly behaved himself to his great larde[113] and worship, in which batell was slayne the said Sir Henry Percy, and many others with hym; and on the kynges party there was slayne in the kynges cote armoure, chef of al other the Erie of Stafford, Erie Richards auntes son, wyth many other in greet nombre, on whoes sowles God have mercy, Amen." In this battle one of the knights has sleeves of chain to his wrists, others to their elbows, and in brigandine jackets. The archers appear in brigandine jackets, with short sleeves and skirts of mail. They have also bucklers or small round shields, hanging on the hilts of their swords.

The fourth "shewes howe the noble Erie Richard was made Knyght of the Garter at that tyme to his greet worship; and after, by marvallous acts by hym ful notably and knyghtly acheved in his propre persone, did greet honour and worship to the noble ordre of Knyghtes of the Garter, as by the pageants[114] hereafter following more pleynly is shewed." The figures are in the same kind of armour as before, but with the bricliettes more visible. Among the weapons are spears, bills, benches, glaives, and pole-axes.

The fifth shows "howe atte place and day assigned, resortyng tliidre all the contre, Sir Pandolf entred the place ix speres born before hym, then tliacte of speres to the Erie Richard worshipfully finished, after went they togedres with axes, and if the Lord Calcot hadde not the sonner cried peas, Sir Pandolf sore wounded on the left shuldre hadde been utterly slayne in the felde." The knights are on foot, the tilting spears lie broken on the ground. They are both in full armour with the visors and beavers of their helmets closed; the tops of the helmets rise to pinnacles, called charnels, and on these are the crests. They are fighting with their pole-axes, and the Earl of Warwick has on his tabard. The squires are standing by each, holding in one hand the horse, and in the other a sword by the point, so as with expedition to present the hilt to their

---

[113] Laud.

[114] The delineations on each page.

masters, if required. In the back is the king and his officers.

The sixth "shewes howe Erle Richard from Venise toke his wey to Russy, Pettowe, and Velyn, and Cypruse, Westvale, and other coostes of Alinayn toward Englond, by such coostes as his auncestors had liaboured in; and specially Erle Thomas his grauntfader, that in warre had taken the kynges son of Pettowe, and brought hym into Englond, and christened liym at London, namying hym after hymself Thomas, and in this journey Erle Richard gate hym greet worship at many turnamentes and other faites of werre." This, therefore, represents him at a tournament. He, and another knight, whose crest is a dragon, are exhibited engaged on horseback with two others. Instead of tilting they are cutting with their swords. They have all the beavers and visors of their helmets closed. The Earl of Warwick has a padded and stitched jacket, probably an arming doublet[115] on, without sleeves, as his armour is visible on his arms, as well as his legs; on his thighs, however, he wears cliausons, or breeches of mail. The others are equipped with the usual armour of the times.

The seventh "shewes howe Erle Richard on the first day, that was the xn day of Christmasse, comyng to the felde, his face covered, a busch of estrich feathers on his hede, his horse trapped with the armes of oone of his auncestres, the Lorde Tony, and at the third course he cast to the grounde at his spere poynt, behind the horse taile, the knyght called the Chevaler Ruge; and then the erle with cloose visar retourned unknowed to his pavilyon. And forthwith he sent to the said knyght a fair courser." In this the two knights are tilting armed cap-a-pie. The company seem, by the fleur de lis on their tabards, to be the French court. A herald supports two spare shields for the combatants.

The eighth follows immediately, and represents "ho we Erle Richard the second day came into the felde, that is to say the morowe after the xii day, his visar cloos, a chaplet on his basnet, and a tufte of estrich fethers alofte, his hors trapped with his armes of Haunslape, silwer two barrys of gewles, and their mette with liym the blank knyghte, and they ran togider; and the erle smote up his visar thries, and brake his besagnes*[116] and other harneys, all his apparaile saved; and so with the victory, and hymself unknown rode to

---

[115] Such are mentioned in the Paston Letters.

[116] Nothing in, tbe illumination leads to an understanding of wbat .part of the armour tbis could be. I presume, tberefore, the two circular pieces, about the size of a shilling, wbich covered the pins on which the visor turned, is here meant, and tbat they were so called from tbeir resemblance to the coins called Besants, or Bézans. Tiley were a long time current in France.

his pavilyon ageyn, and sent to this blank knyght Sir Hugh Lawney, a good courser." In the drawing, which represents the knights tilting, the visor of the blank knight appears pushed upwards; but the Earl of Warwick seems to wear a visored helmet, rather than a visored basnet. He is armed cap-a-pie, and the only difference in his armour, from what is usual, is that, instead of a skirt of mail below the brichettes, the fabric appears to be coarse hair. The herald too, holds two saddles instead of two shields, perhaps in both instances as prizes.

The ninth, "howe on the morowe next folowyng, that was the last day of the justes, the Erie Richard came in face open, his basnet as the day afore, save the chapellet was rich of perle and precious stones, in Guy his armes and Beaucliampe quarterly, and the armes also of Tony and Haunslape in his trappure, and said like as he hadde his owne persone performed the two dayes afore, so with Goddes grace he wolde the third, then ran he to the chevaler name Sir Colard Fymes, and every stroke he bare him backwards to his hors bakke; and then the Frenchmen said he was bounde to the sadyll, wherfor he alighted down from his horse, and forthwith stept up into his sadyll ageyn, and so with worsliipe rode to his pavilion, and sent to Sir Colard a good courser, and fested all the people; gevying the said three knyghtes gret rewardes, and rode to Calys with great worshipe." The basnet here again appears to be a helmet with the visor open. He wears his tabard, as does his squire, who holds a horse by the bridle. There is nothing else beyond what has been before noticed.

The tenth "shewes how a mighty duke clialenged Erie Richard for his lady sake, and he justyng slewe the duke; then the empresse toke the erles livery a here, from a knyghtes shuldre, and for grete love and favour she sette hit on her shuldre; then Erie Richard made oone of perle and precious stones, and offered her that, and she gladly and lovingly received hit." There is nothing particular to distinguish this, except that the breech appears to be of leather slit at the end into a kind of fringe, and that the just being a outrance, there is no barrier.

The eleventh represents "howe Erie Richard in his comying into Englond, wanne 2 greet carykkes[117] in the sea." In this are archers and cross-bowmen habited alike, in brigandine jackets, and spearmen in plate armour. They have all salades.

The twelfth "howe Erie Richard in the warres of Fraunce toke Denfront; and entred first into Cane; but inasmoche as he was there with and

---

[117] Great ships.

under Lorde Thomas duke of Clarance, the kyng's next brother, he sette on the walle the kyng's armys, and the duke's, and made a crye a Clarence, a Clarence; and then entred the duke, and gave the erle many greet thankes. After the erle beseged Cawbeck on the water of Sayn, and they appoynted to stande under the Fourme of Reone; and then brought he up vessels by water to Reone, and then by his policy was it beseged both by londe and by water. After he wanne Mount Seynt Michell and many townes, and the kyng made him Earle of Aumarle." The peculiarity in this is, that the French cross-bowmen have long pavises which curve outwards, supported by a stay behind, which stand before them,[118] and that cannon are introduced.

The thirteenth, "howe Erie Richard was atte the sege of Reon, there set first betwen the kyngs tent and Seynt Katheryns, and when Seynt Katheryns was wonne, he was sette to kepe Port Quartevyle." This affords us nothing new in point of armour; we have, however, a fortified camp and a town blockaded.

The fourteenth "shewes liowe Kyng Henry from Reon sent Erie Richard to the Kyng of Fraunce, and the Erie of Kyme with him in the begynning of May with 1000 men of armes, for the mariage of dame Katheryne, daughter of said Kyng of Fraunce." All the knights are in salades; but the only circumstance worthy of remark, is a hood of mail, worn by one, which terminates in Vandykes.

The fifteenth, "howe the Dolphyn of Fraunce leide in the way 6000 men of armes, with the Erles of Vandon and Lymosyn, and bothe the French erles were slayn, and 2000 of his men taken and salyn; all the other put to flight, and Erie Richard slewe oon the saide Erles with his owne handes." There is nothing remarkable in this drawing, except that the cross-bowmen in the French service have sabres, while the English archers have straight swords.

The sixteenth "shewes how Philip Due of Burgoyn beseged Caleys, and Humfrey Due of Gloucestre, Richard Erie of Warrewyk, and Humfrey Erie of Stafford, with a greet multitude, went over the see, and folowed the Due of Burgoyn; he ever fleyng before them; and they there sore noied the countrey with fire and swerde." In this the earls have sleeves of mail attached to the garment, under their breast-plates, with merely half vambraces.

The seventeenth, which is the last connected with our subject, "shewes how Kyng Henry the Fourth made Erie Richard Lieutennant of Fraunce

---

[118] This was a great relief, as in the preceding reign we see the cross-bowman was incumbered with a Jarge pavise or a man was required to protect him with one.

and Normandy," and is merely curious from the variety of bills, glaives, spears, &c.

It had been a custom of the highest antiquity to display the arms and armour of deceased chieftains, at their funerals. This increased in magnificence, with the improvements of time, but "what shall bi don on the demyse of a king, anoynted" in the time of Edward IV, is contained in a MS. which belonged to Thomas Astle, Esq. In that we are told, that after the body was to follow a "lorde or a knyghte w^t a courser trapped of his arrnez, his herneysz upon hyin, his salet, or basenet on his hed crowned, a sliylde and a spere till he come to the place of his ent'ring." The manuscript then goes on to describe the funeral of Edward IV, at which the writer was present, and observes that, after the church ceremony had commenced, "atte the begynnyng of the Masse of Requiem, the whiche was songen by the Archebisshop of York, officers of armes went to the vestyary, wher they receyved a rich embrow-dred cote of armes, which garter king at arms hyld w^t as grete reu'ence as he cowde at the liede of the herse, &c." "In likewyse Clarenceux and Norroy resceyved the shilde, &c." "And Marche and Ireland received a rich swerde whiche had be sent from the Pope, &c." "Also Chest'r and Leycest'r herauldes receyved a basenet w' a riche crown of gold, and p'sented it to the Lorde Stanley and the Lorde Hastings. And Gloucest'r and Bukingh'm herauldes, w^t Rouge Crosse, Rosse, Bla'che, Caleys, Ginez and Berwyk, and Harrington p'syu'nts, went wt the knyghts and esquiers for the body, to the cliurche dore for to resceyve of John Cheyney maist' of the horse, the man of armez, whiche was Sir Will'm Parr, armed at all peces, saving he was bareheded, having an axe in his hand, the polle downward, and thus accompanied to the quere dore, wher he did alight."

Another manuscript, about the same date, contains:

The Manner of burienge great persons in ancient tymes.

"This is the ordinaunce and guyding that perteyneth unto the worsliipfull beryyng of ony astate to be done in manner and fourme ensewing:

"Item, in lyke wyse his shelde, his cote of worship, his helme and creste.

"Item, to behadde a baner of the Trinite, a baner of our Lady, a baner of Seynte George, a baner of the Saynt that was his advoure[119] and a baner of his armes.

"Item, a penon of his armes.

---

[119] Avowed protector.

"Item, a standard and his beste there inne.

"Item, a geton[120] of his devise with his worde."[121] After stating several other things, it adds:

"Item, the hors of the saide astate trappid with his arms, and a man of armes beyng of his kyn upon the same hors, or ellis ony other man of worship in his name, havyng in his liande a spere, swhirde, or axe, so to be presented to the cliurche, with ii worshipful men, oon goyng on yat eon side of the hors and yat other on that other side of the hors, and a man ledyng the same hors.

"Item, the heire of the saide astate, after he hathe ofered, shall stand up'on the lifte side of the priste receyvyng the offeryng of the swhirde, helme, and crest, baner of armes, cote of worshipp, and penon. It'm, ii men of worship to stonde on the same side of the priste, haldyng a basyn w^t mony therinne for the offeryng." Ten barons of Roslyn were buried in a vault beneath the pavement of Roslyn chapel, and it was customary, says Hay, to encase the corpse in a suit of armour, and thus lay it on the floor, without a coffin.[122] According to Slezer,[123] the bodies have been found entire at the end of eighty years, but this is a very doubtful story.[124] My friend, Sir Walter Scott, in his Lay of the last Minstrel, thus beautifully expresses this tradition:

"Where Roslyn's chiefs uncoffin'd lie,
Each baron, for a sable shroud,
Sheathed in his iron panoply."

The carrying of the king's banner on the day of battle, was still highly rewarded, as appears by the following grant. Roulfe Vestynden held £10 per annum, by letters patent, under the great seal, till rewarded with an office "for the good and agreeable service which he did unto us in berying and holding of oure standard of the black bull, at the batayl of Sherborne, in Elmett."[125]

A fine suit of armour, with its appurtenances for the tournament, quite

---

[120] Guydon.

[121] His motto.

[122] Tbe last baron in the time of Charles II, was the first buried in a coffin. This was against the opinion of the Duke of York, but his widow thought it "beggarly" to continue the practice.

[123] Slezer's Theatrum Scotioe, 1693.

[124] Chalmers' Caledonia, Vol. II. p.765.

[125] Rot. Parl. Edw^{di}. 4^{ti}.

complete, and in all probability, the oldest in England,[126] is in the collection of Llewelyn Meyrick, Esq. and enables me, for the first time in this work, thus early to give, in Plate LVIII a representation from actual armour. This curious suit was brought from Naples, having belonged to one of the Caraffa family, from the descendant of whom it was purchased.

It has, over the breast, for the purpose of justing what was called the grand guard, which is screwed on by three nuts, and protects the left side, the edge of the breast, and the left shoulder: Fastened by the same screws is the volant piece, which covers the bever of the helmet, and presents a very sharp salient angle in front.[127] To this is attached a piece to protect the right shoulder, but sufficiently raised to allow for the elevation of the arm. This piece is engraved at the bottom of Plate LIII, that its appearance, when taken off, may be understood. On the front of the right elbow-piece is fastened a large plate, and on the left, one is screwed by a nut, which may be regarded as an elbow-sliield, or rather a garde-de-bras. These pieces being removed, the armour is rendered fit for war. The visor of the helmet is so contrived as to be back in the head, as it were, by means of that part under it projecting; and what is curious, there are perforations behind to give air when the volant piece is screwed on.

There are two tasses, and appendants to them by straps and buckles, two tassets: but what is very curious, one of these has the appearance of a pointed tuilette, and therefore this suit may be regarded as shewing the origin of tassets; the act of change being here represented. The soliereis are not absolutely pointed, though nearly so, being in the state of transition to the square toe. The gauntlets are large and heavy, not fingered, but formed of several plates instead.

There is another suit in my son's armoury, exactly like this, excepting that the armour for the legs ends at the ankles. This, however, is supplied by footed[128] stirrups, with ankle-guards of steel. This suit, instead of tassets, has actually tuilettes, one of which is given at the foot of Plate LVIII, and which shews it to be of an earlier period.

These suits of armour have been fixed to a date referable to English armour, but, when it is considered, that the fashions seem to have passed from

---

[126] With the exception of one greatly resembling it, but with tuillettes, greaves instead of jambs, and footed stirrups in the place of sollerets, which is of the time. of Henry VI, in the same armoury.

[127] So difficult was it to strike when these were worn, that it often formed an agreement, at tournaments, that they should not be used.

[128] These are of the same shape as the sollerets of tho other suit.

Italy and Germany into France, and thence to England, they might have been attributed to a still earlier time. In the same manuscript copy of Froissart, in the Bibliothèque du Roi, at Paris, before mentioned to have been illuminated at this time, is a delineation representing the arrest of Charles the Bad, King of Navarre, by the orders of John King of France. This has been engraved for Montfaucon's Monarchie Française;[129] and in it are no less than three suits of armour, all that are completely visible in the picture, every one ending at the ankles.

Another plate of Montfaucon's,[130] taken also from the same illuminated manuscript, and which is intended to represent the battle of Rosebecque, represents many of the combatants as wearing jazerine jackets, instead of cuirasses, but with the rest of the armour of plate. Many of the figures, however, have the plate armour ending at the ancles, and soliereis only of jazerine work. This picture is worth examination, containing, as it does, a great variety of helmets, salades, and capellines, as well as of weapons and armour. There are also some cannon introduced, of which only a part is visible, but still it may be seen, that they are somewhat embedded on a plank of wood running their whole length, and placed between two wheels. It is to be regretted that more is not visible.

In the year 1474, King Edward the Fourth directed all the bombs, cannons, culverines, fowlers, serpentines, and all other cannons whatsoever; as also powder, sulphur, saltpetre, stones, iron, lead, and other materials, fit and necessary for the same cannons, wherever found, to be taken and provided for his use, paying a reasonable price for the same.[131]

It has been observed, that the archers of Lewis the Eleventh wore jacques at the commencement of this reign: at the close of it, these seem to have been exchanged for a lighter protection, called jacquetons a species of jackets, stuffed and quilted. Thus it is said in a document:[132]—"Item, Hectori de Montebruno capitaneo gardee idem Dom. noster Rex exsolvi ordinavit per dictum christianissi-mum Dom. Regem Francorum hseredein suum universalem xxv. marcas argenti per ipsum Dom. capitaneum gardæexbursatas in faciendo fieri jacquetanos sagittariorum sive archeriorum dicti domini regis." "Also, to Hector de Montebrun, captain of the guard, our said lord the king has directed to be paid by the aforesaid most Christian Lord the

---

[129] Pl. cviii.
[130] Pl. cxxxix,
[131] Pat. 14, Edwd[di]. 4[tl]. p.2, m. 16.
[132] In Codice, 2 Car. Andegav. last Count of Provence, anno 1481.

PLATE LIII

A SUIT OF ARMOUR,

In the possession of

Llewelyn Meyrick, Esq.

A.D. 1480.

King of France, his universal heir, twenty-five marks of silver, disbursed by the said lord, the captain of the guard, in causing to be made jacquetons for the bowmen or archers of our said lord the king."

Doublets were at this time worn, and often over the armour, as may be seen in that plate in Montfaucon's Mon. Franç. before mentioned.[133] The price charged by a London taylor, at this period, for making one of these, with lining, for the use of King Edward the Fourth, was six shillings and eightpence. According to the inventory[134] in which this is stated, its texture is thus described: "Item, a doublet of crymyson velvet lined with Holande cloth, and interlined with busk." In the Paston letters,[135] written, some during the last reign, and some in this, mention is made of "a doublet of velvet mailed," that is, forming the covering to a shirt of mail. The doublet, although greatly resembling the jacke, was undoubtedly not the same, for, in an enumeration of articles,[136] they are thus distinguished, "25 doublettes, 25 jackkas, &c." The shape of the military jacket was like a flapped waist-coat, with sleeves, and made to fit close to the body. Ducange says, it origi-nated in France, and tells us that it was stuffed with wool and cotton. It was called, in the corrupt Latin of the middle ages, dobletus and dublectus, and received its name from having a lining, which made it two-fold, or double.

The brass plate of Sir Anthony Grey,[137] who died in the year 1480, gives us a fine specimen of the immense elbow-plates which continued till the time of Henry the Eighth, the double pauldrons, the globular breast, with three placards; the double-ornamented plates, above and below the knee-pieces, and the ponderous sword worn in front. Such a sword is in the collection of Llewelyn Meyrick, Esq. and with a miséricorde, with two knobs, instead of cross-bar, for a guard hung on the suit, exhibited in Plate LIII. That suit has also a tilting-lance with a cronel at the end, consisting of three curved spikes, about two inches in length; and having, just above the gripe, a very fine vamplate, formerly in the Arsenal at Vienna. The diameter of it is eleven inches, and the rise four inches perpendicular. At the aperture, where it slips over the lance, it is so constructed as to fit the fluting of the shaft.

It has been mentioned, that a mark, on some of the figures in illumina-tions, shewed that they had been done in Flanders. Philip de Commines, in

---

[133] Pl. CVIII.
[134] MS. in Harl. Lib. marked 4780.
[135] In the Lansdown Collection, in the British Museum.
[136] Rymer's Fœd. Vol. VIII. p. 384.
137 In the Abbey Church of St. Albans. See Gough's Sepul, Monts, Vol. II^d.

the 5th book of his history[138] says: "I saw at Milan, since the death of the Duke of Burgundy, a signet that I have often seen him weare at his breast, which was a ring set with a camée, having very curiously cut into it an iron to strike fire, wherein his armes were graven." In the note on this passage it is observed, that "Claude Paradin, in his Devises Héroïques, p. 46, and Annal. Burgun. lib. 3, p. 711, say that he took the striking iron because it is made in the forme of B, which is the first letter of Burgundie. Further, he took the said iron, striking against a stone, with infinite sparkles flying from them, to signifie that the cruell wars betweene the Duke of Burgundie and the realine of Fraunce, had set all their neighbours on fire." Commines also mentions some Italian troops at this period, called Braciques, which a note[139] informs us "were so called from Bracio de Fortibraci, a greate captaine in his time." Another note in this translation,[140] says that the Duke of Burgundy had his head clove down to the teeth by a halberd, and that this, together with two thrusts of a pike, occasioned his death. If the weapon was really a halberd, and not a pole-axe, this is the earliest mention of it we meet with, in the middle of Europe, though its name had long been known to the nations of the north. Some of the poorest class, at this period, who followed the camps, armed themselves with a kind of strong, heavy quarter-staff, called waroquiau. Thus, in a letter remissory, dated 1474, we read: "Sur icelle charette le suppliant print ung grand baston, appelle waroquiau." "On that car the suppliant took a great staff, called waroquiau."

The javelin we find sometimes to have been called javrelot, at this period. Thus, in a letter, dated 1480, it is said: "Le suppliant embastonné d'un javrelot et garny d'une escrevisse en sa poictrine par dessoubs sa robe, &c." "The suppliant, having for a weapon a javrelot, and having his chest protected by a cuirass of scale-work, called escrevisse, under his robe, &c."

There was also a kind of lance, called by the French janetaire, and by the Spaniards gineta, used at this time by light cavalry, particularly those of Spain. It is spoken of in a letter remissory, dated 1474. "Le suppliant tout en riant print une lance genetaire ou javeline, qu'il trouva en son chemin." "The suppliant, entirely in joke, took a genetaire lance, or javelin which be found in his way." In another, dated 1477, is written: "Le suppliant ensemble Jehan Barrière son cousin, prindrent chacun une arbaleste garnie, et avec ce le dit Barrière son cousin une janetaire." "The suppliant, together with

---

[138] Ch. 9. Same translation as before.
[139] Ibid, note to Ch. 11. Book 7.
[140] To Ch. 4, B. 5.

John Barrière, his cousin, took each a cross-bow, furnished, besides which, the said Barrière, his cousin, had a janetaire." In another, dated 1478, it is called lance genestaire. But in one of the year 1480, the country in which it originated, is pointed out: "Une javeline ou une genetaire, autrement appellee javeline d'Espaigne." "A javelin, or a genetaire, otherwise called a Spanish javelin."

Vials filled with combustibles, were not only attached to arrows, but to lances, or at least, some combustible substances were wrapped round the ends of them, at this period. Thus, in a letter, dated 1472, it is said: "Lesquels archiers allèrent en la ville de Dieppe pour quérir des lances à feu, et autres choses necessaires pour la tuition et deffense de la place d'Arques." "Which archers went into the town of Dieppe, to look for fire-lances, and other things requisite for the safety and defence of the square of Arques." We have seen that the hand-guns, or hand-cannons, were used in the early part of this reign, and towards the close of it, we learn from Philip de Commines, that the harquebuss was invented. This seems to have been an improvement on the hand-gun. The commentary of Francis Carpezani observes: "Ducebat primum aciem ipse cum sexcentis equitibus levis armaturæ, totidemquesclopetariis ac pari numéro arcubu-sariis, nomen certe novum, nee liactenus, quod sciarn latinitafe donatum." "He led the first line himself, with six hundred horse, light armed, and as many with hand-guns, and the same number of arcubusiers, a name certainly new, nor as yet, that I know, given in Latin." The Latin word, however, used for this weapon, was arcusbusus, evidently derived from the Italian, arca-bouza, i. e. a bow with a tube or hole.[141] To that people, therefore, are we to ascribe the application of the stock and trigger in imitation of the cross-bow. Hitherto the match had been applied by the hand to the touch-hole, but the trigger of the arbaleste suggested the idea of one to catch into a cock, which having a slit in it, might hold the match, and by the motion of the trigger, be brought down on a pan which held the priming, the touch-hole being no longer at the top, but at the side.

The first introduction of liand-guns into England, we find, was soon after their invention in Italy. In the year 1471, King Edward landed at Ravenspurg, in Yorkshire, and brought with him, among other forces, three

---

[141] MS. in the Brit. Mus. cited by. Grose; who supposes this to be the first introduction ʻ.of them. I have seen a hangegun, being a simple barrel, furnished ʼwith trunnions, and hung like. a cannon on wood, by which it was held in the hand.

hundred Flemings, armed with "hange-gunnes."[142] Monstrellet, who concluded his Chronicles in the year 1467, speaks of them.

Arquebusiers, or harquebusiers, are mentioned as troops, by Philip de Commines, in these words, where he speaks of the battle of Morat, fought on the 22d of June, 1476.[143] "The said towns had in their army, *as some that were in the battle, have informed me,* 35,000 men, whereof fower thousand were horsemen, the rest footmen, well chosen and well armed, that is to say, 11,000 pikes, 10,000 halberds, and 10,000 harquebusiers."[144] Again, in the next chapter, he says, "Among those that were besieged within the said towne of Nancy, was a worshipful knight, called Monsieur de Beures, of the house of Croy, who had under him certain harquebusiers."

When gunpowder was first discovered to possess a projectile power, its military application was confined to a kind of mortar or bombard, intended as a substitute for the enormous battering machines then usually constructed. None of the countries of Europe having convenient roads, and all many strong castles, engines of war, less bulky and more portable, had long been desirable for invading armies. The commencement of the fifteenth century was, as we have seen, the time of their origin in the field; for, though the more modern author, Vilani, asserts, that they were used at the battle of Cressy, the more accurate Froissart is entirely silent about them.[145] A full century, however, elapsed from the first invention of cannons, before the discovery of hand-guns.

The first bombards were made of bars of iron, strengthened with hoops of the same metal, welded together. They were short pieces, with large bores, and in imitation of the tubes which ejected the Greek fire, were usually made with chambers.

These chambers consisted of the lower half the cylinder, the upper being open for the admission of the can or cannister which held the charge, from whence probably arose the term cannon.[146] One of these may be seen in the tower of London, and there is another lying under an arch at Rhodes.

---

[142] MS. in the Brit. Mus. cited by. Grose; who supposes this to be the first introduction of them. I have seen a hangegun, being a simple barrel, furnished with trunnions, and hung like a cannon on wood, by which it was held in the hand.

[143] Same translation, Ch. 3. B. 5,

[144] This is a great number for the time.

[145] John Barbour, in his Romance of Robert Bruce, calls cannons "Crakys of War."

[146] There is, however, another derivation, viz. their resemblance to a cane, canna. Some of these antient pieces are preserved in the arsenal at Woolwich, and some in the chambers at Alnwick Castle.

The precise purpose for which they were used, was to throw, on the principle of the Balistæ, balls of lead or stone, over the walls, to ruin the roofs of houses, the parapets, and other defences of a town; the ranges describing parabolic curves of little more than three hundred yards radius. There was, as yet, no necessity for the invention of trenches; and the slender protection of the pavisers, was deemed sufficient to shield the gunners against the quarrels, arrows, and stones of the besieged.

In an illuminated copy of the Roman de la Rose, done at the commencement of this reign,[147] is a delineation of an iron cannon. The piece is placed in a kind of trough, or bed of wood, which is continued to the earth, not unlike a modern horse-artillery trail. The whole rests on a pintle, or moveable pivot, fixed in a strong upright, erected on a square timber frame. This apparatus is sufficiently distinct to prove, that the powder used for such artillery must have been very feeble.

In a manuscript, in the Royal Library, in the British Museum,[148] is another cannon, lighter than this, and such as was used towards the latter part of this reign. It is wide near the mouth, but the longer part is of much smaller diameter. It is embedded in a flat piece of timber, the end of which is so shaped as to form a handle. It rests on four legs, when in an horizontal position, which stand on a platform of wood: but, attached to the hinder ones, are two long levers, by which the piece can be lowered or elevated at discretion. Another manuscript of this period, and in the same library,[149] is embellished with several representations of cannons, and machines for war. One of these is a large mortar, raised to a very high elevation, in a frame of wood, and held in its position by being fastened to two upright posts.

There is another piece of ordnance, fixed on the swivel principle, being suspended between the arms of an enormous fork of iron, shaped at top like a pruning-hook or hedger's bill. The cascable is perforated by a large iron bar, in the form of a scythe, standing in a vertical position, and terminating at top in a kind of hook, by means of which it is connected with the after-part of the fork: upon this bar the elevation or depression of the gun is regulated, by means of holes made at certain distances, through which passes a pin, or stopper. The whole apparatus is fixed in a strong iron-plate, fastened down upon a heavy bed of solid oak.

The same manuscript, contains a delineation of a moveable tower, such

---

[147] In the Harl. Lib. in the Brit. Mus. marked 4425.
[148] Marked 16, G. VI.
[149] Marked 14, E. IV.

as used at this period. It is composed of a huge frame of timber, placed on small rollers; open from the first floor downwards, probably for the convenience of moving with greater facility: from the height of what appears to be about ten feet, it is boarded vertically, with the boards perforated at a certain distance, by triangular loopholes, for shooting or casting missiles. The top is embattled with embrasures, each furnished with a lid or shutter; two upright timbers issue out of the centre of the tower, by means of which a large bridge is suspended in the air, with the foremost edge inclined like a roof, to serve the purpose of an immense pavis, or mantlet, and protect the soldiers stationed on the battlements, from the arrows of the besieged. These uprights were constructed so as to be capable of dropping jointly forward, in the two foremost embrasures of the tower, while by some mechanic power, the bridge was at the same time poised in an horizontal direction, and projected upon the ramparts of the besieged. Then the men at arms, who had hitherto stood inactive, protected by the impending surface of the bridge, rushed forward on the enemy's battlements, and carried the town by storm.

Philip de Commines tells us, that "the Lord of Cordes (in the year 1472) had two cannons, which shot twice at the towne gate, and brake downe a peece thereof."[150] In a letter from the Master of the Knights Hospitallers, at Jerusalem, to the Pope, on the siege of Rhodes, by the Turks, in the year 1480, we find "colubrinis et serpentinis deturbant fatigantque." "With culverines and serpentines they disturb and fatigue us." And again: "Colubrinis et serpentinis nostros deturbant." "With culverines and serpentines they disturb us." The word colubrina is derived from coluber, a snake, as the serpentine was from the serpent. This latter was made of copper, as in a deed, dated 1461, mention is made of a serpentine de cuivre.

---

[150] Ch. 10, Book 3, of the same translation.

Edward the Fifth.

1483.

DWARD'S reign was so very short that it cannot be expected to have given any distinctive character to armour. Plate liv, however, may be assigned to it, which represents a man at arms, armed at all points, except his helmet, and holding in his hand a standard. On this is embroidered St. George and the Dragon, with the motto, "Honi soit qui mal y pense," which belonged to the Knights of the Garter. The armour on one arm differs greatly from has a pauldron, turned up so as to form something like a pass-guard; at the elbow too, is a small palette. The pauldron of the right arm is plain, but the elbow-piece is large, and projects to a long point. Over the left cuisse is a tuile, and over the right a tuillette, the upper plate of which is differently cut from the lower one. His gauntlets are with over-lapping plates, instead of fingers; his sollerets pointed, and spurs large. His shield, which is of a singular shape, has its inside turned towards the front, so as to shew that written within is the word

"Anime," and the guige or straps unbuckled.[1]

Underneath is the gauntlet of a Scotch knight, taken from a figure of St. Andrew, in a picture at Windsor Castle, painted about the time of Henry VII.

The armour, represented on the monumental brass plate of Sir Henry Gray, in Ketteringham Church, Norfolk, seems to be of this period. He has a pauldron on his left shoulder, while liis right is protected merely by epaulettes. His tasses are no less than seven in number, on which account he has remarkably small tuilles The lance-rest on his right breast is made to turn up like a hook. His spurs too are very curious, being furnished with a thin piece of steel, placed on the n£ck, which rises over the rowel. This probably bends by pressure, and yet prevents the point of the rowel from penetrating deeply, while, at other times, it keeps it clear of getting entangled.

As the cognizances of the house of Lancaster have been already noticed, it may, perhaps, be equally as curious to insert here those of the house of York. They have been thus collected by Dugdale:[2]

"A stump of a tree, sprouting.[3]

"The sun issuing from the clouds.[4]

"A white hart kneeling, a crown about his neck, and chained gold.[5]

"A peascod branch.[6]

"The faulcon on the fetterlock."[7]

This had been the device of his great grand-father, Edmond of Langley, first Duke of York, fifth son to king Edward III, who, after the king, his father, had endowed him with the Castle of Fotheringhay, which he now

---

[1] Was it not for the pointed toes and tuillettes, there arc many circumstances that would incline me not to give this specimen an earlier date than the time of Henry VIIth.. The figure in the initial letter is from a MS. in the Royal Library, in the British Museum, marked 14, E. V. and has been before noticed; but as the vizored salade worn in the original, has been introduced at the foot of Plate LlI, the simple salade has been made to supply its place.

[2] In his Miscel. lib. xiv. fol. 30.

[3] Adopted by king Edward III.

[4] Edward Black Prince. Speed, however, refers its origin to the battle of Mortimer's Cross, in 1461, "wherein before the battail was strok, appeared visibly in the firmament three sunnes, which, after a while, joined altogether, and became as before; for which cause, (some have thought) Edward afterwards gave the sunne in his full brightness, for his badge and cognizance."

[5] Richard II.

[6] Ditto.

[7] Edward IV, who added to it an equivocal motto, which Mr. Walpole observes "had not even delicacy to excuse the witticism."

PLATE LIV

MAN AT ARMS WITH A STANDARD.

A.D. 1483.

built in form and fashion of a fetter-lock, assumed to himself his father's falcon, and placed it on a fetter-lock, implying thereby, that he was locked up from the hope and possibility of the kingdom. Upon a time, finding his sons beholding this device, set upon a window, asking what was Latin for a fetter-lock, whereupon the father said, "If you cannot tell me, I will tell you: Hie haec hoc taceatis," revealing unto them his meaning, and advising them to be silent and quiet, as God knoweth what may come to pass. This his great-grandchild Edward IV, reported, and bore it, and commanded that his younger son royal, Duke of York, should use the device of a fetter-lock, but opened, as Roger Wall, a herald of that time, reporteth.

To this account of Dugdale we may, in addition, observe, that Shakspeare alludes to the second cognizance in his play of Richard III in the line which recounts the victory of Edward IV over Henry VI.

"Made glorious summer by this tun of York."

There is a MS. entry in the College of Arms setting forth that six gentlemen challenged "all commers at the just roial to be runne in osting harnies[8] alonge a tilte, and to strike thirteen strokes with swordes, in honor of the marriage of Richard Duke of York[9] with the Lady Anne, daughter to the Duke of Norfolk."

The following very curious account of the creation of the Knights of the Bath, contained in a MS. illuminated about this period, is also in the Herald's College. [10]

"1. When an esquire comes to court, to receive the order of knighthood in the time of peace, according to the custom of England, he shall be honourably received by the officers of the court, sc. the steward, or the chamberlain if they be present, but, otherwise, by the marshalls and ushers. Then there shall be provided two esquires of honour, grave and well seen in courtship, and nurture; as also in the feats of chivalrie, and they shall be esquires, and governours in all things relating to him, which shall take the order abovesaid.

"2. And if the esquire do come before dinner, he shall carry up one dish of the first course to the king's table.

"3. And after this the esquire's governours shall conduct the esquire, that is to receive the order into his chamber, without any more being seen

---

[8] Armour worn at justs.

[9] He lost his life with his brother in the tower.

[10] Marked L. 5, fol. 28, a.

that day.

"4. And in the evening the esquire's governours shall send for the barbour, and they shall make ready a bath, handsomely hung with linnen, both within and without the vessell, taking care that it be covered with tapistrie, and blankets in respect of the coldness of the night. And then shall the esquire be shaven, and his hair cut round. After which the esquire's governours shall go to the king and say: Sir, it is now in the evening, and the esquire is fitted for the bath, when you please: whereupon the king shall command his chamberlain, that he shall take along with him, unto the esquire's chamber, the most gentile and grave knights that are present, to inform, counsell, and instruct him touching the order, and feats of chivalrie: and in like manner, that the other esquires of the household, with the minstrells, shall proceed before the knights, singing, dancing and sporting, even to the chamber dore of the said esquire.

"5. And when the esquire's governours shall hear the noise of the minstrells, they shall undress the said esquire, and put him naked into the bath: but, at the entrance into the chamber, the esquire's governours, shall cause the musick to cease, and the esquires also for a while. And this being done, the grave knights shall enter into the chamber without making any noise, and doing reverence to each other, shall consider which of themselves it shall be that is to instruct the esquire in the order and course of the bath. And when they are agreed, then shall the chief of them go to the bath and, kneeling down before it, say with a soft voice: Sir, be this bath of great honour to you; and then he shall declare unto him the feats of the order, as far as he can, putting part of the water of the bath upon the shoulder of the esquire; and, having so done, take his leave. And the esquire's governours shall attend at the sides of the bath, and so likewise the other knights; the one after the other till all be done.

"6. Then shall these knights go out of the chamber for a while; and the esquire's governours shall take the esquire out of the bath, and help him to his bed, there to continue till his body be dry; which bed shall be plain, and without curtains. And as soon as he is dry, they shall help him out of bed; they shall cloath him very warm, in respect of the cold of the night; and over his inner garments shall put on a robe of russet with long sleives, having a hood thereto like unto that of an hermite. And the esquire being out of the bath, the harbour shall take away the bath with whatsoever appertained thereto, both within and without for his fee; and likewise for the coller (about his neck) be he earl, baron, baneret or batchelor, according to the custom of the court.

"7. And then shall the esquire's governours open the dore of the chamber, and shall cause the antient and grave knights to enter to conduct the esquire to the chapell. And when they are come in, the esquires sporting, and dancing shall go before the esquire, with the minstrells, making melodie to the chapell.

"8. And being entered the chapell, there shall be wine, and spices ready to give to the knights and esquires. And then the esquire's govenours shall bring the said knights before the esquire to take their leave of him; and he shall give them thanks, all together for the pains, favour and courtesie which they have done him: and this being performed they shall depart out of the chapell.

"9. Then shall the esquire's governours shut the dore of the chapell, none staying therein except themselves, the priest, the chandler and the watch. And in this manner shall the esquire stay in the chapell all night, till it be day, bestowing himself in orisons and prayers, beseeching almighty God, and his blessed Mother, that of their good grace they will give him abilitie to receive this high temporall dignitie, to the honour, praise, and service of them, as also of holy church, and the order of knighthood. And at day-break, one shall call the priest to confess him of all his sins, and having heard mattins and mass, shall afterwards be commended if he please.

"10. And after his entrance into the chapell, there shall be a taper burning before him; and so soon as mass is begun one of the governours shall hold the taper untill the reading of the gospell; and then shall the governour deliver it into his hands, who shall hold it, himself, till the gospell be ended; but then shall receive it again from him, and set it before him, there to stand during the whole time of mass.

"11. And at the elevation of the host, one of the governours shall take the hood from the esquire, and afterwards deliver it to him again, untill the gospell In principio. And, at the beginning thereof, the governour shall take the same hood again, and cause it to be carried away, and shall give him the taper again, into his own hands.

"12. And then having a penny or more in readiness, near to the candlestick, at the words Verbum caro factum est, the esquire, kneeling, shall offer the taper and the penie; that is to say, the taper to the honour of God, and the peny to the honour of the person that makes him a knight. All which being performed, the esquire's governours shall conduct the esquire to his chamber, and shall lay him again in bed, till it be full day-light. And when he shall be thus in bed, till the time of his rising, he shall be cloathed with a covering of gold, called singleton, and this shall be lined with blue cardene. And when the governours shall see it fit time, they shall go to the king and say to him: Sir, when doth it please you that our master shall rise? Where-upon the king shall command the grave knights, esquires and minstrells to go to the chamber of the said esquire for to raise him, and to attire and dress him, and to bring him before him into the hall. But before their entrance, and the noise of the minstrells heard, the esquire's governours shall provide all necessaries ready for the order, to deliver to the knights for to attire and dress the esquire.

"And when the knights are come to the esquire's chamber, they shall enter with leave and say to him: Sir, good morrow to you, it is time to get up and make yourself ready; and thereupon they shall take him by the arme, to be dressed, the most antient of the said knights reaching him his shirt; another giving him his breeches, the third his doublet, and another putting upon him a kirtle of red tartarin: two others shall raise him from the bed, and two others put on his nether stockings with soles of leather sowed to them. Two others shall lace his sleives, and another shall gird him with a girdle of white leather without any buckles thereon: another shall combe his head, another shall put. on his coife: another shall give him his mantle of silk (over the bases or kirtle of red tartarin) tyed with a lace of white silk, with a pair of white gloves hanging at the end of the lace. And the chandler shall take for his fees all the garments with the whole array and necessaries werewith the esquire shall be apparelled and clothed on the day that he comes into the court to receive the order: as also the bed wherein he first lay, after his bathing, together with the singleton and other necessaries. In consideration of which fees, the same chandler shall find at his proper costs, the said coife, the gloves, the girdle and the lace.

"13. And when all this is done, the grave knights shall get on horsback and conduct the esquire to the hall, the minstrells going before, making musick: but the horse must be accoutred as followetli: the saddle having a cover of black leather, the bow of the saddle being of white wood quartered. The stirrup leathers black; the stirrups gilt; the poitrell of black leather gilt, with a cross paté gilt, hanging before the breast of the horse but without any crooper: the bridle black with long notched raines, after the Spanish fash-ion, and a cross paté on the front. And there must be provided a young es-quire, courteous, who shall ride before the esquire, bare-headed, and carry the esquire's sword with the spurs hanging at the handle of the sword: and the scabbard of the sword shall be of white leather and the girdle of white leather without buckles. And the youth shall hold the sword by the point, and after this manner must they ride to the king's hall, the governours being ready at hand.

"14. And the grave knights shall conduct the said esquire, and so soon as they come before the hall dorè, the marshall and huisliers are to be ready to meet him, and desire him to alight: and being alighted, the marshall shall take the horse for his fee, or else C. s. Then shall the knights conduct him into the hall up to the high table; and afterwards up to the end of the second table, untili the king's coming, the knights standing on each side of him, and the youth holding the sword upright before him between the two governours.

"15. And when the king is come into the hall, and beholdeth the esquire ready to receive this high order, and temporall dignitie, he shall aske for the sword and spurs, which the chamberlain shall take from the youth, and shew to the king: and thereupon the king, taking the right spur, shall deliver it to the most noble and gentile person there; and shall say to him: Put this upon the esquire's heel; and he, kneeling on one knee, must take the esquire by the right leg, and putting his foot on his own knee, is to fasten the spur upon the right heel of the esquire; and then, making a cross upon the esquire's knee, shall kiss him; which being done, another knight must come, and put on his left spur in like manner. And then shall the king, of his great favour, take the sword, and gird the esquire therewith: whereupon the esquire is to lift up his armes, holding his hands together, and the gloves betwixt his thumbs and fingers.

"16. And the king, putting his own armes about the esquire's neck, say: Be thou a good knight, and afterwards kiss him. Then are the antient knights to conduct this new knight to the chapell, with much musick, even to the high altar; and there he shall kneel, and putting his right hand upon the altar, is to promise to maintain the rights of holy church, during his whole life.

"17. And then he shall ungirt himself of his sword, and with great devotion to God and holy church, offer it there; praying unto God, and all his saints, that he may keep that order which he hath so taken, even to the end: all which being accomplished, he is to take a draught of wine.

"18. And at his going out of the chapell, the king's master-cook, being ready to take off his spurs, for his own fee, shall say, I, the king's master-cook, am come to receive your spurs, for my fee; and, if you do any thing contrary to the order of knighthood, (which God forbid) I shall hack your spurs from your heels."

"19. After this the knights must conduct him again into the hall, where he shall sit the first at the knight's table, and the knights about him; himself to be served as the others are: but he must neither eat, nor drink at the table, nor spit, nor look about him, upwards or downwards, more than a bride. And this being done, one of his governours, having a handkerchief in his hand, shall hold it before his face, when he is to spit. And, when the king is risen from his table, and gone into his chamber, then shall the new knight be conducted with great store of knights, and minstrells proceeding before him, unto his own chamber, and at his entrance, the knights and minstrells shall take leave of him, and go to dinner.

"20. And the knights being thus gone, the chamber dore shall be fastened, and the new knight disrobed of his attire, which is to be given to the kings of armes, in case they be there present, and, if not, then to the other lieraulds, if they be there; otherwise to the minstrells, together with a mark of silver, if he be a knight batchelor; if a baron, double to that; if an earl, or of a superior rank, double thereto. , And the russet night-cap must be given to the watch, or else a noble.

"21. Then he is to be cloathed again with a blew robe, the sleives whereof to be streight, shaped after the fashion of a priest's; and, upon his left shoulder, to have a lace of white silk, hanging: and he shall wear that lace upon all his garments, from that day forwards, untill he have gained some honour and renown by arms, and is registred of as high record, as the nobles, knights, esquires, and lieraulds of arms; and be renowned for some feats of arms, as aforesaid, or that some great prince, or most noble ladie, can cut that lace from his shoulder, saying: 'Sir, we have heard so much of the true renown, concerning your honour, which you have done in divers parts, to the great fame of chivalrie, as to yourself, and of him that made you a knight, that it is meet this lace be taken from you.'

"22. After dinner the knights of honour, and gentlemen, must come to the knight, and conduct him into the presence of the king, the esquire's governours going before him, where he is to say: " Right noble and renowned sir, I do, in all I can, give you thanks for these honours, curtesies, and bountie, which you have vouchsafed to me and having so said, shall take his leave of the king.

"23. Then are the esquire's governours to take leave of their master, saying: "Sir, we have, according to the king's command, and as we were obliged, done what we can; but, if through negligence, we have in ought displeased you, or by any thing we have done amiss at this time, we desire pardon of you for it. And, on the other side: Sir, as right is, according to the customs of the court, and antient kingdoms, we do require our robes and fees, as the king's esquires, companions to batchelors, and other lords."

Richard the Third.

1483.

O higher degree of perfection was ever attained in armour than during this reign. The outline of the suit was most elegant, the workmanship most elaborate, and the choice of ornament full of taste.

The monumental effigies in brass of this period fully prove this assertion, and one of them has therefore been selected for Plate lv. It represents Sir Thomas Peyton anned with all pieces except his helmet, on which ac count a salade has been inserted at the bottom of the Plate taken from the works of Albert Durer. It will be perceived that this does not protect the face, but when worn, the lower part was supplied by the hausse-col or gorget which was so formed on purpose. That it may be thoroughly comprehended, that has also been added. The breast of this armour is globular, and furnished with a demi-placard. The pauld ons are beautifully ribbed, and on the right one is placed the moton, which answers the purpose of a palette. But the ornaments at the elbow-pieces are superb beyond comparison. The gauntlets have overlapping plates instead of fingers, and two fine tuilles hang pendant from the lowest tace. The sword belt is so disposed that the ponderous sword may keep in front while a dagger is attached to the right hip.

My son has a fine inlaid suit of the close of this reign which was brought from Modena, but, though the elbow pieces are foliated they are by no means so fine and large as in this brass plate. The inner part however is curiously formed by the upper vambrace being made to turn up at the bend of the arm so as to close the aperture on raising it in the manner of Plate lix. This suit however is for justing solely, and therefore it has armour merely for the outsides of the thighs and legs, being without sollerets. But its greatest curiosity is its very large elbow shield, which is square or rather oblong, and made to screw on the elbow piece in the same manner as the other in my son's collection engraved for this work.[1] This shoulder shield or gardebras was called by the Italians bracciaiuola. The ancient statutes of Florence thus speak of it: Possit portare quselibet anna defendibilia, et etiam bracciaiuolam. "He may bear any defensive arms, and even a bracciaiuola."

A statute passed in the first year of this reign, ch. 11. complains that owing to the seditious confederacy of Lombards using divers ports of this realm, the bowstaves were raised to an *outrageous* price, that is to say, to eight pounds an hundred, where they were wont to be sold at forty shillings. This act therefore provides that ten bowstaves shall be imported with every butt of Malmsey or Tyre wines, brought by the merchants trading from Venice into this land, under a penalty of thirteen shillings and four pence, for every butt of the said wines in case of neglect.

The seal of Richard III exhibits that monarch on a horse caparisoned with the arms of France and England, but wearing himself a plain surcoat with wide sleeves. In the initial letter has been inserted another representation of him from a genealogical table of the Beauchamp family by John Rous in the Cottonian Library[2] which seems to shew that he sometimes wore a tabard of his arms with flat sleeves like those used by the heralds.

This king wore his crown on his head at the battle of Bosworth, and, chancing to espy Henry Earl of Richmond, spurred his horse forward exclaiming: "Treason, treason, treason."

He slew, with his own hand, Sir William Brandon, the bearer of the hostile standard, struck to the ground Sir John Cheney, and made a desperate blow at his rival, when he was overpowered by numbers, thrown from his horse and slain. Lord Stanley, taking up the crown, placed it on the head of Richmond, and he was instantly greeted with the shouts of "Long live King Henry."[3]

---

[1] Plate LIII.
[2] Marked Julius E. IV.
[3] Ross, 218.

PLATE LV

SᴿTHOMAS PEYTON,

A.D. 1484.

𝕳enry the 𝕾eventh.

1485.

AVING arrived at that reign with which most large armouries begin, materials for the remainder of this work, are in ample abundance, yet other authorities must not be disregarded. In the City Library, at Mons,[1] is preserved a sheet of vellum, on which is painted a knight on horseback, in the costume of the commencement of this reign. The helmet is of the large tilting kind, as in Plate lix, one of which, of immense weight, is in the possession of my friend, John Murray, Esq.[2] commissary general. It is put over the head, without being opened, and rests on the shoulders. Attached, by a hinge, to the lower part behind, is a cylinder of steel, in the inner side of which is a hook, that fastens into a hole in the back plate, and at the ears are three rows of rollers, intended, no doubt, to turn off the point of the lance, while the appertures give air to the wearer. In the delineation, the knight wears on his helmet, instead of the cointise, a scroll which, though not yet the earliest specimen, had not become frequent. Heralds consider this as

[1] It was formerly in the Cathedral at Tournay, and since in the possession of Josephine Empress of France.
[2] Of Ardleybury, Herts.

representing the cointisse, or kerchief of Plesaunce, in a torn state, after an encounter, so that such representation soon superseded, generally, the simple ornaments to his genouillieres, with pointed sollerets. The caparison of his horse is covered with music, the notes of which are made of fleurs de lis, on five lines, and he has a handsome chanfron on his head. In front of him is a lady, who holds the horse by the bridle, notwithstanding he is in the attitude of galloping, and points to a chaplet, made *de lettres et de fleurs*, as it is expressed, which is said to have wonderful powers. This chaplet seems to be an enigma, which the song, written partly on the horse, and partly by the side of it, tends to illustrate.

The monumental brass of Edmund Clerc, Esq. in Slokesby Church, Norfolk, who died in 1488, is the next specimen. The helmet, or visored salade,[3] is like that under Plate LV, as is also the gorget. Instead of tuilles there is an indented border of chain-mail, attached to the lowest tace, and on the breast-plate are two placards. The elbow-pieces are large, and the gauntlets with over-lapping plates, cut into a pointed form. The cuisses, genouilliers, and jambs, are much ornamented, and the sollerets consist of over-lapping plates, laid on a sock of chain mail, so as to have a somewhat pointed form. The sword is worn at the left side. The German knights, engraved by Albert Durer, one of whose visored salades is introduced under Plate LV, are habited nearly in this manner, but their sollerets much more pointed at the toe. Their shields are oblong, but terminated at the bottom with a spike.

A foreign illumination shews, that the men at arms sometimes carried a semicircular concave shield, but with a very large boss, in what, if the shield had been round, would have formed the centre. That they wore their elbow-pieces terminating in sharp points, and had to their salades, when worn without the hausse-col, cheek-pieces, formed of several successive plates, with hinges. Their horses had a long feather placed between their ears, and the stirrups had tassels appended to them.

The great change, however, in armour, during this reign, was in the shape of the solleret, which became square at the toe. Previous to this, indeed, they were made perfectly round, as may be seen in the monumental effigy of John De la Pole, Duke of Suffolk, in Wingfield Church, in that county. His elbow-plates are fastened with little ornaments, in the form of an S. He wears four large tuilles, under which is the apron of chain-mail. His sword is at his left hip, and his dagger at the right. The hilt of the for-

---

[3] Ohe of these with moveable visor, and another without, pierced for the sight, are in my son's collection.

mer is green, and elegantly covered with cross-cords of red, fastened by gilt rosettes. The letters J. H. S. are on the top locket of the scabbard, which is tipped at the bottom with an elegant chape. The pommel of the sword is like an inverted pear, but Jhat of the dagger wide in the centre, and eight sided. In this monumental figure may plainly be seen, the hinges on the left side, by which the culettes are attached to the tassets, and, on the right side, the straps and buckles, which fasten them.

Next to this, is the fine and singular suit of armour which, undoubt-edly, belonged to King Henry the Seventh, still preserved in the Tower of London, the greatest curiosity in that collection, as being unique in it, and prior to any in date; it has, therefore, been chosen for Plate LVI.[4] That part which covers the body has a very cylindrical appearance, notwithstanding the convexity of the breast-plate, but is engraved all over, together with the large puckered plates of steel, which cover each thigh to the knee, and con-tinue behind, except where hollowed out for the saddle. These plates are its curiosity, being in imitation of cloth, and called lamboys.[5] The toes of his soliereis too, are almost square, and a little slit is made in the heel to ad-mit of the spur, a mode that continued throughout the next reign. On his casquetel[6] I have placed a plume of feathers, worn in the manner peculiar to this period, and in his hand a sword, copied from one in my son's collec-tion, ridged down the centre, and having the figures of four saints engraved on it, by Albert Durer, in the most exquisite stile. Behind has also been attached, the dagger; all authorized by cotemporary delineations. On the horse's head is the chanfron, on his neck the manefaire, and on his chest the poitral, all as in the Tower. Behind is the croupiere, from another specimen in the Tower, ornamented and completed from one in Montfaucon's Mon. Franç PI. CXCVI. This consists not only of the covering plate for the back, but three hanging pieces on each flank, and one under the tail.[7] A complete one may be seen at Warwick Castle. By the side of him is a billman, in a

---

[4] It is believed that this representation is pretty accurate, ,but tbe disposition at the-Tower, to prevent the use of the pencil, bas obliged the sketch to be made, as it were by stealth,

[5] Tbere is at Vienna a suit which belonged to the Emperor Maximilian I on a similar principle, with pieces to put before and behind, to .cover the openings for the saddle, when used on foot,

[6] One of these, in my son's collection, has been introduced at the foot of PI. L. On further inspection at the Tower, 1 find Henry's to be a helmet.

[7] See PI. xxv of Grose's Treatise, copied from the Tower, where the plate under the tail is wanting.

jazerine jacket of this period,[8] in my son's collection, the front of which is crimson velvet, ornamented with brass studs, The salade and bill are from specimens in the same armoury. The rest of the costume of the figure is taken from Plate CXCV, in Montfaucon, copied from an illumination, in a poem composed by Jean des Marets, and dedicated to Anne of Bretagne, the wife of Louis XII, King of France. It represents great varieties of jazerine jackets,[9] and other armour, salades, helmets, caps, bows, bills, and other weapons, targets, and cannon.

Among others, are two figures with cloaks on, and specimens occur of wearing them with armour, from the time of Edward the Second, to that of Charles the First; a circumstance which I here notice, as it is generally supposed, that cloaks with armour are incongruous. This plate represents Castellas taken by the armed Genoese. The next plate is also from the same work, and represents Louis the Twelfth, on horseback, in armour, much resembling that already described as belonging to Henry the Seventh. His breast-plate and lamboys of steel, have on them the bee-hive and bees, as that of Henry the Seventh has the figure of St. George, &c. His poitrail and croupiere are ornamented in like manner, as is the flanchard or plate under his legs.

But all these pieces, as well as the lamboys, are edged with a broad border, on which are these words: "Non utitur aculeo rex." "The king does not make use of the point of a needle." The raised plate, which goes along the crupper, and forms an arch over the tail, though usual, deserves notice, and has been introduced in that on the horse of Henry the Seventh.[10] The helmet of the king is the casquetel, having no covering for the face, but merely an umbril, and this engraving shews a variety of ways of wearing the plume of feathers. The next print, however, which represents the French taking the forts from the Genoese, is the one from which the hind-plate of the croupiere, or buttock-piece has been taken. It exhibits, also, a good specimen of the steel lamboys, and the back part of the helmets, which is very curious. From

---

[8] Or rather earlier, the skirt being longer in the reign of this monarch. Two of Henry the Seventh's time are preserved at Warwick Castle.

[9] The inside of the jazarine jacket may be seen in Grose's' Treatise on Antient Armour, Pl. XXX, Fig".3.

[10] PI. LVI. Since this engraving has been made, by the order of his Grace the Duke ,of Wellington, I have been admitted to a closer inspection of the armour in the Tower, and have discovered in different parts of the room, the whole of the horse-armour belonging to Henry the Seventh, which has the royal motto "Dieu et mon Droit,". running round Its borders, as in the print of Louis the Twelfth, with the portcullis and sheaf of arrows, the badges of this king.

PLATE LVI

HENRY VII.ᵗᴴ KING   OF ENGLAND,
AND   A   BILLMAN.

A.D. 1490.

this it seems, that the vizor and bever are attached to a piece which goes round the back of the head, without covering the crown. To supply which, a skull-cap is used, that has a large button behind, made to slip into a cleft, formed in the piece that goes at the back of the head. This is the armet, and being so singular in its form, it has been introduced at the bottom of Plate lvi. One of this kind, formerly in the charnel-house of Fulham Church, is in my son's collection, but without the button, having the liind-plate rounded on each side, instead of being angular. One of a later date, with the button, may be seen, hanging up in the Percy Chapel of Beverley Minster.

The lances, in this engraving, are also worthy of notice, proving, among many other instances, that the vamplate, or roundel, were not often used in battle; and that the blade of the lance was very small. An original of this kind, the only one in England, is in the armoury of Llewelyn Meyrick, Esq. painted white, with numbers of red spread eagles on it; the gripe is covered with crimson velvet.

The next plate exhibits Louis the Twelfth, with a sword in his hand, exactly like that which I have given to Henry the Seventh, and with a demi-chanfron on his horse's head, which has a serrated ridge down its front. The next engraving exhibits him with his arming sword at his side, and the estoc, or shorter stabbing sword, at the bow of his saddle. This last is worn on the left side, and, therefore, we may conjecture, that the mace is appended at the other. The attendants of the king carry halberds, the edge of the blades being slantwise, of which kind there are several in my son's collection. All these engravings of Montfaucon are very well worth studying, by any one anxious to comprehend, accurately, the armour of this period. There is another[11] from the same, illuminated, that is also curious. It represents Louis the Twelfth writing a dispatch, with his officers in waiting. On a table, near him, is placed his cuirass, with the tuilles hanging over the edge; behind, the jambs and euisses, and on the side, the helmet, with its plume, consisting of two successive circles of short feathers, and the two swords before noticed.

A manuscript, containing all the sovereigns of the house of Bavaria, until the end of the fifteenth century, has an illumination, purporting to be Charlemagne, where the armour ends at the anckles, so as to be worn with footed stirrups.[12] Montfaucon, in Plate CCXX, of his Mon. Franç has engraved the figure of Michel de Chaugy, of the time of Louis the Eleventh,

---

[11] Plate cc..

[12] See an engraving of it in Baunier's Costumes Françaises.

and his armour, not only ends at the ankle, but the jambs have, as it were, a piece cut out of them, up the middle of the leg, which seems the first step towards wearing the demi-jambs, that covered the outside of the legs only.

A splendid suit of tilting armour of the time of Henry the Eighth, upon this principle, is in my. son's collection, into the tasteful borders of which have been repeatedly introduced the pomegranate.

Louis the Twelfth, King of France, was the first who took into his service the troops called stradiots, or estradiots. These were Greeks who followed the profession of soldiers, and who, under their leader, offered their services alike to the Turks or Christians. Hence they call themselves Στρατιότης, or soldiers, a word abbreviated to stradiots.

They were first known to the French during the wars in Italy, under Charles the Eighth, and are thus mentioned by Philippe de Commines, in his account of the battle of Fornoue.[13] "Hitherto the war had not commenced on our side, but the Marshal De Gie asked the king how he had passed these mountains, and how he had sent forty horses to reconnoitre the enemy's army, who were cut off by the estradiots, that killed a gentleman named Le Bœuf, and, having struck off his head, hung it to the banderole of a lance, and in that manner presented it to the President, to have for it a ducat? The estradiots are troops, like the Janizaries,[14] equipped as horse and foot, like the Turks, with the exception of their heads, not wearing that fabric twisted round them, called a turban. They are a hardy race, and sleep out of doors, as well as their horses, all the year round. They were all Greeks brought from such places as were in possession of the Venetians; some from Naples, and from Romania, on the Morea, others from Albania, towards Durachium,[15] and their horses all good, and of the Turkish breed. The Venetians make great use of them, and place in them great confidence. I have seen them go down to Venice, and be mustered in an isle, in which stands the Abbey of Saint Nicholas, when they amounted to full 1,500. They are brave men, and are indefatigable in an army, when joined to it.

" The estradiots, as I said, made a sortie as far as the quarters of the said Marshal, where were lodged the Germans, and killed three or four of them, carrying oif their heads, for such was their custom. For, when the Venetians

---

[13] Liv.8, c.5.

[14] Genetaires. The Janizaries were originally Greek youths, called Yenghid Zari, in the Turkish language; but the Génetaires were Spanish light cavalry, probably eopied from' tbe Moors; and to these, rather than the Janizaries, does Commines refer. However, I have followed Père Daniel.

[15] Duras.

were at war with the Turc, who was father to the present, named Mahu-met-Ottoinan, he did not choose that his troops should take any prisoners, and therefore assigned them a ducat for every head, which occasioned a retaliation on the part of the Venetians. They, indeed, conceived that, by so doing, they should effectually terrify these estradiots, but they were more frightened at the artillery; for a ball, fired from a faulcon, killing one of their horses, made them instantly retire, not being accustomed to face cannon."[16]

Marshal de Fleurange, in his Memoirs, tells us, that in the army of Louis the Twelfth, when he went to chastise the revolte of the inhabitants of Ge-noa,[17] there were two thousand of these stradiots, commanded by Captain Mercure. They were generally called, in France, Albanian Cavalry.

Their armour, according to M. De Montgommeri-Courbousson, seems to have consisted of a cuirass with sleeves and gloves of mail, over which was put a jacket without sleeves, and on tlieir heads an open salade. They wore a large sabre, one of which is in the armoury of Llewelyn Meyrick, Esq. It resembles, in its blade and hilt, a Turkish sabre, but has a cross-bar, which, together with the chape and lockets of the scabbard, is ornamented with devices from the Greek mythology. As these are embossed, however, it is probably of a later date, and worn during the reign of the French King, Henry the Third, the Albanian cavalry being, even then, continued in the service of France.[18] Besides this, the stradiots carried at their saddle-bows, a mace, and used the zagaye, or arzegaye, which was a lance twelve feet long, and in the antient Greek stile, pointed with iron, at both ends. With this weapon, according to the book attributed to M. Langey, they could sometimes dismount and act as pikemen against cavalry, and one of their principal exercises was to practise the use of it with both hands, sometimes giving one point, and sometimes the other. They were of the utmost use in skirmishes and desultory warfare, and were not rallied by the sound of a trumpet, but by the display of a large banderole, on the end of a lance.[19]

In the year 1485, Henry the Seventh raised the Yeomen of the Guard,

---

[16] It is astonishing that the Greeks retain the same feelings at -this day. -Tbe regiment raised by England, and officered by Englishmen, being sent to take the fort of Santa Mau-ra, as soon as the battery opened, all the privates fell on their faces, alledging, that they were afraid to proceed, although bravé enough on other occasions, and leaving their officers standing, so that two companies of British troops were obliged to be sent to perform that service,

[17] De Gênes.

[18] Brantosme, in his Eloge de .M. de Fontrailles.

[19] De Montgommeri-Courbousson, p. 133.

which may be considered as the first formation of a regular standing military force in England. Rapin, however, who calls them archers, says they were instituted on the day of his coronation, w'liich was the 30th of October, and that they then consisted of fifty men, to attend him and his successors for ever; a precaution which he, probably, thought necessary, at that juncture.

By the first regulation, every yeoman of this band was to be of the best quality, under gentry, well-made, and full six feet high. Their numbers have varied, under almost every reign, and originally consisted of a certain number in ordinary, and an indefinite number extraordinary; and, in case of a vacancy in the former, it was supplied out of the latter number.[20] One half of them formerly carried bows and arrows, the other half harquebuses, and all had large swords by their sides. The harquebuses were disused in the time of William the Third,[21] and the partuisans which they now carry, then first introduced. A part, however, were armed with halberds, in the time of Henry the Eighth, when they acquired their present form and cloathing.[22]

Philip de Commines tells us, that the Venetian men at arms were well accompanied with cross-bowmen on horseback, estradiots, and footmen, at the battle of Fournoue; and he also speaks of the Scotch archers and French valets, at the same battle, having long swords. The Venetians, in this instance, imitated the French, and departed from the usual practice of Italy, which did not allow any archers to the men at arms.[23]

The archers, in the illuminations of this period, are clad in a shirt of chain mail, with short wide sleeves, such as that worn by the cross-bowmen in the time of Henry VI, and over this, a small vest of red cloth, laced in front, with pantaloons or tight hose on their legs, and bracers on their left arms.

The conduct of the English archers, under the Lords Daubeney and Morley, at the battle of Dixmude, in 1489, is worthy of remark. They attacked the French camp, though defended by a strong battery, poured a volley of arrows into the trenches, fell on the ground till the guns had been discharged, rose on their feet, poured in a second volley, and rushed precipitately into the camp. Such was the resolution of these troops, that John Person, of Coventry, having lost his leg, by a cannon shot, continued to

---

[20] Miege's New State of England, A. D. 1703.
[21] Chamberlain's Present State, A. D. 1735.
[22] Burnet's History of the Reformation.
[23] Mémoires, LIV. VIII, c. 5, and 15. See also LIV. VII, c.5.

discharge his arrows, kneeling or sitting, "and, when the Frenchmen fledde, he cried to one of his felowes, and saide, have thou these six arrowes that I have lefte, and folowe thou the chase, for I may not."[24]

The cross-bows used in this reign consisted of two kinds, the latch, with its wide and thick bender, for quarrels, and the prodd, for bullets. The stock of the the former was short and straight, not much exceeding two feet, and the bow was bent by a moulinet, or windlass as it was called by the English, which consisted of a bar of iron, shaped at its end into a claw, and having teeth the whole length of one edge. This slipped through an iron box, in which was a wheel, the coggs of which fitted the teeth of the bar; and, as a handle was affixed to the axle, on turning it the string was wound up. This apparatus was attached by a loop, which slipped over the stock, and was kept in its place by two iron pins, which projected from the side, and then, when bent, it could be easily removed. One of these, with its stock of horn, and rudely inlaid, in length one foot one inch and a half, is in the armoury of Llewelyn Meyrick, Esq.

An illumination, in a manuscript of this period, in the British Museum,[25] shews us the mode of using this cross-bow, and exhibits a school for its practice, with the butts or dead marks as they were called, so frequently alluded to by the authors of this period. Henry VII, however, towards the close of his reign, by statute,[26] forbad the use of the cross-bow.

The prodd was used at this time, however, by the Genoese, and this was lighter, far more elegant, and expeditious. Of this kind is that beautiful stock of yew which was dug up at Bosworth Field, and which has passed from the Museum of Mr. Green, of Litchfield, to the armoury of Mr. Gwennap, in Pall Mall. It is curiously carved, and three feet three inches in length, and though the bow is wanting, the lever and perpendiculars for the sight ball still remain.[27] But, in the collection of Llewn. Meyrick, Esq. are two far more elaborately carved, and perfect; one, indeed, is quite splendid, and has several rare Greek and Roman medals inlaid in its stock.[28] It is, in length,

---

[24] LeI. Collectanea, iv. 247.

[25] Royal Library. marked 19, c. viii. dated 1496.

[26] Statute 19, Hen. VII, o, 4, AD. 1508. There is, however, a reservation in favor or'the nobility: "No man shall shoot with a cross-bow, without the king's licence, except he be a lord, or have two hundred marks of land."

[27] There is an engraving of it in the Gentleman's Magazine for February, 1784, where it is, fully described.

[28] See it represented, PI. XLIV, Fig. 2, where will be found a variety of quarrels of this period in the same collection.

three feet eight inches, and at the distance of two feet five, takes a curve, equal in cord, to the space required to string the bow. This is of great service when shouldered for the purpose of marching, as well as to prevent any interruption to the projectile force of the bullet by friction.

At the commencement of this curve is placed a small lever, being four inches in length, which forms a hook at one end, and turns on a moveable axis: this hook is to lay hold of the string, which, when the lever is pushed down, is held so by means of the trigger, this being furnished with a hook, to catch into a hole in the lever. This hole is prettily made to represent the open mouth of a face, and the hook the tongue in it. Over the lever is placed the sight, in imitation of a triumphal arch, at the top of which is a little crescent, to look through. This is made to lift up and down, turning upon two nails, driven into the stock. When this plate is raised, it answers to a globule, no bigger than the head of a chaplet, which is suspended at the end, just beyond the bow, by a fine wire, and fastened to two small perpendicular columns of steel, most tastefully inlaid with gold, one on the right, the other on the left. By bringing the globule and the sight in the same line as the objet, the aim is rendered certain. The bow is only five-eighths of an inch deep, and six-and-twenty inches long, but it has great elasticity. Different from those of the latches, its cord is double, each parallel set of strings being separated from the other by two little cylinders of wood,[29] equi-distant from the extremities and centre. To these two cords, in the middle, is fixed a ring of cord, whipped round with string, which serves to coniine it in the hook of the lever, when the bow is bent, and immediately before this, a little square of string, in which is placed the bullet. The whole of the stock is most exquisitely chiseled with representations of helmets, shields, grotesque heads, and foliage; and on the top is a most elaborately carved winged dragon, the whole being in the finest taste. The bow is kept in its place by two entwined serpents; the two pillars have dolphins twisted round their shafts, and trophies on the four sides of their pedestals, and these are fixed on a plate, inlaid with gold: the trigger is similarly formed and ornamented. In short, all the steel-work is superbly inlaid with gold, and the stock has, at the bow-end, a ram's head gilt, and at the other a carved top of ebony.

The object of Henry VII, in discouraging the use of the cross-bow, was to induce the more frequent practice of archery. In his youth he had been partial to this exercise, and, therefore, it is said of him, in an old poem, writ-

---

[29] These may have been, originally, of iron, for such are described by Father Daniel, ,in his Milice Françoise.

ten in praise of the Princess Elizabeth, afterwards his queen:[30]

> " See where, lie shoteth at the butts
> And with hym are Iordes three,
> He weareth a gowne of velvette blacke,
> And it is coted[31] above the knee."

He also amused himself with the bow, after he had obtained the crown, as we find the following memoranda, in an account of his expenditure:[32] "Lost to my Lord Morging, at the buttes, six shillings and eightpence," and "paid to Sir Edward Boroughe, thirteen shillings and fourpence, which the kynge lost at buttes with his cross-bowe."

Both his sons followed his example, especially the eldest, Prince Arthur, who used frequently to visit the society of London Bowmen, at Mile-End, where they usually met, and practised with them. From his expertness in handling the bow, every good shooter was called by his name. The captain also, of the fraternity, was honoured with the title of Prince Arthur, and the other archers were stiled his knights.

The Italian armour, at this period, was made very strong and heavy, hence, P. de Commines, speaking of the battle of Fournoue, in the year 1495, says,[33] "We had a number of followers, consisting of valets and servitors, who all came round these Italian men at arms, and killed the most part. Almost all these valets had hatchets to cut wood, with which they broke the vizors of their armets, and gave them great blows on the head, for it was very difficult to kill them, so strongly were they armed, and no one was seen to be killed unless he had about him three or four men." The armet was probably that helmet which is given under Plate LVI, and so called from being armed with additional pieces.

The same author also describes the Venetian men at arms, as being, not only in complete armour, but with their armets furnished with brave plumes of feathers, and as using hollow lances called bourdonasses, handsomely painted. He observes, however, that these horsemen's lances were not worth much, on account of their being hollow, and hardly so weighty as a javelin. At a much later period, they were used for running at the ring, and several of them are still to be seen in the Tower, one of which has been falsely called the lance of Charles Brandon, Duke of Suffolk. An apparatus,

---

[30] Harl. Lib. 365, fol 96.
[31] Marked.
[32] An. 7 et 9, MS. in the Remembrancer's Office.
[33] Liv, viii, c. 6.

with lance-rest, for running at the ring, made to fix into a belt, may be seen at the foot of Plate LVII.

The Cardinal de Richelieu employed Philip de Champagne to paint the portraits of several illustrious Frenchmen, to adorn his gallery. Among others, is one, intended for Gaston de Foix, Due de Nemurs, but, on a comparison with the engraving in Montfaucon, Plate ccxii, the portrait is evidently ideal. He, however, is painted in armour, which is copied from a suit, such as worn at the commencement of the reign of Henry VII, but evidently put together by a person who did not understand it. It has fine tuilles, and very large ornaments at the knees. The sword, instead of being ponderous, and worn, as was usual at that period, is light, and buckled up high, in the modem French fashion. On the contrary, in Montfaucon's plate, he wears a dagger in front of him, the hilt inclining towards the left hip, and having a great tassel appended to it.

There is extant, a rare print, by Hans Burgmair, of the Emperor Maximilian, in armour, on horseback, which, by altering a little the position, has served as the subject of Plate LVII. The armour for the horse's legs, however, has been added, from a coin which he struck, on undertaking a war against the Venetians, in 1509.[34] This coin represents the emperor much in the same costume as Burgmair's print, but the horse, in it, has his throat protected by a piece, which, meeting the mane-faire, renders it completely enveloped.

This plate affords the earliest specimen of fluted armour, which is so extremely beautiful, and which had its origin in Germany. It also gives us, as well as the armour of Henry VII, an example of what are properly called pass-guards;[35] viz. plates set perpendicularly on the pauldrons, being screwed on the upper piece of them. The vizored beavor of the helmet is very elegant, and exactly resembles one in my son's collection. The back-plate has but two culettes attached to it, the lower part being covered by the lamboys of puckered cloth or velvet. There are no tuilles, but the tassets are lengthened, over each thigh. The horse's chanfron has cheek-pieces. The crest, however, which is an eagle's head in a coronet, does not belong to the emperor, but to some other Knight of the Golden Fleece; yet probably was put on the suit of armour which Burgmair copied, and that he did copy the armour is clear, from the solleret, of which, in his engraving, the underpart is shewn, not having any foot in it. Besides the curb, there is a snaffle-bit of steel, with three joints on each side, highly ornamented. The manefaire is

[34] See it in Sylloge Numismatum elegantiorum, by John James Luck, in 1620.
[35] To guard against a pass, as it was called, or thrust.

held on the neck by two straps, covered with steel plates, which pass underneath, and similar ones held on the croupiere. On that which runs down the back, in the manner of a modern crupper, is placed the rerebrake. All the horse-armour is beautifully fringed with gilt foliage. The steel-guard on the bow of the saddle may be observed, at the top of which is a ring, to which was attached the estoc. Pendant from the back of the helmet may be seen the scroll. The armour for the legs of the horse, which, as has been observed, have been taken from a medal, consist of pieces of plate, with joints only at the knees and fetlocks.

I have met with but with one other instance of armour for the horse's legs, and that is in the triumph of Maximilian,[36] where the knight who carries the standard of antient Austria, and he who has that of Alsace, have short pieces of over-lapping plates on the upper part of their horses fore legs.

In my son's armoury is a fluted suit, greatly resembling this, with small pieces of chain-mail below the knees, as in some of the plates in the Triumph of Maximilian, and in Mr. Gwennapp's collection is another very fine one which belonged to Albert, Grand Duke of Bavaria, and also a part of his horse-armour, consisting of the poitral, chanfron, manefaire and steel saddle, but the croupiere is wanting. This has been put on a wooden horse, and another suit of fluted armour mounted on it, also of German workmanship.[37]

At Warwick Castle is another fine fluted suit, of nearly the same date, which the late earl purchased in Germany.[38]

A curious antient Frenoh work, entitled "La Mer des Histoires," printed in the year 1506,[39] gives us specimens of the men at arms, the Italian foot-soldiers, those of France, the Swiss halberdiers, the Venetian lansquenets, the estradiots, &c. These last are on horseback, in quilted tunics, with cylindrical caps on their heads, at the bottom of which appears a turban; oblong shields, having their bouches or mouths at the upper angle on the right, and with their arzegayes. The men at arms have tuilles attached to their tassets, and a vest, which opens with lappels, is placed between their placards and breast-plates, and has short sleeves. It is evident that this cos-

---

[36] Pl. LVII and Pl. LIX.

[37] There are several suits of fluted armour now in England, but not one set up in the Tower, Windsor Castle, or Hampton Court. I have, however, discovered in the Tower, the fluted armour of Henry VIII, and his horse marked with the double rose.

[38] See two plates of it in Grose's Treatise on Antient Armour.

[39] At Lyons.

PLATE LVII

MAXIMILIAN 1ST EMPEROR of GERMANY.

A.D. 1498.

tume must be referred to the commencement of this reign. The Italian foot-soldiers have pointed shields, which curve upwards at the point, and curved swords, wearing salades on their heads. The French infantry, on the contrary, have straight swords.

The sabres of the estradiots were called, at this time, braquemarts, from the Greek words, βραχυς, short, and Μάχαρα, a sword. Thus, in the Hist. Meld, anno 1493, we read . "Neque portent enses, braquemardos, venabula, javelinas, aut alios invasivos baculos per villas aut qusevis oppida." "Nor may they cany swords, braquemarts, hunting-knives, javelines, or any staves for attack, through the villages or any town." And in a French poem of the year 1496, it is said:

> "Qui tenoient tous entre leurs mains
> Bagamars et grans gysarmes."

> "Who hold every one in their bands
> Bagamars and large gysarmes."

Many of the Italian infantry were, at this period, arnfed with a sort of wide-bladed spear, called by them spontone, by the French esponton, and by the English spontoon. It is thus noticed in the Statuta Avellæ of the year 1496; "Nulla persona portare audeat aliquem cultellum seu expontonum majorem et longiorem uno pede et dimidio." "No person shall dare to carry any knife or spontoon, the blade of which shall be greater or longer than one foot and a half." Some of these weapons are in the collection of Llewe-lyn Meyrick, Esq.

The battle-axe was considered, at this time, a royal weapon, and was, therefore, borne as such, at the funerals of Henry VII and Queen Mary, and solemnly offered up at the altar with the helmet, gauntlets and crest.

The favorite colours of the House of Tudor, were green and white, and therefore with these Henry VII tinged the ground of one of the banners which he set up in Bosworth Field, whereon was painted a red dragon, in allusion to his descent from the Welsh king, Cadwaladyr. On his arrival in London, after the victory, Henry offered up this banner in the church of St. Paul, as a trophy; and, in further commemoration of his success, instituted the office of Rouge Dragon, poursuivant at arms.

A similar banner is on his monument, in Westminster Abbey, and has therefore been depicted in the hand of Sir John Cheney represented in Plate LVIII, his standard bearer on this occasion. This Plate, although placed at

PLATE LVIII

SIR JOHN CHENEY,

A.D. 1499.

the close of this reign, is a specimen of the armour worn at its commencement, but, being taken from the monumental effigy, had been dated at the
time of Sir John's death.[40] The helmet by it is from one in Grose's Antient
Armour, said to have been found at Bosworth Field. The armour of Sir Rhys
ab Thomas, in his effigy in St. Peter's Church, Caermarthen, greatly resembles this, but he there has on a kind of juppon, and underneath appear his
tuiles.[41]

The uniform of the English soldiers, during this reign, was white with
a red cross upon it; for, we are told by Bacon,[42] that Sir Edward Wydeville
with four hundred men, etc. sailed privately from the Isle of Wight to assist
the Bretons against the French. In the disastrous battle of St. Aubin he was
slain with all his countrymen, and seventeen thousand Bretons who, to de-
ceive the enemy, had adopted the white coats and red crosses of the English
troops.

The following indenture gives a very full idea of the various kinds of
troops forming the English armies in the year 1492.

"This indenture made betwene the King our Soverain Lorde Henry the
Seventh, by the grace of God, King of Englond and of Fraunce, and Lorde
of Irlande a that oon partie, and his right trusty and right welbeloved cousin George Erie of Kent on that other partie, witnesseth that the said erle is
retaigned and bilest with oure said soverain lorde to serve in his werres beyond the see, in all suche places, rowmes, commissions, and faictes of werre
as it shal at any time please oure said soverain lorde, to commaunde for and
during oon hool yere next and immediately ensuying the day of his first
mousters, and so forth as long after as it shal please oure said soverain lorde,
with the retynue and nombre of vi men of armes his owne persone comprised in the same, eveiy of theim havyng with him his custrell and his page,
xvi Di. launces, xxi archers on horsbak; lx archers on fote, of good and hable
persones for the werre, horsed, armed, garnished, and arraied sufficiently, at
all peces and in every thing as unto every of tlieim after the rowme that he
is appoincted unto shal or after the custume of werre aught to apperteigne,

---

[40]   It was no unusual thing for monumental effigies to be carved in more antient armour. This is the case of John Bleuhayset, Esq. who died in 1500; in his brass plate in Frense
Church, Norfolk, where he-is represented with three tuiles, a gorget of chain and pointed
toes.

[41]   See an engraving of him in Major Smith's Antient English Costume. In' Carter's
Specimens of sculpture ànd painting is a figure in glass ofthis time, whose tuiles represent
two different kinds of shields.

[42]   Bacon; 33. .

at the consideration and sight of oure said soverain lordes commissioners committed and deputed for the taking of the said mousters. Of the which retynue, arraied after the maner and fourme abovesaide, the said erle shal, without faulte in any behalve concerning the same, make his hod mousters at Guldeforde the fourth day of the monetli of Juyn next and immediatly ensuying the date of thise presentes, withoute further dilay or longer respite. And at his commyng to Portesmouth after the said mousters made he shal receive of our said soverain lord, by the handes of his tresouer of werres, or his deputie or deputies, the conduyte money due for the bringing of his said retynue to the said Portesmouth, that is to say, for every of theim for as many xx miles as there be betwene the houses from whens they or any of theim departed and the said Portesmouth vi^d. For the veray knowledge of which distaunce the tresourer of the kinges werres or his deputie or deputies shal take of the said erle and iche of his souldiours an othe upon a boke, and from the furst day of his said commyng to Portesmouth forthwarde during the tyme that he shal as above is said, serve oure said soverain lorde in the werre he shal have and receyve of oure said soverain lorde by the handes as above, for eveiy of the said men of arms garnished as before is said, with his custrell and page xviii^d by the day, and for eveiy of the said Di. launces ix$d$ by the day; and for every of the said archers, be they on horsback or on fote vi^d by the day. Of alle whiche wages the said erle, for his retynue shal at his commyng to Portesmouth receyve the hool paiement of and for oon moneth next and immediately ensuying the said furst day of his commyng to Portesmouth, accompting alweyes xxviii dayes for the moneth. The whiche wages as far as it shal concerne any personne of his said retynue, he shall within in the ship or it departe out of the havon, and not before, deliver and pay, or cause to be delivered and paied unto every personne of the same in as ample wise as it is before saide, and as he shal receyve for theim withoute any parte or peny thereof rebating or diminishing for any cause or in any manerwise; and the last day of the said moneth the said erle shal for his said retynue, according and after the rate above reherced, receyve of our said soverain lorde by the handes as above newe hool wages for oon moneth then next ¿nsuying, the whiche he shal within six days next and immediatly folowing hooly deliver nnto his retynue after the said rate and as before reherced and so forth from moneth to moneth during his reteyndre with our said soverain, he shal receyve and truly pay his wages in alle thinges after the fourme above reherced, of . whiche wages for as moche as shal concern him and his said retynue a this side the see, he shal be paied in sterling money, and beyond the see in sterling money or other money havying course be-yond the see.

"And as touching the paieng of the thridd, and thridd of thriddes of al maner wynnynges of werre taking and delyveryng of prisonners to our said soverain lorde, keping of watclie and warde, stale and foreyes, the said erl not only for himself, but also for his said retynue, and every persone therof, bindeth him to the parfourmance and observation of the same in al maner of wise, aftre and undre suche maner as is comprised in a certain boke of the statutes and ordenaunces of the werre maid by our said soyerain lord, by the advise of suche lordes of his blode, capitaignes of his armee, and other folk as be of his counsaill, whereof a copie is delyvered to the said erle, to th' ob-servation and due keping wherof, and of alle and every statute, ordenaunce, and other thing whatewer it be, comprised in the said boke, the said erle, as wele for his said retynue, and every persone of the same, as for himself, as far as it toucheth him or any of theirn over and above the premisses, bindeth him by these presentes undre and upon such multes, penalties, and puni-tions as be conteyned in the same (that is to say) that, as often and whenso-ever the said erle do thinges contrary to the said statutes, or any of theim, he shall do, suffre and receyve the multe, penaltie, and punition in that caas by the said statutes or statute ordeined and provided, and if any of his retynue do thinges contrary to the said statutes, the said erl shal, withoute fraude or dole put him in his best devoir to bring forth him that so offendeth, to aunswer to his offense and stand to justice after and according to the said statutes. In witness whereof to the oon partie of this Indenture remaigning towards oure said soverain lord the said erl hath sett his seal the ix day of May the seventh yere of the reigne of oure soverain lorde abovesaide.

G. KENT.

Sealed with red wax appendant to a slip of the parchment. There are similar indentures subscribed by the following:

Richard Lord Latymer to serve the king beyond see an hole yere In his werres with iii M. himself com-prised, eche having his custrell andpage, x Di Lane. ii A. on horsb. vi on fote . . . . } iii M.xDiLanc. horsb. ii A. foot vi A.

John Lord Powys to serve the king in his werres beyond See, an hole yere with one M, that is himself with his custn and page, and Ix Di Lane. horsed . . . . } one M. lx DiLanc. H.

John Lord Barnes to serve the king in his werres beyond see an hole yere with ii speres himself accompted and eith of them to have his custrell and page vi Di Lane. iv). on horsb, and vii A. On foote . . . .

ii speres vi. Di Lane. iv. A. horsb. foot vii A.

Henry Lord Grey to serve.the king in his werres beyond see an hole yere with ix M. hirnself comprised, each havin, his custrell and page; x Di Lane. xxv A. on horsb. and Ix on foote . . . .

ix M. x Di Lane. H. xxv A. F. lx A.

Edward Erl of Devon to serve the king: in his werres beyon d see an hole yere &c. with vi M. of Armes, himself comprised, every of them having his cus-trell and page, ii Di Lane. xxv A. H. lxvi A. F. . . . . . .

vi M. ii Di Lanc. xxv A. H. lxvi A. r.

The Lord Scrop of Bolton to serve the king in his werre beyond see an hole yere &c. with iii M. himselfe comprised, every of them having his custrell and page xii Di L. x A. H. and x A. foote . . . .

iii M. xi DiL. Hi x A. F. x A.

Thomas Lord Scrop of Upsall to serve the king in his werrers beyond the see an hole yere &c. with one M. videlicet; himself, having his custrell and page, xv A. H. and xv A. fote . . . .

One M. H. xv A. F. xv A.

Thomas Erle of Surrey to serve the king in his werres be-yond see an hole yere &c. with v M. himself com-prised, every of them having his custrell and page, xii Di L. xx A. on H. xlvi A. F. and xiii billes on foote . . . .

v M. xiii Di L. xx A. H. xlvi. A. F. xiii B.

James Lord Audeley to serve the king in his werres be-yond see an hole yere &c. with iii M. himself com-pr. every of them having his custrell and' page, Di Lé xx A. H. xi A. F. xx . . . .

iii M. xxDi L. H. xi A. F. xx A.

George Lord Straungeto serve the king beyond see an yere &c. with x. M. himself compr. every of them having his custrell and page. Also v. Mèn. Di L. xxiv A. H. A. F. . . . .

x M. v M. xxiv ccxlix

Thomas Brian one of the squiers for the king's body to serve him in his werres beyond see for an hole yere with one spere, videlicet himself, having his custrell and page, iv A. horsb. xiv Ar. on foote and ii billes.

One spere iv A. H. xiv A. F. ii billes.

John Viscount Welles to serve the king in his werres beyond see for an hole yere, etc. with iii M. himself comp, eche having his custrell and 'page xx Di. L. xv, A. horseb. xlv A. foote and xx halberdes on fote

iii M. xx Di. L. xv A. H. xlv A. F. xx Halb. F.

Sir Reynold Bray knyght counsaillour to serve the king in his werres beyond see an hole yere &c. with xii M. himself accompted, eche having his custrell and page, xxiv Di.La. Ixxvii, A. on horseb. ccxxxiA, and billes on fote xxiv . . . .

xii M. xxivDi. L.lxxvii A. H. ccxxxi A. and B. F. xxiv.

Sir Charles Somerset knight for the king's body to serve him in his werres beyond' see an hole yere &c. with one M. viz. himself having his custrell and page vi. Di. Lane. and vi A.on horsb . . . .

One M. vi D. L vi. A. H.

Sir Roger Cotton knight to serve the king in his werres beyond see an hole yere Sec, with ii M. himself compo either having his custrell and page ii Di. Lane. vii A. horsb, xxi A. and billes on fote . . . .

ii M. ii Di L A. vii A. H. xxi A. and B. F.

Lewis ap Rice to serve the king in his werres beyond see an hole yere Sec. with one A. videlicet, himself on horsb. viii A. on fote and vi byllis on fote. . . . . . .

One A. H. viii. A. F. vi billes F.

Sir Richard Hault knight to serve the king' in his werres beyond see an hole yere &c. with ii M. himself comprised, eche having his custrell and page, ii Di. L. vi A. H. and xvi A. F. and vi billes on foote. . . . . .

ii M. ii Di L. vi A. H xvi A.F.B. vi F.

John Crokker squier to serve the king in his werres be yond see an hole yere &c. with one M. viz. the said squier having his custrell and page, xvi A. on foote and and iv billes . . . .

vi M. ii Di Lanc. xxv A. H. lxvi A. r.

Sir William Courteney knight to serve the king in his werres beyond see an hole yere &c. with one sp. viz. himself having his custrel and page vi Di. Lane. viii A. H. xxxii A. F. and iv billes on foot . . . .

One sp. vi Di. L. viii A. H. xxxii A.F. iv B. F.

Sir Ric. Corbet knighte to serve the king in his werres beyond see an hole yere &c. with one M. viz. him-self having his custrel and page iv A. H. xii, A. F. . . . .

One, M. iv A. H. xii A. F.

Sir William Stanley knight counsaillour and cham-berlain to serve the king in his werres beyond see an hole yere &c. with xl A. on horsbak . . . .

xl A. horsb,

Sir John Saint John knight for the king's body to serve him in his werres beyond see anhole yere &c. with ii speres himself. accounted for one, iv Di Lane. v A. horb. x A. F. v billes on fote . . . .

ii sp. vi Di. L. v A. H. x A. F. v B.F.

Sir Thomas Darcy knight to serve the king in his wèrres beyond see an hole yere with one M. viz. himself having his custrell and page xvi A. and iv billes vi H. Rem^t. F. . . . .

One M. xvi A. and iv billies vi H. Rem^t. F.

Sir Walter Hungerford knight to serve the king in his
 werres beyond see an hole yere &e. with ii speres }   ii sp. x A. H. xxx A.
 himsell comprised, either having his custrell and }   F. xx B.
 page, x A. horsb. xxx A. E. and xx byllis . . . .

From these various documents it appears that, at this time, the cavalry of the English armies consisted of men at arms with their custrells and pages also mounted, demi-lancers and liorse-archers, and the infantry of bowmen, bill-men, and halberdiers. This last kind of troops first made their appearance during this reign, and the distinguishing mark of their weapon, from that of subsequent periods, was, that the axe blade had a diagonal termination. Its precise form may be seen in the Triumph of Maximilian the First, and some of this kind are in the armoury of Llewelyn Meyrick, Esq.

When Henry VII created his second son Henry[43] Prince of Wales, four gentlemen offered their services upon the occasion. First they made a declaration that they did not undertake this enterprize in any manner of presumption, but only "for the laude and honour of the feaste, the pleasure of the ladyes; and their owne learning and exercise of deedes of armes, and to ensewe the ancient laudable customs."

They then promise to be ready at Westminster on the 24th day of November, to keep the justs in a place appointed for that purpose by the king. To be there by "eleven of the clock before noone to answer all gentlemen commers, and to runne with every commer one after another, six courses ensewingly, and to continue that daye as long as it shal like the kynges grace, and to tilt with such speares as he shall ordeyn, of the which speares, the commers shall have the choise: but if the said six courses by every one of the commers shall not be performed, and the day not spent in pleasure and sport according to the effect of these articles, it shall then be lawful for the said commers to begin six other courses, and so continue one after another, as long as it shall be at the king's pleasure. If it shall happen to any gentleman that his horse fayleth him, or himself be unanned in such wise as he cannot conveniently accomplish the whole courses, then it shall be lawful for his felowe to finish up the courses."

Again they promise, upon the 29th of November, to be in readiness to mount their horses at the same place and hour as before, to tourney with four other gentlemen, with such swords as the king shall ordain, until eighteen strokes be given by one of them to the other; and add that it shall be

---

[43] Afterwards Henry VIII.

lawful to strike all manner of ways, the foyne[44] only excepted, and the commers shall have their choice of the swords.

"Whosoever," add they, "shall certifye and give knowledge of his name, and of his comming to one of the three kings of arms, whether it be to the justs or at the Tourney, he shall be first answered, the states always reserved which shall have the prehemhinence. If any one of the said commers shall think the swords or spears be too easy for him, the said four gentlemen will be redye to answer him or them after their owne minde, the king's licence obteyned in that behalf."

The gentlemen then intreat the king to sign the articles with his own hand, as sufficient licence for the heralds to publish the same, in such places as might be thought requisite. The king accepted their offer, and granted their petition, at the same time promised to reward the best performer at the justs royal, with a ring of gold, set with a ruby; and the best performer at the tournament, with another golden ring, set with a diamond, equal in value to the former.

There were, also, certain gentlemen, who styled themselves the servants of Ladye Maie,[45] in honor of that month, who gave a challenge to be performed at Greenwich; the articles of which were: "*Imprimis*—The fourteenth daie of Maie simile be redye in the field certaine gentlemen perteyning to the Ladye Maie, armed for the tilt, in lmrneis thereunto accustomed; and there to kepe the fielde, in such place as it shall please the kynge to appoint, from 2 of the clocke, till 5 at the afternoone, to run with every commer 8 courses: and thus the answerers all answered and served, that then if there be any that desiretli for their ladyes sake other 4 courses, it shall be granted, so the hower be not past, if it be then at the Queene's pleasure.

"The seconde daye to shoot standart[46] arrowe and flighte with all commers; he that shootes the standartf furthest to have a prise, and so in like case of the arrow of the flight.

"The third day, with swordes rebated, to strike with every commer 8

---

[44] The foyne is the thrust as in fencing, which, of course, was exceedingly dangerous when the swords were pointed, which might have been the case; as the particular ones are not specified. The author orthe MS. poem, in the Cotton Library, marked Titus, A. XXIII, part. I, fol. 7, entitled: "Knyghtode and Batayle," says, in fighting with an enemy, "to foyne is better than to smyte," and afterwards two inches "entre foyned" hurteth more than a broader wound with the edge of a sword.

[45] The same as the Maid Marian.

[46] A pole, on the top of which was set a mark.

strokes, in waye of pleasure; and four strokes more for any of the commers mistress sake, under the above restrictions, and the Queene's pleasure.

"The fourth day, to wrestle all manner of ways, at the pleasure of the commers.

"The fifth day, armed for to fighte on foote with speares in their hands rebated, and their swords by their sides for the battle; and there with speare and sword to defend their barriers; that is to say, with speares 8 strokes, whereof two with faone,[47] and 6 with strokes; and that done, to drawe their swordes and strike 8 strokes every man, to his best advantage, with gripe[48] or otherwise; and four strokes for a lady, under the above restrictions.

"The sixth daye, to caste the barre on foote, and with the arme both heavie and light.

"At these tournois, the challenger doth engage to come in lmmeis for the tilt, without targe or brochett,[49] woolant piece over the head,[50] rondall[51] over the garde, rest of advantage, fraude, deceit or other malengine."

Some time after this, four gentlemen challenged all commers at the same place, "to the feate called the barriers, with the casting speare, and the targatt, and the bastarde sworde. And one with the speare liedded with the morn, and 17 strokes with the sworde point and edge rebated; without close or griping one another with handes upon paine of such punishment as the judges for the tyme being should thinke requisite."

How early the fashion of mock or satyrical tournaments was introduced is not easy to determine, as there is no account of them on record; but, in a print dated 1500, in the possession of my friend, the critical antiquary, F. Douce, Esq. are not only fools supplying the places of heralds and pages, but even the knights themselves have their salades ornamented with the symbolical hanging bells. A collection of paintings, done at this time, representing satirically a tournament at Nuremberg, in the year 1446, has fools carrying the lances of the combattants, on their way to the great square, where the ceremony was to be performed, and one attending each knight, cloathed in the same fanciful manner as the horse, Avliich he urges on with

---

[47] Foyne.

[48] Laying hold of oné another.

[49] Query—Whether the same as brichette Brochette signifies a spike, and perhaps, in this case, fixed on the arm.

[50] This is seen at the foot of Plate LIII.

[51] The rondelle was put on the lance, and differed from the vamplate in being flat, but of the same diameter. There is one in my son's collection, elegantly inlaid with scrolls in gold, and engraved.

his bladder. The knights are all named, have their proper crests, and the old tilting helmet, like that belonging to General Murray, and their horses are armed a la haute barde, as in Plate LIX. The drawings are in a spirited style, forty-nine in number, and in my son's possession.

For tilting at the quintain, a small breast-plate, before noticed, on which was a lance rest, was used at this time. It was furnished with a flat piece of iron within side, which slipped into a belt or hole, made in the vest, and was thus held tight. One of these rare pieces of armour is in the collection of my son, and has been copied at the foot of Plate LVII.

About the close of Henry the Seventh's time was introduced, an exceedingly gross and indecent appendage to the taces, being an artificial protuberance, placed just over the os pubis. It was copied in armour, after having been first adopted in ordinary dress, aud, indeed, in this manner formed part of the costume of every class, from the sovereign to the lowest mechanic; and what is astonishing, instead of shocking the delicacy of society, spread over all the civilized part of Europe. The French called it baguette,[52] and the English cod-piece, a word still retained in Wales, to signify the modern flap Indeed, it appears, from inspecting Plates cex and ccxvm, of Montfaucon's Mon. Fr. that the flap was the origin of it, and this flap became at first convex, and then protuberant, as may be observed in several of the plates of the Triumph of Maximilian.

The cod-piece is attached to that suit of armour made for Henry VIII, when only eighteen years of age, in the Tower of London, of which it may be worth while to mention here; the distinctive character is the breast, being made flexible by means of two plates over the abdomen,[53] and its being rough from the hammer, as was the case with the black armour. This disgusting fashion continued unabated till the close of Queen Elizabeth's reign; and if any thing can be more absurd than the introduction of so filthy an idea, it must be the purpose to which ordinary ones were applied. The dress of John Winchcomb, the famous clothier of Newbery, in which he went to King Henry VIII, is thus described in his history. "He had on a plain russet coat, a pair of white kersie slopps (or breeches), without welt or guard, and stockings of the same piece, sewed to his slopps, which had a great cod-piece, whereon he stuck his pins."

---

[52] Rabelais calls it gaudipise. In the north of England the word cod implies a pillow, or stuffed cushion"

[53] This suit has lost one of its pass-guards, the screw-holes remaining for that of tbe right pauldron.

P. de Commines mentions that there were at the battle of Fournoue, in 1495, German harquebusiers on foot and on horseback.[54] The harquebuss underwent an improvement during this reign. Hitherto in imitation of the arbaleste it had only a straight stock to hold the barrel, but now it was formed with a wide butt end, which might be placed against the right breast,[55] and thus held more steadily. To render this object more effectual, a notch was made in the butt for the purpose of admitting the thumb of the right hand. When the butt was bent down, or hooked, which it was at a later period, it was called from the German word hake, a hackbutt, haggebutt or hagbut, the smaller sort being denominated demi-hags.

A good account is given of the use of field artillery at the battle of Fournoue in the Memoires of P. de Commines, but their execution was not great, for, throughout the battle, that author tells us the number thus killed on both sides did not exceed ten. There is still lying exposed at Rhodes an antient cannon of this period on its original carriage and a stone ball to fire from it. The cannon is in length nineteen feet, in diameter two feet eight inches, and its calibre two feet, so that the thickness is four inches. About half the length, however, is of a less diameter, and in this, as a chamber, was placed the powder while the ball was in the larger part. On it is an Arabic inscription placed there since it fell into the hands of the Turks, but the original inscription is in Latin, and shews that it belonged to Peter Daubysson, master of the Knights Hospitallers, and that it was made in 1486. The inscription runs thus: F. Petrys Dabysson m. hospitalis iher, opvs Francisi Mantvani, mcccclxxxvi. The carriage is made of timber, placed longwise and crampped together, on which the cannon is laid, while a portion is raised higher behind the piece. It has not any wheels.

---

[54] Lib. VIII, c. 7.

[55] Many of the antient pieces were held to the breast instead of the shoulder which will account for their being so short in the butt.

Henry the Eighth.

1509.

ERE must be noticed the armour in the brass plate of Edward Whyte, Esq. at Shottisliam Church, Norfolk, who died in 1528; and that of Peter Rede, Esq. in St. Peter's Mancroft Church, Norwich, who died in 1508; yet, properly speaking, they are of the early part of Henry Seventh's time. The former has a gorget of chain-mail and an apron of the same, both indented and tuillets over the last. The latter has four tuilles, pointed sollerets and a visored salade, such as worn in Edward the Fourth's time. The inscription, accompanying this effigy, is worth notice. "Peter Rede, Esq. who not only served his prince, but the EmperorCharles V at the conquest of Barbaria, and at the siege of Tunis, and other places, whence the emperor gave him tlie order of Barbaria."

The monumental effigy of Richard Knightly, Esq. in Upton Church, Northamptonshire, who died in the year 1537, is like that worn in the middle of Henry the Seventh's time; but it may be remarked that the fashions, which arose in Italy and Germany, were slow in finding their way into England so as to become general.

It has been observed that the fluted armour was used at the close of the last reign; it was also continued until the middle of this, and, although there is but one in the armoury at the Tower,[1] yet all the men at arms are thus equipped in that curious old painting given by his late Majesty to the Society of Antiquaries, which represents the battle of the Spurs.

The fluted armour of Henry VIII was, therefore, in all probability, made in Germany, and perhaps presented to him by the Emperor Maximilian I. The battle of the Spurs was fought on the 16th of August, 1513. While the Lords Shrewsbury and Herbert were before Terouenne, Henry arrived at their camp from Calais.[2] The Emperor Maximilian joined him with four thousand horse. This subtle prince, to flatter the vanity of his young ally, and to avoid any dispute about precedency, called himself the volunteer of the King of England, wore his badge of the red and white rose, put on the cross of St. George, and accepted one hundred crowns as his daily pay. Louis XII determined to relieve the town, but was advised not to hazard his person in battle. The French cavalry, therefore, that had been collected at Blangy, dividing into two bodies, advanced along the opposite banks of the Lis under the Duke de Longueville and Alençon. Henry had the prudence to consult the experience of his imperial ally, who was acquainted with the country, and had already obtained two victories on the very same spot. By his advice the army was immediately mustered. Maximilian hastened to meet the enemy with the German cavalry and the English mounted archers, while the king followed with the principal part of the infantry. The French gendarmes, formed in the Italian campaigns, who had acquired the reputation of superior courage and discipline, fled on the first shock of the advanced guard: the panic went through the whole army, and one thousand of the best cavalry in Europe were pursued about four miles by the German and a few hundred English horse. Their officers, in the attempt

---

[1] That one has been whimsically divided: the breast plate and gard de reine, on which is engraved the red and white rose, are put on the figure of Queen Elizabeth, the other pieces are nailed upon different parts of the walls, and the corresponding horse" armour exhibited with an inferior suit behind therange of kings. As the pomegranate is on the horse armour it was evidently made in the early part of this reign.

[2] Hall thus describes Henry's armour on his landing, "He was appareilled in Almaine ryvet crested and his vambrace of the same, and on his head a chapeau Montabyn with a rich coronal; the folde of the chapeau was lyned with crimsyn satyn and on y^e a rich brooch with the image of Sainet George. Over his ryvet he had a garment of white cloth of gold with a redde crosse." In the above mentioned painting he is in bright steel armour, inlaid with gold.

PLATE LVIX

KNIGHT ARMED À LA HAUTE BARDE.

A.D. 1512.

to rally the fugitives, were abandoned to the mercy of the enemy. La Palice and Imbrecourt, though taken, had the good fortune to make their escape, but the Duc de Longueville and the Marquis de Rotelin, the Chevalier Bayard,[3] Bussy d'Amboise, Clermont and La Fayette, warriors distinguished in the military annals of France, were secured and presented to the united sovereigns.

The Turnier Buch or Tournament Book of Wilhelm der Vierten of Bayern, with coloured illustrations, representing different Bavarian Tournaments from the year 1510 to that of 1545, and just published at Munich with fac-simile engravings from the original manuscript, aifords very full information relative to the costume at those amusements during this reign.

Very much like these engravings is a tournament roll preserved at Malta representing the costume at one given by the family of Fiigger to that of de Montfort, in celebration of a marriage between the two houses at this period.

Plate LIX represents a knight armed for the joust as it is called a la haute barde, the barde or armour of his horse rising so high in front as to protect the rider as high as the abdomen.[4] He, therefore, needs no other armour below his breast-plate than short cuisses. At his shoulders are palettes, and the upper half of the vambrace is made to lap over, and also to turn up within the bend of the arm, having the appearance of being an additional piece but, in reality, only one half the vambrace,[5] the pondrous tilting-lielinet, before described, is over his head,[6] and he holds in one hand the thick tilting-lance with its cronel and vamplate, while on his bridle arm hangs the shield painted red and white, the colours which he has adopted.

On his horse's head is a beautiful chanfron with an indented ridge

---

[3] A suit of armour with pass-guards now in the Rotunda at Woolwich and brought from the Château of St. Germain, in France, certainly of this period, is attributed to the Chevalier Bayard. If this be really tbat whicb be wore, he does not appear by any means, to bave been a tall man.

[4] There is some armour of this kind in the Tower, but, as it is only partially exhibited, never strikes the observer.

[5] This is ascertained by inspecting two suits belonging to my son, but of an earlier date, which came from the Ducal Palace at Modena.

[6] One of these occurs.on a piece of German stained glass in the possession of William Reader, Jun. Esq. dated 1531. On another bit of the same date is one with a moveable pierced beaver,having from its top a wide par that protects the sight from a transverse cut; and on a third, dated 155'2, one with a uniber and a bar over the ocularium. The two last helmets are made to open perpendiculary, one being furnished with two hinges, the other with a strap passing through a ring, but all are on the ponderous principle before noticed.

down its length, a fashion that has been already noticed; it is also furnished with gratings to protect the eyes.

One of these fanciful chanfrons, brought from the arsenal at Vienna and which belonged to the Emperor Maximilian, is in my son's collection. It represents the head of a griifon and the various undulations of surface, the muscles, hair, etc. are beat out of the solid steel in a most astonishing manner. There is, likewise, a piece to cover the top of the horse's tail made in the same fine style and in the form of the head of an ideal fish.

The horse has also a manefaire, and round his neck a string of large bells, a fashion adopted from the Asiatics. The poitral, as has been observed, rises up very high in front of the saddle, and, as armour was only needed before, we observe none behind. Just by the horse's shoulder the poitral is beat out into a convex form, and such may be seen in those at the Tower, it being invariably the practice at this time. It was made incase the lance should by any means strike so low that it might the more readily glide off.

This plate has been taken from one of those in the triumph of Maximilian cut in wood by Hans Burgmair, in the year 1512. Indeed, these curious representations are so interesting as to merit, as far as relates to armour, a concise description. The first military appearance is made by a number of fifers and drummers on horseback dressed in the fashion of the last reign with long sabres, and the former with their fife cases by their sides. The drums do not differ from those in present use, but the fifes are much longer. They are under the command of Anthony Dornstall, who is made to say: "I have played on the fife in many countries for the valourous Emperor Maximilian in several great battles, as well as in the lists of combat both a plaisance and à outrance."

The stag hunters are represented with spears with blades leaf-shaped on one side and straight on the other, and the wild boar hunters have large swords made spear-shaped at the ends and perforated just below for a cross-bar. Two such originals I have met with but not so broad.

The next that claim attention are the combatants on foot. These are headed by John Holly wars or Holubar, celebrated for his combat with Mathias King of Hungary, master of the science of arms at the court of the emperor. First are five men with flails, a mode of fighting as old as the time of Henry III. Their staves only are of wood, the striking part being of leather, as these were only intended for practise. Then come five men with quarter staves, next five with lances, then as many with halbards.[7] M. de Bellay

---

[7] Several precisely like these are in the armoury of Llewelyn Meyrick, Esq.

says: "I have been told, by a Switzer, that the antient manner of using this weapon was to tell off the front rank of lialbardiers alternately into pushers and strikers, so that, while one half charged with their spears, the others struck and cut with the hatchets of their halberts." This weapon is said to have been invented by the Switzers, from whom it was adopted by the Germans, and became very prevalent under the Emperor Charles V. Then five with long battle axes were thus followed by five men with targets and long swords, and next as many with fencer's bucklers[8] and short swords. Five men armed in the Bohemian manner next appear, having large shields of an oblong shape, but a ridge down their whole length to receive the arm, called in their language poweza, i. e. pavise, invented by Ziska, and with square or round headed maces. Last of all, are five men with two handed swords[9] in the Swiss manner which they carry on their shoulders.

Henry VIII was very skilful in the use of this weapon; for Hall tells[10] us that the King of England, (in 1510), being twenty years of age, repeatedly fought at barriers with the two handed sword or the battle axe, and was always successful. Something however, may be attributed to the courtesy of his antagonists.

Next in procession came the tourneyers. These are preceded by Anthony d'Yffan, master of the tourneys who is said to be armed for a tournament. He is in complete armour as well as his horse; but the latter, instead of a manefaire, has the criniere of chain-mail which covers the upper part of the neck, reaching to the ends of the mane where it is indented. Behind the saddle is seen a flat plate[11] and its utility is also visible, viz.: for attaching the croupiere by straps. It may here be observed, once for all, that the poitral and croupiere[12] are composed of three pieces each. The large helmet given in Plate lix is called, in this work, alte stech helme, or old justing helmet, while that worn by Anthony d'Yffan is termed neue stech helme, or the modern one. Next follow five tourneyers armed at all points like their leader, and, like him, having tuiles. They have lances with small heads which do not project beyond the staff and large swords. Five mounted tourneyers follow these. They have, however, the grand guards a la mentoniere that is, made high so as to cover the chin screwed on to the centres of their breast-plates.

---

[8] There is one like theseand two .square ones of this time in my son's collection.

[9] There is a very great variety of these in the collection of Llewelyn Meyrick, Esq.

[10] Chron I, 12.

[11] It may also be observed in the representation of the Emperor Maximilian, Platè LVII.

[12] In some instances, however, the croupière is made of from four to six.

In some instances this is made to cover the left side and the right breast, while, in others, it protects the whole body. They have the vamplates on their lances; their horses are completely barded and some have the mane-faire with criniere below. In the Turnier Buch, before noticed, are some of these large grand guards with mentonieres, which, instead of screwing to the breast-plate, are fastened to the lower part of the helmet. One of this kind has been introduced at the bottom of Plate LX.

Next are represented the combatants in the jousts, headed by Wolfgang de Polheim, master of the jousts and courses, who is made to say: "That the games of chivalry were never exercised in the world, in such variety as at the court of the emperor, instituted with my assistance." He has, screwed to the right side of his back-plate, a large piece of iron, which projects behind, and is then made to curve down. This curious contrivance was called a queue or tail, and its intention was to relieve the combatant from the weight of his lance, as, while it was supported in front by the rest, this prevented the end rising up behind, and in this way are several knights represented charging in the Turnier Buch. His thighs and knees are protected by large convex plates, screwed on the saddle, through which he has placed his legs. These are called sockets, and they render tassets sufficent armour, without cuisses. The first who follow Wolfgang, are the Italian jousters, who are armed just like the figure in Plate LIX, but their horses have no other armour than chanfrons, being covered instead with rich caparisons; indeed, the horse of Wolfgang is with the caparison only. The German jousters follow next, who do not differ from these, except in having the queue, and their horses' fore-heads protected by a round plate. They have also the haute bard with a drap-ery over it; crests on the tops of their helmets, and wreaths of laurel twisted round their lances. Next follow the jousters a la haute barde, one of whom is represented in Plate LIX. After these are five jousters, armed like those in the Italian joust, from the middle upwards, but from that downwards like the tourneyers; they have also queues, and ride on high fronted steel saddles. Their horses are completely barded, except manefaires or crinieres.

Next follow those armed for the course, the first of which are the Italian courses. They are armed like the last, except having the modern helmets, and being without queues, but they ride on saddles like the last. Their lances have small points rebated or bent down, called monies.[13] Their horses are only protected by chanfrons, having nothing else over them but ample ca-parisons and collars of bells. These are succeeded by the course called bond,

---

[13] The points of the cronel were called mornettes, or little mornes.

because the horses eyes were covered, and the whole party fastened their horses together before they started, to run at their adversaries. They had sockets on their saddles, and sabbatines on their feet, with queues to their back-plates. They wore on their heads a kind of visored salade,[14] which was called, in German, rennhute, or coursing hat. Before their faces were placed two bars, joined by a cross one, on which was a ring, into which was hooked the grand guard a la mentoniere, while it rested on two pins on the chest. This was covered with a drapery, and when struck was thrown up in the air in acknowledgment. The lance has at its end the morne rebated, but, instead of the ordinary vamplate, one is used which extends only on the outside, and at top, so as not to make quite three-quarters of a circle. These were called floating vamplates, and by the Germans, from their resemblance to a tanner's utensil, garbeisen. Their extent was greater upwards and downwards than on the side.[15] These jousters have been considered so very curious, that one of them is represented in Plate LX.

The next set of coursers are the Swabian, who have the same coursing-hats and lances as the last, and also a grand guard à la mentoniere fixed close to their breast-plates. On this is a protuberance and two rings to hold a shield, made also with a mentoniere, and called pavoise futée. It derives its name from being composed of various pieces, which loosen on being struck, when all are thrown up in the air and separate. The sollerets of the knights are made pointed, but not in the antient manner with heels to them. The horses are without any armour, but are ornamented with bases. Next follows the course with helmets, the rest being in coursing-hats.[16] After these come the coursers with targes futées, which differ from the last but one in the component shield, being a target instead of a pavise. Their horses too have chanfrons and caparisons. After these come the tilters à la poêle, so called from wearing on their chests a square shield or plate, called poêle. It had a raised edge, and had on it a grating, whence its name, from its resemblance to a German chafing-dish. As the champions fought bare-headed, and without armour, this kind of course was very perilous.[17] The horses

---

[14] One of these is in my son's collection.

[15] Two fine ones of this kind, falsely called croupieres, one being of several pieces, are in the Rotunda at Woolwich.

[16] The usual coursing-hats, however, at least such as were used about the middle of this reign, greatly resembled a morian with oreillets. A beautiful specimen of this kind belongs to a jousting suit in the possession of Llewelyn Meyrick, Esq.

[17] It is said to have been So dangerous, that a coffin was placed in the course before the combatants commenced.

PLATE LX

A KNIGHT ARMED   FOR THE BOND,

A.D 1512.

were also blindfolded in this course. Fencer's bucklers on the principle of the poêle, being of a square form and grated, are in the armoury of Llewelyn Meyrick, Esq. They have hooks on the outside, for hanging them on the sword-guard, so that the handle might be outwards, for the more readily taking hold with the left hand, while the sword was drawn by the right one. These came from Vienna.

Next follows the field-course, where the combatants and their horses are fully armed, but they have grand guards with mentonieres, and cours-ing-hats; a bell on the crupper of the horse, and another hanging from the poitral. Next to this is the course in the stile of Gaspar Wintzer, a celebrated jouster, the champions having shields. Then the course au garde bras. The garde bras screwed on the elbow of the bridle-arm, acting as a shield above it, and extending half way below it, in the form of the vambrace. There is an ornamented one of this kind in the Tower of London; and six varieties in my son's collection. The knights in this had helmets. Then comes the course à la queue so called from the use of that contrivance, but the appearance of the antagonists scarcely differs from that given in Plate LX.

Last of all is the course au bourrelet, so called from the knights wearing wreaths of their lady's colours on their heads. They have no helmets and are merely protected by grand-guards with visored mentonieres, one of which has been given at the foot of Plate LIX. They have the queue, and the sabba-tines, and their thighs are protected by sockets. Their horses are blind-fold-ed but without armour. Next follow standard bearers in whole armour; there is some variety, but the general character marks this period, though there is an attempt at more antient fashions. The horse of the knight, who carries the standard of Styria, has a large criniere of mail pendant from the manefaire. That of the one who has the colours of modern Austria, has the manefaire along the top and the whole of the rest of the neck envelopped in mail, while that of the knight, holding the arms of antient Austria, has half a manefaire coming from the horse's ears, and half a criniere attached to it reaching from thence down to the saddle. These two last horses have flexible cuisses of plate. The knight who carries the standard of Kybourgli has a manefaire on his horse of little plates rivetted on cloth, with a criniere below, and that with the flag of Reineck, a poitral on his horse, with a piece bending out from it at top so as to fit the neck of the animal.

Then follow triumphal cars on two or three of which are depicted of-ficers of infantry in allecrets, whose flexible cuisses come only half way of their thighs and who carry halberds in their hands.

PLATE LXI

A KNIGHT AND ONE OF THE KING'S GUARDS,

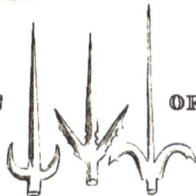

A.D. 1525.

After these follow various troops, among them are the lansquenets who were first raised among the Germans by this emperor, and then only for each campaign. These kind of troops were, after this, adopted by the English, Henry VIII having served as a volunteer in the army of Maximilian. Thus in a convention, dated 1543,[18] we read of, Duo millia peditum lanskenetorum. "Two thousand foot soldiers lansquenets."

The triumphal procession concludes with the baggage, &c.; but just before these are a party of harquebusiers. Their bandileers, the earliest specimens I have met with, are hung round their necks like a collar,[19] and suspended in the same way, in front are the powder flasks, some of which resemble horns, and others are of a circular form, but plain behind and convex in front. Both kinds most elegantly ornamented are in the collection of Llewelyn Meyrick, Esq. Those with the bandileers were intended to hold the fine powder for priming, while those worn without are for the charge. In a bag, suspended at the right hip, were the balls, and, at the left, is a sword, the belts crossing over the abdomen. All these liarquebusses are matchlocks, and the soldiers carry the match cord in their hands. The pieces are rather short, and therefore no rests are used, a contrivance of later date than this. Their breasts, backs, abdomens and thighs are protected with armour, as well as their arms, and on their necks they wear chaiii-raail gorgets. This armour was probably the allecret as that was a light armour, greatly resembling the corselet which succeeded it, and for which it seems to have been the prototype. It is called alecret in the Chronicle of Charles VIII, under the year 1511. Plusieurs alecrets et utencilles pour le fait de la guerre. "Many alecrets and utensils for the materials of war."

Marot, the french poet who wrote in the year 1545, has:

> Fort bien armés du corps, testes, bras et gorges,
> Aussi dit-on de ballecrets, de horges.

> "Very well armed in bodies, heads, arms and throats,
> Such they call hallecrets de horges."

Two specimens of the allecret, but of the middle of this reign, are in my son's collection.

In a book of drawings by Albert Durer, which belonged to Sir Hans Sloane, and now in the British Museum, is a knight on horseback in com-

---

[18] In Rymer's Fœdera.
[19] I am not certain however whether they are bandileers or merely tassels.

plete armour, in the attitude of striking with a morning-star, held with both hands. The plate armour of his horse is covered with spikes, and spiked-balls are suspended from the poitral and croupiere. The form for the appurtenances of a lance are drawn on the same sheet of paper.

In the Cotton Library[20] are several military figures of the middle of Henry the Eighth's reign, two of which have been selected for Plate lxi, representing a knight dismounted and one of the king's guard. The former holds in his hand a martel de fer of the ordinary form, used by the officers when commanding infantry, and intended to strike through the chain-mail armour with one end, or to stun a person by a blow of the other. These were made of various shapes which admitted of much elegance, and there are, at least, ten in the collection of my son, all different. Grose has supposed them to be the same as the horsemen's hammers, but two of the latter in my son's armoury completely disprove this. These horsemen's hammers have square handles covered with steel, and perforated to attach them to the saddle bow, and a hook, to fix them, when necessary, in a belt. The heads are much smaller and almost like a modern hammer, except that one end is made to a point. The drapery, besides making lamboys, is made to cover one half the breast.

The other figure wears the arming-doublet with its sleeves of chain-mail, carries on his shoulder a spontoon,[21] and has hanging to it behind his convex roundel. These kind of shields became very prevalent at this period, and were made of wood covered with leather. One of this sort, with figures gilt on it and also colored inside, one red and gold, another with the mode of besieging a town, are in the armoury of Llewelyn Meyrick, Esq. but the finest thing of the period of this sort is the target of the Emperor Charles V, on which are engraved twelve subjects of his history, and thirty-six others from sacred and profane authors, gilt upon niello, in the same collection.[22] It is of steel and lined with sky-blue velvet.

The first of these subjects is the elevation of Charles to the throne of Spain in 1519, and the last exhibits his imperial state and alliance; the fabrication, therefore, of this splendid target, cannot be dated earlier than the year 1550. Among the other incidents are the capture of François I at the battle of Pavia, in 1525; the taking of the Castle of St. Angelo and the pope,

[20] In the British Museum, marked Augustus 2.

[21] Several of these are in my son's collection.

[22] By unscrewing the spike in the center and taking off the raised foliage, is seen the following inscription HIER. SPACINUS. MEDIO. BON. FACIEBAT. The ornament of the initial letter to this reign is taken from it.

by the Prince of Orange, in 1527; the defeat of Barbarossa and release of the Christian slaves at Tunis, in 1535, and the Duke of Cleeves compelled in the most abject manner to implore mercy, in 1538.

The armour said to have been worn by the King of France at the time of his capture is in the salle d'artillerie at Paris, having been, during the last war, brought from Germany; and of the recovery of his sword from Spain, Dr. Southey gives the following interesting account.

"Bonaparte having intimated to Ferdinand King of Spain, through Murat, that the restoration of the sword of François I, would greatly gratify him; this trophy of Pescara's victory, which had lain since the year 1525 in the royal armoury at Madrid was yielded up for the gratification of the Parisians. It was carried in a silver basin under a silken cloth, laced and fringed with gold to Murat's head quarters in a coach and six, preceded by six running footmen, and under the charge of the superintendant of the arsenal the grand equerry and the Due del Parque followed in a second equipage with the same state; a detachment of the guards escorted them, and the sword was presented by the Marquis of Astorga to Murat."[23]

In the College of Arms is a tournament roll of vellum, seventy feet in length and eighteen inches broad, containing one hundred and seventy figures and seventy three horses painted by the armorial artists of the time on which is written:

Justes at Westminr. the 12th of Feb^r. by the King my Lord of Levon S^r. Thos. Knyvet and Edw. Nevill. A°. 1°. H. VIII.

"The noble Queen Lade Renome considering the good and gracious fortune th^t y^t hath pleased God to send hyr deyre and best beloved cosyns the King & Quene of England and of Fraunce that is to say the byrth of a yong prynce, hath sent iiii knights borne in her realme of CEURE NOBLE that is to say CEURE NOBLE, VALLIANT DESYRE, BENVOLYR AND JOYEUX PENSER to fornyche and cōply the certen articuls as foloeth.

"And for as moche as after the order & honnor of arms hyt is not lefull for any man to enterpryse arms in so high a presens without his stocke and name be of nobles descended. In consyderation theis iiii knights be of so fer & straunge partes, they shall present themselff w^t their names and arms portend[24] in their shylde.

---

[23] Southey's Hist, of the Peninsula war, Vol. I.
[24] Pourtray'd.

"Item these four knights shall prsent themselves in the feyld at the Paleys of Rychmond[25] or elles where hyt shall please the kynges grace at the tyme of Candelmas next or nigh theirupon in harneys for the tylt w^{t}out tache,[26] or breket,[27] wolant pece[28] on the hedde, rondell on the garde rest,[29] adūntag, fraude, deceyt or any other malengyne.

"Item to evry comer shall be runne vi courses pvyed[30] all way yf the comers be of so greate number that they cannot resonably be for on[31] day, hyt shall be lefull for the iiii chalengers to enter the felde the second day and so to answere all the comers to the full nomber be served of soche as be noble of name or of armes and w^t out report.

"Item all speres to be garnished[32] and brought to the field at the pvision and chardge of the chalengers, of the wch speres the answerers to have the choice.

"Item yf y^t happe any man as God defend to kyll his fellows horse by way of foule runnyng he shall be bound, y^t so doth, to give the horse y^t he rydeth on to his felow or the pryse of the horse so kyld at the dyscresion of the judges.

"Item who stryketh his felow beneth the wast or in the sadell with full course by way of fowle runnynge he shall be dysalowed for ii speres before broken.

"Item, who stryketh his felow uncharged and disgarnyslied of his speare he shall be disalowed at the descression of judges.

"Item, who breaketh his spere above the charnell[33] to be allowed ii speres well broken after the old custom of armes.

"Item who breaketh his spere morne to morme[34] to be allow'd iii speres after the custome of arms.

---

[25] Tbis tilt-yard may be seen in a collection of original drawings of tbe time of Queen Mary, in possession of Messrs. Colnaghi

[26] Tbe piece whicb covered the pocket and therefore tbe belly.

[27] Tbe briebette or else tbe brochette.

[28] Volant piece, a piece of steel which presents an acute angle to tbe front and is put on the helmet as in Plate LIII.

[29] The flat vamplate for the lance.

[30] Provided.

[31] One.

[32] Furnisbed with the usual appendages as coronelIs, mornes, etc.

[33] That part which, when held upright, would be above the charnel or pinnacle of the helmet.

[34] The morme or morne is the étui de fer or short point on the end of the spear to prevent injury.

"Item who breaketh most speres ys better worthey the pryse.

"Item who stryketh down horse and man is better worthe the pryse.

"Item who stryketh his felow clere out of the sadell is best worthe of the pryse.

"Item if any gentleman chalenger or defender breake a staff on the tylt[35] to be dialow'd a staff.

"Item yf y[t] is the pleasure of the kynge our most dred souaigne lorde, the queens grace and the ladies with the advice of the noble and dyscret judges to give pryses after their deservings unto both the partes. Item that every gentleman ans were do subscrybe his name to the artyculles.

"Item yt ys the humble request of these iiii gentlemen that yf in these articles be comprised more or ells then amowne[36] or curtese requereth ever to submit them to the quene and the ladyes, and their alwayes to adde and menyshe[37] at their noble pleasure.

"The kings grace, Cœur Loyal.

"L[d] W[m] of Devon, Bon Yoloir.

"S Tho. Knyvet, Valliant Deser.

"Sr Edw. Neveyl, Joyeux Penser."[38]

At the end of the roll five stanzas of seven lines each in praise of Henry VHI, make him surpass the " noble nyne" while they constitute him " the tenthe" as well as they "the nyne."

"Sethe non of them more nobyll for the tyme."

These, in the enumeration which follows, are Ector, Julyes, Judas, Josewe, Charles of Fraunce, Arthure the Worthe, Alexander the Great, David and Godfras; but, as the verses throw no light on our immediate subject, I omit them. Those who are curious may see them in the first Volume of the Vetusta Monumenta together with a reduced engraving of the tournament roll.[39] On this the procession is as follows: Le maistre de l'armurerye du roy on horseback preeceded by men on foot with truncheons followed by others carrying tilting-lances tipped with coronels. Then a man on horseback bearing a mace, after whom are les trompettes also on horseback. These are

---

[35] On the saddle by the thigh.

[36] Gentleness: mwyn in Welsh is gentle.

[37] Diminish.

[38] See Hall's Chrono 1, Henry VIII, p. 9, and Hollingshead's ditto, anno MIO

[39] One of tbe figures, viz. Ie Roy Desarmey, may be seen of tbe size of the original in Dallaway's Heraldic Inquiries.

followed by six gentlemen mounted, two and two, called les gorgyas de la court, one of whose horses wears a chanfron without cheek-pieces. Next come six officiers d'annes bare-headed except one. After these, mounted on a horse armed with chanfron and criniere and duly caparisoned, is Joyeulx Penser in full armour with a tilting-lielmet, such as that in the possession of my friend John Murray, Esq. Commissary General at Ardleybury, Hert-fordshire, and like that in Plate LIX, and with a puckered skirt or lainboys in a war-saddle so contrived as to afford protection to his thighs. He is at-tended by six truncheon-men who support a canopy over him powdered, as well as his skirt, with the letter K with his title in the border at bottom. In like manner follow Bon Vouloir and Vaillant Desyr. Then comes the king as Noble Cueur Loyal in the same style, except that his attendants amount to twenty-two, all wearing collars and the canopy, which is more splendid, sur-mounted by a crown. Next are seen two led horses with chanfrons, crinieres and war-saddles called les selles d'armes. Then are les pages du roy, nine in number and mounted. Next a led horse fully caparisoned with a war-sad-dle[40] over which are the words la selle d'honneur. After this appears mount-ed le grant escuyer and then le maistre des pages. The procession, from one side, is now supposed to have reached the ground, there is, therefore, next represented the lists with two combatants tilting with the paling between them, one of which appears to be the king and attended by two squires on foot. At the back is the gallery containing the queen, her ladies, and the officers of the court, the entrance to which is through a portico ascended by steps. On the right hand side of this gallery are the four canopies, and three of les quatre tenants ready for the encounter. On the left hand side are les venants with plumes or cointises on their helmets[41] and fully equipped for the tilt.

Besides the one engaged there are eight in number, the foremost of whom has a tilting-lance, with its morne, ready to engage. Their caparisons are decked with their armorial bearings. Next after these are six trumpeters sounding le son des trompettes a l'hosteL Then l'yssue du champ, which seems to mean the return from the field, and is represented by sixteen gen-tlemen on horseback with truncheons in their hands two and two. Next a man on horseback, supporting on a staff, le heaulme du roy,[42] on which

[40] The stirrup to this saddle has a bar in front to prevent the foot slipping forward.
[41] There is only' one witb a cointise, and his belmet and armour are gilt witb green spots like flames of fire, what the heralds call guttee,
[42] The til ting helmet before noticed.

is placed his crown. In the back is the gallery with the queen, ladies and officers as before and this concludes the roll. On the crupper of each horse is a large bell, and smaller ones of divers shapes are attached to the bridles, caparisons and other trappings.

Hall gives the following account of another tournament which took place in honor of the birth of Prince Arthur in the 2nd year of his reign.[43]

"The morrow being the xiii day of February after dynner, at tyme convenient, the quene with the ladyes repaired to see the justes. The trompettes blew up, and in came many a nobleman and gentelman, rychly appareiled, takynge up their horses, in clothe of golde and russet tynsell; knightes in clothe of golde and velvet; and a greate number of gentehnen on fote in russet satyn and yealow, and yomen in russet damaske and yealow: all the nether parte of every man's hosen skarlet, and yealow cappes. Then came the kynge under a pavilion of clothe of golde and purpul velvet embroudered, and poudered with H and K of fyne golde, the compass of the pavilion above embroudered rychely, and valenced with flat golde, beten in wyse with an imperiall croune in the top of fyne golde, liys baser and trapper of clothe of gold fretted with damaske gold, the trapper pendant to the tail; a crane[44] and cliafron of stele, in the frount of the chafron was a goodly plume set full of musers or tremblyng spangles of golde. After followed his three aydes, every of them under a pavilion of crimosyn damaske and purple, poudred with H and K of fine golde, valanced and frynged with golde of damaske: on the top of every pavilion a great K of golde smythes worke. The number of gentehnen and yomen attendant a fote, appareiled in russet and yealow, was clxviii. Then next these pavilions came xii chyldren of honor, sitting every of them on a greate courser ricliely trapped and embroudered in several devises and facions, where lacked neither brouderie nor goldesmythes worke, so that every childe and horse in device and facion was contrarye to other, whiche was goodly to beliolde.

"Then on the counterpart entered Sir Charles Brandon fyrst on horsebacke, in a long robe of russet satyn, like a recluse or religious person, and hys horse trapped in the same sewte, without dromme or noyse of mynstrelsye, puttinge a byll of peticion to the queene, the effecte whereof was, that if it would please her to licence hym to runne in her presence, he woulde do it gladly, and if not, then he woulde departe as he came. After that hys request was graunted, then he put of hys sayde habyte, and was armed at all pieces,

---

[43] Hall's 'Unicn.' fol. 8:
[44] Criniere.

with ryche bases, and horse also rychely trapped, and so did run hys horse to the tylte ende, where divers men on fote, appareiled in russet satyn, awaited on hym. Next after came in alone young Henry Guylford, esquier, hymself and hys horse in russet cloth of golde, and clothe of silver, closed in a devise, or a pageant made lyke a castel or a turret, wrought of russet sarcenet Florence, wrought and set out in golde with hys worde or posye, and al his men in russet satyn and white, with hosen of the same, and their bonettes of like colours, demanding also licence of the quene to runne, whiclie to hym graunted, he toke place at tliende of the tylte. Than came next the marques of Dorset and Syr Thomas Bulleyn, like two pilgrims from Sainct James, in taberdes of blacke velvet, with palmers hattes on their hellmettes, with long Jacob's staves in their liandes, their horse trappers of blacke velvet, their tabardes, hattes and trappers set with scolloppe schelles of fyne golde, and stripes of blacke velvet, every stripe set with a scalope shell; their servauntes all in blacke satyn, with scalop shelles of gold in their breastes. Sone after came in the Lord Henry of Buckyngliam Erie of Wylshire, hymself and his horse appareiled in cloth of silver, embroudered with a poyse, or his worde, and arrowes of golde in a poyse, called la maison du refuge, made of crymosyn dainaske, broudered with roses and arrowes of golde; on the top a grey-hounde of silver bearinge a tree of pomegarnettes of golde the braunches thereof were so large that it oversprede the pagent in all partes. Then entered Syr Gyles Capell, Sir Roulande, with many other knightes, richely armed and appareiled. And thus beganne the justes, whiche was valiauntly acheved by the king and his aydes, emonges whome hys grace atteyned the price. These justes fynished, every man withdrew; the kynge was disarmed, and at time convenient he and the quene heard even song, and that night all the ambassadours supped with the kyng and had a great banket. After supper hys grace, with the quene, lordes and ladies, came into the white hall, within the sayde pallays, which was hanged rychely; the hall was scaffolded and ray led on all partes, there was an interlude of the gentlemen of hys cliapell before hys grace and divers freslie songes. That done, hys grace, called to hym a great man or a Lord of Ireland, called Odonell, whom in the presence of the sayd ambassadours he made knight, then the mynstrells beganne to playe, and the lordes and ladyes beganne to daunce.

And in the middest of this pastyme, when all persones were moste attentyve to beliolde the dauncyng, the kyng was sodenly gone, unknowen to the moste parte of the people there, onless it were of the quene, and of certayne other. Within a littel while after his departing, the trompettes at thende of the hall began to blow. Then here was a device or a pageaunt upon wlieles brought in, out of which pageaunt issued forth a gentelman rychelye appareiled, that shewed, how in a garden of pleasure there was an arbour of golde, wherein were lordes and ladyes, moche desirous to shew pleasure and pastyme to the quene and ladyes, if they might be licenced so to do, who was aunswered by the quene, how she and all other there were very desyrous to se theirn and their pastyme. Then a great cloth of arras that dyd hang before the same pageaunt was taken awaye, and the pageaunt brought more nere: it was curiously made and pleasaunt to beholde; it was solempne and l-yche, for every post or pillar therof was covered with frise golde; therm were trees of hathorne, eglantynes, rosiers, vynes, and other pleasaunt floures of divers colours, with gillofers and other herbes, all made of satyn, damaske, silk, silver and golde, accordingly as the natural trees, herbes, or floures ought to be. In which arber were 6 ladyes, all appareiled in white satyn and grene, set and embroudered full of H and K of golde, knytte together with laces of golde, of damaske, and all their garmentes were replenyshe with glytteringe spangles gylt over; on their heddes were bonettes all opened at the 4 quarters overfrysed with flat gold of damaske, the orrellettes were of rolles wrethed on larnpas douck holow, so that the golde shewed throw the lampas douck, the fassis of their head set ful of new devised facions. In this garden also was the kyng and 5 with him, appareiled in garmentes of purple satyn, all of cuttes with H and K; every edge gar-nished with frysed gold, and every garment ful of poysees, made of letters of fyne gold in bullyon, as thick as they might be, and every persone had his name in like letters of massy gold; the fyrst *Cuer Loyall*, the second *Bone Volure*, in the 3 *Bone Espoir*, the 4th *Valyaunt Desyre*, the fyft *Bone Foy*, the vi *Amour Loyall*; their hosen, cappes, and cotes were full of poyses, and H and K of fyne gold in bullion, so that the grounde could scarce apere, and yet was in every voyde place spangels of gold. When time was come, the said pageaunt was brought forth into presence and then discended a lord, and a lady by copies, and then the mynstrels, which were disguised, also daunced, and and the lordes and ladyes daunced, that it was pleasure to beholde.

"In the meane season the pageaunt was conveyed to the ende of the place, there to tary till the daunces were finished, and so to have receyved the lordes and ladyes againe; but sodenly the rude people ranne to the pa-gent, and rent, tare and spoyled the pagent, so that the lord steward nor the head officers could not cause them to abstaine, excepte they shoulde have foughten and dravven bloude, and soo was this pagent broken.

"After the kyng and hys coinpaignions had daunced he appoynted the ladyes, gentelwomen and the ambassadours, to take the letters of their garmentes, in token of liberalitie, whiche tliyng the common people perceyving ranne to the kyng, and stripped liym into hys hosen and dublet, and all hys compaignions in likewise. Syr Thomas Knevet stode on the stage, and for all his defence he lost hys apparell. The ladyes likewise were spoyled, where the kynges garde came sodenly, and putte the people backe, or els, as it was supposed, more inconvenience had ensued. So the king, with the quene and the ladyes, returned to his chamber, where they had a great banket, and all these hurtes were turned to laughyng and game, and thought that all that was taken awaye was but for honor and larges: and so this triumphe ended with rnyrthe and gladnes.

"At this banket a shipman of London caught certayn letters, which he sould to a goldsmyth for 3*l* 13*s* 8*d* by reason wherof it appeared that the garmentes were of a great value.

Hall already quoted, whose work was publishedin the time of Elizabeth, introduces the story of the Dukes of Aumarle, Excester, &c. planning a tournament at which they might murder Henry IV just after his accession to the throne. This is probably founded on the assertion of Walsingliam, who, though a cotemporary, dedicated his book to the king's son, and who states their intention to stir up a rebellion, raise troops and gain the cooperation of the French. But Hall is not satisfied with the fabrication of the tournament. He therefore undertakes to go into the detail of the preparation, and in his attempt to describe a most magnificent entertainment prior to his own days, gives in reality a copious account of the armour used in the time of Henry VIII. For this reason I have introduced it here serving, as it does in this place, the purpose of an historical document. His words are "All the lordes of this cospiracie departed to their houses (as thei noised) to set armorers on work for trimmyng of their harneis against the solemn justes. Some had the helme, the visiere, the two bauiers,[45] and the two plachardes[46] of the same curiously grave and conningly costed: Some had their collers fretted, and other had them set with gilte bullions, one

---

[45] Bevers. They may have been said to be two, when composed of two pieces, either drawing up over one another from the chin, or forming as it were cheek-pieces, and meeting in the centre as in Grose's Antient Armour, Plate IV, Fig. 5 and 6; but more probably the mentoniere is here meant, which resembles an additional bever,

[46] The plackard or placket, was an additional breast-plate.

company had the plackard, the rest, the port,[47] the burley,[48] the tasses, the lamboys,[49] the backpece, the tapull,[50] and the border of the curace all gylte: And another band had them all enameled azure:[51] One sorte had the vambraces, the pacegardes, the grandgardes, the poldren, the pollettes[52] parted with golde and azure: And another flocke had theym silver and sable: Some had the mainferres, the close gauntlettes,[53] the guissettes,[54] the flancardes,[55] drooped and gutted[56] with red, and other had the spekeled with grene: one sorte had the guishes, the greues, the surlettes,[57] ye sockettes[58] on the right side and on the left side silver. Some had the spere, the burre,[59] the cronel[60] al yelowe, and other had them of divers colours. One band had the scafferon, the cranet,[61] the bard[62] of the horse all white,[63] and other had them all gilte. Some had their arming sweardes freshly burnyshed, and some had them conningly vernished. Some spurres wer white, some gilt, and some cole blacke. One parte had their plumes all white, another had them all redde, and the third had them of severall colours. One ware on his headpece

---

[47] The port was either fixed to the saddle, or the stirrup, and was made to carry the lance when held upright.

[48] The burley was the place over which was slipped the burr, i. e. the butt end of the iance. Hence the tilting spear itself was sometimes called a burdare.

[49] From the French lambeau. It signifies the drapery which came from below the tasses over the thighs, sometimes imitated in steel.

[50] Perhaps the projecting edge perpendicularly along the cuirass, from the French taper, to strike.

[51] In my son's collection is a pair of stirrups enamelled blue and white, of this time.

[52] Pollettes or epaulettes were sometimes placed on one shoulder while the poldron protected the other.

[53] These were such as had immoveable fingers, and one of which kind is in my son's collection.

[54] Short thigh-pieces.

[55] The flancardes, or flançois were coverings for the horses flanks.

[56] From the French gutté " with drops of blood."

[57] The surlettes were probably coverings for the feet corrupted from solerettes.

[58] Pieces of steel affixed to the saddle to protect the thighs, as in Pl. LX.

[59] A broad ring of iron behind the place made for the hand on the tilting spear, which burr is brought to the rest when the tilter is about to charge; serving both to secure and balance it.

[60] The coronel or little crown as it were, which was placed at the end of the lance.

[61] Small criniere.

[62] The poitrinal or breast-plate of the horse, in this place, from the old French bardé" covered," But according to Richelet the whole armour for the horse was generally included in that expression.

[63] The term "white" in armour .invariably means polished steel.

his ladies sleue, and another bare on his helme the glove of his dearlyng: But to declare the costly bases,[64] the rich bardes, the pleasant trappers bothe of goldesmithes work and embrawdery, no lesse sumptuously then curiously wrought, it woulde aske a long time, to declare, for everye man after his appetite deuisedhis fantasy verifying the olde proverbe, *so many heades, so many wittes.' "

The circumstances of the helmets being adorned with plumes is sufficient to place this account of armour after the reign of Henry IV, and the mention of pass-guards enables us to fix it to the time of HenryVIII.

Persons of rank were taught in their childhood to relish such exercises as were of a martial nature and, as has been before noticed, the veiy toys that were put into their hands as playthings, were calculated to bias the mind in their favor. There is a curious engraving on wood by Hans Burgmair, which makes one of a series of prints representing the history and achievements of the Emperor Maximilian I, which exhibits these toys made to imitate two knights justing, pushed by the hand upon a table towards each other, and one of the knights fallen back from the blow he had received. There is also, in the possession of Sir F. Eden, one of these toys about four inches in height, the knight and his horse being both of brass. Four wheels, now wanting, were originally attached to the pedestal which has a hole in the front for the insertion of a cord. The lance is also wanting, but the hole in which it was inserted under the right arm and that for the queue to hold it behind, still remain. The man may be readily separated from the horse, and is so contrived as to be thrown backwards by a smart blow upon the top of the shield or front of his helmet, and replaced again with much ease. His shield covers his face, both sides of his body and reaches to the saddle, having a bouche or piece cut out for the lance. It was one of these shields or rather grand-guards which has been noticed as in a German Tournament Book, and which is given at the bottom of Plate LX.

He wears a basnet, has on his feet the surlettes, and on his saddle the sockets mentioned by Hall. Two such toys were requisite, each of them having a string made fast to the front of the pedestal. Being then placed at a distance, in opposition the one to the other, they were violently drawn together in imitation of two knights justing, and, by the concussion of the

---

[64] The base was the drapery thrown over the horse, and sometimes drawn. tight over the armour which he wore.Where Hall in another part of his chronicle describes the justs in honor of Queen Catherine at the commencement of the reign of Henry VIII, he says "some of the knights had their basses and trappers; of clothe of golde, every of them his name embroidered on his basse and trapper."

spears against the shields, if dexterously managed, one or both of the men were cast to the ground. Those before described, being pushed instead of drawn, are without wheels.

In an antient picture of the time, presented by his late Majesty King George the Third to the Society of Antiquaries, representing the interview between Henry VIII and Francis I at the Champ de Drap Or,[65] is a representation of a tournament that then took place. The account given of this is the following: Orleans, king at arms for France, came to the English court and there made a proclamation, that the King of England and the French King, in a camp between Ardres and Guiñes, with eighteen aids in June next ensuing, should abide all comers, being gentlemen at the tilt, tournaye and barriers; and the like proclamation was, by Clarenceux king at arms of England, made in the courts of France and Burgundy, and in other courts in Germany and in Italy. According to Hall the lists contained, within their area, a space of nine hundred feet in length, and three hundred and twenty feet in breadth. In the representation of these in the picture there is, on one side, a scaffold or long gallery for the reception of the royal personages and their attendants; and the whole, except the entrance, is fenced with a rail and barrier, as well as the barrier in the centre, and guarded by a great number of demi-lancers and men at arms. Du Bellai says, that the lists had a barrier on the side of the French King and another on that of Henry. The English archers and captain of Henry's guard kept the French King's side, and the captain of the French King's guards, his archers and the Swiss, kept the English King's side, and suffered none to enter but the combatants. Thus, in the picture, the entrance into the lists is guarded, on the one side, by French troops cloathied in blue and yellow with the badge, a salamander embroidered thereon; and, of Francis on the other, by English yeomen of the guard with their partizans[66]

On a rising part of the ground, at the left hand corner of these lists and close to the end of the gallery, stands a large artificial tree of honor. Its trunk is wrapped round with a mantle of red velvet embroidered with gold; and, upon its branches, agreeable to the practice of the time, hang the shields of arms of the two challengers, those of their respective aids, and the tables of the challenges. Under them are the shields of arms and subscriptions of the several answerers. This tree, as we are informed by historians, being thir-

---

[65] In the year 1520.

[66] A variety of partizans in the possession of Llewelyn Meyrick, Esq. are given at the foot of Plate LXI.

PLATE LXII

HENRY THE EIGHTH   KING OF ENGLAND,

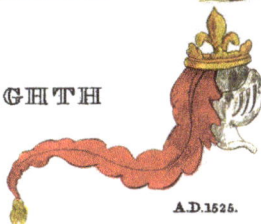

A.D.1525.

ty-four feet in height, spreading one hundred and twenty-nine feet, and from bough to bough forty-three feet, was composed of the framboisier or raspberry; another badge of Francis I, and the hawthorn which Henry had chosen as his cognizance from his father having borne it enclosing a crown, in allusion to the crown of Richard III having been found in a hawthorn bush[67]. These are artificially entwined together, as emblematical of the mutual friendship then subsisting between the two monarchs; and of their union as challengers in the several exercises of arms then to be performed. The leaves of this artificial tree are said to have been made of green damask, the branches, boughs and withered leaves of cloth of gold, and the flowers and fruits of silver and Venice gold. In the gallery appear the two kings Francis being on the right; and at some distance from them are the two reigning queens, attended by the ladies of their respective courts, as spectators of the justs. The front of that part of the gallery, appropriated for the reception of Henry and Francis is covered with cloth of gold, and the rail before the queen is hung with rich tapestry. Within the area are two combatants armed cap-a-pie mounted on horses richly based and barded and tilting against each other. Near these is a herald picking up the pieces of broken spears to which, by the law of arms, he was entitled as his fee. Larrey in his history,[68] says that, on the 11th day of the interview, the two kings entered the lists, and tilted against each other; that each of them broke several spears, but without its being possible to determine which of them had the advantage. Our historians do not mention this circumstance;[69] but there was, at Cowdry, in Sussex, a small picture, exquisitely well painted, in which Henry and Francis, each in complete armour, with their regal crowns on their helmets, and mounted on horses, fully harnessed, are represented justing with each other. Near, to the lists appears the group of tents in which the combatants put on their armour and prepared themselves for the conflict.

There is a volume in the Cotton library, marked Augustus 3, in which

---

[67] Cognizances may be considered in the literal meaning of the word as preceding coat-armour, but, in an heraldic sense, date their origin from the adoption of the planta genista, or broom sprig. For many succeeding centuries they appeal to have been confined in England to tbe royal use; but after the reign of Richard II, some of the nobility adopted them. In the war between the houses of York and Lancaster, they were on banners, and in the celebrated joust at Hereford, Thomas Mowbray, Duke of Norfolk, had his horse trappings of velvet embroidered with lions and mulberrp trees, to typify his name.

[68] Tom: II, p. 139.

[69] Except Hall whose words are—"Then began a new encounter hard and sore, many of them bare great strokes of the kinge's to their honor. When these bendes were delivered, the heralds cryed à l'ostel, and the princes then disarmed, and went to lodgynge."

are the portraits of some of the principal warriors who were with Henry VIII in France, as well as of the king himself. The former part of the manuscript is filled with an account of the marches and actions of Henry and his army during their stay in that country. The king is represented in blue steel armour with pass-guards. On his breast-plate and pauldrons is the red cross, and he is with the visor of his helmet, which is ornamented with a plume of blue and pink feathers, open. The gauntlets, which come high, on his arms appear to have separate fingers, an unusual circumstance in this reign. The armour is also edged with gold. The lamboys covers his thighs entirely and is ornamented with red crosses, and stripes, being dressed out in large puckers. From underneath the manefaire hangs a criniere of chain-mail vandyked, and the horse is not only ornamented with feathers coloured like those of his rider, standing upright on the testiere, but hanging pendant from the same someway down his neck. His head is armed too with a chanfron from which projects a spike. He is, in other respects, completely barded and based, the bases covering the bardes. These are white with a deep gold fringe. Upon them is seen the white and red roses united, surrounded by entwining branches of rose trees. On the poitrine is a lion's head with a ring in its mouth. The king rides on a saddle armed with steel on the bow, and wears a sword in a red and white sheath. Besides the broad red bridle, he has one of chain. See Plate LXII.

Charles Brandon the Duke of Suffolk is represented much in the same manner, except that his horse is merely trapped.

As the king does not wear the armour which, at this time, was appropriated for justs, I conceive him to be represented as when commanding his troops in France. Indeed, in the painting at Cowdry, in Sussex, of the siege of Boulonge, he appears in complete armour inlaid and otherwise ornamented with gold. Hollinshed, in his Chronicle, says: "It was a matter in the camp of ease to discern which was the king; for none of the rest came near to him in tallness by the head. As for his proportion of limbs, it was answerable to his goodly stature, and making a memorable description whereof, as well as of his artificial armour, I find reported as followeth:

Rex capite Henricus reliquos supereminet omnes,
Heros praevalidus, seu fortia brachia spectes,
Seu suras quos fulvo opifex incluserat auro,
Sive virile ducis praestanti pectore corpus,
Nulla vi domitum, nullo penetrabile ferro."

"Henry the king out topped all others by the head,
A most mighty hero, whether you regard his strong arms,
Or his thighs which the artisan had cased in tawny gold,
Or the manly body of the general, with his fine broad chest,
Not to be subdued by any force, nor penetrated by steel."

In a letter from Thomas Allen to the Earl of Shrewsbury, dated 1516, he says: "Upon Mondey and Tewsday last ther was a gret justing at Grene-wiche: The kyng's gee, my Lord of Suff. my Lord of Essex, Sr. Georg Caro wer challenge. I her say the kynge hath p'mysed nevr to just again except hit be wᵗ as gud a man as liymselfe.".

Stow relates[70] that, " in the year 1540, the 32nd of Henry VHI, on May Day, a great and triumphant justing was liolden at Westminster, which had been formally proclaimed in France, Flanders, Scotland and Spain for all comers, that would undertake the challengers of England, which were Sir John Dudley, Sir Thomas Seymor, and Sir Thomas Ponings, and Sir George Carew, knights, and Anthony Kingston and Richard Cromwel, Esq., all which came into the lists that day richly apparelled and their horses trapped all in white velvet. There came against them the said day forty-six defen-dants or undertakers, viz: The Earl of Surrey foremost, Lord William How-ard, Lord Clinton and Lord Cromwell son and heir to Thomas Cromwell, Earl of Essex, and chamberlain of England, with others. And that day, after the justs were performed the challengers rode unto Durham House in the Strand, where they kept open household and feasted the king and queen with her ladies, and all the court. The second day Anthony Kingston and Richard Cromwell, were made knights there. The third day of May, the said challengers did tourney on horseback with swords, and against them, came forty-nine defendants, Sir John Dudley and the Earl of Surrey running first, which at the first course lost their gauntlets, and that day Sir Richard Crom-well overthrew Master Palmer and his horse in the field, to the great honor of the challengers. The fifth of May, the challengers fought on foot at the barriers, and against them came fifty defendants which fought valiantly, but Sir Richard Cromwell overthrew that day at the barriers, Master Culpep-per, in the field; and the sixth day the challengers brake up their house-hold. In this time of their housekeeping, they had not only feasted the king, queen, ladies and all the court as is afore shewed; but also they cheered all the knights and burgesses of the Common-House in Parliament, and entertained the Maior of London, with the aldermen, and their wives at a

---

[70] Survey, B. 5, p. 2.

dinner, &c. The king gave to every of the said challengers and their heirs for ever in reward of their valiant activity one hundred marks and a house to dwell in of yearly revenue out of the lands pertaining to the hospital of St. John of Jerusalem."

This extract plainly shews the magnificence and expence of such kind of entertainments at this period, and how much they were encouraged by Henry VIII. In order that the head might remain steady, notwithstanding the force of any blow that might be given on the breast-plate or helmet, it was usual for the armourers to attend on the knights who entered the lists, after their armour was put on, and, with their rivetting hammers, to close the rivet up which came through the bottom of the tilting-helmet. This rivet may be observed in many existing suits, projecting from the top of the breast-plate, with a slit in it like the eye of a needle. After it had passed through the hole at the bottom of the helmet, a kind of lynchpin was driven through it by the armourer. To this circumstance Shakespear alludes in his play of Henry V.[71]

"The armourers accomplishing the knights
With busy hammers closing rivets up."

The grand-guard, volant piece and gard de bras were put on with nuts which rendered pincers necessary.[72]

When the ordinary helmet was used instead of the tilting-helmet, the gorget was worn and then this rivet served to hold a sash by, which, passing under both arms, was tied behind.[73]

In Caxton's Epilogue to the Book of the Ordre of Chyvalry or Knyght-hode, he exclaims: " I wold it pleasyd our soverayne lord that twyes or thryes in a yere, or at the lest ones, he wold do crye justes of pees, to thende that every knyght shold have hors and harneys, and also the use and craft of a knyght, and also to tornoye one ageynste one, or ii ageynste ii, and the best to have a prys, a dyamond or jewel, such as shold please the prynce. Thys shold cause gentylmen to resorte to thauneyent customes of chyvalry, to gret fame and renomee and also to be alwey redy to serve theyr prynce

[71] Act, IV, Sc. I.

[72] See them mentioned under the reign of Edward IV. See also Variétés Historiques, 1752, 12mo. Tom. II, p, 73.

[73] See some of tbese in the triumph of Maximilian. In more antient suits a strap was put in tbe place of the rivet, which fastened to a buckle at tbe bottom of tbe tilting belmet, and tbe boles tbrougb which passed tbe nails to hold the strap may be seen on many exist-ing breast-plates. Specimens of botb kinds are in the armoury of Llewelyn Meyrick, Esq.

when he shall calle them or have nede."

A great deal of the armour of this period has a coat of arms stamped on its various pieces, which is one half of a spread eagle impaling three bends. This is the arms of Nuremberg, where, as well as at Milan, was a famous foundery at this time for arms and armour. Other stamps often occur from the same cause. Sometimes the knights had their arms and crest engraved on the upper part of their breast-plates. One of this kind, very finely fluted, is thus proved to have belonged to a Margrave of Baden, in the early part of the reign of Henry VIII, and is now in the possession of my friend William Reader, jun[r]. Esq.

The Hungarians seem to have worn elbow shields, but probably round as in the life of the Duke of Alva; it is said that they had very small shields with spikes or nails[74] in them which they wore on their left elbows.

In the wood engravings by Hans Burgmair, to represent the Triumph of the Emperor Maximilian I, is one representing the fencers of the court who are all armed with swords and bucklers; the latter similar to some in the possession of Llewelyn Meyrick, Esq.

This art seems to have shared the same fate as the justs and tournaments, having been first prohibited and then sanctioned by royal favor. Henry VIII of England made the professors of this art a company or corporation by letters patent, wherein it is entitled the Noble Science of Defence. The word 'fence,' therefore, was a contraction of 'defence.'

The manner of proceeding in the schools of this corporation was this: "First they, which desire to be taught, at their admission are called *scholars*, and, as they profit, they take degrees and proceed to be *provosts* of defence; and that must be wonne by public trial of their proficiencie, and of their skill at certain weapons, which they call prizes, and in the presence and view of many hundreds of people; and at their next and last prize well and sufficiently performed, they do proceed to be *maisters* of the science of defence, or *maisters of fence*, as we commonly call them." The king ordained "that none, but such as have thus orderly proceeded by public act and trial, and have the approbation of the principal masters of their company, may profess or teach this *Art of Defence* publicly in any part of England."

In the British Museum are the designs for sword and dagger hilts by Holbein, for the court of Henry VIII, engraved by Hollar. These are very elegant with beautiful scroll work, foliage, etc. and the dagger for the king himself is particularly splendid.

---

[74] These were the brochettes.

There is at Strawberry Hill a handsome dagger said to have belonged to this monarch, and at Hull a sabre, which he is supposed to have presented to some favorite there, with a representation of the siege of Boulonge, inlaid with gold on its blade and also beneath the following lines:

> Henrici octavi certare Bolonia ductu
> Purpuréis turres oonspieienda rosis.
> Jam detracta jacent male olentia lilia, pulsus
> Gallus, et invicta regnat in arce leo.
> Sic tibí nec virtus décrit, nec gratia formæ,
> Cùm leo tutelæ, cùm rosa sitdecori.

The art of inlaying in gold was called "damasquinée," it having been borrowed from the Asiatics, and introduced by Benvenuto Cellini. The mode of effecting it may be seen in Felibien's Principes de l'Architecture, de la Sculpture, &c. chap. xv.

A superb specimen of a two-handed sword of this period, is that of state belonging to the regalia of Scotland, presented by Pope Julius II to James IV, in 1507. Lesly mentions another given by a Pope, in 1536, accompanied by an intimation, which James V had the wisdom to disregard, that the edge of the weapon would be well employed against his heretical neighbour Henry VIII of England. This seems to have been lost in the dilapidation of the royal treasure in the reign of Queen Mary.[75]

During the latter part of Henry the Seventh's reign, and the early part of this, whether the armour was fluted or plain, the breast-plates had a globose form, and they were terminated at top by a straight line composed of a round piece of nearly an inch in diameter in the centre, which was intended to prevent the thrust of a lance driving the point into the throat. Similar pieces were also on the gussets of plate, which turning on a nail, moved at the upper end on the slit of an almaine rivet, to allow the wearer the more readily to close his arms, the straps of the back-plate bringing them back to their places when the arms withdrew. About the middle of this reign, the breast, although globose, took an edged form down the centre which, as before observed, was called the tapul, an old fashion revived. A suit made in this manner and one in my son's collection of a German knight belonging to the order of St. George of Ravenna, instituted by Pope Paul III, in the

---

[75] The raised piece, put down the centre of the blade on each side, during the reign of Henry VII, for strength, was in the early part of Henry VIII removed, and its purpose supplied by a thickness near the point; Such a one, said to have belonged to Colonna, in 1525, is in the possession of 1. H. Allan, Esq.

year 1534, to oppose the Barbary Corsairs,[76] in the same style, have been selected for Plate lxiii, they are black with gilt edges or borders, the first on horseback with chanfron, bridle, manefaire and poitral to correspond. The chanfron has in its centre a small shield, on which are the owner's arms; but the principal circumstances of singularity are, that the cuisses are but very short, and the tassets taking a curved form and reaching within six inches of the knees. In my son's suit this is not quite so great; but the helmet is curious from having no other opening but for the purpose of putting it on the head, and from being perforated all round for a gorget of chain-mail to hang over the liausse-col; it is perforated down the back part to hold the crest and a piece of drapery like that to the helmet of the Duke de Bourbon, given under Plate LXII. As the liausse-col is made with shoulder caps, it is exhibited separate underneath. The other suit is furnished with the guard de reine which succeeded the culettes, and extended over the hind-part of the saddle.

Henry VIII instituted the first permanent corps of cavalry, and denominated it "the band of gentlemen pensioners." His object was to form an honorable body-guard on which he could, in all cases, rely, and, at the same time, to create a nursery for officers of his army, and governors of his castles and fortified places. His orders and regulations on this occasion are preserved in the Cottonian library,[77] written on five quarto leaves of indented vellum, and are as follow:

"Certain ordinances and statutes devised and signed by the king's majestie for a retinewe of speres or men of arms,[78] to be chosen of gentlemen that be commen and extracte of noble blood. With the forme of their othe.

"Henry R.

"Forasmoclie as the king oure souveraine lorde, of his great noblenesse, wise-dom and prudence, considreth that in this his reame of England be many young gentlemen of noble blod, which have non exercise in the feate of armes, in handling and renying the spere, and other faits of werre on horsebacke, like as in other reames and cuntreys be dailey practised and used, to the greate honor and laude of theim that soo dothe, his highnes hath ordeyned and appointed to have a retynue daily of certaine speres called men of armes to be chosen of gentlemen that be comen and extracte

---

[76] At tbis time they made frequent descents on the Marches of Ancona, under tbe celebrated Barbarossa. The order was dissolved by Pope Gregoryin 1572.

[77] Marked Titus, A. XIII, N. 24.

[78] The heavy armed cavalry-were called speares, launees, or men at arms, as the light-horse were demi-launces,

PLATE LXIII

TWO SUITS OF  BLACK ARMOUR.

A.D. 1534.

of noble blod, to thentent that they shall exercise the said feate of armes, and be the more mete and able to serve tlieire prince, as well in tyme of werre as otherwise, and to have good wages to leve upon accordingly.

"And to thentent alsoe, that every of them shall knowe howe to order and demeane themselfs, his highnes hath made, ordeyned and established certaine orde-nances and statutes followinge.

"Furst, Eviy of the said gentlemen shall have his harneys complete and all other habiliments mete and necessary for him, with twoo double horses at the leeste for himself and his page, convenient and necessarye for a man of arms, also his coustrell,[79] with a javelyn or demy-launce, well armed and horsed as it apperteyneth. And they shall obeye, in everye condicion, the captaine that shall be ordeyned and deputed by the king's highnes, or his deputie lieutenante, to have the rule, conduite, and gov'nance of tliemm, in all things that thei shall be commanded to doo on the king's behalf.

"Itm. That they shall make their abode in suche places as the king's grace shall appoint theim, or the said captaine, or the deputye lieutenante in the king's name, whedder it be in places nigh his person, or elsewhere, upon pain for every such defaulte to lose six dayes wages.

"Itm. Evry of the said speres and coustrellys shall, at every time, cary with theim thire horses, harneys, and other habiliments of werre as thei have, and shall muster with, not lacking, at any time, pece or parcel of theire said liabilyments of werre, nor horses, upon payne of losing six dayes wages for every suche daye and tyme as he shall be founden in defaulte, being afore commaunded by the king, captaine or lieutenante.

"Itm. In likewise that non of the said speres nor coustrells shall in no wise departe oute of the place, where they be assigned to make theire said abode, withoute the special licence of the king our souvraine lorde, or of theire said captaine, or deputie lieutenante: and to suche as license shall be granted unto by the king's grace, or the said captaine or lieutenante, and the daye appointed theim for theire returne not to faille, withoute lawfull excuse of sicknesse or otherwise duly proved, upon paine of the losse of double theire wages for every daye, as tliei shall faille in comying after the said daye to them lymited and assigned.

"Itm. That evry of the aforesaid men of armes shall furnyshe and make redy twoo good archers, well horsed and harnessed,[80] and to bring them to

---

[79] His cultellarius, or attendant, armed with a long knife.

[80] In the original painting of the battle of the spurs, given by his present Majesty to the Society of-Antiquaries, is one of these archers attendant on the men at arms.

muster before the king's grace, or suche persones as his grace shall appointe, within a moneth at the farthest after the daye that they shall be commanded soo to doo by the king's grace, or theire captaine or lieutenante, and not to faille soo to doo, upon paine of losing their romes, and their bodies to be ponyshed atte the king's pleasure.

"Itm. If any of the said archers after they be admitted, fortune to dye, the said speres shall not admitte any other in theire place, but shall name oon mete person for that rome of archer unto the king's highnes, and bring him to his presens, to be admitted at his pleasure, or els to the said captaine or lieutenante.

"Itm. For the wages and ent'teyning of the said speres and archers, the king's highnes hath ordeyned and appointed, that every spere shall have and receive for himself, his coustrell, his page, and his two archers, three shillings and foure pens strlings by the daye, to be paid by the hands of the treasurer of the king's chambre, whiche is appointed by the king's highnes to paye them the same. And furthermore the said speres shall receive theire said wages for them and for theire archers at thend of every moneth.

"Itm. The king's pleasure is, that the said lieutenante shall have for the wages and entertaining of himself, his custrell, page, and six archers, six shillings by the daye, to be payed in like manner as the said speres shall be.

"Itm. The king's grace woll that the saide captaine or lieutenante, with suche other psones as his grace shall appointe, shall evry quarter of the yere, as it slial be the king's pleasure, see the musters of the said men of armes and theire company, if any of them lakke horse, harneys, or if any of theire said horses and harneys be not sufficient as they should be, if thei be not, that they be commanded by the foresaid captaine or lieutenante, to provide for suche, as shal be good and sufficient, upon raisonable daye, by the saide captaine or lieutenante to be appointed. And suche as soo be founden in defaulte, that the saide captaine or lieutenante, shall restrain his wages in the hands of the saide treasurer of the cliambre, till he be sufficiently apparelled of suche thinges as he soo shall lakke, and thus the saide captaine or lieutenante to doo upon payne of the king's displeasure, and losing of his rome.

"Itm. To tlientent that the said speres shall alwayes be in the more arredynes with theire retynue, and suche horse and barneys, and other things as shal be necessarye in that behalf, the king's pleasure is, that the said speres shall be redy always to muster befor the said captaine or lieutenante at such tyme or tymes as they shal be by them commaunded soo to doo.

"Itm. It is the king's commandement, that the said speres and theire com-panye shall observe and kepe good rule and gov'nance, and notliynge attempte againste the king's subjects, contrarye to his lawes; and that tliei duely and truely content and paye in redy money for vittals and all other necessaries, that tliei shall take for themselfs, theire said servants and horses, upon payne to be ponished after the king's pleasure. And if any of theim shall be founde three times culpable in any such defaults, then he or tliei to be deprived of his rome, and his body to be ponished at the king's pleasure.

"Itm. It is the king's pleasure and commaundement, that none of the said speres shall presume to take his lodging by his owne auctoritie, but be ordered theirin, and take such lodging, as by the king's herbergiers[81] for that purpose deputed shall be appointed untotheim, upon ponysliment afore-said.

Next to this follows the oath, which, after swearing allegiance to the king, binds the party to the observance of the foregoing regulations; but, as it is rather long, and not particularly connected with the subject of this work, may be omitted.

As there is no date to these regulations, it is uncertain when they were made , but, from several concurrent circumstances, there are good reasons for assigning to them the year 1509, being the first of Henry's reign. What was the original number of men is not mentioned in them, but most of the chronicles fix it at fifty. The establishment, however, being, it is said, found too expensive, the corps was disbanded a short time after its institution, and before the year 1526, revived on smaller pay, as it is mentioned that year in the household statutes made at Eltham. About this time they appear to have done duty, on foot, in the court; and, most probably, with the pole axes[82] they still use; the appearance of those weapons being such as to au-thorise their being attributed to the reign of Henry VIII.

According to Dr. Chamberlayne's Angliae Notitia, of the year 1672, the band had two standards, one St. George's cross, the other four bends; but he has not stated the blazoning.[83]

James II ordained, that "every gentleman pensioner should provide three great horses, a case of pistols, a broad sword, an iron back, breast and

---

[81] Harbingers.

[82] The pole-axe differs very little from some of the martels-de-fer except in name, and having besides a spear-bead; some derive its appellation from: that kind of-axe being much used in Poland, saying, that its true name is Polish axe; while others assert, that it was so called from its supposed use to strike at the head or poll; there are some too, with more probability, say it was thus named from being fixed on a long pole.

[83] Probably this was the arms of their captain.

headpiece, with proper furniture and accoutrements to the same appertaining."

The globose breast-plate with but slight edge in the centre, was succeeded by one where the edge was more raised, and made to project in the centre of the breast. A specimen of this kind may be seen in what is called John of Gaunt's armour, in the Tower, and which has been engraved for Grose's Treatise.[84] This armour is of a very large size, and probably, therefore, was that which belonged to Charles Brandon, Duke of Suffolk. It has pass-guards, and formerly a large cod-piece; but this was removed a few years back owing to its unsightly appearance, when lent for an entertainment given by the Duke of Devonshire to the three sovereigns after Buonaparte's abdication.[85]

This projecting part was afterwards removed from the centre lower down, and two very fine suits in my son's collection, one fluted which belonged to Ferdinand King of the Romans, brother to the Emperor Charles V, and the other exquisitely engraved of Italian workmanship, are represented in Plate lxiv. The helmet of the fluted one is a bourgoinot that is made with an hollow ledge at bottom, which fits on the corresponding top of the hausse-col and thus enables it to turn round. The beaver of it is moreover made to open in the centre, so as to hang to the right and left. The arms have in the bends of the elbow those curious contrivances called splints, sometimes applied to whole suits, but in this and others confined to the arms. They are made by a piece laid across first, and overlapping pieces extending from it up the brassart, and the same down the vambrace. In this suit the edges are what the heralds would term embattled. The gauntlets of both these suits as well as the two black ones last described, and indeed most suits of this period are without fingers, but made of overlapping plates instead. Some of those in the Tower of London are made extraordinarily wide in the part above the wrists, but these are only for the bridle arm and used in justing, and sometimes were made to screw on ordinary ones underneath; which is the case with one in my son's collection. The breast-plates, from the time of Edward IV to the close of Elizabeth's reign, were furnished with

---

[84] Plate XXII.

[85] It is, however, preserved in the Tower. Gayton alludes to the custom of fools being provided with this unseemly part of dress in a more remarkable manner than other persons, when speaking of the decline of the stage in his Festivous notes upon Don Quixote, p.270. He says: "No fooles with Harry cod-pieces appear ," an epithet which alludes to the time of its introduction into Bugland. So Shakespeare, in King Lear, Act III, Sc, 2, makes the fool say: H Marry, here's grace and a cod-piece, that's a wise man and a fool."

gussets of plate, which were small pieces held to them by rivets just under the arms, and so contrived as to give way with the motion of the arms. The cuisses in this suit, and from the latter part of Henry the Seventh's time to this period, had a similar contrivance on their tops to give way with the motion of the legs, and just below them a large projecting ridge to stop the point of the lance, should it run under the tassettes. This may be observed in the fluted suit as represented in the plate. The left shoulder has a pauldron complete, but the right one has a piece cut out at bottom to assist in the movement, and its place supplied by a palette or roundel. The figure holds in his hand a fine sword on which an antient German inscription runs down each side of the blade and over the cross-bar. It is as follows.

On the blade:

Heiet dich—Hab acht auf mich—Truf ich dich—ich verschneid dich.
"Beware you—Have a care of me—If I find you—I will mince you."

Luog unb sich dich—Gben sir vor aim der dir schaben, don wil un brew ist yets sast eil.
"Look up and observe—have a care of one who will barm you
—Want of faith is prevalent."

On the cross-bar of the sword:

Gin neuwer Harlig haist Grobian,
"A new favorite named Ruffian,"

Den will netz sir ein yeder man.
" And he is ready for every man."

The engraved suit has a pair of large palettes at the arm-pits most beautifully engraved, and the centre spikes made in an elegant form. Like the monumental effigy of Richard Gres wold, Esq. engraved in Dugdale's Warwickshire, who died in the year 1537, it has under the shoulder plates, brassarts and vambraces as well as elbow pieces. This suit has a cod-piece; its cuisses reach to the knees, but without knee-pieces. It may be observed here that the flexible cuisses are composed of pieces overlapping each other, not downwards as erroneously represented at the theatres and in many modern paintings, but upwards; and the reason is, that, should the lance strike the thigh of the knight when mounted, it may glance off instead of passing between the plates. This is a suit belonging to a demi-lancer or light-horseman, while the fluted one is such as was worn by the men at arms. Conse-

PLATE LXIV

TWO SUITS OF ARMOUR,
In the possession of Llewelyn Meyrick Esq.ʳ

(A.D.1540.)

quently to this suit is an open casque with orielets and fixed umbrel but beautifully engraved, as is also the hilt of the sword with its large round flattened pommel. The demi-lance only half the weight of the lance and held at half its length, has a long blade, on which are figures exquisitely engraved. Underneath this plate is represented a footed stirrup also engraved and one of a pair in the armoury of Llewelyn Meyrick, Esq.

The officers of infantry had their hallecrets made after this fashion, two of which are in my son's collection. The cuisses of them extend only half way down the thigh in the same manner as those in the triumph of Maximilian I;[86] but the sole armour for the arms are epaulettes which reach nearly to the elbow, but only protect the outside. They have also gorgets of plate and open casques with ear-pieces. Sometimes gauntlets were added.

The book attributed to M. Guillaume de Bellay, on military discipline, distinctly points out[87] the different kinds of armour worn by the men at arms, the horse arquebusiers and the light cavalry in France, according to the ordonnances of Francis I: "The arms of the cavalry shall be according to the expence of each, for a man at arms should be anned differently from a light horse-man,[88] and this, again, from the estradiots and the arquebusiers.

"In the first place, a man at arms shall be armed with soullerets, greaves, entire,[89] cuissots, cuirasses with tassettes, gorget, armet with its beavers,[90] gauntlets, vambrace, gussets and grand pieces.[91] These men at arms, whose orders are to remain firm, and not to ride here and there, should be loaded with heavy harness, and, in order properly to sustain this weight, they ought to have large strong horses, besides which they should have them barded. These men at arms ought to have an arming sword at their sides, the estoc at the bow of the saddle on one side, and a mace on the other; their lance should be thick and very long.

"The light cavalry ought to be well mounted and armed with a haussecol,[92] a hallecret with the tassettes[93] to just below the knee, gauntlets, vam-

---

[86] See Plate XCVIII of that work.

[87] Liv. I; fol. 29.

[88] Cheval Léger.

[89] Entières means for the back as well as front of the legs.

[90] Sesbavieres implies the vizor and beaver or a double one. In Charles I of England's time the umbrel was called a beaver.

[91] The grand pieces, were probably the pauldrons and brassarts.

[92] Here is a difference therefore made between the gorgerin and haussecou.

[93] By tassettes here is meant cuishes or thigh-pieces made of several successive plates instead of in one which was the case with the cuissot. We learn from this that the cuirass of the light cavalry was called hallecret, and indeed it greatly resembled that of the infantry.

braces and large epaulettes,[94] and a strong salade well cut so as to give an open sight.[95] They ought to wear a large sword, have a mace at their saddle bows, and a lance very long in the shaft.[96] These, as their harness is neither so heavy nor secure as that of the men at arms, give less trouble to their horses, who could not suffer the weight of complete harness, and move about in every direction with facility.

"The arquebusiers should be well mounted, and their harness like that of the estradiots, with the exception of the salade; for these should have merely a cabasset, in order to command a better view, and their head less loaded. They should wear a sword at their sides; and, on one side of the saddle-bow have a mace, and, at the other, the harquebuse in a case of boiled leather, which may hold it firm without rubbing. This harquebuse should be two feet and a half long, or three feet at the utmost, and as light as possible.

"The estradiots should have sleeves and hand-coverings of mail to their jackets and an open sighted salade, a large sword at their side, a mace at the bow of the saddle, and a zagaye which they call arzegaye, the shaft of which should be ten or twelve feet pointed with iron at both ends."[97]

In the Cotton library[98] is a manuscript of Henry the Eighth's time which is as follows:

"The order to be had when the king goeth to battle.

"First the conestable, and Lord Marshall, ought to send out ryders to discover the countryes together, as the army draweth nearer every day.

"After them one marshall, or other valiant man, conjoin'd with good esquierye, of good men and horse; and they to have with them good ordenaunce, and store of shott, sufficient for to succor the distress (if neede be of the spyers).

"After them the marshall of the lodginges, the knight harbenger, steward, pourveyors, and sergeaunts of the tents, with theyr trayne to decipline the lodging.

---

[94] The epaulettes differed from the brass arts in being composed of several successive plates covering only the outside of the arm, and.not having any pauldrons.

[95] Bien coupée, à veuë coupée .... something is wanting here.

[96] Blen longue au poing.... something wanting again.

[97] An Asiatic and an African arzegaye or hassegaye are in my son's collection both made on this principle.

[98] Marked Tib. E. viii.

"The Forewarde of the Battle to he in order as followeth:

"The constable, and marshall as chefe, to give order there, as the tyme and place may require; with the ordenaunce in order followinge; as esquers, knights, bannerets, barons, and officers at arms, to ride here and there, where they shall be commanded. The constable the first in the foreward, then the barons, knights and esquyers; next after the maister of the ordinaunce with the ordinaunce, and all thinges to him appertainynge.

"The master of the horse ought to beare, or cause to be borne, the kynges standard unto the tyme of the battle; then he must beare it himself.

"The kinges henchmen[99] upon bardett horses, having the armour of the kynge both for the body and the head.

"Then the trumpetters next after the henchmen; then pennons of the bachellers knights; next banners of the bannerets two and two, after their degree.

"The barons two and two.

"The banners of the noblemen of the blood two and two, after their degree and dignity.

"The banner of the kynge; which ought to be borne into the field, or battle.

"The chief chamberlayne.

"And two ranks from the barons, the kinges of armes, heralds and pursevants; to be sent here and there as cause shall be.

"Then shall folowe the kynge, accompanyed with princes of the blood royal, dukes, lords, earls, and other noble men, to a great power.

"The chief carver, ought to beare the kinges pennon, there where the kinge goeth most, next and behynde, to the ende that every man may knowe where the kynge is.

"*Memorandum.* They that bear banners, standards or pennons on horseback, the voiage accomplished, it is their right to have them.

"The Rerewarde.

"After cometh the Rerewarde, where the dukes, earles, and marshalles,

---

[99] They were generally armed with axes; but their name is derived from the Saxon henʒeƿc a horse. Chaucer speaks of them as horsemen in "the floure and the leafe."

> "And every knight had after him riding
> Three henshmen on him awaiting."

be well accompayned with the vahentest men; and with the sliott apper-
tayning to the armye.

"After the rerewarde, at a little distance, some companyes of good
horsemen.

"After them horsemen well furnished, which shall tarrye behynde, and
shall go on bothe sydes, to discover that they be not taken, or rather that the
rereward should not be suddenly attacked: and on the two sydes, shall be
two wynges; and therein gonnes, conducted by two princes, where the ad-
mirall, or the marshall, or the maister of the ordinaunce, or other captaynes,
wyse and vaulient, shall suddenly send to the right, and left sydes, good and
sufficient men at armys on horseback, for to discover the countries, passages, and lands, &c."

There is another copy of the order of battle in the same manuscript,
which farther explains the subject: thus,

"The Ordynaunce of the Kinge, when he goeth to hattayle.

" When the kynge will goe to warre, in the countrie of his enemyes, and
intendeth to make batayle; he must have in the forewarde; the maister of
his cross-bowes, to be before the kynge; and after the forewarde, the high
stewarde, and the marshall of his lodgynge, the which is for the battaylle
of the kynge; and then the kynge, accompanied with dukes, and earlles of
liys bloode, and barons of his realme; and then in the rerewarde must be
put a duke, or an earle, or one of the inarshalles, if the forewarde be stronge
enough to resist the enemies.

"The Order of a Kynge, if he intend to fyghte.

"The kynge arrayed in his own coat of armes, must be on horseback,
on a good horse, covered also with his armes. The kynge must also wear a
crown upon his head-piece, and on each syde of liym two dukes or knyghtes
of the valiauntest that he hath in hys armye, well mounted, and armyd at
all poyntes, covered with the armes of the kynges bearynge; in their handes
eache of them to bear, a banner of hys armes: and before the kynge to be appoynted five hundred speares with hys banners; behynde the kynge hys gentleman carver shall go bearynge hys pennon, wheresoever the kynge goeth.
And if it happen the kynge to go from the battayle, to make ordinaunces, or
other thinges, then shall the constable and marshalles ryde alonge the bat-

tayle, to ordayne and keep good order, and arraye in the armye. The kynge ought to be accompayned with dukes, and earles, and to contynue under liys banners. If the enemie will fight on foote, the kynge must still bide on horsebacke, and those that carry his banners must be on foot, accompayned as beforesaide. The kynge must be on horsebacke, because that the dignitye of a kynge hath that priviledge; and for that it ought to suffice, to see hys people fight; and it is requisite that he see from one ende of the fielde to the other, to comfort his armye and give them courage: also if it happen that the fielde should be lost, he may save hymself; for it is better to loose a battayle, then to loose a kynge, for the loosyng of a kynge, is often the loss of a realine.

"How to maintayne a Duke in battayle and in what arraye.

"The duke must ordeyne his battayle as aforesaid;[100] and must have his horse with hys armes, and himself likewise arrayed in hys owne coate; and to have a corownett of golde and pretious stones upon hys heade-peece, signifienge that he is a duke. To have a banner, and pennon of hys armes and to be accompayned with 300 speres, and his banner in the mydst, and archers for the winges, and hys earles and barons: and if lie ordeyne hys battayle on foote, he must stande undyr his banner, accompayned with hys earles and barons, on eyche syde of hym; and to do hys devoir untill he be taken or slayne. For the kynge his soveraigne is bownd to revenge, and ayde hym, and to releese hym also from prison: and for this cause the duke ought more to adventure hymselfe than a kynge, in any battayle that is.

"How to maintayne an Earle in battayle.

"An earle must have 200 speares, and also archers with hym, if he goe into the battayle he must have one hundred speares before hym to fyght: and to have a banner of hys armes, and penons, with the other hundred speares, to keepe hys bodye, and the bowmen before in the winges, to proceed in good arraye.

"The same number of men and the same ordinaunce belong also to a marquis.

---

[100]   Like the king: for, in this case, he is supposed, to be commander-in-chief during the king's absence.

"How to maintayne a Baron.

"The baron must have 100 speares: 50 to fight, and the other 50 for to keepe his bodie, and hys banner: but he must have no pennon; which is the difference between the earl and the baron.

"How to maintayne a Bannerett.

"A bannerett must have 50 speares and bowmen; 25 to fight, and 25 for to keepe hys bodye, and hys banner. He is to be under the barons, and if there be any other banners of honor, according to their nobilitye, and in like wise all men that bear armes.

"How to ordeyne battayles, and to arrange the hoste.

"1st They must not be set too thick together, lest one should encumber the other.

"2nd^ly Not too thin, least the light armed of the enemy should easily enter amongst them to annoy them.

"3rd^ly To set the best armed, strongest, and best weapon'd men in front, the weakest in the rear.

"4th^ly The general may divide his army into four or five battles, as he may see occasion; but if the enemy be stronger than himself, he should bring all his men together, and endeavour to force in upon the enemy unawares.

"Seven Precepts shewing how the Enemy may be stronge.

"1st When they are assembled in good order.

"2nd^ly When they have the advantage of any passages of water, mountains, straights, &c.

"3rd^ly When the wind, the sun, or the dust is in their backs.

"4th^ly When they assail their opponents suddenly, while at meat or otherways employed, thinking themselves secure.

"5th^ly If they have been some time at ease, untired with long marches, watches, &c.

"6th^ly While they hold together in firm league without dissention and quarrels.

"7th^ly If they are well acquainted with the state and condition of their adversaries.

"Seven other Precepts contrary.

"1st The chieftain must endeavour to assault, and break the ranks of his enemies.

"2nd[ly] He ought to secure all passages, straights, mountains, &c. where he can post himself to advantage.

"3rd[ly] He should be careful so to contrive his battle, as to have the advantage of the sun, the wind, and the dust, &c.

"4th[ly] He should be careful to let some part of his host, as well men as horses, have both meat and drink before they approach the enemy, that they may then guard the rest against any sudden assault.

"5th[ly] He should constantly (if possible) assail the enemy, when they are weary and harassed with long marches, and fatigued with watchings, &c.

"6th[ly] He should by spies and emissaries, strive to breed debates and quarrels in the army of his adversaries, to hurt their order and divide them.

"7th[ly] He ought to be very close and secret in his own intentions, yet striving by all manner of means to discover the state, the number, and the motions of his adversaries."

So powerful is the force of custom, that, notwithstanding the statute of Henry VII in 1508, it was found necessary to renew the prohibition for the use of the cross-bow; and, therefore, in seven years after[101] another statute was passed to this purport. This interference, however, of the legislature, does not seem to have produced the intended effect; for, in less than twenty years after, the use of the cross-bow had become so prevalent, that a new statute was judged requisite, which inflicted on every person, that kept one in his house, the penalty of twenty pounds. It is from this period, therefore, that we may date the decline of the arbalest in this country, as these statutes produced, by degrees, the reformation sought for. Not a single cross-bow man is to be seen in the paintings at the Society of Antiquaries, nor at Cowdray-House, representing the battles of Henry VIII, and painted at the period; and, to give a finishing blow, another statute soon followed,[102] still more decisive. That act of parliament complains, that "divers murders had been perpetrated by means of cross-bows, and that malicious and evil-minded persons carried them ready bent, and charged with quarrels, to the great an-

[101] The 6th of Henry VIII, c. 13.
[102] The 33d of Henry VIII, c. 6.

noyance of passengers on the highways." This act, therefore, again restrains the custom, and ordains, that those who are possessed of lands to the value of one hundred pounds per annum, shall alone use the cross-bow; and that they shall not ride with them on the king's highway, nor shoot within a quarter of a mile of any city, or market-town, under a penalty for so doing.

Not totally to discourage the use of the arbaleste, for the king himself wished rather to limit than eradicate the practice; a patent was granted in the twenty-ninth year of his reign to Sir Christopher Morris, master of the ordinance, Anthony Knevyt, and Peter Mewtas, gentlemen of the Privy Chamber, empowering them to be overseers of the science of artillery. That the use of the cross-bow was included in this term, we learn from the Gesta Grayorum, printed in the year 1594; for, in an enumeration of the different species of artillery, are reckoned long-bows, cross-bows, slur-bows, and stone-bows,[103] scorpions and catapults. The statutes of both our universities, however, forbid them, though they permit the scholars to use the long-bow in their exercises.

The use of gunpowder, and the great improvements in the art of gunnery completely superseded the cross-bow as a weapon of war, though Father Daniel[104] says, that there was but one arbalester at the fight of Bico; but so skilful was he, that "an officer named Jean de Cardonne, having opened the vizor of his helmet to take breath, this man struck him in the unguarded part with his arrow, and killed him." So likewise "at the siege of Turin, in 1536, though there was but one arbalester in the French army, yet he was so expert, that he killed more persons than any of those using the harquebuss." In a document, cited by Du Cange, and dated 1511, are three distinct kinds of cross-bows mentioned, balista calcibus fulcita subingenio, strung by props under the lever; balista fulcita suo ingenio, strung by its own lever; and balista fulcita suis utilibus vel utensilibus et tractibus, strung by its own utensils and apparatus. Bows of these three kinds are in the armoury of Llewelyn Meyrick, Esq. The last, if not the one with the moulinet, is a latch which has an iron-bar within its stock, so as to render unnecessary the removal of the apparatus. The stock of this is longer, but that with the moulinet is shorter than during the reign of Henry VII. There is at Hull a German cross-bow of this period, with a moulinet of twice the ordinary size of the time. The next kind is that with the pied de clievre, or goat's-foot lever,

---

[103] This was the prodd. Probably the slur-bow was one furnished with a barrel, through a slit in which the string slided when the trigger was pulled.

[104] Milice Françoise, Vol. I. p. 427.

as it was called, which is moveable[105] This is formed of two legs, a catch and a handle, all acting on one pivot; the legs are applied to the projecting pieces of iron on each side the stock, and then the purchase is very great. That with *suo ingenio*, I take to be the prodd, which has merely a small lever made on this principle, and fixed to the bow.

How long the whistling arrow had been known in England is uncertain; but, from a story told by Hollinshed,[106] they seem to have been but just introduced at the beginning of the sixteenth century, otherwise the exhibition of them would have been scarcely worth the attention of the king and his company. The account is this: "In the year 1515, the court lying at Greenwich, the king and queen, accompanied with many lords and ladies, rode to the high-ground of Shooter's-hill to take the open air; and as they passed by the way they espied a company of tall yemen, cloathed in green hoods, and bows and arrows, to the number of two hundred. Then one of them, which called himself Robin Hood, came to the king, desiring him to see his men shoot, and the king was content. Then he whistled, and all the two hundred shot, and loosed at once; and then he whistled again, and they likewise shot again. Their arrows whistled by craft of their head, so that the noise was strange and great, and much pleased the king and queen, and all the company. All these archers were of the king's guard, and had thus apparelled themselves to make solace to the king."

Henry VIII, it seems, was very fond of shooting, and seeing any feats in archery; the same author, therefore, relates the following droll circumstance relative to this: "Now at the king's returning, many hearing of his going a maying, were desirous of seeing him shoot; for, at that time, his grace shot as strong, and as great a length as any of his guard. There came to his grace a certain man, with bow and arrow, and desired his grace to take the muster of him, and to see him shoot. The man put one foot in his bosom, and so did shoot, and shot a very good shot. Whereof not only his grace, but all others greatly marvelled. So the king gave him a reward for so doing. Which person afterwards, of the people and the court was called foot-in-bosom.[107]

By statute 3rd of this king, ch. iii, all men under the age of forty, some certain persons only excepted, were ordered to have bows and arrows, and to use shooting. But this was not found sufficient, as in the thirty-third year

---

[105] See it introduced under Pl. LXVI.
[106] Chrono Vol. III, p. 836. A quarrel made with a whistling head, is in the collection of Llewelyn Meyrick, Esq.
[107] Hollinsh. Chrono Vol. III, p. 806.

of his reign,[108] another act passed for the encouragement of the long-bow. It opens with a complaint on account of the decay of archery. It ordains that all men, under sixty, except spiritual men, justices, &c., shall use shooting with the long bow, and shall have a bow and arrows ready continually in their house. That every person having a man-child or men-children in his house, shall provide a bow and two shafts[109] for every such man-child being seven years old and upwards, till of the age of thirteen, in order to promote shooting. And if the young men be servants, the expence of the articles shall be abated in their wages. When of the age of seventeen years, the young men are to provide a bow and four arrows for themselves, and use shooting; and if a master or father permit his servants or children, being seventeen years of age, to lack a bow and arrow for the space of a month, the said master or father shall forfeit six and eight pence for every offence. Also every servant upwards of seventeen, and under sixty years of age, shall pay six and eight pence if he be without a bow and four arrows for one month.

It is also enacted, that no person, under the age of twenty-four, shall shoot at a standing mark, except it be a rover,[110] where he may change his ground every shot; under a penalty of four pence each shot. And no other person above twenty-four shall shoot at any mark of eleven score yards, or under, with any prick shaft, or flight arrow, under pain of six shillings and eight pence every shot.

No person under seventeen shall use a yew bow, under a penalty of six shillings and eight-pence, unless he have lands of the value of ten pounds yearly, or have moveables of the value of forty marks.

The inhabitants of every city, town and place, are ordered, by this act, to erect butts, and use shooting on holydays, and at every other convenient time. On account of the greater price and excellence of yew, it is enacted by this law, that bowyers, shall make four bows of ordinary wood, as elm, ash, wych, hazel, &c., for every one of yew, and on neglect they shall incur a penalty of three shillings and four pence for every such bow deficient. All artificers of bows, arrows, &c., are, by this statute, obliged on the command of the king, lord chancellor, &c., to go from London to inhabit any town destitute of such artificers, where they may be ordered, on the penalty of

[108] Ch. 9. Bows were kept in canvas cases, Hence Sir William Davenant says: "With Ioynes in canvas bow-case tyde."

[109] Arrows were frequently so called.

[110] Roving is shooting to the greatest distance, and in such case the bow is elevated so that the arrow may form an angle of forty-five degrees. For this purpose the flight-arrow was used.

forty shillings a day during their abode, after receiving proper notice.

Aliens are prohibited from shooting without the king's licence; and may not transport bows into foreign countries.

No bowyer is permitted to sell to a person between seven and fourteen years of age, any bow for more than one shilling, and was to have bows of all prices, from six-pence a piece to a shilling for persons of that age. And no bowyer was to sell any elk-yew bow, for more than three shillings and four pence.

Henry VIII, besides making laws in favor of archery, in the 29tli year of his reign, instituted a society for the practice of shooting, under a charter, in the name of the fraternity of St. George. It has been observed, that he was fond of witnessing the skill of archers; thus it is said, that, one day having fixed a meeting at Windsor, a person of the name of Barlow, far out shot the rest; which pleased the king so much, that he told Barlow he should be called the Duke of Shoreditch, being an inhabitant of that place. This dignity was long preserved by the captain of the London archers, who used to summon the officers of his several divisions, by the titles of Marquisses of Barlow, Clerkenwell, Islington, Hoxton, Earl of Pancras, &c.

The king granted also to this fraternity a privilege, that, if any of the members shooting at a known and accustomed butt, having first pronounced the word fast, (or stand fast) should happen to kill any person passing between the shooter and the butt,[111] he should not suffer or be imprisoned. The bow was practised by the inhabitants of Gascony, and was continued in the army of Francis I; but, towards the close of his reign, it seems to have been almost entirely disused.

But that it might not be so in England, Ascham published, in 1544, his Toxophilus, which contains instructions for archers, what to do, and what to avoid. The strings of bows were made of hemp,[112] and, from a passage in this writer, it appears that the old adage: "It is good to have two strings to your bow," was literally the case in his time. "In warre," says he, "if a stringe brake, the man is lost, and is no man; for his weapon is gone; and although he have two strings put on at once, yet he shall have small leasure and less roome to bend his bowe; therefore God send us good stringers, both for warre and peace!" But the two strings were not always put on the bow at the same time, owing to the inconvenience of which Ascham speaks; the archers, however, carried them with them though of two different kinds,

---

[111] This had been done by Henry I and was copied from the Roman law.

[112] Yet in the ballad of Adam Bell, we read, that " theyr stringes were of silke ful sure."

the thick and thin. "The one," says he, "is safe for the bow, but does not shoot strong; while the other is infinitely preferable in long distances, but, at the same time, does not direct the arrow so true, and is sooner broken." This author has enumerated fifteen sorts of wood, of which arrows were made in England at the time he lived, viz: "Brazell, Turkie-woode, fusticke, sugercheste, hardbeame, byrche, ashe, oake, servistree, aulder, black-thorne, beclie, elder, aspe, salow of these aspe and ash were prefered to the rest; the one for target shooting, the other for war.

The archers at this time wore, on their sword-hilts, a small buckler, which had been the custom ever since the time of Edward IV. One of these, formerly in the possession of Dr. Green, at Litchfield, and now in that of Mr. Gwennap, is engraved in Grose's Treatise,[113] and there stated to be thirteen inches diameter. Similar ones may be seen in the painting of Henry the Eighth's embarkation at Dover,[114] belonging to the Society of Antiquaries which clearly ascertains the date; and, in the Philosophical Transactions,[115] is the engraving of another. Of this Mr. Thoresby gives the following account: "It is fifteen inches diameter, whereof a little more than a third-part was possessed by the umbo or protuberant boss, which is made of an even convex-plate, wrought hollow on the inside to receive the hand. On the centre of this is a smaller boss, wherein there seems to have been fixed some kind of sharp offensive weapon.[116] From the said umbo, the shield is four inches and a half broad on each side, in which are eleven circular equidistant rows of brass studs of that size that two hundred and twenty-two are set in the outmost circle, which is four feet wanting three inches, the circumference of the buckler, the inmost circle, is placed upon the umbo itself, the next eight upon as many circular plates of iron each a third of an inch broad; the two outermost, on one thicker plate an inch broad. In the middle intervals, between these circular plates, are plainly discovered certain cross laminae that pass on the back of the other from the umbo to the exterior circle, and these iron plates are also about the third part of an inch at the broader end towards the circumference, but gradually contracted into a narrower breadth, that they may be brought into the compass of the umbo at the centre. The inner coat, next to these iron plates, is made of very thick, hard, strong leather, which cuts bright somewhat like parchment. Upon

---

[113] Plate XXXIV, fig. 1. See also the ballad of Adam Bell.
[114] Particularly worn by the figures on the Pier.
[115] No. 241, p. 205.
[116] That at Mr. Gwennap's is complete. There is another at Hull.

this is a second cover of the same, and on the outside of this are plaited the iron pins that run through the brass studs, for the above-mentioned brass studs are cast purely for ornament upon the heads of the said iron pins, the sixth part of an inch long that none of the iron appears. The next cover to the plaiting of the said nails (which pass through the circular and cross iron plates, and both the leather covers) is a pure linen cloth but discoloured, though perhaps not with age only, but sour wine and salt, or some other liquid wherein it seems to have been steeped. And lastly, upon the said linen is the outmost cover which is of softer leather. All which coats that compose the shield are narrow one towards the centre, and a thicker and larger one an inch broad at the circumference, which is curiously nailed with two rows of very small tackets, above four hundred in number. The vacant holes, whence some of the nails are dropped out, are little bigger than to admit the point of a pair of small compasses, both which rims do likewise fasten the handle (the only part of wood) which has also six other iron plates about three or four inches long to secure it."[117]

The concavity of this target was very little, but Mr. Thoresby had another in which it was was very great, and which was a foot larger in circumference.[118] "From the skirts of the protuberant boss, in the middle, it rises gradually to the circumference, which is nearly three inches in perpendicular height from the centre. This has fourteen rows of the like brass studes; but the circular plates of iron into which they are fixed, do not lie upon other cross-plates as the last described, but each from the centre upon the outer edge of the other, which occasions its rising in that concave manner." Grose in Plate XXXVII, of his Treatise, has given the representation of another which is one foot in diameter, but instead of being made with circular plates of iron, is "formed of three skins of leather, covered with a plate of iron, strengthened and decorated with ten concentric circles of brass nails, and secured within by three thin hoops of iron; the umbo, its spike included, projected five inches, it was hollow and stuffed with hair, the handle was of wood much decayed and fastened by thin iron plates."

In the Memoirs of the Marquis de Fleurange,[119] it is stated, that the English archers used mallets in the time of Louis XII who died in the year 1524, and in the antient poem of the battle of Flodden field, leaden mallets

---

[117] Another found at Hên Dinas, in Shropshire, bas been engraved in tbe Vetusta Monumenta, by the Society of Antiquaries.

[118] The diameter one foot seven inches.

[119] MS. in the library of the King of France.

PLATE LXV

A SUIT OF GENOESE ARMOUR,

In the possession of *Llewelyn Meyrick. Esq.ᵗ*

A.D. 1543.

are several times mentioned. From the following description there given, it seems as if the head of the mell, maule or mallet, was entirely of lead, hooped round the ends with iron:

> "Some made a mell of massey lead
> Which iron all about did bind." [120]

They appear to have been tremendous weapons in the hands of strong active men such as are described in this poem to have weilded them:

> "Two Scotch earls of an antient race,
> One Crawford called the other Montross,
> Who led twelve thousand Scotchmen strong,
> Who manfully met with their foes
> With leaden mells and lances long."

Indeed the mells, at this battle, seem to have been mixed with the bills and Moorish pikes, for so the following lines import:

> " Then on the English part with speed
> The bills stept forth and bows went back,
> The Moorish pikes and mells of lead
> Did deal there many a dreadful thwack."

In Plate LXV has been introduced a suit of Genoese demi-launcers' armour in the collection of Llewelyn Meyrick, Esq. This differs but little in outline from that in the preceding plate, but is here inserted to shew a specimen of the raised armour, the prototype of the embossed. The ground of the armour is nearly black, and all the foliage is raised about the tenth of an inch and made to shine; the pauldrons, elbow-pieces, and knee-pieces have raised lion's heads on them. Underneath this plate is a curious weapon in the same collection, and of this period for breaking swords. It is made like a short broad bladed sword, with a point and one edge sharp. The other is formed into several teeth about two inches long, at the top of each of which is a small moveable piece cut transversely, but reaching to the other. When held up to guard the holder from the cut of his antagonist's sword, that weapon forces down the moveable piece, which closes again from a spring inside the moment the sword is within the teeth. By moving the hand a little the blade of the antagonist's weapon is broken, and he is either stabbed

---

[120] I bave never met with any of these, but, in my son's collection, is one of wood, bound witb iron and studded with spikes, called a holy-water-sprinkle.

or cut with the sword breaker as the user chooses.

In this reign was introduced a weapon called pertuisan or partizan. The etymology of the word has been much controverted, but seems to lie between the Latin pertica, and the German bart an axe. Its blade was much broader than that of the pike, and much like that of the spontoon, but not so long nor quite so broad. It differed from these in having that part of its blade which was next the staff formed in the manner of a crescent. Three kinds in the armoury of my son are introduced at the bottom of Plate lxi. It was found more serviceable than the pike in trenches, mounting breaches, and in attacking or defending lodgements. That it was in fashion in Elizabeth's time is evident from the following passage in Shakespeare.[121]

"Let us make him with our pikes and partisans a grave."

It was used as late as the time of William III, and is still earned by our yeomen of the guard.

Several pole-axes, battle-axes and other weapons of the time of Henry VIII may be seen depicted in the pedigree of the Earls of Warwick in the College of Arms.

In the procession of Henry VIII to meet Francis I at Ardres, in the original painting at the Society of Antiquaries, he is represented as preceded by his billmen, who are followed by the yeomen of the guard with pertuisans, and next his henchmen, and the rear is brought up by the demi-lancers. In that book,[122] in the Cotton library noticed before, is a curious delineation of the march of this monarch against his enemies.[123] First go a strong party of horse, guarded on both sides by two cannons attended by two troops of horse, one to the right and the other to the left, then follow a large party of liarquebusiers and henchmen ranked alternately, preceded by a small, and followed by a large, party of liarquebusiers only, and at both ends as wings is a small guard of archers, and on the right and left several pieces of cannon. Then follows the main body, flanked at each end with a strong party of archers, and on each side a large wing of horsemen well armed. The main body is composed of pikemen and henchmen; the henchmen being placed in the middle to guard the king's person. After the main body follows a detachment of liarquebusiers, then a larger one flanked on each side by a

---

[121] Cymbeline, Act IV, Sc. 2.
[122] Marked Aug. 3.
[123] It took place in 1514 and is described by Holinshed, p. 1479, who has given the names of the leaders.

company of archers, and followed by another party of liarquebusiers only; behind, and on each side, are many pieces of cannon. The rear is brought up by the baggage, women, and cattle guarded by a strong body of cavalry.

The standard of the Earl Marshall at Flodden field, A.D. 1513, was red, and had on it three goat's heads couped with the motto, Veritas vincit.

The following military cautions are extracted from the work of Jacobus Comes Purliliarum, de Re Militare, published in the year 1527.

"Quid agendum ubi timetur ne ob gementium et machinarum strepitum milites terrore afficiantur.

"Si timetur ne ob nimium machinarum et gementium strepitum milites magno afficiantur terrore, qua ex re et animi et corporis vires amittant, consilium salubre est, ut militum aures aliqua obturentur materia, et sic absque metu ullo, ad praelium attenti erunt, neque vulneratorum gemitus, neque machinarum strepitus exaudientur, quibus milites terrore affici possint. Nec hodie hoc inutile erit consilium contra Teutones, qui magno pilulariorum numero utentur.[124]

"Quid agendum, ubi hostium exercitus sagittariis abundat.

"Ubi in hostium exercitu rnagnus est sagittariorum numerus, contra ipsos scutarii[125] ponantur, quod in exercitibus orientalibus frequenter contigit. Hoc enim pacto tutus erit exercitus.

"De balistariorum et scorpionariorum multitudine.

"Ubi propter magnam pilulariorum et scorpionariorum[126] inultitudinem, in muris defensores consistere tuto nequeunt, optimum est consilium, ut per parva murorum foramina hostes sclopetis et sagittis petantur, ne tuti extra urbem oppugnare valeant.

"De equitibus sclopeteriis.

"In bello non inutile erit quos Theutorum more assuefacere pati cum sclopetis assessorum neque liorrido strepitu terreri. Illis enim in exercitu nullum milituxn genus utilius erit; nam nemo in hostium exercitu tarn munitus ullo armorum genere erit: qui tutus sit a sclopeti ictu, tanta tamque terribilis in eo bellico instrumento vis est. De mediis curribus cum ser-

---

[124] That the savages of America or the Southseas should be terrified 'at the sound 'of artillery is not to be woudered at; but that European soldiers should be so much alarmed a.s to, render It necessary to stop their ears, is astonishing: yet it shows how much fire-arms were dreaded and esteemed at this period.

[125] The pavisers,

[126] The harquebusiers,

pentinis seu spingardis[127] et organis.

"In exercitu magnum serpentinarum numerum super medios habere currus, valde utile erit: nam nullus tain robustus et rnagnus exercitus erit, quin illis plusquam dici possit terreatur,[128] quoniam ipsis a longe etiam milites, et equi prosternuntur. Et nullus denique neque prope, neque longe tutus erit: terrore omnibus militibus et vires decidunt et animi deficient.

"De arcubus in exercitu habendis.

"Pedites cum arcubus quibus Britannici utuntur in exercitu habere multum plurimum que confert: nam ob ipsarum sagittarum ictum, nec toracibus quideip homines muniti satis tuti erunt tanta in arcubus vis est."[129]

Stubbs describes the doublets at the middle of the sixteenth century as "reaching down to the middle of the tliighes, though not always quite so low, being so hard quilted, stuffed, bombasted and sewed, as they can neither work nor yet well play in them through the excessive heat and stiffness thereof, and therefore are forced to wear them loose about them. They make their bellies appear to be thicker than all their bodies besides. They are stuffed with four, five or six pounds of bombast at the least, and made of sattin taffata, silk, grograine, chamlet, gold, silver and what not? slashed, jagged, cut, carved, pinched and laced with all kind of costly lace of divers and sundry colours."[130] In an inventory of apparel,[131] made at the latter end of the reign of Henry VIII, is mentioned "an armyng doublet of crimson and yellow satin embroudered with scallop shells, and formed down with threads of Venice gold." The arming doublet is seen in Plate LXI.

The large belly which Stubbs notices extended to armour, and Henry VIII is thus represented in a statue in a niche in the wall at Gorhambury, Hertfordshire, the seat of the Earl Verulam. But in my son's collection there is actually a suit with this large low belly, which has also very large passguards on the shoulders. As it is curious in shewing the gradual changes in the fashion of armour, it has been copied for Plate LXVI. The monumental effigy of George Talbot Earl of Shrewsbury is another instance of this long bellied armour.

The tubes which had formerly been made to cast the Greek fire being formed to represent the mouths of monsters, not only gave origin to the

---

[127] This shews that even at this time some of the antient machines were used as well as cannons.

[128] Hère is another proof of the dread which artillery occasioned,

[129] A strong corrobation of the skill of the English archers.

[130] The English gallant.

[131] MS. in the Harl. lib. marked 1419.

legends of fiery dragons, &c., but to the name of each species of ordnance. These, however, had only such supposed animals engraved on them as supplied the various appellations of serpentines, culverins,[132] flying dragoons, &c.[133]

Of these the basilisk was the largest. It was sometimes called a double culverine, and was much used by the Turks at this period. It must have been of a prodigious size as it carried a ball of near two hundred pounds weight. Coryat[134] mentions that he saw in the citadel of Milan, "an exceeding huge basiliske which was so great that it would easily contayne the body of a very corpulent man."

Father Maffei, in his History of the Indies, relates that Bador, King of Cambray, had, at the siege of Chitor, four basilisks of so large a size, that "Each was drawn by a hundred yoke of oxen, so that the ground trembled beneath them."

Robert Borthwick was master of the artillery to James IV, King of Scotland, and cast, among other pieces, the beautiful train of guns called the seven sisters, so much admired by the victors, whose prize they became on the fatal field of Flodden. He put on his cannons this rude legend:

Machina sum Scoto Borthwic fabricata Roberto.

It required, however, all the patronage the great mind of the Emperor Charles V could bestow, to acquire any satisfactory ideas relative to the calibres or dimensions of ordnance.

Chambers[135] observes, that "ordnance in England is distinguished into two kinds: field-pieces, which are from the smallest to 12-pounders, and cannon of battery, which are from a culverin to a whole cannon. Each of these divisions is again subdivided: the first into base, rabinet, falconet, falcon, minion ordinary, minion largest, saker least, saker ordinary, demi-culverin least, and demi-culverin ordinary: the second into culverin least, culverin ordinary, culverin largest, demi-cannon least, demi-cannon ordinary, demi-cannon large, and royal whole cannon. Different nations, it is to be observed, give different proportions to pieces of the same denomination, so that we have an Italian, a German, a French, and an English set of cannons,

---

[132] In French couleuvre, a snake.

[133] And yet in a print by Israel the pupil of Callot; dated 1635, there is a cannon in the shape of a monster, but it appears quite ideal.

[134] Crudities, p. 104, quarto.

[135] See his Dict. sub voce.

PLATE LXVI

LONG BELLIED ARMOUR.

AD. 1645.

all differently adjusted."

The following account[136] of the furniture of the ship, called the Harry Grace de Dieu, will give a good idea of the state of ordnance at this time.

Gonnes of Brasse.		*Gonnes of Yron.*	
Cannons	iiii	Port pecys	. xiiii
D. cannonc	iii	Slyngs	. iiii
Culveryns	iiii	D. slyngs	. ii
D. culveryns	ii	Fowlers	. viii
Sakers	iiii	Baessys	. lx
Cannon perers[137]	ii	Toppe peces[138]	. ii
Fawcons	ii	Hayle shotte pecys . . .	xl
		Hand gonnes complete . .	c

Gonne Powder.		*Shotts of Yron.*	
Serpentyn powder in barrels	ii	For cannons	. c
Corn powder in barrels . .	vi	For d. cannons	. lx
		For culveryns	. cxx
		for d. culveryns	. lxx
		For sakers	. cxx
		For fawcons	. c
		For slyngs	. c
		For di. Slynges	. l
		Crosse barre shotte . . .	c
		Dyce of yron for hayle shotte iiii^m	

Shotte of Stoen and Lead.		*Arrows, Morry Pyles, Byllys, Darets for Toppys*[139] *Bowes Bowestrynges.*	
For cannon perer	lx	Bowes of yough	v^c
For porte pecys	. ccc	Bowe stryngs	. x grocys
For fowlers	c	Morrys pykes	. cc
For toppe pecys	xl	Byllys	. cc
For baessys shotte of leade .	ii^m	Daerts for toppis iii doussens	c

---

[136] From a MS. in the Pepy-   sian lib. in Magd. Colt Cambridge.
[137] For stone balls.
[138] To be used in the tops, i. e. the stands on the masts.
[139] To be used in tops, i, e. the, stands on the masts.

Munycions.		Habilliments for Warre.	
Pych hammers	xx^{ti}	Ropis of hempe for wolyng and brechyng	x coyll.
Sledges of yron	xii	Naylis of sundree sorts	i^m
Crows of yron	xii	Baggs of ledder	xii
Camaunders.	xii	Frykyns with pursys	vi
Tampions	v^m	Lyme potts	x douss.
Canvas for cartowches.	1 quar.	Spaer whelys.	iiii payer
Paper ryal for cartowches[140]	vi	Spaer truckells	iiii payer
		Spaer extrys	xii
		Shepe Skynnys	xxiiii
		Tymber for forlocks	c

There is an indenture, among the deeds in his Majesty's Office of Ordnance, dated 20th January, in the 30th year of the reign of King Henry VIII, for the delivery of the castle of Berwick, together with all its military stores, by Sir Thomas Clifford to Sir William Ewers, who thereby, among other things, received the following: "The towne, castell and towre, with all the ordinaunces, municyons, artillarye, and habyllyments off warre thereto belonginge, as by particular parcelles hereafter ensuyth, besydes the implements whyche ar conteyned in a cedull unto thys present indenture annexed; that ys to saye fyrste, at the hall doore w^{t}in the said castell, a double cannon of brasse unmountyd, with seven score and two shotte of iron for the same, two bombardilles[141] of iron, unmountyd and a chambar[142] of iron for either of the same, with 39 shotte of stonee for the same bombardelles, foure score and five shotte of iron for a demy cannon, 31 stonee shotte and no pece for them.

"Item, in the Bownkell towre, three serpentynes stokkyd and bound with iron with forlookks, and two chambars of iron for every of the same, two sledges of iron, a fowler of iron[143] stokked and bounde with iron, with

---

[140] These are for large guns; cartridges for small arms being a much later invention.

[141] The smaller kind of bombard.

[142] The chamber held the charge, and was put into a place made to receive it in the cannon; thirty or forty were often kept ready charged. Some of these .antient chambers may be seen at- Aluwie Castle.

[143] Mr. Lodge, in his illustrations of British History, Vol. I, p.4, in an account-of "ordeJnce and artilery," Temp. Henry VIII, has the following: "Fowlers with their apparell, with two chambers."

forlok and syxe chambars for the same, and upon the hed of the same tow-re a saker[144] of brasse of the fyer brande of Homfrey's makinge, mountyd uppon shod wlielys, with ladell and sponge, a fawcon[145] of brasse called the Porteculles of Homfrey's makinge, mounty'd upon shod whelys, with ladell and sponge.

"Item, in Clayton's towre, three serpentynes, stokked and bounde with iron, a payre of old saker whelys bounde with iron, and uppon the same towre hed a saker of brasse of Scottyshe makinge, mounty'd upon shod whelys, with ladell and sponge.

"Item, upon the walles at the bakehouse ende a saker of brasse of Scot-tyshe makinge, called the Thysell, mountyd upon shod whelys, with ladell and spounge, a faucon of brasse of Homfrey's makinge, mountyd with shod whelys, with ladell and spounge.

"Item, a fawcon of brasse of the fier brande with oon olde stokke uppon shod whelys, with ladell and spounge.

"Item, upon the olde towre hed, a fawcon of brasse, of the fyre brande mountyd upon shod whelys.

"Item, in the littel house in the walle besyde Bownkill towre, 22 straks of iron for saker whelys, 28 shotte of leade for a fawcon, two bollts of iron with rampaires, and thre houpes of iron, a payre of olde saker whelys bounde with iron.

"Item, in the hawke howse, halfe a laste of gunpowder, 41 black bylls helvyd,[146] 44 byll heeds unhelvyd, 24 shotte of iron for a saker, four shott of iron for a demy culveryn,[147] a greate brasse morter, with a pest ell of iron for making of powder.

"Item, in the gonner's chambar 28 hagbushes of brasse,[148] 11 chambars for serpentyne, a chambar of iron without a hawll, a stamp of iron for hag-busshes wyth a worme at the ende.

"Item, in the ordenaunce house in the dungeon 53 bowes of yough wraiks, 26 dosyn bowestrings, 27 hoole barelles, and fifty and 7 half bar-

---

[144] It appears from Sir William Monson's Naval Tracts, that the sacar was apiece, of ordnance of three inches and a half bore, weight of shot five pounds and a half.

[145] From the last authority we learn, that the falcon was of two inches and a half bore, weight of the shot two pounds.

[146] With handles fitted into them.

[147] The bore of the demi-culverin, according to Monson, was four inches, 'Weight of the shot nine pounds and a half.

[148] The same as the haquebut, or hagbut, with the barrel of brass.

relles of gonne-powder, 15 pece of letter calteroopes,[149] 14 payr of dowlays for wheles, 23 bolts of iron for ordenaunce, 5 boundes of iron for gonne stokks, a barre of iron for oon axeltree, 5 lynspynnes of iron, two forlookks for stokk to ordenaunce, a mould of iron for a serpentyne, thre chaynes of iron, a barre of iron, 23 stracks of iron for saker and fawcon whelys, six hondreth shotte of leade for a serpentyne, thre hundredth shotte of leade for a fawcon, four score shotte of leade for a slang,[150] 16 shotte of leade for a saker, two hundredth shotte of leade for hagbushes.

"Item, in the armery above the hall 9 old sallets, foure payr alinane ryvetts[151] good, 15 payr almaine ryvetts rusty and brokyn, syxe stele gorgets, 5 payre of splents,[152] a barrell and a hawlk[153] for a gynne.

"Item, in th' ordenaunce house above the armery 13 score and 5 sheves of arroes, 13 hedstalles, 51 horse-collers, 51 old liorse-tracys, 5 score and 13 morys-pykes, three shevers of brasse, 11 cressetts of iron, two chests for arrowys.

"Item, in the towre at th' end of the whyte walle, 8 double hagbushes.

"Item, in the towre of the bridge upon the hed of the same a serpentyne of brasse mountyd upon oon olde stok, with shod whelys with ladell and spounge, 12 shotte of leade for the same.

"Item, benethe in the same towre, ten hagbushes of iron with thre score shotte of lead for the same, a sledge of iron, 30 shotte of lead for a fawcon, thre trestelles[154] for hagbushes, a ledder bag wyth powder, &c."

As a supplement to this account, may be added the following extract from Lord Dacre's Memoir on the state of Norham Castle, dated the 5th of February: "the xiij yere of the Pontification of the Lord Bussliop of Duresine."[155]

"And as for ordinance, it is knowen by indenture, whereof one part remay-nyth wᵗ maister Chancellar, what remaynth in the said castell; first,

---

[149] The calthrop, or cheval-trap, was a little instrument of iron made with four spikes about an inch long each, and so placed, that, whenever thrown on the ground, one spike is sure to stand upwards. These were scattered in numbers, to lame tile horses. One of this period is in my son's collection.

[150] Probably a sling.

[151] Moveable' rivets, first made in Germany, whence the armour to which they were applied was so mined. Several such are in the armoury of Llewelyn Meyrick; Esq.

[152] Composed of several little plates that run over each other, and defend the inside of the arm.

[153] Or haque, The hacked-butt, so called.

[154] Trestles, on which were placed, one above another, the hagbutts.

[155] A. D. 1521.

of grete peces, a saker, two faucons, a fawcon of maister Chancellar's, viij
small serpentyns going upon iiij pare of wheles of metall, a grete slaing of irh,
and iij serpentyns wherof one has no cliambres. As for liaggbusshes ther is
metely enowe. And so we have never one pece nor a serpentyne for the four
bullwarks wᵗ the two yatehouses in the ultro ward. As for gonpowder there
is metly of it to be doing wᵗall. And ther must be certain brimstone and sauf
peter be provided for to th' intent that a gonner may sharp it, for I fere me
that ther is overmiche cole in it, wherby it is something flatt, as I perceive
it upon my hand when I burn it. And as for arrowes ther is certain of them,
howbeit be reason of evill keping they want fedres whereby many of them
will do no good unto suche tyme as a fletcher[156] have them throwglie hand:
and as for bowes ther is none but only xlᵗⁱ whiche is of none effect, x of them
not able. And therfor ther must be provided for cᵗʰ or ccᵗʰ of good bowes,
for common store bowes are of none effect. And in this case stands my lord's
castell, wᵗ myn opynyon in every thing, &c."

Hitherto the ordinance used by the English had been made by foreign-
ers; but, in the year 1521, says Stowe,[157] "John Owen began to make brass
ordnance, as canons, culverins, and such like; he was the first Englishman
that ever made that kind of artillery in England."

From the same author we learn when bomb-shells were first made.[158]
His words are: "In the year 1543, 35th Henry VIII, the king minding wars
with France, made great preparations and provision, as well of munitions
and artillery, amongst which at that time one Peter von Collen a gunsmith
conferring with Peter Bawd, devised or caused to be made certain mortar
pieces, being at the mouth from 11 inches unto 19 inches wide, for the
use whereof the said Peter caused to be made certaine hollow shot of cast
yron, to be stuffed with fire worke, or wild fire, whereof the bigger sorte for
the same has screws of yron to receive a match to carry fire, for to break in
small pieces the same hollow shot, whereof the smallest piece hitting a man
would kill or spoyl him."

"After the king's return from Bullen, the said Peter Bawd by himself,
in the first year of Edward VI did also make certain ordinance of cast yron
of divers sorts and forms as fawconet, falcons, minions, sakers, and other
pieces."

Valturius, however, assigns an earlier date to the invention. The first edi-

---

[156] The fletcher was the arrow maker, so called from the French flèche.
[157] Chrono p. 572.
[158] Chrono p, 584.

tion of his book was published in 1472, and he there describes an engraving of a mortar as "Machina qua pilse seneae tormentarii pulveris plense, cum fungi aridi fomite urentis, emittuntur," a machine by which brazen cannon-balls, filled with powder and with fuel formed of dry inflammable spunge, may be ejected.

That they were known in the reign of Henry VIII, is further confirmed by the frontispiece to the book of Nicholas Tartaglia, a mathematician of Bresse in Italy, printed in the year 1538, where a mortar is represented throwing a burning ball; Peter von Collin, therefore, only carried into effect what, in all probability, had been described to him.

Another species of artillery of the field kind were the war carts, each carrying two pierrieres, or chambered pieces. Several of these carts are represented in the picture of the siege of Boulogne, formerly at Cowdry, engraved by the Society of Antiquaries, and that of Henry the Eighth's encampment at Dover. They seem to have been borrowed from the Scotch, as they are thus described in the following acts of the Scot's parliament.[159] The first, dated 1456, recites that, "It is tocht speidfull, that the long mak requiest to certain of the great burrows of the land that are of ony might, to make carts of weir, and in elk cart twa gunnis, and ilk ane to have twa chalmers, with the remnant of the graith that effeirs thereto, and an cunnand man to shute thame." By the second, of the year 1471, the prelates and barons are commanded to provide such carts of war against their old enemies the English.

The small arms of this period consisted of the hand-guns, the harquebuss or hagbuss or haquebut, the demi-haques and the pistol. By the statute of the 33rd Henry VIII it was enacted, that no hand-guns should be used of less dimensions than one yard in length gun and stock included. This could do but little execution on men mostly in armour, and therefore, in some measure, accounts for small arms being so slow towards general adoption. By the same statute the haquebut or hagbut might not be under three quarters of a yard long, gun and stock, as before, included. The demi-haques were still smaller,[160] and gave occasion to the origin of pistols, which were invented during the latter part of this reign at Pistoia in Tuscany; according to Sir James Turner, by Camillo Vitelli.

M. de la Noue says, that "the Reitres first brought pistols into general

---

[159] Black acts: James II, act 52, and James III, act 55.

[160] Some of these, but of the time of Elizabeth and James I, are in the. armoury of Llewelyn Meyrick, Esq.

use, which are very dangerous when properly managed."

But the grand invention of this period was the wheel-lock, which continued in use till the the time of Charles II, and even still has its admirers. This was also an Italian invention, and, according to M. de Bellai, one of the first occasions on which it was used, was in the year 1521, when Pope Leo X and the Emperor Charles V confederated against France, and their troops besieged Parma, which was defended by the Marquis de Foix. It might be supposed, that this novelty would be at once communicated to the Germans, but Luigi Collado, in his Treatise on Artillery, printed at Venice in 1586, says, that they only began in his time to use the wheel-lock in Germany.[161]

This was a contrivance for exciting sparks of fire, by the friction of a furrowed wheel of steel, at the bottom of the pan, which, with a quick revolution, grated against a piece of pyrites.[162] The spring, which turned this wheel, was wound up, or, as the term was, spanned with a small lever, termed a spanner. When this instrument was put on the projecting axle of the wheel, which was made square, and fitted a corresponding hole at one end of it, the spanner was turned from left to right, which made the wheel instantly revolve; and, by this movement, a little slider, which covered the pan containing the priming, retired from over it. The spanner was then removed, and the cock, like that used in modern firelocks, containing the pyrites, was brought down upon the wheel, it being placed contrary to the modern fashion, beyond the pan. The trigger being pulled, as in ordinary pistols, the wheel revolved, and, grating against the pyrites, produced the fire, and communicated it to the priming.

At this time the spanner was the simple instrument described, and one such is in the armoury of my son. It is appended by a leathern strap to a powder-flask very curiously inlaid with brass and ivory, and having attached to one side the leathern bag for the purpose of holding the bullets.

In the same collection too, is a brace of these first-invented pistols, the date of which is evident from the costume of some of the figures on them; for they have stocks of ebony, beautifully inlaid with ivory, on which several subjects from sacred and profane history are engraved in the most masterly

---

[161] His words are, "Nell' Alamagna etiandio fu ritrovata l'invenzione degl' archibugi da ruota." The wheel-lock never became common in England.

[162] The sulphuret of iron was so called from being applied to this use. Flints would have been too soon worn out by the friction. Such pieces are in several of the cocks of the small arms in the possession of Llewelyn Meyrick, Esq.

style. The barrels too, as well as the locks, ramrods, &c,[163] are exquisitely inlaid with silver in elegant foliage.

The iron of the barrels is an eighth of an inch in thickness, which shews the dread of bursting at this period, and the butt has a spheroidal nob at the end. The length of these pistols is one foot eight inches and a half, and they have long iron hooks on them by which they may be held in the girdle.

The patent was granted to Sir Christopher Morris, Knight, master of the ordnance, Anthony Knevett, and Peter Mewtes, gentlemen of the privy chamber, overseers of the fraternity, or, guild of St. George, granting licence to them to be overseers of the science of artillery, viz: for long-bows, cross-bows, and hand guns; and the said Sir Christopher Morres, Cornelys Johnson, Anthony Anthony, and Henry Johnson, to be masters and rulers of the said science of artillery, during their lives; and to them and their successors for ever, being Englishmen, or denisons, and the king's servants, authority to establish a perpétuai fraternity or guild, and to admit all honest persons whatsoever, as well strangers as others, into a body corporate, having perpetual succession, by the name of masters, rulers, and commonality of the fraternity or guild of artillery, of long-bows, cross-bows, and hand-guns, with the usual powers granted to corporations of purchasing lands, and using a common seal. This society might elect four under masters, either

---

[163] The superb appearance of these pistols, justifies the tradition that they belonged to the Grand Duke of Tuscany. The silver has the finest appearance from the barrels being blacked, or covered with what was called the niello. This was formerly much' used "by tbe German and Italian goldsmiths, but as the art of making it is now, I believe, obsolete, I am induced to mention the composition as stated by Theophilus Presbiter.

"To make niello-take one ounce of fine silver, two ounces of copper well purified, and three ounces of lead. The silver and copper must be first melted with bellow's heat, then the lead should be added, and stirred with a coal to make the lead throw off its dross, and the whole incorporate properly. Then take an earthen pot, the size of a thumb, witb a narrow mouth, fill it half full with powder of brimstone, tbe blackest that can be got; pour into it the three metals well melted, closing up the mouth of the vessel with clay; shake the whole till it is cold, and well mixed. Break the vessel and melt this composition again in a crucible, adding toit a drachm or two of borax. This is for nielling gold and silver only. For other metals the niello must'be thus used: boil the.metal to be nielloed in water mixed with oak ashes, then clear it well with a brush and cold water. Bruise tbe niello on a marble in particles the size of grains of millet; wash it well witb water in a glass vessel. Spread it with a little shovel of tin or copper over the metals to be nielloed about the thickness of the back of a knife, sprinkling it with a little borax. Makè a little fire or flame with twigs of wood or faggots, and gently melt the niello, so tbat it does not tun too fast to spoil the process. When tbe mixture begins to run like wax, spread it over tbe work with a bit of hot wire, and, when cold, polish with tripoly and charcoal."

English, or strangers of good character, to oversee and govern the company, and to have the custody of their property, real and personal; these might be chosen annually. The fraternity were also authorised to exercise themselves in shooting with long-bows, cross-bows, and hand-guns, at all manner of marks and butts, and at the game of the popymaye,[164] and other game or games, as at the fowle and fowles, as well in the city of London and suburbs, as in all other places wheresoever within the realm of England, Ireland, Calais, and the marches of Wales, and elsewhere within the king's dominions, his forests, chases and parks, without his especial warrant, reserved and excepted; as also game of heron and pheasant, within two miles of the royal manors, castles, and other places where the king should fortune to be or lie, for the time only.

The masters of this corporation were authorised to keep long-bows, crossbows, and hand-guns in their houses, and their servants to carry the said weapons, when and where ordered by their masters, which servants carrying such cross-bows or guns, might not shoot at any sort of fowl, under penalty of paying the forfeiture of the act. No other fraternity of this sort might be formed or kept in any part of England, without the licence of these masters and rulers. The patent also permitted them to use any sort of embroidery, or any cognisance of silver they should think proper, on their gowns and jackets, coats or doublets, and to use in them any kind of silk or velvet, satin or damask, the colours of purple and scarlet only excepted; and also to have on their gowns, or other garments, all sorts of furs not above that of martyns, without incurring the penalty of any act or proclamation respecting apparel.

The masters and rulers of this fraternity were exempted from serving on any inquest within the city of London, or any where else within the realm: and the king further granted, that, if any of the fraternity shooting at a known and accustomed butt, having first pronounced or spoken the usual word, 'Fast,'[165] should, after that, happen by mischance, to kill any passenger, he should not suffer death nor be impeached, troubled, or imprisoned for it.

The earliest patent of incorporation, however, of the Honourable Artillery Company, in its present form, is dated the third year of King James I, i. e. 1606.

---

[164] The popinjay, or, artificial parrot.
[165] That is, stand fast.

END OF THE SECOND VOLUME.

www.ingramcontent.com/pod-product-compliance
Lightning Source LLC
Chambersburg PA
CBHW040412110426

42812CB00033B/3365/J